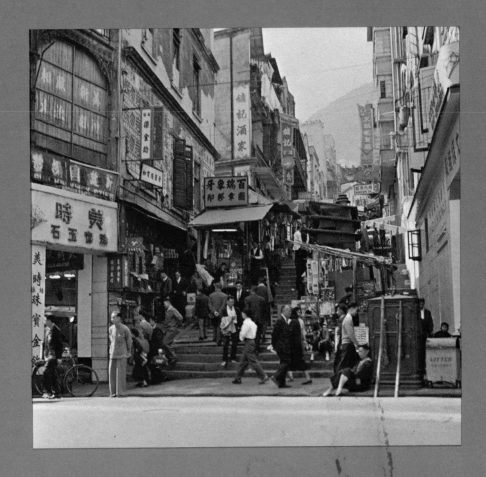

the

nations

of

ASIA

Edited by Dr. Donald Newton Wilber

Maps by Delos D. Rowe Associates

HART PUBLISHING COMPANY, INC. • NEW YORK CITY

CONTENTS

Contents

Contents

Authors' Credentials

RICHARD BUTWELL

Director, William Andrew Patterson School of Diplomacy and International Commerce, University of Kentucky. Visiting Professor of Political Science, University of the Philippines, 1964-1965. SEATO Research Fellow (Thailand), 1962. Fulbright Professor of Political Science, University of Rangoon, 1959-1960. Institute of Pacific Relations Research Scholar (Malaya), 1953. D. Phil., St. Antony's College, Oxford University; M.A., Indiana University; B.A., Tufts; Phi Beta Kappa, Pi Sigma Alpha.

Member, American Political Science Association, Association of Asian Studies, Mid-West Conference of Political Scientists, (Mid-West) Conference on Asia Affairs. Rockefeller Foundation Field Staff Member for the Social Sciences and Humanities.

Author: Southeast Asia Today—And Tomorrow, 1964; Southeast Asia Among the World Powers, 1957; many magazines articles.

JOHN F. CADY

Professor of History, Ohio University. Lecturer, University of Rangoon, 1935-1938; O.S.S. and State Department, Burma and South Asia, 1943-1949; Fulbright and Guggenheim Fellow, Burma, 1955-1956; Guggenheim Fellow, London, 1961. A.B., DePauw University; A.M., University of Cincinnati; Ph.D., University of Pennsylvania; H.L.D., Franklin College; ΦBK, DePauw; Chairman, Southeast Asia Committee.

Member, Association for Asia Studies, American Historical Association.

Author: Development of Self-Rule and Independence in Burma, 1948; BURMA chapter, L.A. Mills, New World of Southeast Asia, 1949; The Roots of French Imperialism in Eastern Asia, 1954; A History of Modern Burma, 1958; Southeast Asia: its Historical Development, 1964.

KIWON CHUNG

Graduate student of Harvard-Yenching Institute. Research assistant at Center for International Affairs, Harvard University. M.A., Harvard; B.A., University of Wisconsin.

Author: China Quarterly article, The North Korean People's Army and the Party, 1963; Asian Survey article, Japanese-North Korean Relations Today, 1964.

Engaged at present in research on the Korean-Chinese Communist Movement in Manchuria.

VERA MICHELES DEAN

Professor of International Development, Graduate School of Public Administration, New York University. A.B., Radcliffe; M.A., Yale University; Ph.D., Radcliffe. French Legion of Honor; Radcliffe Alumnae medal.

Member, AUUP, American Association of Public Administration, American Association for Asian Studies.

Author: New Patterns of Democracy in India, 1959; Builders of Emerging Nations, 1962; The Nature of the Non-Western World, 1957; The United States and Russia, 1947; The United States and the New Nations, 1964.

Many sojourns in India. Taught U.S. foreign policy at India School of International Studies, New Delhi, 1957; Studied community development projects in India, 1953. Serves as United Nations correspondent for In-

dian News and Feature Alliance. Writes for Opinion magazine, Bombay.

LOUIS DUPREE

Associate, American Universities Field Staff; Associate Professor of Anthropology, Pennsylvania State University Research Associate, American Museum of Natural History. A.B., A.M., Ph.D., Harvard University.

Author: Shamshir Ghar: Historic Cave Site in Kandahar Province, Afghanistan, 1958; Deh Morasi Ghundai: A Chalcolithic Site in South-Central Afghanistan, 1963; numerous articles and reviews.

Archaeological-anthropological research in Afghanistan, Iran, and Pakistan; travel in Soviet Central Asia and India.

GEORGE B. ENDACOTT

Master, Robert Black College, University of Hong Kong. Formerly, Senior Lecturer, History Department, University of Hong Kong. M.A., B. Litt., (Oxon); B.A., (Lon).

Author: A History of Hong Kong, 1958; A Biographical Sketchbook of Early Hong Kong, 1962; An Eastern Entrepot, 1964; Government and People in Hong Kong 1841-1962, a Contitutional History, 1964; A History of Hong Kong, 1965.

Has traveled extensively in Southeast Asia.

WESLEY R. FISHEL

Professor of Political Science, Michigan State University. Consultant, Operations Research Office, Johns Hopkins University, in Japan and Korea, 1953; B.S., Northwestern University; Ph.D., Chicago University; Guggenheim Fellow, 1961-1962; Chairman, American Friends of Vietnam.

Member, American Political Science Association, Association for Asian Studies, American Society of International Law. Hon. Mbr., Association for Administrative Studies of Vietnam.

Author: The End of Extraterritoriality in China, 1952; Language Problems of the Eighth Army in Korea, 1958; Problems of Freedom: South Vietnam Since Independence, 1962; Vietnam: Is Victory Possible?, 1964; articles in Yale Review, Journal of Asian Studies, New Leader, United Asia, Western Political Quarterly, and others.

Consultant on Governmental Reorganization, Foreign Operations Administration and International Cooperation Administration, Saigon, 1954-1955; Chief, Michigan State University Vietnam Advisory Group, 1956 to 1958; Research in Japan and Southeast Asia, 1959, 1962, 1964.

MARGARET W. FISHER

Associate Research Political Scientist, Institute of International Studies and Lecturer in Political Science, University of California. A.B., Mount Holyoke College; M.A., George Washington University; Ph.D., University of Pennsylvania.

Co-author: Himalayan Battleground: Sino-Indian Rivalry in Ladakh, 1963; India in 1963: A Year of Travail, 1964, Asian Survey.

Extensive travel in Asia.

GISBERT H. FLANZ

Professor of Political Science, New York University. J.U.C., Faculty of Law, University of Prague; Dipl. Sc.-Pol., Free School of Political Sciences,

Authors' Credentials

Prague; Ph.D., Graduate School, Princeton University.

Member, Phi Beta Kappa, American and International Political Sciences Associations.

Author: Federal Experiments in the West Indies 1958-66, 1966; many articles in technical journals.

Long residence in Turkey, and extensive travel. Advisor, Constitution Deliberation Committee, Supreme Council of National Reconstruction, Republic of Korea, 1962; Advisor, Administration Reform Improvement Commission, Republic of Korea, 1964.

ROY JUMPER

Consultant, Ford Foundation, 1962 to present. Associate Professor of Political Science, Wake Forest College, 1956 to 1962. Ph.D., Duke University. Formerly, Fellow, Harvard University, Center for East Asian Studies.

Co-author: Governments & Politics of Southeast Asia, 1964.

Ford Foundation Fellow, Indochina, 1954 to 1956. Consultant, AID in Saigon, 1962.

PRADYUMNA P. KARAN

Professor of Geography, University of Kentucky. Lecturer in Geography at Patna University, India (1950-1954). Ph.D., Indiana University; Fellow, American Geographical Society, Association of American Geographers, Society for International Development, Association for Asian Studies, National Geographical Society of India.

Author: Nepal: A Cultural and Physical Geography, 1960; The Himalayan Kingdoms, 1963; numerous articles in technical journals.

Travel in Nepal, Sikkim, and Bhu-

tan. Led geographical expedition to Bhutan Himalaya in 1964.

HYMAN KUBLIN

Professor of History, Brooklyn College; Executive Officer, Ph.D. Program in History, City University of New York. Fulbright Research Professor in Japan from 1955 to 1956. A.B., M.A., Boston University; Ph.D., Harvard University.

Member, Association for Asian Studies, Japan Society, Asia Society, Phi Beta Kappa.

Author: Meiji Rodo Undo-shi no Hito-koma, 1959; The Rim of Asia, 1963; Asian Revolutionary; the Life of Sen Katayama, 1964; author of numerous articles.

Traveled throughout Asia and the Pacific. Consultant to Office of Foreign Area Studies, New York State Department of Education.

PALDEN THONDUP NAMGYAL

Chogyal of Sikkim. St. Joseph's College, Darjeeling and Bishop Cotton School, Simla, India. Indian Civil Service School, Dehra Dun, India.

Founder and President, Sikkim Namgyal Institute of Tibetology.

BRYCE F. RYAN

Professor and Chairman, Department of Sociology and Anthropology, University of Miami. Professor and Chairman, Department of Sociology, University of Ceylon, 1948 to 1952. A.B., University of Washington; M.A., University of Texas; M.A., Harvard University; Ph.D., Harvard University. President, Southern Sociological Society, 1964 to present; Fellow of the American Sociological Association.

Authors' Credentials

Author: *Caste in Modern Ceylon: The Sinhalese System in Transition,* 1953; *Sinhalese Village,* 1958; co-author: *Integration of Sinhalese Society,* 1954.

HARRISON E. SALISBURY

Assistant Managing Editor, *The New York Times.* B.A., University of Minnesota.

Author: *American in Russia,* 1955; *Moscow Journal,* 1961; *A new Russia?,* 1962; *The Northern Palmyra Affair,* 1962.

Visited Mongolia in 1959 and in 1961.

DAVID J. STEINBERG

Secretary and Chief Economist of the Committee for a National Trade Policy; Director of Program, Foundation for International Trade Research. B.Ph., University of Vermont; M.A., Harvard University.

Member, American Economic Association, American Political Science Association, National Planning Association.

Co-author: *The Sterling Area, An American Analysis,* 1951; *Cambodia, Its People, Its Society, Its Culture,* 1957; *U.S. Senate Committee Reports: Soviet Bloc Latin American Activities and Their Implications for United States Foreign Policy,* 1960; *and The United States and World Trade,* 1961.

WALTER F. VELLA

Associate Professor of History, University of Hawaii. Ph.D., University of California; Ford Fellow at Cornell and Harvard for post-doctoral studies in international relations.

Author: *Impact of the West on Government in Thailand, 1955; Siam under Rama III,* 1957.

Affiliated with O.S.S. in Burma, Thailand, and Cambodia, 1945 to 1946.

RICHARD LOUIS WALKER

James F. Byrnes Professor of International Relations and Director of Institute of International Studies, University of South Carolina. Assistant Professor of History, Yale University, 1950-1957. Professor of Political Affairs, National War College, Washington, D.C., 1960-1961. Visiting Professor, National Taiwan University, 1954-1955. Visiting Research Scholar, Institute of Modern History, Academia Sinica, Taipei, Taiwan, 1965-1966. B.A., Drew University; M.A. and Ph.D., Yale University.

Member, American Historical Association, American Oriental Society, American Political Science Association, International Studies Association.

Author: *Multi-State System of Ancient China,* 1953; *China Under Communism, the First Five Years,* 1955; *China and the West: Cultural Collision,* 1956; *The Continuing Struggle,* 1958; *The American Secretaries of State and Their Diplomacy — Edward R. Stettinius, Jr.,* 1965.

Chinese interpreter, MacArthur's Headquarters, World War II; Served U.S. Government in Far East During Korean War; SEATO Conference in Philippines, 1957; Lecture tour in Far East, 1958-1959; Congress of Orientalists, Moscow (U.S. Delegate), 1960.

DONALD NEWTON WILBER

Chairman, Board of Directors, The Iran Foundation. B.A., M.A., Ph.D., Princeton University.

Authors' Credentials

Member, The Middle East Institute, The Asia Society.

Author: The Architecture of Islamic Iran: The Il-Khanid Period, 1955; Persian Gardens and Garden Pavilions, 1962; Afghanistan: its People, its Society, its Culture, 1962; Annotated Bibliography of Afghanistan, 1962; Contemporary Iran, 1963; The Land and People of Ceylon, 1963; Iran Past and Today, 1964; Pakistan: its People, its Society, its Culture, 1965.

Extensive travel and some residence in Afghanistan, Pakistan, India, and Ceylon.

CHITOSHI YANAGA

Professor of Political Science, Yale University. B.A., M.A., University of Hawaii; Ph.D., University of California. Fulbright Research Professor in Tokyo, 1955-1956. Fellow, Carnegie Endowment for International Peace, Tokyo, 1934-1935; Fulbright Research Professor, Tokyo, 1955-1956; Yale University Senior Faculty Fellow, Tokyo, 1962-1963.

Member, American Political Science Association, Association for Asian Studies.

Author: Japan Since Perry, 1949; Japanese People and Politics, 1956.

Picture Acknowledgments

Grateful acknowledgment is made to the following sources, which have generously provided photographs for this work. The photos appear on the enumerated pages.

AGENCIA-GERAL DO ULTRAMAR, Praca do Comercio, Lisbon, Portugal

321

THE ASSOCIATED PRESS, 50 Rockefeller Plaza, New York, N. Y.

490

CHINESE NEWS SERVICE, 1270 Sixth Avenue, New York, N. Y.

509, 512, 513

MR. KIWON CHUNG, Washington, D. C.

399

CONSULATE GENERAL OF JAPAN, 235 East 42nd Street, New York, N. Y.

267, 268, 272 (2), 237-A, 276, 278, 282-C, 291, 294-B, 299

DEPARTMENT OF BROADCASTING AND INFOR-

MATION, Sabah, Malaysia

332 (3), 339

DR. LOUIS DUPREE, American Universities Field Staff

38-39, 50-A, 50-B, 50-D, 50-E, 51-C, 60, 62

GOVERNMENT INFORMATION SERVICES, 5th Floor, Beaconsfield House, Hong Kong

200

HONG KONG TOURIST ASSOCIATION, 501 Madison Avenue, New York, N. Y.

193, 194, 197, 198, 199, 202, 203 (2), 205, 206

INFORMATION SERVICE OF INDIA, 3 East 64th Street, New York, N. Y.

67, 70, 73, 213, 215, 220, 224, 225, 228-A, 229-C, 235, 246, 255, 258, 262 (3), 561-A

Picture Acknowledgments

PRADYUMNA P. KARAN AND UNIVERSITY OF KENTUCKY HIMALAYAN EXPEDITION, Lexington, Kentucky

66, 69, 76, 77, 370-371, 375, 376, 377, 383, 478, 479 (2), 481, 482, 569 (4), 572-B

KOREAN INFORMATION OFFICE, Embassy of the Republic of Korea, 1828 Jefferson Place N.W., Washington, D. C.

467, 474

MALAYSIAN INFORMATION SERVICE, Malaysia

330, 333 (2), 336, 342-343, 346 (2)

METROPOLITAN MUSEUM OF ART, New York, N. Y.

166-B, 166 (4)

MINISTRY OF CULTURE, Singapore

340

JONATHAN MIRSKY, Oriental Studies, University of Pennsylvania, Philadelphia, Pa.

520 (3)

PAKISTAN MISSION TO THE UNITED NATIONS, 8 East 65th Street, New York, N. Y.

444, 448, 449

PERMANENT MISSION OF THAILAND TO THE UNITED NATIONS, 20 East 82nd Street, New York, N. Y.

531, 534, 535, 538-A, 539 (2), 543, 544, 545 (3), 547-A

PICTORIAL PARADE, INC., 130 West 42nd Street, New York, N. Y.

131, 142-C, 143, 151, 156 (3), 157-B, 158, 159, 163, 164, 174, 175, 178 (3), 179-A, 179-C, 183, 184, 186-B, 188, 211, 212, 218-219, 221, 223, 227, 228-B, 228-C, 229-A, 229-B, 238 (2), 239-A, 243, 248-249, 251, 252, 259, 263, 273-B, 275, 280, 282-A, 282-B, 283 (3), 285, 268-287, 290, 292, 294-A, 295 (2), 298 (2), 300, 410, 411, 412 (2), 413, 418, 419, 443, 461, 465, 470, 556, 561-B, 563, 572-A, 5 photographs on jacket

ROYAL AFGHAN EMBASSY, 1875 Connecticut Avenue N.W., Washington, D. C.

50-C, 55

SMITHSONIAN INSTITUTION, Freer Gallery of Art, Washington, D. C.

166-A, 166-C

TOURIST ORGANIZATION OF THAILAND, 20 East 82nd Street, New York, N. Y.

526, 528-529, 538-B, 540

UNITED NATIONS, PHOTO LIBRARY, Room 994, 1st Avenue and 42nd Street, New York, N. Y.

36, 41, 43, 47, 51-A, 51-B, 56-57, 63, 80, 86, 87, 91, 92-C, 95, 98, 104, 106-107, 109, 112, 113, 117, 118, 122, 125, 137, 142-A, 230, 233 (2), 239-B, 245, 253, 256, 301, 306, 329, 331, 344, 350, 372, 373, 379, 380, 382, 434, 436, 440 (2), 441-A, 451, 532, 547-B, 549

UNITED PRESS INTERNATIONAL, 220 East 42nd Street, New York, N. Y.

132, 433, 441-B, 446-A, 447-A, 457

UNITED STATES DEPARTMENT OF THE ARMY, Washington, D. C.

425, 429

WIDE WORLD PHOTOS, INC., 50 Rockefeller Plaza, New York, N. Y.

83, 85, 92-A, 92-B, 93 (2), 100, 105, 148, 152-153, 155, 157-A, 169, 170, 172, 176, 179-B, 181, 186-A, 187 (2), 281, 304, 307, 309, 310, 312 (2), 313, 314 (2), 315, 319, 323, 327, 328, 354-355, 356, 358, 359, 360-361, 363 (4), 364, 369, 387, 390, 393, 394, 405, 406, 407, 409, 423, 426, 446-B, 447-B, 460, 463, 464, 468, 473, 489, 491, 495, 496, 499, 500, 502, 505, 510, 517, 521, 523, 555

DR. DONALD NEWTON WILBER, Princeton, N. J.

134, 139, 142-B, 453, 454 (2), top photograph on front of jacket

Editor's Introduction

The Nations of Asia, as covered in this book, include some twenty-four countries and special areas. The geographical range is from the heartland of the continent to its rim, and beyond to those islands most closely related by history to the mainland.

Areas of the Soviet Union within Asia proper are omitted: not, however, as a reflection of the insistence of the Chinese Communists that the U.S.S.R. is not an Asian country. Afghanistan, on the western edge of the chosen area, has historical, ethnic, and linguistic ties with Iran and the Middle East which are stronger than those with Pakistan. In the extreme northeast Afghanistan does have a few miles of common frontier with the People's Republic of China. Hong Kong and Macao are included because of their value to the Western world as observation posts on the Chinese mainland. The islands described are those of the Japanese chain, Taiwan, and the island communities associated with Malaysia.

Recent events have led to the severance of Singapore from Malaysia. Because the rupture is so recent, no current statistics on Singapore as a country are available. Because of this fact, it has been deemed best to include Malaysia and Singapore as one entity.

Readers of this volume will read about these lands in articles written by outstanding authorities. I am grateful to these scholars for their willingness to put aside pressing obligations in order to distill their experience and knowledge. Their longer works are recommended—the titles are listed under the name of each author in the Authors' Credentials. All these writers have traveled in or have lived in the countries about which they write. They speak to those peoples in the native tongue. All are deeply sympathetic with the problems and aspirations of these nations; in their articles the emphasis is not upon critical judgment but on factual, constructive presentation.

Asia is a vast region of such diversity that it is very hard to pick out common threads and themes which can serve to relate nations or groups of nations to each other. This diversity is found in topography, climate, peoples, languages, cultures, religions, and, of course, kinds of government.

Basically, much of Asia is too hot or too cold, too dry or too wet, too rugged or too unfertile to favor human life. Scarcely ten percent of its area is under cultivation, but this land must feed nearly two billion people—well over half the total population of the world.

The topography of Asia is varied in the extreme, with vast stony wastes, rolling steppes, upland plateaus, great rivers with wide food plains, and endless stretches of forest and jungle.

Some of the major features of the landscape require mention. From the Pamirs, a great knot of lofty peaks, important mountain ranges radiate: to the west the Hindu Kush, to the north and east the Altai and Tien Shan, and to the east the Himalaya, Karakorum, and Altyn Tagh. The major rivers include the Indus, Ganges, Brahmaputra, Mekong, Yangtze, and Hwang Ho (Yellow); most are not suitable for long-distance water transport. Wide plateaus are found in Tibet, Mongolia, and the Deccan region of India, while the great deserts are those of Takla-makan in western China, the Gobi in Mongolia, and the Thar in northwestern India.

Climatic conditions vary widely, and only along the rim of Asia and its islands is the annual rainfall abundant enough for dry farming. Partly for this reason the greatest density of population is found in India, in China, and in the regions which lie between these nations.

The population of Asia ranges in coloring of skin from white to yellow to brown, and from small, wiry people to tall, vigorous types. The classification of Asians by races, once done with more confidence than is the case today, distinguishes the Ainu, Dravidian, Hindu, Classic Mongoloid, Mongoloid, Negrito, North Chinese, Southeast Asian, Tibeto-Indonesian, and Turkic. Some of these races, such as the Ainu and Dravidian, are regarded as remnants of aboriginal populations. A more subjective classification singles out different types: Ainu, Dravidian, Indo-Afghan, Indonesian-Malay, Negrito, Sino-Mongoloid, and Turanian. However, anthropologists tend to concentrate their studies on distinctive ethnic and tribal groups—and there is a bewildering number of these groups. Afghanistan, a comparatively small country, has sixteen distinctive groups, and there are scores of peoples in India. Patterns of living, long residence in an area, diet and occupation, special customs and traditions, religion, and languages are factors which combine to make each group distinct from all others.

If the problem of classifying the kinds of people who live in Asia is difficult, that of identifying their many languages is still more perplexing. Languages are classified by major families. Those found in Asia are the Indo-European, Dravidian, Sino-Tibetan, Malay-Polynesian, and Turco-Tatar. While each family may contain many tongues, a few of the languages of Asia, such as Japanese, Korean, Manchu, and Mongolian do not belong to any of these families. It should be clear that language is not a synonym for race, or for any other classification of peoples. Powerful religious, cultural, and migratory movements act as carriers for languages which replace those formerly in use. As examples, the movement of the Aryans into the upper part of the Indian subcontinent drove out the Dravidian language, which continued to be spoken in the south; the expansion of Buddhism to Ceylon introduced the Sinhalese language to the island.

Other factors operated to multiply the number of languages of Asia: small groups of people in isolated pockets in mountain ranges developed separate languages, while closely knit ethnic groups and occupational castes worked out their own tongues. Languages die hard. In India some 845 languages are spoken, twelve of them by fewer than one thousand people each. In contrast, Chinese predominates in that country, and local variants appear in numerous dialects rather than in separate languages. There are five major dialects in China of which Mandarin, spoken by at least 300 million people in North China, is the most important.

Statistics on the religious affiliations of the Asians are so fragmentary that the following figures represent bare minimums. Hindus number 385 million, mostly in India; Buddhists, 270 million, with densest concentrations from Burma on into China; Muslims, 120 million, largely in Afghanistan, Pakistan, India, and Malaysia; Shintoists, 80 million in Japan; and Christians, scattered throughout the region, some 20 million. There are vast numbers of Confucianists and Taoists in China, but the Communists both discourage religious practices and decline to give figures. In spite of the pervasiveness of these great religions, countless animists, who relate natural phenomena to spiritual forces, still carry on age-old practices. Over many centuries great cultures have sprung from these religions, but today both religious majorities and minorities enter the political field. A striking example is the forceful activity of the Buddhist monks—who traditionally should remain aloof from temporal things—in the politics of Ceylon and South Viet Nam.

The vital cultures of Asia are briefly considered in the separate articles which follow. Over many centuries, they waxed and waned according to the relative strength and prestige of the empires and kingdoms to which they offered inspiration and motivation. While the empires have vanished, a few kingdoms have survived. Their life expectancy may be short. These nations have turned away from ancient ways of government and have adopted Western institutions and political ideologies. Each now has a constitution and strives to establish the political systems of either Communism (Marxist-Leninist socialism), or socialism, or democracy.

Almost every government is committed to promoting a social-welfare state; that is, a polity in which each citizen is assured of a job, adequate food, necessary lodging, free medical care, and security in his old age. However, those governments lack the financial and other resources required for such a goal. Democracy, as we know it, is losing out in Asia, with India the most notable exception. The trend is toward a one-party government, with the party controlled by a single politician who presents himself as the "father" (Mao Tse-tung and Ayub Khan) or "brother" (Sukarno) of the people. Beset with economic difficulties, these leaders may attempt to divert public concern away from the internal problems by undertaking a campaign of hostility against a neighbor. And, unfortunately, every nation has claims against its neighbors. The extreme example of this attitude is the campaign of Indonesia against Malaysia.

In the field of international relations, a variety of national attitudes is apparent. Those countries which have a close association or an alliance with the West—Pakistan in the Central Treaty Organization (CENTO), Pakistan and Thailand in the Southeast Asia Treaty Organization (SEATO), Japan, and Malaysia—are motivated by the desire to maintain political stability and national independence; SEATO also provides for the protection of Cambodia, Laos, and South Viet Nam against an external attack. A few countries maintain an aggressive, expansionist foreign policy. The People's Republic of China and its satellites, North Korea and North Viet Nam, are committed to aggression; it is perfectly clear that China intends to absorb South Viet Nam, Laos, Cambodia, Burma, Thailand, and Malaysia, aided by a fifth column of the large Chinese minorities within the countries mentioned.

The majority of the countries describe themselves as nonaligned, or as neutral, or even as nonaligned neutrals. There are no generally accepted definitions of these terms; in practice, these nations take positive positions on international questions. For example, the Communist bloc has been so successful in branding the European powers who once controlled much of Asia, and in branding the United States, as unrepentant imperialists and colonialists that the nonaligned nations reflect this attitude in their voting record at the United Nations.

However, new circumstances will obviously affect a national attitude. The viewpoint of India, formerly the self-elected leader of the nonaligned nations of Asia and scornful of the so-called menace of the People's Republic of China, changed overnight when India was invaded by the Chinese. And Cambodia expects to strengthen its neutrality by seeking closer ties with China. No broad pattern of future international and intraregional groupings in Asia is discernible, but it seems unlikely that effective, purely Asian defensive alliances will come into being.

The economic life of Asia is plagued by the interrelated problems of overpopulation and underproduction of food. For centuries, the population of this continent was quite static; then it began to rise at the rate of 1 to 1.5 percent annually. Today, nearly every country of the area has an increase of over two percent a year—in Malaysia it is 4.7 percent

—and the rates are rising. At a rate of two percent a year, a population doubles in 35 years; at three percent, in 25 years; at the rate of three percent, Asia would add one billion people by 1975, and would exceed four billion by the year 2000. Most countries are following the lead of Japan, which has lowered its rate of increase to about one percent by promoting birth control and family planning. The principal factors causing this population explosion are better medical facilities and improved sanitary conditions, although both remain inadequate. Also, in earlier periods, floods, famines, wars, and epidemics exercised a more devastating effect on these peoples.

In some countries—India, China, and Japan—food production long has barely met the demand; in others—Ceylon and those of the Indo-China peninsula—crops have been abundant. However, all these countries must now raise far more food. The key to greatly increased production is to be found in irrigation, in erecting dams, and in building canals to bring water to the waste lands. A heavier yield per acre must be obtained through the use of fertilizers, the use of improved varieties of seeds, and by employing modern farm machinery. Nor can the human factor be neglected: each government has the choice of persuading its farmers to work harder and more efficiently, or of forcing its farmers to do so in communes and in collective farms.

Many Asian countries suffer from an unfavorable balance of trade; that is, the value of their imports exceeds that of their exports. An even balance is sought in two ways: (a) by increasing exports; and (b) by producing at home items which previously had to be imported. The major exports of Asia, such as cotton, rice, jute, tea, rubber, and tin, meet with stiff competition in the world's markets, while any increase in their total production diminishes the land available for food crops. Major import items include vehicles, machinery, electrical equipment, metal products, and countless other products of the highly industrialized countries. In response to the basic need of their countries, the nations of Asia are in a period of rapid industrialization. Since local financial resources are inadequate to establish heavy industries, loans are obtained from the industrialized countries themselves. However, the pace of industrialization is limited by the ability of the borrowers to repay loans and interest charges from factory earnings and national savings. Asia's capital expansion is also limited by the fact that it is not one of the petroleum-rich areas of the world.

In these paragraphs too much may have been said about the problems of Asia and too little about the favorable prospects. Throughout the region, educational facilities are expanding at a rate even greater than the population increase. By far the largest age group is that of children and young people, who are being trained in the skills and techniques of the modern world. The women of Asia have been released from social bondage to contribute to the productivity. As the people become better educated, more mobile, and aspire to the material benefits of life, family-centered and tribal-oriented structures will lose their hold over them. They will learn the value of cooperative effort and identify themselves with national hopes and goals.

Finally, each of these countries is trying to employ the best local and foreign talent to plan long-range programs of economic development and social progress. These plans are the carefully charted future: they provide for annual increases in the national production and for a steady rise in the per capita income. Economists agree on the soundness of such planning; but only political stability and freedom from aggression will enable Asia to achieve any measure of prosperity.

Frictions between the inhabitants of an Asian country arise from the presence of one or more important minority groups. A minority religious group or a minority linguistic group may not enjoy equal rights and privileges, and may actively express its resentment. Minority ethnic groups, such as the Chinese throughout the Indo-China peninsula, the Vietnamese in Laos, and the Indians in Ceylon, are also distinguished by their different languages and religions and by the fact that they are often more hardworking and enterprising than the natives of their host countries. Finally, there is persistent mistrust, if not enmity, between the rice-growing farmers of the lowlands and the tribes of the hills who survive on the slash-and-burn cultivation of lands of marginal productivity.

The divisive factors in Asia have been exceptionally well presented in an essay entitled "Discrimination & Discord in Asia" which appeared in the April 9, 1965 issue of *Time Magazine*. Because this essay makes this prime fact about the nations of Asia so clear, the article has been reprinted in full on the following pages, with the kind permission of the publishers of *Time Magazine*.

DONALD N. WILBER

Discrimination and Discord in Asia

REPRINTED FROM TIME MAGAZINE, ISSUE OF APRIL 9, 1965

"If you see an Indian and a cobra, strangle the Indian first," the saying goes in Indo-China, Javanese peasants say, "When you meet a snake and a slit-eye [Chinese], first kill the slit-eye, then the snake." Among Punjabis the proverb is, "If you spy a serpent and a Sindhi, get the Sindhi first."

VARIATIONS of this ugly axiom are heard the length of Asia and are as universal as the antagonisms they express. The continent's greatest single cause of turmoil is not the struggle for food or political power but simple—and not so simple—hatred among peoples, classes, races. The U.S. is deeply and rightly troubled by its own problems of racial discrimination. They are mild compared with Asia's endemic and murderous grudges, and America's problems are subject to a system of social and legal redress that, tragically, most of Asia lacks. The Asian paradox is haunting: on the one hand the brooding, jewel-eyed idols from which flow a spirit of contemplation and moral nobility, and on the other hand swirling violence and blind prejudice. These are some of the passions that years ago were described by André Malraux as "troubled shapes which in the evening swarm up from the rice fields and hide behind the roofs of the pagodas."

Such passions are not unknown elsewhere, from Cyprus to the Arab-Israeli frontier to the Congo. But in intensity and in the numbers of people they embroil, Asia's hostilities are the world's most serious and in many ways most troubling to the U.S., which now must consider Asia its foremost foreign-policy problem. These quarrels sadly refute the Gandhian view that Asian spiritualism is superior to the rationalism of the West. Gandhi liked to call for spiritual tranquillity. "Virtue," he preached, "lies in being absorbed in one's prayers in the presence of din and noise." Spirituality has proved powerless to return rioting mobs

24

to their prayers, while Western rationalism in Asia has been equally unable to mute the "din and noise" of communal clashes.

GEOGRAPHY OF ENMITY

• VIET NAM, LAOS AND CAMBODIA, the former states of Indo-China, would be locked in a vicious cycle of nationalistic enmity even if Communist aggression disappeared overnight. Vietnamese armies have harried Laos for centuries, earning the Laotians' hate and dread. North and South Vietnamese alike look down on Cambodia, which they helped France rule. Cambodia's dyspeptic Prince Sihanouk snubs Laos, hates neighboring Thailand (a Thai premier once called him publicly "a pig"), and gibes disdainfully that "all Vietnamese are married to women with black teeth."

• INDIA AND PAKISTAN are rent by the ancient hatred between Hindus and Moslems. In 1947, after the British withdrew, 750,000 members of both faiths slaughtered one another. India's Moslem minority and Pakistan's remaining Hindus still lead fear-filled lives, saved only by the knowledge that each side holds hostages from the other; each regards the other as a more immediate menace than Red China. In riots last year 4,000 from both groups were killed after a holy hair from the prophet Mohammed's head was stolen from a Kashmir mosque. The two nations' conflicting claims to Kashmir have created a diplomatic impasse that may outlast the East-West stalemate on Berlin.

• MALAYSIA AND INDONESIA are locked in an equally ominous enmity. Even without open war, both may come apart at the seams. Indonesia's Sukarno, whose own regime has been plagued by revolts among distant islanders, wages guerrilla war against British-backed little Malaysia (one-tenth Indonesia's size). Malaysia itself, a precarious geographical creation, is sapped by hatred between its Malay and Chinese population (each 40% of the total). Easygoing Moslem Malays claim that the Chinese, who dominate Malaysia's economy, reek of money, while Singapore's Chinese Premier says, "The Malay does not respond to the profit motive." In last year's Singapore riots, Chinese and Malays murdered one another with daggers and rice-wine bottles.

• JAPAN, though Asia's most modern nation, has two despised minorities. Members of the pariah Eta caste are scorned because their impoverished ancestors were forced to perform the most degrading tasks—including the clearing of corpses from samurai battlefields. Etas perennially try to "pass" into respectable society, often commit suicide if caught. The 600,000 Koreans in Japan are called "senjin," the Nipponese equivalent of nigger. Japanese look down on them because Japan ruled Korea as a slave state for 35 years. In Author Kobo Abe's celebrated novel, *Woman in the Dunes,* one character, a socialist, notes "that he liked a Korean's soul but couldn't stand his smell."

• CHINA has imposed more central control than most Asian nations on its peoples. Yet southern Cantonese still sneer at "barbarians" from North China who speak a different tongue. Friction arises when Chinese from different regions are forced to work together. All Chinese consider themselves vastly superior to minority groups within their borders, such as the newly enslaved Tibetans and the Moslem Uighurs in the west. Formosans, themselves ethnic Chinese, dislike the Nationalist mainland refugees who have made them prosperous, and some hire thugs to prevent *mésalliances* between mainlanders and Formosan girls.

Taken country by country, Asia's manifold enmities seem hopelessly complex, but certain patterns repeat themselves. Essentially, the hatreds flow from a few major causes: religion, language, race, and the accumulated grudges of history—all underscored by the failings of today's Asian leaders.

RELIGIOUS FEUDS

Religious antagonism is caused by friction between South Asia's three great religions: Hinduism, Buddhism and Islam. Though all three have undergone schisms and changes, they have nonetheless escaped the equivalent of the Reformation, which split the less flexible Christian faith but also moved it into the modern era. Relatively unharried by reformers and modernizers, Hinduism, Islam and Buddhism reached the 20th century with their ancient, fossilized social doctrines nearly intact. Hinduism's caste system, Buddhism's ambiguous attitude toward worldly institutions, Islam's hatred of infidels—all perpetuate intermittent communal discord.

Theoretically tolerant, Buddhist bonzes make immense mischief when they meddle in politics (TIME cover, Dec. 11). Troublesome Islamic minorities chafe in China, Thailand, the Philippines, as well as India. A leading Bombay Moslem complains: "Hindu customers never allow me in their offices at lunchtime because they feel my presence would pollute their food. How can we ever live as brothers?" Hindus return hate for hate. Nehru himself once remarked that Hindu communalism was "the Indian version of fascism." Social, let alone sexual intercourse between young people of the two religions has been known to lead to murder.

In theory, Indian law has done away with the caste system, but higher-caste Hindus still abuse the country's near 65 million Untouchables. Custom still requires them to live in the shabbiest quarter of each village and perform the most menial tasks, like gathering night soil for the fields. In many areas their womenfolk are forbidden to wear jewelry or pretty clothes of any kind. While a Moslem theater in New Delhi not long ago staged a local version of Shaw's *Pygmalion,* the original *My Fair Lady,* modern-minded Indians point out bitterly that a Hindu version would be unthinkable: as the daughter of a dustman, Eliza Doolittle would be an Untouchable. Hence Brahmin Henry Higgins' housekeeper would never let her use the same plates and bedding as the rest of the household. And if the high-caste guests at the famous tea party guessed they were socializing with an Untouchable, they would drop their teacups and rush to a temple to purify themselves.

The fate of India's Untouchables is special—and yet it is also typical. It is almost a metaphor for the condition of all minorities in Asia, for to some degree each Asian country has its Untouchables.

LANGUAGE AND RACE

Linguistic enmities hamper understanding and cause bloodshed among Asians, who speak more than 3,000 languages and dialects. The most recent linguistic flare-up came in February, after New Delhi tried to establish Hindi as the official tongue, although it is understood by less than 45% of India's population. Scores of pro-Hindi partisans were beaten, stabbed or trampled to death in protest riots by South Indians, who fear losing government jobs to Hindi speakers.

Racial hatreds plague all Asian nations, which present a vast, graduated racial spectrum, from the blonde ethnic Russians of bleak Sinkiang through the anthracite Tamils of India and Ceylon, whose daughters were of such black velvety loveliness that in World War II lonely American servicemen were wont to sigh, "I'd walk a mile for a Tamil." Now a new G.I. generation is entranced by Saigon's graceful Cochinchinoises but is surprised to find Asian girls just as sensitive to racial nuances as the snobbiest New Orleans debutante.

Asians save their sharpest prejudices for their own minorities, including Burma's harried Indians, Japan's Koreans and — throughout Southeast Asia—the overseas Chinese. Sixteen million Chinese live outside China, and everywhere their prosperity, diligence and clannishness arouse jealousy. Often they are accused of disloyalty to their host countries. Indonesians have stripped rich "slit-eyes" of their holdings, and Chinese in Laos are scornfully called "Mao-Tse-tung." International airlines make sure that no Chinese stewardesses work on their flights to India.

Many Asian countries have not yet absorbed backward peoples in their midst. Marauding tribesmen inspire almost psychotic fear in Pakistani officers; India has been plagued with demands for self-determination by her half-civilized Nagas. Aboriginal tribes like Viet Nam's montagnards have virtually no voice in their central governments, occasionally take up arms in protest; they are now more loyal to the newly arrived American Special Forces advisers, who arm and pay them, than to the Saigon regime.

BURDENS OF HISTORY

To Asia's burden of religious, linguistic and racial antagonism is added the weight of history. New grievances as well as old goad Asians to seek what Calcutta Philosopher Abu Sayeed Ayub calls "the appeasement of the ghosts of our ancestors by slaughtering members of another

community." Conquerors have come and gone across Asia, sowing ran-
cor as they marched. For generations after the Burmese raped Siam,
Thai women wore crew-cuts to avoid being hauled off by the hair. During World War II, brutality by the Japanese earned them loathing
throughout Asia; until recently, any Japanese who toured the Philippines risked getting a balisong (switchblade) between his ribs.

Unfortunately, in the past the Western colonial powers often used
communal hatreds to rule, by playing nationalities and races against one
another. Says Professor Theodore Hsi-En Chen of the University of
Southern California, "From China to Indonesia, nationalism in Asia is
totally negative; it expresses deep-seated hatred of anything resembling
foreign control." This applies to control by other Asians as well. While
such antagonism would exist even without Communism, the Reds exploit it. The small Communist organizations in Cambodia and Thailand are recruited mainly from long-suffering minority Vietnamese. The
Malayan Communist Party, which fought a twelve-year guerrilla war
before the British finally beat it down, was composed almost entirely of
dissident Chinese. On the other hand, ethnic antagonisms sometimes
work against the Communists. Hanoi seems loath to call in Chinese
help against America's stepped-up war effort because most Vietnamese
hate the Chinese, remembering that China ruled Viet Nam for over
1,000 years.

It would take a generation of Asian Atatürks to knit unified nations out of what are all too often simply shreds of geographic motley.
Today's Asia, however, is short on Atatürks. Since Nehru's death, most
leaders of Asia's developing countries fall into one of two categories:
those too weak to overcome hatred as such and those who try to exploit
it to build up their personal power.

To the first category belongs India's Shastri, who tries to mediate
between antagonists rather than strike at the roots of their antagonism.
Malaysia's jovial Prime Minister, Tunku Abdul Rahman, also finds it
hard to be a true national leader because the bulk of his support comes
from his anti-Chinese fellow Malays—even though he warns them, "You
can't throw all of the Chinese into the sea."

Of the second, demagogic, category of Asian leaders, the worst is

Indonesia's Sukarno, whose campaign to "crush Malaysia" as a "neo-colonialist" plot furnishes Indonesia with a phony national purpose and distracts attention from his own disastrous misrule. Even Sandhurst-educated President Ayub Khan of Pakistan plays up "the Indian menace" to strengthen his political hand, warns darkly: "India wants to settle every dispute with force and aggression."

LACK OF IDENTITY

Obviously none of these antagonisms are unique to Asia. For centuries, the West's highly advanced nations have fought the world's most disastrous wars, even before the Bomb, and any sense of European superiority must be badly shaken by the memory of Buchenwald. Yet since World War II, the peoples of Europe, for all their lingering animosities, have begun to develop more of a common loyalty to the whole region and idea of Europe. Moreover, adds Harvard Sinologist Professor Benjamin Schwartz, "The West has achieved the modern secular state, and its machinery does tend to control internal strife. But most Asian countries are not yet modern nations in this sense."

Ironically, the fading of the "imperialist" enemy, a menace that the Communists try so hard to keep alive, aggravates the crisis. Making common cause against colonial masters often gave Asian countries—and groups within countries—a solidarity they are now losing. But there are some encouraging signs. Interracial schooling, notably in Thailand and Malaysia, is binding young overseas Chinese closer to their host nations. Officers and men of different races serve happily together in units of the Indian and Malaysian armed forces, where the military-command structure replaces communal loyalties. Above all, as industrialization spreads in Asia, traditional cleavages, based on almost exclusively agricultural ways of life, may tend to blur. In the short run, industrialization and economic competition may bring further strains, but in the long run, the machine does homogenize people. And a better life—even the mere prospect of a better life—can establish a sense of community.

What the countries of Asia need to develop is a far stronger sense of national identity. Ultimately, only a common patriotism can subdue the internal enmities between classes and races; and a strong, self-reliant patriotism should eventually exist without having to be artificially whipped up through hatred of other countries. That kind of patriotism may offer the only real resistance in Asia to Communism and its ready-made formulas for "emerging nations."

The growth of such national feelings will also require the growth of individualism, for a sense of nationhood can probably be achieved only by people who respect themselves and their own worth. A generation ago, the great leader of India's Untouchables, B. R. Ambedkar, asked Gandhi: "How can I call this land my own homeland wherein we are treated worse than cats and dogs, wherein we cannot get water to drink?" Yet gradually, very gradually, Untouchables have begun to speak of India as their nation. And so it must be for all the other "untouchables" of Asia, if the great Asian peoples are to acquire a real sense of loyalty to nation and eventually to the ideal of order.

the

nations

of

ASIA

AFGHANISTAN

A Monarchy in the Mountains

Afghanistan is one of the world's few completely landlocked independent countries. Roughly the size of Texas, the nation holds a strategically important position, being bordered by Pakistan, Iran, the Soviet Union, and China.

THE LAND AND THE MOUNTAINS

Mountains dominate this country and profoundly affect the Afghan way of life. The rugged mass of the Hindu Kush and its affiliated ranges form a central core, and are the source of the melt water that irrigates much of Afghanistan's crops. The mountains divide the country into three major geographic zones—the mountains themselves constitute the central zone, the northern zone consists largely of arable and non-arable plains, and the south is mostly desert.

On the Turkestan Plains in the north, Uzbek and Turkoman shepherds raise karakul, or Persian lamb, and fat-tailed sheep. In this zone, well-farmed irrigated areas in the river valleys supply the greater part of the nation's wheat.

DESERTS THAT SHOULD BLOOM

In the south and west are deserts and semi-deserts, cut by the Helmand-Arghandab river system which drains 40 percent of the country. A strange feature of Seistan, in the extreme southwest, is the *bad-i-sad-o-bist ruz*, the "Wind of 120 days" which blows from June through September, sweeping down from the north, and sometimes reaching a velocity of more than 100 miles an hour.

This area has not always been a desert wasteland. In ancient times, the land was famous as one of the garden spots of Asia, its rich crops supporting flourishing civilizations. But repeated invasions and massacres decimated the population and destroyed most of the irrigation systems, with the result that desert conditions now prevail over much of the area. Today, irrigation projects are underway, but it will be many years before the Helmand River region once again reaches full productivity.

The ancient *kariz* irrigation system required careful engineering and good maintenance. Underground channels were dug by hand. They were skillfully designed to lead the water, which collects underground at the bases of slopes or mountains, out into the plains. In some areas, water was stored in deep tanks of masonry. Some of these have survived, and even today are used to provide water in bad times for the herds of the nomads.

RURAL GIRL   She is helping during wheat harvest.

TUNNEL THROUGH THE HINDU KUSH

In the central region, there are over a hundred mountains which soar between 20,000 and 25,000 feet above sea level. The highest peaks are in the eastern Pamirs, which is the home of the famed Marco Polo sheep.

In the western Hindu Kush is located one of the most notable spots in the land—the *Band-i-Amir,* a region of five lakes known for its beauty and the deep blue color of its waters. Nearby is the ancient site of Bamiyan. In the early centuries of the Christian era, colonies of Buddhist monks dug cells and grottoes here in the sandstone cliffs. They decorated these retreats with painted murals. On a sheer face of one of these cliffs, two gigantic figures of the Buddha were carved into the rock, the taller of these representations being 175 feet high. Originally, these statues were draped in robes of gilded plaster and were elaborately painted. In ancient times, Bamiyan was far off the beaten track; today, it has become a prime tourist attraction.

The important effect of the central mountain ranges is that they divide the country, making communication difficult between north and south. In 1964, a paved highway was completed through the Hindu Kush; its showpiece is a mile and a half long tunnel. Now traffic can move through the mountains even in the dead of winter. This should lead to more extensive links—both social and economic—between the speakers of Persian in the north and the speakers of Pushtu in the south.

MELTING POT OF ISLAM

Afghanistan has been a melting pot of many peoples. The people who emigrated to Afghanistan have adopted the faith of the land, but not the language nor the institutions. Nevertheless, this sort of melting pot has been effective in creating an Afghan nation.

THE MUSLIM FAITH

The religion of Afghanistan is Islam, to which over 99 percent of the people adhere. The *Hanafi Sunni* group, an orthodox sect, is dominant. *Shi'a* groups, or Muslim breakaway sects, are found among the

BUZKASHI *In this rugged game, Afghani mountaineers use a beheaded goat or calf instead of a ball. Here, men of the Panjshir River valley thunder after a player who has retrieved the goat and is just about to carry it for a goal. The mountains of the Hindu Kush loom in the background.*

Hazara, Qizilbash, and some Wakhan groups. Among the *Shi'a* sects, the *Imami*, which also predominates in neighboring Iran, is the most significant.

Few in Afghanistan can read, and many village *mullahs,* analogous to parish priests, are illiterate. The *mullahs* often use their religious authority to protect their economic and political interests against the uneducated who depend on them for guidance.

A TRIBAL POPULATION

Physically, most Afghans—a group name that includes Pushtuns (or Pathans), Tajiks, Qizilbash, Baluchi, Nuristanis—are members of the Caucasian race. But in the north there are large groups who are of Mongol descent: the Hazara, Aimak, Uzbek, Turkoman, Kirghiz.

The seasonal movements of the nomad tribes make it practically impossible exactly to determine the distribution of the population. No census has ever been taken. Most qualified observers estimate the population to be around 12 million, or about 50 persons per square mile. The major population groups are estimated as: Pushtuns, 6,500,000; Tajiks and Qizilbash, 2,200,000; Uzbeks, 1,000,000; Aimak, 850,000; Hazara,

800,000; Turkoman, 200,000; Nuristanis, 60,000; Hindus and Sikhs, 30,000.

About one-fifth of the people live in the fertile valleys of Kabul and Jalalabad; fewer than eight percent live in towns or cities. Most Afghans are village farmers or nomads. Small groups classed as semi-sedentary farmers travel to the mountains in the spring and summer with sheep, goats, cattle. Semi-nomads move seasonally with their flocks.

THE NURISTANIS

Among the least-known of the many small tribal groups are the Nuristanis, who were called *Kafirs,* or "heathens" until their conversion to Islam late in the 19th century. These people have a high percentage of recessive blondism; in the villages I have studied, about 30 percent of the Nuristanis had blond or red hair.

For centuries, the Nuristanis have fiercely defended and preserved their way of life and their ancient languages and customs, retaining their own set of values. Isolated in its own valley among the rugged mountains, each small group has preserved its own peculiar dialect. A Nuristani does not place such a great value on horses as a Pathan does; instead, Nuristanis still raise goats and cattle, which at one time were used for sacrifices to the gods.

Before they were converted to the religion of Islam, Nuristanis took pride in slaying Muslims. After he had dispatched four or five Muslims and returned from raids with booty and with such trophies of victory as Muslim ears or scalp locks, a Nuristani was entitled to wear a special kind of shawl.

TRIBAL SOCIETY

All of Afghanistan remains to this day essentially a tribal-oriented society. Each tribal unit has an elaborate kinship system, and its traditions, passed from father to son, dominate the ideas of the group. Reinforcing the in-group feeling is the fact that relatives are closely united, sometimes with real—often with merely fictional—blood ties.

In the tribal setup, kinship and political institutions coincide—the chief of one's tribe and the head of one's family are one and the

GRAPE CULTURE   *A farmer near Kabul proudly displays a heavy vine. These grapes will be eaten fresh or dried for export. Muslim Afghans do not make wine because their religion forbids them to drink intoxicating beverages.*

same individual. Many Afghans still do not have family names; when modern civilization requires a last name for a passport or a school diploma, they take the tribe's name.

In a tribal society, a man is born into a set of prerogatives and obligations. Moreover, he is born into an *inward-looking* society which takes its methods and ideas from its own past, rather than from teachers or peoples outside the local clan. A tribesman has, by tradition and birth, a set of *answers;* questions of a basic nature rarely arise in his mind. Conversely, in the West, we are born into an *outward-looking* society; that is, we inherit a set of *questions* to which each person must seek his own answers through his own experiences, his own thinking, and his particular teachers.

This difference between a tribal society and a non-tribal society is one of the important differences between East and West. In considering these differences, it should be acknowledged that for a group living in a subsistence economy an *inward-looking* set of values is necessary for survival. Neither time nor resources permit the development of elaborate, question-answering institutions such as the laboratory and the university.

THE CODE OF THE HILLS

The cultural attitudes prevalent in Afghanistan can best be explained by describing the *Pukhtunwali,* the unwritten code of the hills. The *Pukhtunwali* includes such diverse and often contradictory concepts as hospitality to strangers, eternal hostility to enemies (including blood vengeance), and asylum for a specified period of time to all who ask for it—including blood enemies.

A harsh land breeds a harsh people. Characteristic of the Pushtun people is a suspicion of outsiders, modified by a code of obligatory hospitality. They believe in Islam but seldom worship, and are ruggedly irreligious unless an outsider challenges their faith. Their brutality is tempered by a love of beauty. Dynamic when there is work to be done, they are easily swayed to indolence. Avarice is combined with spurts of impetuous generosity. They are conservative in their mountain homeland, but quick to adapt to new ideas and techniques when citified. An anarchistic love of individual freedom is tempered by an acceptance of rule by the aristocratic *khans.* An assertion of masculine superiority nevertheless allows for a tacit recognition of women's rights. A love of isolation is constantly challenged by curiosity about the outside world.

BUZKASHI AND GHOSAI

The national game, *buzkashi,* or "goat-grabbing," is well suited to the essentially tribal Afghan character. Played mainly on the northern plain, *buzkashi* combines, in a loose framework, individualism with group cooperation. Two teams—the number on each side varying from ten to hundreds—play the game, a combination of polo, mounted football, and unorganized mayhem.

A dead goat or calf is placed in the center of a field. A shot is fired and the horsemen make a dash for the carcass and attempt to carry it to

CITIZENS OF KABUL   Men pause outside a mosque to exchange opinions in the sun. The crowd is wholly masculine. Islamic ladies of good family do all their visiting indoors.

the goal. Participants use stout quirts to control their horses—or to strike their heavily padded opponents. Many villages in north Afghanistan have special fields on which they play "sandlot" *buzkashi* all winter.

Although it is played on foot, the game of *ghosai* is somewhat like *buzkashi*. An unlimited number can play, but usually about 20 divide into two teams. One man, the *ghosai*, tries to reach a goal while his team protects him. Each player hops on one foot, and holding one arm behind his back, wrestles with opponents, obstructing them with his free hand.

A MEDLEY OF TONGUES

Tribal, inward-looking, and often isolated in mountain valleys, the Afghans have preserved the tongues that they originally brought with them to Afghanistan. Over 20 languages are in daily use, most of them Iranian. Pushtu and Dari are the official languages. Dari, a Persian dialect, usually serves as the *lingua franca*.

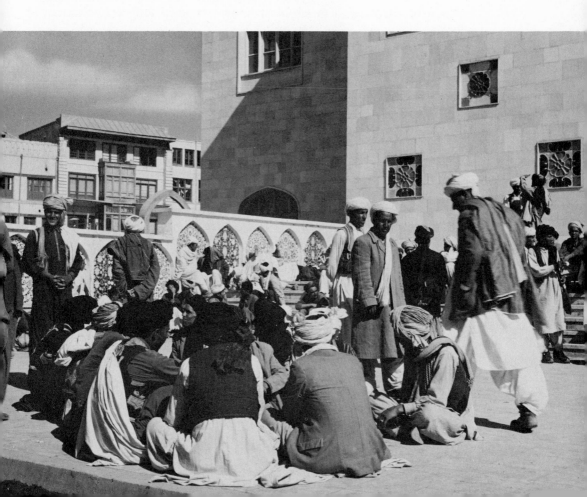

THE AFGHAN WAY OF LIFE

Despite the fact that the peoples and languages of Afghanistan are heterogeneous, the predominant basic ideas and feelings are similar enough to give the people a sense of unity. Not only are the Afghans united through their belief in Islam, but the tribal way of life also provides unity. Even long-time city dwellers and farmers whose families have lived in villages for generations retain much of the tribal outlook.

Just as the clans of a tribe stay together, so in the villages extended families remain together. There will be a house or several houses inside a walled compound. As each son marries, he will bring his wife to live in one of the rooms or, if the family is well off, in one of the houses in his parental compound. In tribal living, each son pitches his tent near his parents' tent, and all the women of the group cooperate in the cooking and in many other housekeeping chores.

For the spring festival, *No Ruz,* clans and families—all on donkey back—come to Kabul or to the nearest town for the games and carnivals. Ordinarily, men spend much of their free time in long conversations at tea houses, where women may not go. But during the holiday the whole family celebrates together. Sometimes women even join in dancing the national dance, the *attan.* In this dance, people join in a great circle and dance to the music of drums and flutes, faster and faster, for as long as two or three hours without stopping.

VILLAGE HOSPITALITY

Hospitality is very important in the tribal code, the *Pukhtunwali.* Every village has a *hujreh,* or guest house. Individuals and villages compete for the privilege of entertaining a guest, and every little boy is carefully taught how to welcome strangers.

When a guest comes, everyone in a village welcomes him individually and every family sends some of its dinner to the guest house. The important men talk with the guest, giving and seeking the latest news, as long as he will stay awake. They come back in the morning with milk and bread. Everywhere in the land, a man is apt to be very hurt if his hospitality is refused.

KABUL, CENTER OF PROGRESS

Kabul is the most progressive city in Afghanistan, but even in this big city many of the simple and friendly tribal customs prevail. For example, no one passes a friend on the street without stopping to talk.

The modern and the traditional are blended. Kabul has movies, modern government buildings, and electric lights, but it also has numbers of tea houses, old style, flat-roofed houses, and bazaars. The streets are crowded with trucks, bicycles, cars, and taxis, intermingled with horse-drawn *gaudi,* men on horses, loaded camels and donkeys, and an occasional flock of sheep.

A villager may feel strange in the modern business and residential sections with their wide streets, but he is at home in the old town, even though it is much busier than his village. He soon adapts to city life because the basic values are much the same as those he has always known.

A TURBULENT HISTORY

Afghanistan was once a pivot point in Asia, the center of the caravan trade between China and Rome. Through its high mountain passes went many conquerors, including Alexander, Ghengis Khan, and Tamerlane. Many a traveler, notably Marco Polo, passed through here on his way to India or the Near East.

Historical records confirm that Alexander the Great, in the course of his conquests, married Roxanna, daughter of an Afghan chieftan. Legend relates that she was his favorite wife and was by his side when he died in Babylon at the age of 32.

Ideas, as well as traders and conquerors, passed through Afghanistan, and sometimes germinated and were spread far and wide. Buddhism reached Mongolia, China, Korea, and ultimately Japan from Afghanistan along the fabled Silk Route.

Also, from the first to the fifth centuries A.D., under the combined influence of Hellenic, Roman, and Indian art styles, a magnificent renaissance occurred in an area then known as Gandhara; today this area is occupied by Afghanistan and West Pakistan. The most spectacular manifestations of this development are to be found today at Bamiyan.

THE COMING OF ISLAM

In the eighth century A.D., when Islam was expanding, the Afghans fought the Arabs with the same ferocity with which they have always faced invaders. However, in the course of three centuries of warfare, various tribal leaders were converted to Islam, and founded local dynasties and spread the new faith throughout most of the land.

In the 10th century, resurgent Hindus invaded, taking over Kabul and eastern Afghanistan. But early in the 11th century, one of Afghanistan's most famous kings, Mahmud of Ghazni, expelled the Hindus and established a great empire, stretching from Central Asia to the Indian Ocean and across to the Persian Gulf. Islam was once again propagated.

Leading raids into India almost every year for loot and glory and for the sake of the true faith, Mahmud was called "the Image Breaker." His soldiers and his treatment of the image-building Hindus were ruthless. Yet Mahmud was not merely a warrior; he created a great center of learning and art at Ghazni, patronizing hundreds of poets, astronomers, musicians, scholars, and craftsmen.

EMPIRES DOOMED BY BROTHERHOOD

Mahmud's Ghaznavid Empire began to break up with his death in 1030 A.D. From that time until 1880, a process which I call *political fusion and fission* became the typical pattern of Afghan history. A strong leader would rise and fuse together large areas into an empire, rather than into a nation-state. Upon his death, there would ensue a struggle for power of brother against brother, of nephew against uncle, and the empire would break up into a number of competing petty kingdoms.

Until 1220, the civilizations of the Muslim world were as brilliant as any this planet had seen. But no unity existed, and each state fought constantly with the other states. The Muslim Turks—most early Afghan kings were Turks—were powerful and they seriously threatened both the Muslim Arabs and the European Christians.

Then out of Mongolia came a man who made history by destroy-

WOMEN OF KABUL *All but one of these ladies wear the black veiling called a "chadri." This traditional garb has an inadequate peephole of heavy net surrounded by embroidery. Until quite recent years, the wearing of the chadri was "de rigueur" for all women in Kabul; it was considered contrary to Islamic tradition for an unveiled woman to be seen in public. Women who flouted this tradition were subject to arrest. In 1959, Kabul police were ordered not to arrest unveiled ladies, but rather to protect them—a radical change, if not in general custom, at least in law. Since then, many young women have eagerly abandoned the cumbersome veil, but most feel more comfortable when their modesty is protected by a coat and scarf. Characteristically, the young lady has thrown a scarf around her head before she ventured into the streets.*

ing the finest civilizations of the 13th century. Ghengis Khan and his Mongols carved a transient empire from the China Sea to the Adriatic.

The many fratricidal wars, the Mongol invasion, and the Turco-Mongol invasions of Tamerlane at the end of the 14th century tumbled Muslim culture from its high pinnacle. The civil wars and the invasions destroyed the one thing without which the high level of the civilization could not be maintained: the vast irrigation projects which supported the people with great food surpluses.

For two hundred years after Tamerlane's incursion, the Persian Safavids and the Indian Moghuls fought for control of Afghanistan. Even though the Afghans were no longer masters in their own land, many tribes maintained their independence.

RISE OF THE DURRANI CLAN

In 1747, a native Afghan dynasty was founded in Kandahar by Ahmad Shah Durrani, a first-rate soldier and administrator, whose exploits rank with those of Mahmud of Ghazni, Ghengis Khan, and Tamerlane. He defeated the Persians, invaded north India, and consolidated an empire which far exceeded Afghanistan's present boundaries. At his death in 1773, his empire began to break up, in the political fusion and fission pattern mentioned earlier.

IMPERIALISTIC INFLUENCES

Fratricidal fights continued to fragment Afghanistan during the 19th century, but external forces brought about the beginnings of a nation-state instead of the usual empire. Czarist Russia steadily expanded into Muslim Central Asia, and the British countered by extending the northwestern limits of their Indian empire. Twice, from 1838 to 1842 and from 1878 to 1880, the British occupied Afghan territory in response to real or imagined Russian threats.

After the second invasion, the British were in a dilemma as to whether to continue to rule the part of Afghanistan they had occupied. With tacit consent from the Russians, they agreed instead to support Abdur Rahman Khan as Amir of Kabul.

During his reign, 1880–1901, Abdur Rahman laid the foundations of the modern Afghan state. He extended his influence—if not control—throughout most of the country. In his own words, the Amir "had to put in order all those hundreds of petty chiefs, plunderers, robbers, and cutthroats. . . . This necessitated breaking down the feudal and tribal system and substituting one grand community under one law and one rule."

Thus, although the Afghans never came directly under imperialist control, they became a modern state because of pressures of an essentially imperialistic nature from both north and south.

To this day, Afghans rankle at the thought that outsiders drew their boundaries. The Russians and British were responsible for those in the north. British and Persians together controlled borders in the west, while the British alone drew the boundaries with Pakistan in the south and east. This resentment is one of the historical sources of Afghanistan's present dispute with Pakistan over the Pushtuns.

THE FIRST ATTEMPT AT MODERNIZATION

Amir Habibullah reigned from 1901 to 1919, continuing the policies of his father, Abdur Rahman. He was assassinated on a hunting trip, and his third son, Amanullah, seized the throne. Partly to save his tottering regime, Amanullah launched the Third Anglo-Afghan War, an inconclusive month-long affair which resulted in British recognition of Afghanistan's right to conduct its own foreign affairs.

In 1923, Amanullah started reforms which included a new constitution and measures to control the Muslim theologians. After an extended trip to Europe, Turkey, and Iran in 1927, King Amanullah attempted to introduce Afghans to further western-type reforms, such as monogamy (Islam traditionally permits a man to have four wives), separation of church and state, and secular education.

TRADITIONALIST REVOLT

In 1928, the Afghans, devoutly Muslim, fiercely independent, illiterate, tribal, and ultra-conservative, revolted against these changes. Amanullah had to flee the country in spite of Soviet attempts to send aid. He had tried to do too much too fast—and without the backing of the army! In the immediate confusion, an illiterate Tajik bandit, Bacha-i-Saqqao, came to power. For nine months, he ruled by torture and extortion. He held court in the lapis lazuli–tiled bathrooms of Amanullah's palace, and staged cockfights in the large reception rooms.

BEGINNINGS OF STABLE GOVERNMENT

Sardar Mohammad Nadir Khan, a distant cousin of Amanullah's was living in exile in France at that time. With his four brothers, he returned to Afghanistan, gathered together his supporting tribes, overthrew the bandit-king and executed him. In September, 1930, the *Loya Jirgah*, the Great National Assembly of tribal leaders and other notables, was called and it proclaimed him Nadir Shah, King of Afghanistan.

PUSHTUN VILLAGER

NURISTANI   *This red-headed, blue-eyed you[ng] man hails from the mountains on Afghanistan's ea[st]ern border.*

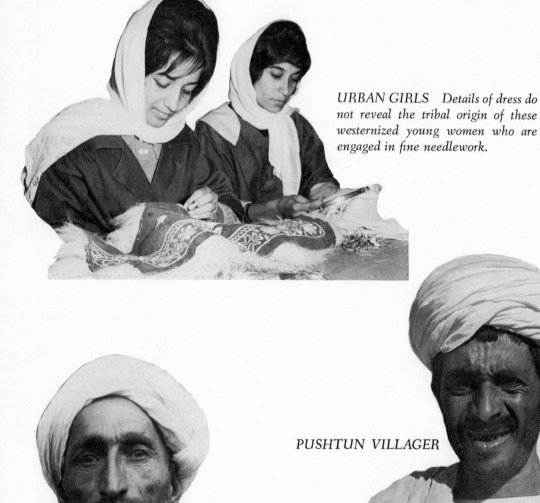

URBAN GIRLS   *Details of dress do not reveal the tribal origin of these westernized young women who are engaged in fine needlework.*

PUSHTUN VILLAGER

UZBEK

A PUSHTUN FATHER AND DAUGHTER *They live in She-waki village, outside of Kabul.*

PUSHTUN VILLAGER

HAZARA *His Mongol ancestry is somewhat apparent in his physiognomy.*

The new Shah's brothers were rewarded with important positions —one was appointed Prime Minister, another War Minister—and they all set out to restore order in the land and to begin the process of economic development. They knew the country needed social reforms, but they also knew their conservative countrymen, and they proceeded slowly.

Before his assassination in 1933, Nadir Shah had formulated a constitution which called for a government based on a liberal interpretation of the Hanafi Code of Sunni Islam. He was succeeded by his 19-year-old son, Mohammad Zahir, who had the support of his uncles, a rare occurrence in Afghan history. For once, family solidarity and dynastic survival overrode personal ambitions. Until 1953, two of the young king's experienced uncles took turns serving as Prime Minister.

The 1930's were primarily years of recovery from the upheavals of the 1920's. A cautious development program was begun, primarily through hiring German, Italian, and Japanese technicians. Among the more important of the projects undertaken were dams and irrigation works.

World War II slowed the development programs because no equipment was delivered. The Afghans remained neutral in the war, as they had in World War I. They accumulated much surplus capital, because they sold freely to Allied armies in India, but could buy almost nothing. At the war's end, they were in a good position to resume the course of development. However, the emergence of new nations and changes in world politics revolutionized Afghanistan's position in international affairs.

AFGHANISTAN'S RECENT PAST

Since the end of World War II, two factors relating to outside influences have dominated the Afghan scene: bad relations with the newly formed Pakistan disrupted the traditional pattern of transit trade; and secondly, development schemes were financed by grants and loans from western countries (primarily the United States) and from nations of the Soviet bloc.

SARDAR DAOUD

In 1953, a cousin of the king, Sardar Mohammad Daoud Khan, commander of the Afghan army (*Sardar* means prince), peacefully and smoothly seized power from the King's uncles. He ruled Afghanistan as Prime Minister for a decade. Under Daoud's vigorous tutelage the country moved forward in many spheres; the solid achievements of his regime are many.

Traditional Afghan neutrality was used to obtain increased foreign aid from both east and west; this aid has greatly speeded up the construction of an economic infrastructure—roads, airfields, a telecommunications network. The status and morale of the armed forces improved when the Soviet Union assisted in modernizing the army and air force after the Americans had refused to help. Educational opportunities increased and the ultra-conservative, anti-progressive religious leaders lost much of their power. Regional economic planning spurred additional development. As the political base of power gradually broadened to include more of the people, each municipal election became more democratic.

Although most of Sardar Daoud's achievements relate to economic development, possibly his most important legacy is the government-sponsored, but voluntary, removal of the veil from women in 1959. It is probable that the government was not only interested in improving the lot of women but also wanted to increase the national labor force—a lady wearing a voluminous *chadri* cannot operate a typewriter or even see well enough to cross a busy street. Some Afghan ladies, especially those who are elderly, still wear the veil, but many younger women have abandoned both the *chadri* and Islam's customs of seclusion. Every year more women become active members of society, usually as nurses, teachers, or office workers.

THE PUSHTUNISTAN ISSUE

A major factor contributing to Sardar Daoud's resignation was the "Pushtunistan" problem, which concerns the fate of the Pushtuns, or Pathans, on the Pakistan side of the Durand Line.

Briefly, the problem is as follows: In 1893 the British demarcated the

Durand Line to separate Afghanistan from British India. The line divided the Pushtun areas approximately in half. Although Amir Abdur Rahman signed a treaty accepting the Durand Line as Afghanistan's frontier, he and subsequent Afghan rulers considered it a formality which merely established zones of influence rather than a permanent boundary.

When Pakistan became independent in 1947, it inherited the British position in the area. The Afghans demanded that their "Pushtun brothers" be given the opportunity to vote for independence, which meant, of course, that the Pushtun area of Pakistan would eventually be absorbed by Afghanistan. Pakistan refused to allow the issue to come to a vote.

The dispute intensified over the years, and in 1961 caused the closing of the Afghan-Pakistan border for two years. Prime Minister Daoud had been a stout supporter of the "Pushtunistan" issue, and as long as he remained in power there was little hope of reopening the border.

The border closure cut off the supply from the west of material for development as well as of trade goods. The closure therefore operated to push the reluctant Afghans into greater economic dependence on the Soviet bloc. Many Afghans and Westerners are seriously concerned over the Soviet experiment with economic penetration in Afghanistan. After the resignation of Daoud, Afghanistan and Pakistan reached a formal agreement providing for the unrestricted transit of goods across the border. Now, the Afghans continue to seek political stability and relative economic viability by accepting grants, loans, and technical assistance from both the West and the Communist bloc.

PROBLEMS OF DEVELOPMENT

Under the guidance of King Mohammad Zahir and his advisers, Afghanistan is progressing in all directions. New roads, irrigation and hydroelectric projects, and airfields are under way or have been completed. Ariana Afghan Airlines now services six stops inside the country as well as half a dozen foreign capitals. Schools to combat the 95 percent illiteracy rate, hospitals and public health facilities to combat high

ZAHIR SHAH   *Surrounded by his advisers, Afghan's moderate and progressive
King is signing the promulgation of the new Constitution.*

infant mortality and such endemic diseases as tuberculosis, are in
progress.

Economically, Afghanistan has been trying to increase its agricultural productivity, both in total acreage cultivated and in production
per acre, especially in wheat and cotton. Another goal is to produce certain items locally, especially textiles, cement, and sugar, which annually
use up much of the country's foreign currency. Progress is also being
made in improving the quality of the major export items, such as
fresh and dried fruit and nuts, karakul skins, carpets, and sausage
casings.

THE CONSTITUTION OF 1964

Probably the most important event since the 1963 change in government has been the writing of a new constitution, approved by the
450-man *Loya Jirgah* in September, 1964.

This liberalized constitution prohibits members of the royal family
from participating in political activities, holding political office, or serving in the judiciary. The separate powers and responsibilities of the
monarch, executive, legislative, and judicial institutions are clearly de-

fined. The King is invested with the right to appoint a Prime Minister (not necessarily an elected member of the legislature), who is empowered to form a government which he must present to Parliament for approval.

Parliament will consist of two branches: the directly elected House of the People, and the House of the Elders, two-thirds elected and one-third appointed by the King. In the event of a national emergency the King can dissolve Parliament and call a *Loya Jirgah,* which will be made up of the members of Parliament and the elected chairmen of the Provincial Councils. Although Islam remains the official religion of Afghanistan, the new constitution secularized most of the legislative and judicial processes.

NOMAD ENCAMPMENT Tents and herds of pastoral clans can be found throughout most of Afghanistan. This characteristic scene shows a summer camp in the foothills of the Hindu Kush. The tents, open to the warm breeze, are rectangular pavilions formed by draping lengths of black goat's hair cloth over supporting poles. Herds cropping the sparse grass include camels, horses, karakul sheep, fat-tailed sheep, goats. The herds are guarded by ferocious dogs trained to stop any stranger.

The new constitution moves Afghanistan slowly along the path to democracy. Meanwhile, the King and the army have the power and resources to preserve stability. In the economic sphere, the ruler strives toward vitality and viability, insofar as it is possible in a nation whose economy is fundamentally agricultural.

In terms of foreign aid, both Russia and America are competing for influence in Afghanistan through long-term commitments to assistance, with neither side winning. The Afghans, firmly neutral, *are* winning, however, and perhaps that is the way it should be.

Afghanistan is still a nation with no railroads and few wheeled vehicles in its villages. Nevertheless, considering the economic, political, and social reforms that have been achieved, Afghanistan has probably made as much progress as any country in Asia—or more,

LOUIS DUPREE

IN BRIEF

AREA   245,000 square miles, smaller than Texas.

TERRAIN   Landlocked behind mountains and deserts. Afghanistan has an average elevation of 4,000 feet. Peaks of the Hindu Kush, which runs through the center of the land, reach heights of over 20,000 feet in the northeast. In these mountain valleys and on the high central plateau, the land is chiefly suitable for grazing flocks or raising highland wheat and barley. In the north, the land drops to plains averaging 1,500 feet elevation and often as low as 900 feet. Parts of these plains are fertile, when irrigated. The southwest is desert.

FLORA   Largely treeless. Extensive forests (pine and oak, with poplar and willow in the valleys) grow only in Pakhtia and Nuristan.

FAUNA   Bears, mountain goats, gazelles, ibex, deer, hyenas, jackals, foxes, wolves, and leopards. Game birds (partridge, grouse, ducks) abound seasonally. Siberian tiger and Marco Polo sheep in the Pamirs.

CLIMATE   Arid, with strongly marked seasonal changes. Annual rainfall is only 10 or 11 inches. Temperatures below zero are common in winter; summer temperatures rise to 100°F. Kabul is famous for its remarkably pleasant spring weather.

CAPITAL   Kabul had an estimated 325,000 inhabitants in 1964.

OTHER CITIES   Kandahar, 115,000 inhabitants. Herat, Mazar-i-Sharif, Jalalabad, Ghazni, and Gardez are the other main urban centers.

POPULATION   About 12 million people, including about two million nomads. No census has ever been taken; estimates range from 8 to 14 million. Rate of population increase is possibly as high as three percent a year; density about 50 persons per square mile.

ETHNIC GROUPS   Caucasoid groups include 6.5 million Pushtuns, 2.2 million Tajiks, 60,000 Nuristanis. Also some Baluchis—nomads of the southwestern desert. Groups of Turkish and Mongol origin include a million Uzbeks, 800,000 Hazara, 850,000 Aimak, 200,000 Turkomen, and some Kirghiz tribes in the Pamirs.

There are also Brahui in the southwest, Hindus and Sikhs in the towns.

LANGUAGES

Four-fifths of the people speak Pushtu or Persian, the official languages. There are about 20 languages, including dialects, in common use. Persian or Dari, which is known as Farsi in Iran, is used by the Tajiks, Qizilbash, and Hazara. Pushtu is the language of the Pushtuns. The Baluchis speak their own Iranian dialect, called Baluchi. The Uzbeks, Turkomens, and Kirghiz in northern Afghanistan use dialects belonging to the Ural-Altaic family.

RELIGION

Over 99 percent of the people are Muslim. Most are Sunnis, but about a million belong to the Shi'a and other Muslim sects.

DATE OF INDEPENDENCE

In 1747, a native Afghan dynasty attained power. Although there were many later invasions, there was no total conquest by a European power. In 1880, Amir Abdur Rahman began to create a modern nation-state.

FORM OF GOVERNMENT

Constitutional monarchy. The 1964 constitution limits and defines the King's duties. The House of the People is directly elected, and the House of the Elders is partly elected and partly appointed. The government is formed by a Prime Minister appointed by the King. There are no political parties, but the first elected Parliament, that of 1964, yill probably pass a political parties law. Afghanistan is a member of the United Nations and other international bodies.

EDUCATION

In 1963, primary, secondary, and vocational schools open to the public enrolled about 310,000 students. There were close to 6,500 teachers, with 2,000 more being trained. The university at Kabul had 2,500 students; another 2,200 were studying abroad. Less than 10 percent of the people are literate. Although eight percent of the budget is used for education, only one out of 10 children starts school, and only one in 300 reaches secondary school.

HEALTH FACILITIES

In 1963, there were some 400 doctors in the government hospitals; there were 475 nurses and 65 hospitals with 2,000 beds. Complete records are not kept, but life expectancy is probably less than 30 years. It is estimated that even in Kabul 15 per-

NURISTANI MUSICIANS *One man is plucking a four-stringed instrument which is much like an ancient lute. At the lower rim, it has a small sound box which is almost exactly like that of his companion's two-stringed relative of the violin. They wear the characteristic hat of the Nuristanis. In winter the rolled rim of the hat is pulled down over the ears.*

cent of the babies die in their first year. Malaria has been largely eradicated; smallpox, typhoid, and typhus are considerably reduced. Tuberculosis, trachoma, cholera, leprosy, anthrax, syphilis, dysentery, and diarrheal diseases remain serious problems.

CULTURAL FACILITIES

In 1961, 12 daily newspapers had about 74,000 circulation. One person in 200 sees a paper every day. The Ministry of Education press publishes about 100 books a year and other presses about an equal number; several magazines appear. There were 20 cinemas in 1960. *Radio Kabul* broadcasts news, music, and educational programs in eight languages. Although film-making is in its infancy, there is a thriving theater in Kabul. Popular entertainment survives mainly in the hands of poets and minstrels who travel among the villages. Songs, recitations, and tribal dancing are universally enjoyed.

CURRENCY AND FINANCE

The *afghani* weighs 10 grams of silver or 0.3 grains of fine gold, but its value fluctuates. Since 1960, on the free market it has usually been worth about 2¢ in U.S. currency. For the year ending March, 1964, the government budget anticipated revenues of 4.89 billion *afghanis* and expenditures of 5.03 billion. Development projects were to use 2.02 billion, including 1.5 billion *afghanis* in foreign loans and grants.

INDUSTRY AND PRODUCTION

Barely begun, industrialization proceeds slowly with foreign assistance; handicrafts and cottage industry remain economically significant. Hydroelectric power plants, cement factories, textile mills, and small factories for such things as soap, ceramics, and matches are in operation. Manufacturing may provide as much as six percent of the Gross National Product; GNP estimates range from 13 to 38 billion *afghanis*. Per capita income is probably close to $50 a year.

CROPS: The principal crops are wheat, barley, rice, fruit, nuts, corn, cotton, sugar, and vegetables. About 70 percent of the population live in agricultural villages.

LIVESTOCK: An estimated 30 million head include 16.3 million sheep, 6.6 million karakul sheep, 2.3 million goats, 3.7 million cattle, and horses, camels, mules, and donkeys. Herds and their products are the largest single source of national income. Perhaps a third of the people, including the nomads, are employed in livestock raising, producing Karakul skins, wool, hides, grease from the fat-tailed sheep, and meat.

MINING: Coal and salt are mined for local use only. Small amounts of gold and lapis lazuli are produced. No survey has been comprehensive, but undeveloped resources are known to include copper, lead, iron, silver, asbestos, mica, sulfur, chrome, and natural gas.

TRADE

Karakul skins, dried fruits and nuts, carpets, hides, cotton, and wool are the chief exports. Machinery, vehicles, petroleum products, textiles, and iron and steel mill products are the chief imports. Trade is mainly with the Soviet Union, Pakistan, India, Britain, the United States, West Germany, and Japan.

TAJIK This traveling smith follows his craft in the Logar River valley, south of Kabul.

March 1963–March 1964:

IMPORTS 6,303,084,000 *afghanis*
EXPORTS 3,459,133,000 *afghanis*
DEFICIT 2,843,951,000 *afghanis*

TRANSPORT

ROAD: There are at least 7,000 miles of road, about two-fifths of it usable in all weathers. An extensive rebuilding program receives U.S. and Soviet assistance. Access to the country from the south is mainly by road through mountain passes —especially the Khyber, Bolan, and Gomal passes. The Salang tunnel road through the Hindu Kush, completed in 1964, eases transport within the country. In 1961, there were about 8,800 trucks and buses, and over 5,000 cars. Internal freight is still largely carried by camels, donkeys, and horses.

RAIL: There are no railroads. Short spur lines approach the borders at six points: two from Pakistan and four from the Soviet Union.

NEW SCHOOLS   A teacher directs a village school. Like most government employees he is dressed in western clothes, but he wears a round Karakul hat. His students wear elaborately embroidered caps made in the style of Kandahar. The older students have wound turbans around their caps. All these boys wear the long shirt of the villagers; some wear sleeveless embroidered waistcoats; two wear the striped "chapan" of the northern regions. The chapan is a long cloak of striped silk or cotton which has a thick cotton lining designed to protect against the cold of the windy plains.

WATERWAY: There is a limited amount of barge traffic on the Amu Darya. There are few navigable rivers within Afghanistan, although timber is floated down the Kabul and Kunar rivers.

AIR: Kabul is the busiest airport, while Kandahar has an international jet airport. The single domestic airline serves four smaller fields and flies to Teheran, Peshawar, Karachi, New Delhi, Beirut, Frankfurt, and Tashkent.

SEA: The closest ocean outlet is Karachi, Pakistan.

COMMUNI-CATION A government-operated telephone and telegraph system provides limited service. There were about 8,500 telephones and 22,000 radios in 1964. *Radio Kabul* reaches most towns by means of loudspeakers installed in public places. Cheap transistor radios are bringing about a revolution in communications.

BHUTAN

Tiny Kingdom High in the Sky

The India-China border dispute has focused the attention of the world on one of the least-known countries—the Himalayan Kingdom of Bhutan. Its location between the rich Assam-Bengal plains of India and Communist-occupied Tibet gives the kingdom considerable strategic significance.

Bhutan may be roughly divided into three regions: the High Himalayan country, the Inner Himalaya, and the *Duars*.

THE HIGH HIMALAYAN REGION

The high Himalayan region, along the Tibetan border, averages over 14,000 feet in altitude. In this section are the snow-capped Great Himalayan Ranges, which attain a height of more than 24,000 feet in some places. This northern part of Bhutan is largely uninhabited, except for a few scattered settlements in the high valleys, where high mountain pastures are used during the summer months for grazing the hardy yak. These alpine pastures form a comparatively broad base from which the snow-capped mountains rise steeply.

Until a few years ago, the tempo of life in the High Himalayan area continued much as it had for many centuries before. Undisturbed, Bhutanese traders carried cloth, spices, and grain across the mountain passes into Tibet, and brought back salt, wool, and sometimes herds of yak.

Since the 1959 Tibetan revolt, Bhutan's trade with Tibet has completely stopped. The India-China border dispute has shaken the tranquil isolation of these remote highlands. Hundreds of refugees from Communist-occupied Tibet swarm through the High Himalayan country, and have become to some extent government charges.

THE INNER HIMALAYAN REGION

The Inner Himalaya is a mountainous area south of the High Himalayan country. The mountains here, in the midlands of Bhutan,

65

CONSTRUCTION WORKERS · *These women are employed in moving earth in a construction project at Thimbu which will become the permanent capital of Bhutan. The women are recruited from each village for work on the new government secretariat. Laborers receive about 50¢ a day in wages for a 12-hour shift. Note that most women are barefoot.* (Courtesy P. P. Karan and University of Kentucky Himalayan Expedition.)

enclose several fertile valleys, located at elevations varying from 5,000 to 9,000 feet. These relatively broad and flat valleys have moderate rainfall, and are fairly well populated and cultivated.

In the valley of the Paro River, substantial houses, peacefully guarded by rows of tattered Buddhist prayer flags, cluster into villages or stand alone amidst lush little fields of wheat or rice.

The spectacular *Dzong* (castle-monastery), built on an outcrop along the steep side of the valley, looms from afar. Its series of vertical prayer rooms and its temples with richly painted windows soar above the landscape in fairy book style.

Paro Dzong serves temporarily as the administrative center of Bhutan. It frequently serves as the venue for the sessions of the *Tsongdu* (The National Assembly), as well as for Bhutanese festivals such as the archery meet and the ritual dances which are attended by the ruler of Bhutan.

The settlement of Thimbu is the site of the permanent capital of the kingdom.

THE DUARS

Bordering the Assam-Bengal plains of India, the *duars* stretch along the northern border of Bhutan to a depth of eight to ten miles. Here, mountains rise sharply from the narrow plains, and are marked by deep gorges. The rainfall is heavy and the hillsides are covered with thick vegetation.

The entire *duars* tract is unhealthy; the narrow valleys are hot and humid; the forested foothills are wet and misty—the section too damp for human comfort. The southern section of the Bhutan *duars* is covered mostly with heavy savanna grass and bamboo jungle. In some areas, these have been cleared for rice cultivation. The *duars* control access to the strategic passes through the Himalayan foothills which lead to the fertile, populous valleys of the Inner Himalaya.

CASTLE   *This building is presently used as the residence of the King when he is in Paro. The elaborately carved wooden tiers are characteristic of the national architecture. The pennants are prayer flags which presumably send wishes to the Buddha with every flap.*

POPULATION

The country has an estimated population of 850,000.

The people who now live in the western half of the kingdom settled in Bhutan centuries ago and are, for the most part, Tibetan in origin. In eastern Bhutan, most of the people are similar in ethnic make-up to the people of adjacent Assam. Both population groups are Buddhist, but those of eastern Bhutan are less strict in their observance of religious customs, and there are fewer monasteries and lamas in this part of the country.

In addition to these groups, there are Nepali-Hindu settlers in southern Bhutan.

RELIGION

Buddhism is the state religion. Approximately 400 lamas, attached to the monasteries of the kingdom, are supported by the state. More than one-fourth of the nation's revenue goes to support the monasteries. Lately, the King has attempted to reduce the number of lamas by leaving unfilled such vacancies as have come about through death.

EDUCATION

Illiteracy is practically universal. In the Paro Valley, where social progress has been most marked, a small, literate class is taking root. Political and cultural alertness mark this group as the prime source of potential in Bhutan.

In the last two years, several government schools teaching Bhutanese, Hindi, and English have been opened.

A RURAL POPULATION

Bhutan's population is almost entirely rural. The kingdom has no towns, no banks, no theaters, no shops worthy of the name. Thimbu, the new permanent capital, is a mere cluster of houses around the Tashi Cho Dzong, combination fortress, administrative and religious center, built in the architectural style of the palace of the Dalai Lama at Lhasa.

MAHAYANA MONKS   These three young men at Thimbu wear the red and saffron robes of Buddhist lamas. Monks in Bhutan generally go barefooted. This is not because of religious reasons, but because they can't afford shoes. There are over 400 monks in Bhutan and they are maintained by the state. These men occupy an important religious and political status in the kingdom. Meditation and concentration are important features of Mahayana Buddhism. (Courtesy P. P. Karan and University of Kentucky Himalayan Expedition.)

A NEW CITY

An Indian team of engineers is completing surveys for the erection of a modern town at Thimbu, which lies 8,000 feet above sea level. Although Thimbu is situated between two mountain ranges rising to 12,000 feet, its regular terrain allows for easy drainage and sewage disposal, and the soil is suitable for building. There is also ample room for expansion without affecting the agricultural land of the neighborhood. Among the first structures to be erected by 1966 will be a Government Secretariat, an Assembly House, a Market Place, a General Hospital with 100 beds, a Secondary School, a Police Station, and an Institute of Cottage Industries.

BHUTANESE DANCERS   *Performers at Paro Dzong display the traditional dress of the Yakwalla tribe.*

Paro, the temporary capital, lies 20 miles southwest of Thimbu, and is linked to the new capital by a new road. Electricity, drainage, and modern facilities are still unknown in Paro and Thimbu. Paro's only modern installation is a small radio transmitter for maintaining contact with the Bhutan House in India.

THE ECONOMY

Of the three major regions of Bhutan, the relatively low, well-watered, and fertile valleys of the Inner Himalaya have the largest percentage of cultivated land, and here agriculture is most intensively developed. Rice and buckwheat grow well up to an elevation of 5,000 feet; from this altitude barley alternates with rice to about 8,000 feet; wheat grows at altitudes up to 9,000 feet. However, centuries of cultivation without manuring has depleted the fertility of the soil.

Pastoral activities are common to all regions of the country. The practice of driving herds up the mountainsides in the spring and down again in autumn (called transhumance) enables the Bhutanese to utilize pastures on the high Himalayan slopes during the summer when they are free of snow. Yak, as well as sheep and goats, are employed by the Bhutanese as beasts of burden.

Although a large part of Bhutan is covered by forest, lumbering is not developed because of the inaccessibility of the timber areas.

Bhutan has no proved mineral deposits of significance. There has been a proposal to mine the small deposit of coal in south Bhutan.

The economic development of Bhutan has long been handicapped by physical barriers which have reduced the accessibility of various areas. Up until 1961, in order to enter this Himalayan Kingdom, the traveler had to trek for six days on foot and muleback from the plains of Assam-Bengal, across a forbidding maze of thickly forested, sharp mountain ridges alive with leeches, and then travel through the Inner Himalayan Ranges to the fertile Paro Valley of central Bhutan.

In February, 1962, Bhutan's first motorable road, linking Phuntsholing on the Indian border with Paro, Bhutan's temporary capital, was finished. The completion of this road has reduced the travel time between Paro and the Indian frontier from six days by mule and foot to ten hours by jeep. This new road has stimulated a tremendous drive for modernity.

HISTORY AND GOVERNMENT

Bhutan's early history is enveloped in great obscurity. Old Tibetan manuscripts found in Buddhist monasteries indicate that the country became a distinct political entity about 300 years ago, when an influential traveling Tibetan lama, Sheptoon LaPha, proclaimed himself King and took the title of *Dharma Raja*.

His successors confined their power to the spiritual role and appointed a *Deb Raja*, or temporal ruler, to exercise temporal power. This custom of having two supreme authorities—a *Dharma Raja* for spiritual affairs, and a *Deb Raja* for temporal affairs—existed until the last *Dharma Raja* died 35 years ago. Traditionally, succession to the spiritual office was dependent upon a verifiable reincarnation of the *Dharma Raja*.

In 1907, with the help of the British, the *Penlop* (Governor) of Tongsa in eastern Bhutan established himself as the hereditary King. The present ruler, 36-year-old *Druk Gyalpo* (Dragon King) Jigme Dorji Wangchuk, is the third to succeed in this line. During his 12 years on the throne, he has shown himself to be a strong, determined ruler, deeply interested in the betterment of conditions for his people.

Queen Kesang, to whom he has been married since 1951, attended Oxford University in Britain. The Queen is a cousin of the Maharaja Palden Thondup Namgyal of neighboring Sikkim.

King Wangchuk is assisted in the administration of the kingdom by an advisory council which consists of civil servants and representatives of the Buddhist hierarchy. An elected 130-member National Assembly, which gives the people a voice in the government, meets twice a year in Paro.

According to a treaty signed in 1949, Bhutan is guided in her external relations by India's advice. All of Bhutan's foreign aid comes from India. In 1962, under Indian sponsorship, Bhutan became a participant in the Colombo Plan. Bhutan also issued its own postal stamps in 1962.

The invasion of Tibet by China and the invasion of India by China in 1962 aroused concern about China's intentions toward Bhutan. There is an area of northern Bhutan which is shown as Chinese territory on Chinese maps.

PRADYUMNA P. KARAN

ARCHERY   These men are expert with bow and arrow. Competitions in archery are regularly held; many Bhutanese still feel it is sacrilegious to fire a gun. Note that these men wear Western shoes, an uncommon sight in Bhutan.

IN BRIEF

AREA

An estimated 18,000 square miles, about the size of Vermont and New Hampshire combined. No complete survey has ever been made.

TERRAIN

Three major regions. There is a band of plains and river valleys, the *duars,* in the south where the climate is hot, steamy, and unhealthy; it is eight to ten miles deep. In the north, a similar band constitutes almost useless land. This High Himalaya region has several peaks over 24,000 feet. Although the climate is arctic, some valleys between 12,000 and 18,000 feet provide summer grazing for hardy cattle and yak. The central region, the Inner Himalaya, has broad, fertile valleys and a temperate climate. Numerous rivers, all of which flow into the Brahmaputra, run south from the mountains. Bhutan lies in the same latitude as Florida; and Thimbu, its new capital, lies in the same latitude as Tampa.

FLORA

Rain forest in the duars area in which grow broadleaf evergreen, pine, and rhododendron. Also areas of 15-foot elephant grass and dense bamboo jungle. In the temperate areas, forests of giant conifers; other forests of birch and oak.

FAUNA

Elephant, deer, tiger, rhinoceros, snakes, and other tropical fauna in the duars. Mountain goat, wild sheep, bear, boar, and snow leopard in the Himalayas. Wildlife is varied and numerous.

CLIMATE

Varies with elevation and exposure to prevailing winds. In general, arctic above 15,000 feet, temperate down to 7,000 feet, subtropical below 7,000 feet. Sheltered northern valleys receive less than 20 inches of rain a year, but the duars may have as much as 130 inches in the same period.

CAPITAL

Thimbu has about 1,000 inhabitants and is being expanded with Indian aid. Paro, with 1,500 inhabitants, is the temporary administrative center.

POPULATION

Estimated at 850,000 in 1963. There has never been a census. Density may be about 47 persons per square mile. Annual rate of increase is estimated at 1.9 percent.

ETHNIC GROUPS About two-thirds of the people are Bhutias (or Drukpas), a people of Tibetan origin, concentrated in the west. There are a thousand or so Lepchas. In the east, the tribes are ethnically related to the hill peoples of Assam, but culturally related to Tibet. Nepali immigrants, about a quarter of the population, are concentrated in the south. Since 1959, several thousand Tibetan refugees have entered the country.

LANGUAGES Bhutanese, the official language, is closely related to Tibetan, and is spoken in many dialects by isolated groups. Nepali is used in the south.

RELIGION Mahayana Buddhism, received from Tibet, is the state religion. Most lamas are of the *Druk Kargupa,* or Red Hat, sect. Over 25 percent of the public revenue is used to support monasteries and lamas. Nepali settlers are predominantly Hindu. Animistic customs remain.

DATE OF INDEPENDENCE The area has been a distinct political entity since the 15th century. In 1907, Sir Ugyen Wangchuk became the first hereditary *Druk Gyalpo,* or Dragon King, of *Druk Yul,* the Land of the Dragons.

FORM OF GOVERNMENT Semi-independent monarchy. Bhutan is in the process of becoming a constitutional monarchy. Each settlement chooses a headman who helps select a district representative. The *Tsongdu* of 130 members is thus an indirectly elected advisory council. There is also a Prime Minister and a Council of District Governors with advisory powers. Bhutan, in a treaty of 1949, agreed to be guided by India in foreign affairs and receives an annual subsidy of $105,000 and all its foreign aid from India. However, the country has recently joined the Universal Postal Union and the Colombo Plan.

EDUCATION In recent years, about 70 government schools have been organized to supplement and, in time, to replace monastic education. Bhutanese, Hindi, and English are the languages of instruction. Over 95 percent of the people remain illiterate.

HEALTH FACILITIES A hospital of 100 beds is to be built at Thimbu with Indian aid by 1966; modern medical facilities are lacking. Witch doctors or lamas are called in case of illness. Malaria is endemic in the south, tuberculosis in the north, dietary diseases everywhere. Life expectancy runs to 32 or 35 years.

**CULTURAL
FACILITIES**

The *dzongs,* or castle-monasteries, are the chief centers of cultural activity. Crafts and arts, as bronze work, silver work, and especially wood carving, are preserved in and disseminated from the *dzongs.* Dance, pantomime, and drama are religiously oriented. There is no newspaper, no national radio station, and very little national consciousness.

**CURRENCY
AND FINANCE**

A Bhutanese coin, the *ngultrum,* exists, but the Indian *rupee,* equal to 21¢ in U.S. currency, is widely used. Barter is the most common method of exchange. As a result, the *dzongs* have large stocks of grain, hides, and other supplies which are held much as a bank holds currency. National budgets cannot be meaningfully reported, since much of the tax is paid in kind. A five-year plan, started in 1961, will use aid from India of about $3.4 million a year, in addition to the annual subsidy, to develop roads, education, medical facilities, electric power, and industry.

**INDUSTRY AND
PRODUCTION**

Virtually all of the people are rural. There is no industry. Handicrafts include embroideries, wool and silk fabric, silver and bronze work, wood carving, fine swords and daggers, basketry, and hand-forged muzzle-loading guns.

CROPS: Rice, barley, millet, tea, temperate and tropical fruit and vegetables, and jute. Lac is collected in the southern forests.

BHUTANESE BOY   *This teen-age beggar boy is carrying a sounding drum and an engraved brass bell. Drums, gongs, and bells provide music for the Bhutanese.*   (Courtesy P. P. Karan and University of Kentucky Himalayan Expedition.)

MONASTERY *The wood carving for which Bhutanese artisans are renowned is evidenced on the windows and roof of this building built about 400 years ago in Tashi Chho Dzong.* (Courtesy P. P. Karan and University of Kentucky Himalayan Expedition.)

LIVESTOCK: Cattle, yak, sheep, goats, elephant, ponies. Yak, sheep, and goats are among the beasts of burden employed in caravans.

MINING: There are no mines. Deposits of coal and gypsum have been located but not exploited. No complete survey has ever been made.

TRADE

Most trade is with India. Until the border with Tibet was closed, Bhutanese exchanged cloth, spices, and grain for salt, wool, and herds of yak from Tibet. Trade averages around $60,000 in imports a year, about the same in exports.

TRANSPORT

ROAD: In February 1962, Bhutan's first motorable road was completed; the capital is now a 10-hour jeep ride from India. while it was formerly six days by a very difficult mule track. About 800 miles of road are under construction, but most of the country still depends on caravans or foot porters following mountain tracks. There is no air, rail, or waterway transport within the country, although air service to Paro and Thimbu is being planned.

**COMMUNI-
CATION**

Paro has a small radio transmitter which maintains contact with Bhutan House in India. Telephone connections now exist from Paro and Thimbu to Gangtok and India; most internal communication is by letter or by human messengers, usually on foot.

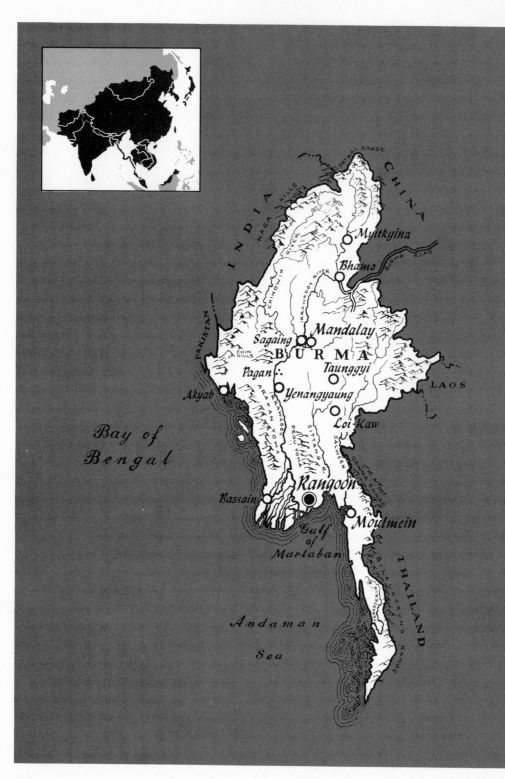

BURMA

A Land of Many Peoples

It was Rudyard Kipling who first brought Burma to public notice with his poem, "The Road to Mandalay." After the verses were set to music, concert artists throughout the United States regaled audiences with the popular lines:

By the old Moulmein Pagoda, lookin' eastward to the sea,
There's a Burma girl a-settin', an' I know she thinks o' me;
For the wind is in the palm-trees, an' the temple-bells they say:
"Come you back, you British soldier; come you back to Mandalay!"
Come you back to Mandalay,
Where the old Flotilla lay:
Can't you 'ear their paddles chunkin' from Rangoon to
Mandalay?
On the road to Mandalay,
Where the flyin'-fishes play,
An' the dawn comes up like thunder outer China 'crost
the Bay!

Through this romanticization, the provincial Westerner came in contact for the first time with Burma, an ancient civilization, the main outlines of whose known history date from the year 700.

Burma constitutes a buffer before India on the west and China on the northeast. In historic times, Burma provided the only feasible avenue to trade from southwestern China to the Indian Ocean.

Burma is just about the size of Texas. The country is important as a source of rice, teakwood, oil, and minerals.

LAND OF MANY PEOPLES

The heart of the country is the valley of the Irrawaddy River, a stream which is continuously navigable from its mouth almost up to the China border. Equally important for interior communication is the valley of the Sittang River. In these two central river valleys, most Burmans live.

WORKING ELEPHANTS   *Close to 1,300 elephants are used in forestry operations in central and northern Burma. The kneeling elephant is receiving his regular inspection by a veterinary, while other elephants still wearing their carrying racks await their turn for attention. The skin of the elephant although covered with spines is surprisingly sensitive. The trained beast responds readily and intelligently to directions of the mahout, applied to the elephant's head.*

In the delta areas, there reside a varied assortment of ethnic and linguistic peoples that give Burma its special character. The Mons and the Karens share the Tenasserim coast in lower Burma. Other minorities of importance include the Shans, the Kachins, the Nagas, the Chins, and the Arakanese. In addition to these major groups, scores of minor linguistic tribal peoples are to be found in remote mountainous areas. Most of the indigenous inhabitants are Mongoloid, the majority Burman group having originated in eastern Tibet.

EARLY HISTORY

The history of Burma can be divided into six major periods. Up to the ninth century A.D., the leading ethnic group in Burma was the commercially minded Mons. This people settled in the delta areas and along the Tenasserim coast running down the isthmus. During that era, a Tibetan people known as the Pyu controlled most of the upper Irrawaddy Valley and the Arakan coast. In the latter part of the eighth century, the Pyu went into decline; their state of North Burma was destroyed around 830 by Nan Chao, a state ruled by Shan or Lolo tribesmen.

In the middle of the ninth century, a second period started with the arrival of the Burmans proper, who occupied several irrigated regions in central Burma which had been developed by the Mons. The Burmans constructed an imposing capital city at Pagan. In the middle of the 11th century, they managed to gain control over their more civilized Mon neighbors, and the country was politically unified for the first time. The substantial Pagan Empire lasted for almost two and a half centuries. During this era, the Burmans absorbed the literary and artistic culture of the Mons who were oriented toward Indian culture. A large number of Buddhist monuments were constructed at Pagan, and even today this city remains one of the world's most spectacular architectural sites. Of the more than 10,000 pagodas once built in this capital, some 5,000 still remain, spread over an area of 16 square miles.

Around the year 1287, the first Burman Empire crumbled before the Mongol-Chinese armies of Kublai Khan.

THE TOUNGOO DYNASTY

Then followed a long period of division during which a succession of Shan leaders ruled the up-country, while a commercially prosperous Mon state re-emerged in the south. Eventually, a fusion of Burman exiles from the Pagan and Ava regions established a precarious Toungoo state in the Sittang Valley. This second unification of Burma was effected by the Toungoo dynasty during the middle half of the 16th century.

However, upon the death of the reigning monarch in 1581, this empire quickly crumbled, and the succeeding Toungoo rulers eventually withdrew to the interior, leaving the delta region to the Mons.

THE KONBAUNG DYNASTY

In the middle of the 18th century, the reunification of the country was again effected, this time by the Konbaung dynasty, whose leader recovered from the threatened domination of the Mons. After the country was unified, the Konbaung rulers initiated a military campaign against Siam. The city of Ayudhya was captured and destroyed in 1767, a deed which the Thai will never forget.

Several decades later the pendulum swung back. The Siamese leadership founded a new capital at Bangkok, and the new Chakri dynasty proceeded to cancel out the Burman conquests. Frustrated to the east, the Konbaung ruler of the early 1820's turned his spirited Burman troops loose in Assam in an attempt to conquer British-ruled Bengal. The response was a landing of British-Indian forces at Rangoon, who forced Burma's king to sign a humiliating treaty in 1826, through which British India annexed the two coastal strips of Arakan and Tenasserim, and exacted a heavy indemnity.

Then the Konbaung dynasty went from bad to worse. In 1851, the Burman ruler, powerless to resist British-Indian occupation of the central valleys, was accordingly deposed, and in 1885, the remnant of the Konbaung state was absorbed into British India as a Commissioner's province.

BRITISH RULE

From 1885 until 1948, Burma lived under British colonial rule. During this period, the country witnessed a rapid expansion of economic productivity. Negatively, during the same period there developed a disintegration of traditional social controls, a steady erosion of popular recognition of governmental authority, and an accompanying tide of lawlessness. This deteriorating social situation lasted until the end of World War I, when it was dispelled by the emergence of nationalist sentiment.

GENERAL NE WIN   Burma's Prime Minister and Chairman of the Revolutionary Council is a man of decision and courage who has proved himself in difficult situations. He was a close associate of U Aung San, Burma's national hero, who was assassinated in 1947. He is also known for his pleasure in gambling and in entertaining at his Rangoon mansion. He was born in 1910 at Rome and is approaching 55. He was educated at the University of Rangoon and speaks and reads English quite well.

NATIONALISM AND INDEPENDENCE

Burman nationalism was quite as much anti-Indian as it was anti-British, though in fact the Burman independence movement owed a great deal to the example of the Indian Congress Party. But it should be pointed out that minority peoples like the Karens, the Shans, and the Kachins, who had suffered in pre-colonial times under Burma's rule, did not support the insistent demand for independence.

After 1937, Burma was granted separation from India. The limited period of parliamentary self-government which ensued prior to the outbreak of World War II was a salutary experience, but of too short duration to accomplish lasting results. The occupation of Burma by Japanese forces in 1942 introduced the period in which Burma fought for and achieved independence.

The war brought to the fore a new group of younger political leaders. Organized as the Anti-Fascist Peoples Freedom League (AFPFL), this vital group was led by General Aung San, General Ne Win, by the Communist Than Tun, the pro-Buddhist U Nu, and the Socialists U Kyaw Nyein and U Ba Swe. The various nationalist factions held together long enough to wrest independence from Britain in 1948, and then the leadership began to fragment.

In July 1947, Aung San was assassinated; and U Nu, taking over
the leadership, became Burma's first Prime Minister. Almost immediately he encountered a multi-sided rebellion composed of Communists,
disgruntled veterans, and dissident Karens, who fortunately for Nu's
regime couldn't agree among themselves.

After recoiling from the very brink of disaster in 1952, Premier
Nu's overburdened government was plagued by inefficiency. Recovery
was painfully slow. The ruling AFPFL, driven by personal rivalries,
fell completely apart in 1958. Civil war was only narrowly averted. The
army, under General Ne Win, set up a caretaker regime which kept
the peace and instituted some reforms.

SOCIAL AND POLITICAL BREAKDOWN

An election was held in early 1960, and U Nu was returned as
Premier. But once again governmental efficiency deteriorated, and U
Nu's promised concessions of self-government to the Shans, the Mons,
the Karens, the Kachins, and the Arakanese threatened to destroy the
state.

Accordingly, in March 1962, General Ne Win and his army as-
sociates again seized power, this time in a naked military dictatorship
shorn of any constitutional authority. Political critics were silenced.
Commercial, financial, and industrial operations were nationalized; and
General Ne Win inaugurated a program which he called the "Burmese
Road to Socialism."

General Ne Win cut off virtually all cultural contacts and economic assistance from the West, while deliberately cultivating rela-

NOVICE MONK *Wearing a gilded crown and elaborately embroidered robes, th*
little boy in his father's arms is being honored in this initiation procession. Like man
Buddhist boys, he is about to become a novice for the duration of his pagoda schoolin
The two older youths are participants in the shin-pyu rites initiating them as novi
monks. The procession moves through the marble-paved courtyard of the greatest an
most important of Burma's temple-monasteries, the Shwe Dagon Pagoda of Rangoo
whose towers are completely covered in glittering gold leaf. The family parades all
its finery in order to accentuate the contrast between the conquest over desire by th
abstemious monks and the desire of the laymen for earthly treasures.

TECHNICAL HIGH SCHOOL   Built in the late 1950's, this attractive building in Rangoon was designed by a United Nations assistance team. The façade is composed of prefabricated concrete units covered with stucco. The moulded concrete and stucco statue shows a classical Burmese dancing figure.

tions with neighboring China. Meanwhile, he continued his opposition to Communist rebels as well as to other forms of domestic dissidence.

Moderate economic gains were realized in the agricultural sector; but industry and transportation broke down to the point where basic foodstuffs had to be rationed. All articulate opposition was suppressed, and in November 1963, the University was completely closed for almost a year.

As of early 1965, the prospect is for an indefinite continuation of economic stagnation and military rule, despite the alienation by the army of virtually every segment of the body politic. Burma reverted in some degree to its traditional xenophobic attitude while paying deference to a powerful China, which Burma must not provoke to hostility. Accommodation to the demands of world relations generally had thus been subordinated to relations with China.

POLITICAL FACTIONALISM IN BURMA

The difficulties which Burma encountered in trying to establish a stable government in 1948 had deep roots in the country's history and social fabric. Traditionally, Burmese national identity is related to popular respect for royal authority; the ruler has always enjoyed prestige as a patron of Buddhism. The King's authority was derived and authenticated by the manifold symbols of his divine status; the sense of nationality was derived from a prideful reputation for military prowess. Government was authoritarian and arbitrary, and in no way identified with the promotion of the public welfare; on the contrary, government was regarded as a kind of predatory scourge to be endured.

British colonial rule effectively demolished the traditional underpinnings of authority. In the place of the royal Court and *Hlutdaw* Council, in the place of the township *myothugyi* and the village headman, the British substituted an alien and impersonal law under which they, and the Indian and Chinese residents, profited most.

The renaissance of Burmese nationalism during the two decades after World War I acted as a unifying factor only because it was directed against the common target of alien control; otherwise, Burmese nationalism was highly fragmented and disparate. The extremist parties

FOREST RECREATION   Elephant handlers and timber workers, isolated in the teak forests during the timbering season, provide their own entertainment with drums, cymbals, whistles, and flutes. Such performances are also associated with placation of the spirits (nats) of the forest. The central performer bears the headdress and facial marking of the shaman priest in the traditional spirit play.

of the 1920's were led by obscurantist traditionalists or by political-minded Buddhist monks. The 1932 rebellion was led by the charlatan ex-monk, Saya San, who had no following among the urban élite and who aimed to revive the trappings of kingship. The better informed proponents of nationalism were divided between those who advocated separation from India and those who feared such separation. There were those who accepted the Constitution of 1935 as a road to the attainment of self-government, and those who sought to wreck that Constitution. A political party often consisted merely of a leader and a coterie of personal followers.

The emergence of the youthful nationalist and leftist AFPFL as the authentic spokesman for Burma's independent political aspirations was an accident of the Japanese occupation. The new group included neither the most experienced nor the best trained or ablest of the Burman élite. Once British-Indian control was lifted, the several disparate nationalist groups began to contend for control. That a semblance of national unity was preserved for a decade was largely due to Premier Nu.

What Premier Nu undertook to do was to bridge the chasm which separated the village agriculturalists, who constituted some four-fifths of the population, from the westernized and urban elements of the population. He addressed the villagers in symbolism drawn from Burmese folklore and animistic superstitions, while attempting to establish his personal prestige as the patron of Buddhism. He also undertook to implement the program for planned economic development as fashioned by his Socialist associates in the government. However, he failed to demonstrate any capacity for exerting the vigorous authority required to discipline his feeble administration or to prevent party meddling at local levels of government. His pro-Buddhist policy encouraged the assertiveness of the politically minded monks, and his lackadaisical attitude permitted radically inclined student malcontents to engage in manifold excesses.

Nu won repeated victories at the polls because of his personal popularity, but he repeatedly proved unable to generate authority and leadership. The eventual disruption of the ruling AFPFL precipitated a showdown between Nu's faction which enjoyed popularity but not authority, a group of westernized Socialist modernizers, and the powerful but unpopular army. Not one of these three Burman groups was able to command the best abilities of the nation.

MINORITY STRIVINGS

Burma's pattern of fragmentation was further aggravated by dissidence from important minority peoples. The coastal Arakanese were embittered because of the failure of the AFPFL government to mitigate the ravages of war suffered by Akyab and other such communities. Despite the general Burmanization of the Mon peoples, Mon nationalist leadership talked of an autonomous Mon state in the Tenasserim area.

THE KARENS

More seriously dissident was Lower Burma's Karen population which distrusted the Burman majority and would have preferred a continuation of British colonial rule. The Karens numbered several millions, occupying considerable portions of the Irrawaddy delta, as well as peripheral hill regions. With the exception of the Pwo Karens (who had long been associated with the Buddhist Mons), the Karens were predominantly animists in religion. Looked down upon as backward by the ruling Burmans, the Karens had found a welcome opportunity for advancement under British rule. They served as delta cultivators, constituted in time the strongest element of the colonial army, and were in many areas the recipients of missionary education. Although far from homogeneous linguistically, politically, or religiously, the Karens shared a common antipathy to Burman rule. It was the dissident Karen National Army which came closest to overturning the new Burman Union government in 1949.

THE KACHINS

Another important ethnic minority, akin to the majority Tibeto-Burmans, were the Kachin tribesmen who occupied the northern provinces and spilled over the border into China. Burma's postwar Kachin population numbered around 400,000, divided into five major family groupings. As comparative newcomers to Burma (since the 16th century), the Kachins are backward culturally, and largely animist. Kachin contingents, like Karens, played a prominent role in the British armed forces. The Kachin State is a constituent member of the Union of Burma, but is currently in rebellion against Ne Win's regime. The political and cultural gap which separates the lower valley Burman majority and the Kachin tribesmen of the remote northern hills is largely unbridged.

THE SHANS

The third major minority people are the two million Shans, Buddhist kinsmen of the Thai. They occupy the eastern Shan plateau area. The Shans use an adaptation of Burmese script. They have long enjoyed a considerable measure of autonomy under their own Sawbwa princes. The hereditary rights of the Sawbwas were extinguished by General Ne Win in 1959.

The Shans actually constitute only half of the population of the Shan States; the other half is split among many tribal groupings of hill people. The Shans control most of the cultivated and grazing areas. Several hundred thousand Karen-related groups live in the southern Shan States. Important mineral deposits are located in the Shan region (wolfram, lead, zinc, silver), and the region has long been a principal source of cattle for lowland Burma.

When the Union of Burma was formed, the Shans were accorded the right to secede after a decade, if they so desired. Premier Nu was apparently preparing to honor this right in March 1962, when General Ne Win seized power. The army imprisoned all the Shan leaders, including a former President of the Union and a number of princely politicians then assembled at Rangoon for the purpose of negotiating with Nu. Army leadership was convinced that the prospective grant of independence to the Shan State would inevitably inspire similar demands from the Karens, the Kachins, the Mons, and the Arakanese, and thus precipitate the breakup of the Union. However, the army

BURMESE CO-OP   *A prosperous farmer and his family purchase cloth and imported groceries in this government-owned cooperative, one of the many established to fight the exorbitant prices charged by small merchants. Note the traditional. long-sleeved aingyi worn by the woman, the top-knotted chignon and perennial cheroot of the man, the knotted Shan bag on the arm of the boy, the tea, milo (milk), and cigarettes in the lower shelf, and the display of Burmese-type weaving. The stall is part of a general bazaar area. The clerk is Burman—not the traditional Indian shopkeeper. The boy's skirt is a longyi like that worn by father and mother.*

CHIN LADIES These tribal women ha
come to Rangoon from the far north to he
celebrate the springtime Thingyan Festiv
which involves tribal dancing and oth
forms of gaiety. The main fun comes wh
everyone goes into the streets to thro
water, a symbolic celebration of the Bu
dhist rites of purification. Hoops or bracele
at wrist, neck, and waist are characteris
of Chin dress. The chest decoration on t
left is made of beaten silver.

WELL-TO-DO KAREN WOMAN She is
probably a resident of the hill area to the east of
the Sittang delta. Her beads are made of colored
paste, but the bangles and disks are of silver, copper, and bronze. The woman, in her twenties,
probably wears on her person all of the family
treasures. The pierced flat disks near the right
temple are silver rupee coins.

RICE HARVESTER This prosperous farmer from t
Irrawaddy Delta holds a sheaf of newly gathered rice. H
ceremonial sickle, probably inherited from his father a
grandfather, has a handle carved to represent a drago
head. The first sheaf of rice from the harvest must be c
furtively in ritual fashion so as not to disturb the fertil
earth spirit involved.

NAGA TRIBESMEN   The Nagas are famous for their warlike prowess. A buffalo's rib is passed through the knot of hair at the back of the head. Both edges of the dah, the curved sword of the Nagas, are sharpened. The buffalo rib is a sacred life symbol. Originally savage head hunters, some of the Naga tribes have been Christianized in recent generations. They live astride the mountainous northwest border of Burma, adjacent to the Indian province of Assam. They enjoy a measure of autonomy in the state of India.

BURMESE WOMAN   A long-necked Padaung woman from the Southern Shan State of the Union of Burma. The concentric brass rings are added over a number of years and actually achieve an elongation of the neck, which becomes dependent on the support of the rings. The cloth at the top softens the abrasive effect. This sort of decoration, although handicapping mobility, is considered a mark of wealth, social distinction, and beauty, much as bound feet were regarded in traditional Chinese society. The family wealth is otherwise displayed in the rings and bracelets, in the ear pendants, and the hair decoration.

was unable to put down the rebellions of minority factions; these revolts continued largely unchecked. Communist rebellion also defied conciliation.

AN UNRESOLVED POLITICAL SITUATION

National unity is still to be achieved in Burma. Burmese kingship is moribund; democracy has proved ineffective; military control is generally unpopular; but no attractive alternative is currently available. It will obviously take time to forge a nation, to modernize the economy, and to find ways to make the popular will effective.

SOCIAL AND CULTURAL LIFE

The population of Burma is predominantly Buddhist, although animistic propitiation of *nat* spirits for daily needs is an almost universal concern. Burma is largely rural. Much of elementary education is still conducted by village monks who receive substantial grants from the wealthy, and alms from the pious, both interested in accumulating merit for their next transmigration. Literacy is estimated at somewhere between 45 and 50 percent of those 15 years old and over.

The Burmese script is an adaptation of the *Pali* script used in the Buddhist *Tripitaka* scriptures. The language includes a substantial literature of fiction, legends, royal chronicles, and religious commentaries. Calendric Buddhist festivals and animistic rites are gala occasions.

Under British rule and until the late 1950's, much of the university instruction was conducted in English; since then Burmese has largely taken over. The principal university is just outside Rangoon, with branches located in Mandalay and Moulmein. Political preoccupations of the students constitute a serious problem for both disciplinary and academic standards. Ne Win's military regime has crushed student disaffection and has revamped the university curriculum in line with the assumed needs of a Socialist state.

ECONOMIC MODERNIZATION

Burma's industrial potential is limited by a number of factors, the most important being the lack of essential supplies of coal and iron, a native population unsuited by experience and temperament to industrial regimentation, and a general lack of capital resources. British and Indian bankers and businessmen, who dominated the economy along with still-resident Chinese, have been excluded and have not been replaced by indigenous leadership. No encouragement is being afforded to private economic initiative under Ne Win's military regime, which is attempting to control all production and trade.

In 1960, the estimated per capita Gross National Product was $57, at the time the lowest in all of Southeast Asia. But Burma is capable of substantial improvement in every economic sphere. Locally grown cotton is available for developing a textile industry; wood is at hand for paper-making. Undeveloped, cultivable land is available to support the substantial increment in population. Timber products are abundant; and once order and transportation facilities are restored, mineral and oil output can be increased. Electrical energy, generated by Japanese-installed plants, is now widely accessible. Electrical equipment is being purchased from China and elsewhere.

HEALTH CONDITIONS

Infant mortality continues high, and general health is poor. Buddhist taboos against the taking of life long prevented the elimination of disease-bearing pests, such as mosquitoes, rats, and the droves of ownerless dogs. Religious scruples have also hampered the development of livestock, which could provide meat and dairy products to supplement the normal diet of rice, fish paste, and vegetables, which is deficient in proteins and minerals.

LLED DRAFTSMAN This well-paid rnment employee in the Town Planning artment of the Burmese National Housing d is working on plans for modernizing goon's central district. Underneath his head-covering, or gamboung, his hair is d up into a knotted chignon. The wearing e neck scarf indicates that the picture was n in the cool season which runs from mber into February.

SPORTS

Soccer is the most popular sport; huge crowds turn out every Saturday afternoon to witness major games.

Like Thai boxing, Burmese boxing permits kicking and jabbing with the foot, and other forms of mayhem popular with the populace.

THE CITY OF RANGOON

Rangoon, Burma's capital since 1885, is a city of 752,000 people. The ravages which it suffered from World War II bombings have only partly been repaired. Beyond its business district are tree-shaded streets, and several beautiful lakes.

Overlooking the city is the Shwe Dagon Pagoda, a shrine that Kipling dubbed the "Beautiful Winking Wonder," and which is regarded as one of the greatest Buddhist monuments in all Asia. It is completely covered with gleaming gold up to the very tip of its 326-foot spire. At its apex is a tiered umbrella (or *hti*) encrusted with thousands of diamonds and semi-precious stones.

In the center of Rangoon stands the less impressive Sule Pagoda, built 2,250 years ago.

OUTLOOK FOR THE FUTURE

Burma's adjustment to the modern world will not be speedy. Although its leadership is intelligent and not without humor (U.N. Secretary U Thant is typical), the people at large suffer from having been uprooted from their traditional moorings. The manifold problems are too intricate for the Burmese to master in a short time.

Diplomatic accommodation to its Chinese neighbor—while at the same time domestically resisting Communist interference—reflects a realistic Burmese approach; but the reversion to traditional xenophobia removes Western contacts and limits the possibility for social and economic progress. Burma's friends will need to be patient, as well as helpful.

JOHN F. CADY

IN BRIEF

AREA　　　　261,789 square miles, slightly smaller than Texas.

TERRAIN　　　Mountains make rugged borders on the east, and extend through most of the north; one minor north-south range separates the lower valley of the Irrawaddy from the parallel Sittang to the east. The Salween River, still further east, bisects the Shan plateau. The Irrawaddy, its tributaries, and the shorter Sittang water most of the fertile central plain.

CLIMATE　　　Except for hill areas and a rain-shadow district in central Burma, the country has a tropical monsoon climate. Temperatures are in the 70's during the dry northeast monsoon from November to late February. The hot season follows. The southwest monsoon, starting in late May, brings heavy rain and cooler—80°F.—temperatures. Up to 200 inches of rain fall on parts of the coast, while the Irrawaddy delta receives 80 to 100 inches.

CAPITAL　　　Rangoon had an estimated 752,000 inhabitants in 1963.

OTHER CITIES　　Mandalay, 212,900; Moulmein, 115,900.

POPULATION　　23,735,000 estimated in 1963. The annual increase is probably 1.8 percent. Density is low for Asia, about 90 persons per square mile.

ETHNIC GROUPS　The dominant Burman ethnic element comprises roughly 60 percent of the population. The Mons, highly civilized before the Burmans arrived, remain a significant minority, but are being steadily assimilated. Shans, Karens, Kachins, and Chins are the important hill peoples, with Arakanese inhabiting the coastal area bordering Pakistan. There are about a million Chinese, Indian, and Pakistani residents, although many of the latter groups have been expelled in recent years.

LANGUAGES　　Burmese, in several dialects, is spoken by 70 percent of the populace. About 126 languages and dialects are used by minority groups. Although Burmese is the official language, English is a compulsory subject in secondary schools. University instruction, previously mostly in English, is shifting to Burmese.

FAMILY DINNER *Rice, broth, and highly seasoned fish sauce are the staple items in a home menu. The large piece of pottery in the background is a Pegu jar, used for storing rice. The head of this prosperous family, who wears his hair in a chignon, is clothed in a skirt-like lower garment or longyi, standard wear throughout lowland Burma.*

RELIGION	About 80 percent of the people are Buddhist; most show concern for *nats,* or spirits. Islam, animism, Confucianism, and Christianity are followed by minorities. Buddhism ceased to be the state religion in 1962.
DATE OF INDEPENDENCE	On January 4, 1948, the Union of Burma formally assumed the governing powers previously held by Britain.
FORM OF GOVERNMENT	Military dictatorship. A parliamentary democracy for 10 years, Burma was taken over by the Army Chief of Staff, General Ne Win in 1958. He returned authority to civilians in 1960, but took over again on March 2, 1962. All legislative, executive, and judicial powers remain in his hands; his Council of Ministers is almost totally composed of military officers. The government is strongly oriented toward its "Burmese Road to Socialism." Member of the United Nations.

EDUCATION   In 1962, there were more than 13,650 primary and secondary schools with almost 2,020,000 students. Almost 2,700 teachers were being trained in six colleges in 1963. Two universities have over 17,000 students. There are five "Intermediate Colleges" and several technical and agricultural institutes. About half of the people over 15 are literate.

HEALTH FACILITIES   There were over 1,960 doctors, 21 dentists, and 3,860 midwives in 1960. In 1954, life expectancy was about 42 years for a newborn child. Some improvement in medical facilities has been made, impeded by lack of political and economic stability. Infant mortality is high. Malaria, typhoid, intestinal diseases, typhus, and tuberculosis are endemic.

CULTURAL FACILITIES   In 1962, there were 31 daily newspapers with a total circulation of 202,000; about one person in a hundred gets a daily paper. Of the 330 books published in 1960, some 35 were translations, mostly from English. Ninety films were made in 1962 for showing in 415 cinemas, with an annual attendance of over 114 million. There were about 157,000 radios in use in 1962, but no television. Films, music, and the traditional drama with dance and song are popular.

CURRENCY AND FINANCE   The *kyat,* theoretically equal to 0.187 grams of fine gold, and worth 21¢ in U.S. currency, is actually worth half that value. Budget estimates for fiscal 1964 expected $285.6 million in revenue and $338.1 million in expenditure. Almost a third of the budget was earmarked for defense.

INDUSTRY AND PRODUCTION   Chiefly processing of natural products. Industry is developing slowly under government control. Manufacturing provides about 13 percent of the Gross National Product which, at about $1.32 billion, gave a per capita product of around $58 in 1962. Rice milling, sawmilling, food processing, footwear, and cottage industry products, such as textiles, furniture, and cigars, were, until 1964, largely in private hands. Major government-owned operations include four sugar mills, a cement plant, a cotton mill, a jute bag plant, brick and tile works, and seven cigarette factories. Production and commerce suffered severely in 1964, when the newspapers and over 12,000 commercial and manufacturing establishments were nationalized and all export-import operations came under government control.

CROPS: Rice is grown on over 10 million acres and accounts for about 60 percent of the total value of the farm output, reaching about 7.7 million tons in 1964. Forest products, especially teakwood, are next in importance. Other crops include peanuts, rubber, cotton, sugar, tobacco, wheat and other grains.

LIVESTOCK: Oxen and buffalo are the common work animals. About 900 elephants are employed in forestry.

FESTIVAL OF LIGHTS   One of the happiest of Burma's Buddhist festivals, Tazaung-Daing, is celebrated by lighting lanterns, staging theatrical performances, and offering gifts to the pongyi monks. Here, citizens in procession are delivering their gaily wrapped gifts to a Rangoon monastery. The gifts include living essentials, towels, brooms, tea cups and dishes, packets of tea, writing paper, handkerchiefs, and sweets.

FISHERIES: Fish from inland waters are important in the local diet. Development of promising coastal fishing grounds has barely begun.

MINING: Tin, tungsten, lead, zinc, iron, and petroleum are produced, but minerals provide less than two percent of the Gross National Product. Undeveloped deposits of inferior coal and iron are known; unsurveyed areas are believed to be rich in mineral resources.

TRADE

Rice and rice products account for almost 70 percent of exports. Teak, rubber, metal ores, cotton, and agricultural products account for the rest. Large rice buyers in 1964 included Indonesia, Ceylon, the Philippines, and the Soviet Union. Tourism, formerly a source of foreign exchange, was effectively discouraged by government regulations in 1964. Machinery, chemicals, textiles, drugs, and manufactured goods are the chief imports.

> 1962: IMPORTS $218,600,000
> EXPORTS $263,700,000
> SURPLUS $ 45,100,000

TRANSPORT

ROAD: Of the 9,500 miles of roadways, less than a third are hard-surfaced. In 1962, almost 45,000 registered motor vehicles included over 21,000 trucks and buses.

RAIL: Government-owned railways have about 1,860 miles of track in service. About 2,060 miles were in service before the Japanese occupation during World War II.

WATERWAY: Almost half Burma's freight is carried on the 3,600 miles of navigable waterway. The Irrawaddy and the Salween, with their tributaries, are the chief arteries.

AIR: Union of Burma Airways, a government monopoly, provides internal service to 38 airports and some external services. International airlines serve Rangoon.

SEA: Rangoon, about 20 miles from the sea in the Irrawaddy delta, handles most of the ocean freight.

COMMUNI-CATION

Telephone, telegraph, and wireless services are state monopolies. In 1963, there were 18,800 telephones in use, mostly in Rangoon.

THAILAND

LAOS

PHANOM DONG RAK

Angkor

Battambang

Siem Reap

MEKONG RIVER

TONLE SAP

Kompong Chhnang

Kratie

CAMBODIA

TONLE SAP

VIETNAM

Phnom-Penh

Kompong Cham

Sihanoukville

PHU QUOC

Gulf of
Siam

CAMBODIA

Nation Aspiring to Remain Free

To Cambodians, independence is a day-to-day concern, a continuing, vital question of national survival.

Cambodia is one of the smallest countries of Asia, only 70,000 square miles, about the size of North Dakota. With about six million inhabitants, it is one of the least populated countries on the continent.

To Cambodians, Thailand and all of Viet Nam—as well as those who support these neighboring nations—are potential sources of danger. The power of mainland China is clear and present. In this environment, Cambodia continues its ancient struggle for independence and security.

THE PEOPLE

Cambodians as such are called *Khmer* (pronounced *k'mer*), and compromise over 85 percent of the population. Most of them earn their livelihood by farming. Cambodian (Khmer) is the official language. French, Vietnamese, and English are heard in the urban districts. Buddhism is the state religion.

Although most of Cambodia's farmers and virtually all its government and religious leaders are Khmer, industry and commerce are primarily in the hands of Chinese inhabitants (about five percent of the population) and to a much lesser extent in the hands of Vietnamese (about five percent of the population), of French, and of Indians. The Khmer have made some inroads in the area of commerce—for example, in rice milling which used to be entirely dominated by Chinese.

Also, the government has taken steps to diminish the dominance of Chinese and Vietnamese in economic affairs by nationalizing the banks, the insurance companies, and foreign trade.

The movement of rural people to the cities has also tended to strengthen the position of the urban Khmer vis-à-vis the Chinese and Vietnamese. When, in recent years, border populations were endangered by warfare in Viet Nam and Laos, the government resettled many

Khmer farmers in urban areas. Many of these farmers were successfully absorbed in new jobs.

ETHNIC TENSIONS

There is considerable friction between the Chinese and the Vietnamese minorities, particularly in certain fishing areas. Many thousands of hard-working Vietnamese fishermen live around the Tonle
Sap, or "Great Lake," in colonies consisting of houses floating on pon-
toons or sampans. The rights to many of these fishing grounds are held
by Chinese who rent these rights to the fishermen. The Chinese are
also moneylenders, and charge high rates. Often, the fisherman must
go to the moneylender for a small loan needed to pay for supplies, or
to cover a family crisis. Friction results because the Vietnamese often
finds himself heavily obligated to the Chinese capitalist.

Friction also exists between the Cambodians and Vietnamese, the
internal counterpart of the external friction between Cambodia and
Viet Nam. The aggressive manner of the Vietnamese in contrast to the
innately more gentle manner of the Cambodian is at the root of much
of this conflict. The Khmer resent the Vietnamese, calling them "va-
grants and sellers of everything." Some Khmer even feel that Viet Nam
gets rid of its undesirables by sending them to Cambodia.

Relations between the Cambodians and the Chinese are, on the
whole, friendly. Except for situations in which a Chinese moneylender
imposes a burden upon a Khmer farmer, the Cambodian respects the
Chinese for his business ability. This respect seems to outweigh such
misgivings as the Cambodians may have over the aggressive Chinese
manner, and this respect even obscures the threat the Chinese pose to
Cambodian political stability and survival.

*MEKONG STEAMER Boats plying
the Mekong carry much of Cambodia's
traffic. Here, a small steamer releases passengers laden with bananas, brief cases,
babies, and baskets. The dock is allowed
to float because the level of the water
changes drastically between the rainy
and the dry season. Passengers must walk
the narrow plank to reach dry ground.*

*HIS ROYAL HIGHNESS, NORODOM SI-
HANOUK This independent prince, Cam-
bodia's dynamic chief of state, was 43 years of age
in 1965 when this picture was taken. He succeeded his grandfather on the throne of the ancient Khmer empire in 1941. Sihanouk was educated in Saigon and Paris.*

THE LAND AND THE WATER

Cambodia's mostly flat and fertile land—only about a fourth of it cultivated—makes it ideal for the growing of rice. The country is an important producer of rice, growing much more rice than it needs to feed its own people. This great wealth in food resources accounts for the covetous attention of its neighbors. "Wealthy as Cambodia" is a Chinese saying, and it conveys a great deal.

Waterways are the lifelines of Cambodia. They maintain the land's fertility, provide huge inland fishing resources, and carry much of the freight and passenger traffic. Most river boats are sampans or canoe-like pirogues; some sailing junks, a few steamers, and some barges towed by tugs are also used. Small ocean-going vessels go up and down the Mekong to Saigon, with Pnom Penh functioning as the main Cambodian terminal for river traffic.

FARMING VILLAGES AND VILLAGERS

Most of the people of Cambodia live near the lakes or rivers in largely self-sufficient villages. Their houses are built on stilts to accommodate the rise and fall of the waters of the Mekong and the Tonle Sap.

A villager's house may have several rooms with palm-leaf partitions; poorer houses have only one room. Joined to the house by a ramp is the kitchen shed, also built on stilts. The farmyard animals are kept underneath the house; however, during the rainy season, when the water rises, these animals must be led to higher ground. Sundry equip-

A VILLAGE ON THE TONLE SAP   These floating houses, and houses perched high on stilts, are typical of the habitation on the shores of Tonle Sap, the "Great Lake" of Cambodia. These villages are mostly occupied with fishing. The woman poling her pirogue across the water may be going to visit a sister five houses or five miles away. In either case, she uses a boat. For miles around, the shore of the lake is a muddy soup. Whenever the rivers are full, the lake expands far across the land.

ment, such as looms or carts, are also stored beneath the house. This kind of house does not provide much privacy; everyone in a village knows all about everyone else. But this type of dwelling is very well adapted to the weather.

Women play a key role in family living and in the making of decisions; the wife is on an equal footing with her husband. Except during the busy season when their help is needed in the rice fields, the women are likely to be attending to household chores. At mealtime in the morning, they prepare extra food which the family will use to put into the bowl of the Buddhist *bonze,* or monk. He comes by only in the morning, for monks are not allowed to eat after midday.

Twice a day, at about ten in the morning and again at five in the afternoon, the family gathers for meals. Serving dishes are set on floor mats. An ordinary meal for an adult might include a ball of rice and three dried fish, seasoned with *prahoc,* a fermented spiced paste made of salted and dried fish.

Buddhism is a very important part of every villager's life. There is no god in Buddhism; but as a carryover from earlier Cambodian religions, spirits are still deemed potent and are consequently placated. Guardian spirits, or *neak ta,* are associated with local mountains, rivers, trees, rice paddies, specific ancestors, or ancient Brahman gods and heroes. Small altars have been erected almost everywhere for the *neak ta,* even in the dark corners of Buddhist pagodas. The villager leaves offerings of rice or incense sticks for the *neak ta,* and whenever he passes an altar, the rural Cambodian will take off his hat, or respectfully raise both hands to his forehead in a traditional gesture.

HIGH LAND AND THE FOREST DWELLERS

Not all of the land is rich, easily flooded, rice-growing mud. There is some high country, even some mountainous country; and there is excellent timberland which provides fuel and construction materials for domestic use and even for export. The tribal minorities live in these hilly areas.

The Khmer call these highland tribesmen *Phnong* and regard them, more or less, as savages. The Khmer do not recognize any ethnic kinship with the *Phnong*. On the other hand, the *Phnong* have maintained their own customs for centuries, and do not consider themselves as inferiors.

The *Phnong* have organized their groups by tribes instead of by villages. To earn a living, they hunt, gather materials from the forests, and farm a few fields by slash-and-burn methods.

A highlander always has his weapons nearby—a sword, a lance of rattan, and possibly a bamboo crossbow. As part of his costume, he might wear in his chignon a lock of hair from a dead enemy. The *Phnong* tribesman is often involved in a blood feud with another clan. Among other factors, enmity and the distances between their scattered settlements prevent the hill tribes from uniting to demand better treatment from the lowland Cambodians.

These fighting highlanders retain their primitive religious rites and have not been deeply affected by the peaceful Buddhist faith. When tribal war is in prospect, or when a new settlement is to be built, or when a leader is buried, or when an epidemic strikes, they sacrifice animals to placate the spirits. Then everyone, including children, comes to a party to drink great amounts of beer and to listen to an impressive gong concert. The gongs are highly valued among them. A man's gongs and his weapons are his only pieces of personal property; everything else belongs communally to the tribe.

A NEW DIMENSION OF INDEPENDENCE

The forests also provide some protection against invasion; but until recently, the same insulation kept the Cambodians from develop-

PREPARING RICE   *A village housewife pounds her rice with a pestle in a huge wooden mortar in order to separate husks from kernels. She takes the grain from the deep basket on her right and puts the finished product in the flat straw tray on her left. The little boy wears his hair in a tuft called a kor sak. When he reaches the age of eleven or twelve, his kor sak will be cut off, and then he will no longer be regarded as a child.*

ing an outlet to the Gulf of Siam. Sihanoukville, now the country's most important port, was begun in the 1950's with French help. The port is growing in importance year by year. In 1959, a road called the Khmer-American Friendship Highway which runs from the port to Pnom Penh, the capital, was completed with U.S. help. A railroad between Pnom Penh and Sihanoukville is under construction with French assistance.

For access to the outside world, Cambodia is thus no longer as dependent as it used to be on the port of Saigon and the Chinese firms that dominate the city's economic life. As Cambodia's own port develops, Saigon will cease to be so dominant in the economic life of Cambodia, and Chinese control of Cambodian commerce will diminish.

INDUSTRY AND TRADE

Most of the country's industry revolves about the processing of rice, rubber, fish, and timber. Rubber is produced by Vietnamese workers on plantations which are owned by Frenchmen. These plantations constitute the major foreign investment in Cambodia.

A new factory assembles motor vehicles. Cigarettes, matches, textiles, plywood, paper, and other consumer goods are produced. Some plants are government-owned—for example, those in textiles and cement.

Rice is produced by Khmer farmers whose reliance between harvests on Chinese moneylenders for credit seriously undermines their independence. Although the Khmer farmer owns his land and tools, he often is not free to seek the highest bidder for his harvest. The local moneylender, who is frequently a rice broker as well, uses his position as a lever to get hold of the farmer's rice cheaply.

THE CITY OF PNOM PENH

Cambodia's capital city, Pnom Penh, is its industrial and cultural center. More than 400,000 persons live in this port city, which is located at the junction of the Tonle Sap, Bassac, and Mekong rivers.

Wares of local craftsmen are displayed in small shops throughout the city where visitors may buy beautiful Cambodian silverware, textiles, and tortoise shell decorative pieces. Pnom Penh also boasts a fine museum of Khmer arts and culture.

ANCIENT PATTERNS AND RECENT PROGRESS

For centuries, Cambodia has been a nation of small farmers who weave their own cloth and build most of their own equipment. For centuries, these farmers grew what they needed, and perhaps just a little extra to pay for the few things they couldn't make for themselves. Since nearly everyone farmed, the excess crop was used to support the *bonzes,* the nobility, and the few craftsmen; no one was compelled to work very hard.

By and large, the Cambodian villager regards his way of life as quite satisfactory. He is conservative. Accustomed to traditional patterns, he rarely comprehends the value of modern methods and the possibility of increasing his yield. In this setting, the task of modernizing the economy is slow and difficult. It is made even more difficult because the government finds it hard to collect taxes. Cambodians, accustomed to avoiding the taxes imposed by foreigners, find it normal to evade their own tax collectors, too.

Some economic growth has been achieved through foreign aid; new roads are a good example. Foreign aid has also been used to build factories and to improve agricultural and health facilities. The government's Five-Year Plan will build a few more factories. However, by and large, foreign aid has affected only the life of Pnom Penh; the villages are little changed. Industrialization is restricted by deficiencies in the supply of capital, labor, and management skills; low incomes limit the market for goods.

THE TRANSMISSION OF IDEAS AND VALUES

Although the most widely used language is Cambodian or Khmer Chinese and Vietnamese are the major languages used in business and trade. Cambodians dealing with merchants in the typical give-and-take of the Asian marketplace use Vietnamese; Khmer, a language full of hints and subtleties, is not to be contaminated by such unmannerly bargaining.

French is the language of administration. In Pnom Penh, officials, professionals, and the intellectual élite acquire status by using French. English is gaining in importance among government officials and among some of the Buddhist clergy. The *bonzes* are finding English very useful in communicating with foreign Buddhists, especially with Buddhists in Japan.

Pali and Sanskrit in their ancient forms are used in Buddhist texts

VILLAGE WELL *Informal social activity often centers around a village well's circular coping. Here, women and children customarily set down their jugs while they exchange news and perhaps wash a few clothes, which they hang on a nearby fence to dry.*

and services, much as Latin is used in some Christian churches. Many of the technical terms introduced into Cambodian come from these old languages. French and Vietnamese used to be the prime sources for technical terms; but today, Cambodians do not wish to depend on their former rulers or historical adversaries—even for words.

MODERN COMMUNICATIONS

Though roughly half of the people can read and write their native tongue, literacy is largely restricted to men. About 10 percent of Cambodians are fluent in French.

The villagers have a strong respect for writing. Often, in poor huts, little pieces of yellow paper with a few words written on them—prayers, birthday greetings, etc.—are pinned near the statue of Buddha. Most boys learn something about the Cambodian alphabet during their pagoda study time.

Radio is becoming increasingly important. The Cambodian, used to learning news from travelers through word-of-mouth reports, takes to the radio more readily than he does to a newspaper. Illiteracy, especially in the rural areas, is a powerful factor in limiting the circulation of the press.

ANGKOR TOWERS   Here is some of the masonry and a few of the great sculptured faces near the top of Angkor Wat's towers. Although the temple was originally consecrated to Brahma and to the multiple Brahman dieties, today many Cambodians mistakenly take these representations of Brahma to be representations of the Buddha.

In 1962, there were 11 daily newspapers and several weeklies in Cambodia. The number is increasing. But the press is still constricted in its freedom to express an independent view on a controversial issue of government policy. Every publication must secure a license to operate from the Ministry of Information.

ARTISTIC EXPRESSION

The most significant mode of cultural expression is through the performing arts. The themes of Cambodian plays and ballets are both old and new. Legends of the old Hindu gods and heroes dominate the folk theater. The pride of the performing arts is the Royal Cambodian Ballet—one of Prince Sihanouk's daughters is the prima ballerina. In the capital, translations into Cambodian of French classics and modern novels are read. Films are also popular in Pnom Penh.

Cambodian poetry recounts the ancient stories and legends of the country. For example, *The Old Man of the Sweet Cucumbers* has a peculiarly Cambodian point of view. One year, an old peasant who planted cucumbers had such a good crop that he offered some to the king who found them so excellent he gave the peasant a present of a lance with which to guard the royal garden. One night, to test the peasant's carefulness, the king sneaked into the garden and was killed with the very lance that he had bestowed as a gift. Whereupon the elders of the country were so impressed with the peasant's watchfulness that they crowned *him* king.

The Khmer are quite clever at improvising lyrics on modern topics, fitting their verse to traditional Cambodian melodies. Such improvisations are the age-old means by which current news and opinions are spread among the villages.

EARLY HISTORY OF CAMBODIA

Some two thousand years before the Christian era, the Khmer tribes entered Cambodia from the northwest, areas that are now China and Tibet. From this direction also came Hinduism, Theravada Buddhism, and other influences on Cambodian life. The folk tales heard in Cambodia today are a blend of legend and fact concerning these early migrations. Many stories center around the symbols of *The River* and *The Mountain.* Ever since the Bronze Age, Cambodians have adopted a set of credos, according to whether a family originally came from high country or from river country. The highland chiefs and the tribal sorcerers were regarded as having descended from a divine bird who controlled fire and lightning; the chiefs of river tribes and their magicians drew power from a divine fish or a divine snake who controlled the rain and thus controlled the waters.

RISE OF THE KHMER EMPIRE

After many centuries of tribal conflict—lasting from the first century A.D. to the beginning of the ninth century—the Khmer emerged as the most powerful tribe in a territory which at that time was known as Chen-La. This territory stretched from the Gulf of Siam to the Chinese border. The legendary hero of this era was Kambu Svayambhuva; it is from his name that the word "Cambodia" was derived.

From about 800 to 1430, a Khmer Empire achieved impressive heights of artistic and social development. Today, Cambodian politicians refer to the great kings of this era with as much pride as Fourth of July orators in the U.S. speak of George Washington. The leading figures of this period were Jayavarman II and Jayavarman VII. The latter is famed for his interest in social welfare; he founded hospitals, schools, libraries, and rest houses for travelers. An inscription on stone taken from his day was the theme used at a recent dedication of a modern hospital; it read: "The pain of their subjects, and not their own pain, is the sadness of kings."

Angkor Wat, site of the world famous temples of the same name, was the capital during the reign of these epic kings. However, this great center of art and learning was abandoned after invading Thai carried off thousands of Cambodian scholars and artists to Siam and made them slaves. Over the centuries, the jungle invaded the city, and only recently was restoration attempted. Symbols of national greatness, these temples are portrayed today on the Cambodian flag.

THE STRUGGLE FOR SURVIVAL

Thai armies invaded the Khmer Empire many times, and Angkor Wat was a military objective which changed hands repeatedly during centuries of fighting. Even after the Khmer Empire ended in 1432, invasions of Cambodia continued. The country was continually in a struggle for survival—against Thailand on one flank, and Viet Nam on the other. By 1603, the King of the Khmer was a puppet controlled by the Thais.

During the 17th and 18th centuries, Cambodia fell under the control of Viet Nam. Thais and Vietnamese continued to fight each other for suzerainty over Cambodia. (Considerable Cambodian territory was lost to both of these predators; and to this day, there are still border areas which remain in dispute.) The conflict was finally resolved in 1846 when the rulers of Siam and of the Vietnamese Kingdom of Annam established a joint regime in Cambodia. In that year, the overlords agreed on a native king for the Cambodians. Their choice, Ang Duong, was the first of the present Cambodian royal line.

THE GAINING OF INDEPENDENCE

Ang Duong, however, was not so easily controlled. At the first opportunity, he sought French protection against both his sponsors; and in 1863, Cambodia became a French protectorate.

But Cambodians were not content to be Asian Frenchmen. After World War II, they took advantage of France's weakened position to demand independence. There was considerable dissension in Cambodia over the negotiations. Some rebels accused the King of helping the French to remain in power. In the end, Norodom Sihanouk, who had been chosen King in 1941, succeeding his mother's father over the heads of her brothers, was successful in convincing the people of his dedication to the nation, but only after he had exiled himself, vowing not to return until Cambodia had been granted independence.

In 1954, independence was finally achieved. A settlement was negotiated in Geneva for all of Indochina. Of the three sections of French Indochina, only Cambodia emerged whole, stable, and united.

A KING ENTERS POLITICS

In 1955, King Norodom Sihanouk abdicated in favor of his father, Suramarit, in order to commit himself fully to a political career. As Prince, he formed a new movement, the People's Socialist Community (*Sangkum Reastr Niyum*), a coalition which has won all the seats in the National Assembly. It has been supported by an overwhelming majority of the people—nearly reaching unanimity—in every election. The party's success is based on the power and prestige of Prince Sihanouk, its leader.

When the father died in 1960, the Prince's mother assumed the throne, and Norodom Sihanouk had himself proclaimed Chief of State, an office for which there is no provision in the Constitution. He thus assumed the duties, but not the rank of King, enabling himself to remain the country's political leader.

THE GOVERNMENT

Since 1960, the central government, nominally headed by the King (there is none at present), actually has been headed by the Chief of State, aided by a Crown Council. It is made up of members of the royal family and political, religious, and judicial leaders of the country. When the Chief of State is out of the country, the Crown Council assumes top authority. If the throne should become vacant, the Crown Council is empowered to select a Regent, or a new King, or a new Chief of State, who must be a male descendant of Ang Duong.

RICE PADDY A rice farmer guides a team of water buffalo through his flooded field. Water buffalo are excellent work animals because they are able to pull plows and wagons in the slippery mud of the paddies.

ANGKOR WAT   *The great temples at Cambodia's national shrine date from about 1100 A.D. Built by Brahman god-kings, these temples are one of the architectural wonders of the world. Angkor was depopulated by enemy raids, and after 1430 the ancient city was allowed to return to the jungle. This was in part because the Cambodians of the region had turned from Brahmanism to Buddhism and the temples were no longer an essential part of their religious life. But about five hundred years later, the temples became a center for Buddhist pilgrimages. Clearing Angkor from the jungle and restoration of the wats moves ahead. Here, a Buddhist monk works in the temple grounds.*

There is a judiciary and a two-house legislature, which is elected by the people. The Chief of State appoints as Prime Minister the leader of the majority party in the National Assembly or lower house. The Prime Minister, in turn, appoints the governmental ministers, who have to be members of the National Assembly, to which they are collectively responsible.

THE POLITICAL STRUCTURE

The governmental structure is like a pyramid. Its base consists of a multitude of semi-autonomous villages combined into groups, the groups into districts, the districts into provinces. The district chiefs and provincial governors are appointed by the central government. To expedite the central government's administration of the country, the provinces are, in turn, grouped into administrative regions.

DIMENSIONS OF NATIONAL UNITY

Unity is a prominent Cambodian characteristic. The people of the rural areas have different economic values than their city brothers; the conservative religious practices of the nobility differ from the religious practices of other groups; there is criticism of the government and frequent changes in ministerial leadership; but whatever differences exist seem marginal compared with the unity of outlook that governs all aspects of Cambodian life.

THE PINNACLE OF UNITY

National unity is personified in the Chief of State, who is also the religious leader and most powerful politician. He is central in every significant event, whether it be the announcement of new policies or the starting of important construction projects. To dramatize his interest in progress, Sihanouk has pitched in and gone to work himself with laborers.

When Prince Sihanouk has deemed it essential for political stability, he has suspended the Constitution. While still King, in 1949, he took over the legislature because personal feuds were leading to chaos in the government. New elections were held in 1951. But once more the winners brought the country close to disorder by giving too many jobs to party members instead of to more worthy civil servants. He took over again, from 1952 to 1955, and ruled by royal mandate.

It was after a near-unanimous popular vote of confidence in his stewardship that Sihanouk gave up the throne to assume political leadership under the system provided by the Constitution. In this way, he could engage vigorously in politics—always a controversial pursuit—without endangering the monarchy which, according to the Constitution, is supposed to be above politics.

SOCIAL UNITY

Although the privileges and symbols of rank are important in Cambodia, barriers to individual ambition are not rigid. Rank can be won, as well as inherited. Education, advantageous marriage, and promotion by royal decree are important stepping stones to positions of prestige.

For those with no other hope, the Buddhist belief in reincarnation provides a special route to preference, ultimately to *Nirvana*, the "heaven" of Buddhist eternity. It is particularly important to a rural family to feel that its members may be wealthy and honored in a later life. They do not resent the privileges of others, because they feel that they are *earned* privileges (earned by meritorious conduct in the cycle of reincarnations). By the same token, they do not complain at privation for themselves because they feel that they, too, earned their status in previous lives. Thus, while the government is actually run by nobles and educated commoners, religion reaches across all classes. The merit system of reincarnation gives the peasant hope that he may, in some future life, rise to the highest councils of government.

RELIGION AND FAMILY UNITY

While the King or Chief of State is the head of both church and state, below the royal level politics and religion are kept separate. The views of the Buddhist clergy command respect; but clerical interference in political affairs is not permitted.

The fact that nearly every Cambodian boy is educated as a *bonze* for at least a few months contributes to the stability of the country. This uniform indoctrination strengthens Buddhist principles, and it also builds loyalty to King and country—to the very land itself as the locale of future incarnations—and to the royal personage who is today Cambodia's dominant political figure.

Great respect is accorded the head of a Buddhist family by the children. A Cambodian child is taught to revere age, even in social inferiors. Prince Sihanouk as King, then as former King, and currently as Chief of State, has been a father figure to most Cambodians, even something of a semi-divinity. This religious support reinforces his political image. He has also reached his people through direct contact, in his travels around the country and through granting mass audiences in the royal palace.

PRESSURES OF CHANGE

Western ideas have stimulated pressure for change in all aspects of Cambodian life, including religion. But on the whole, gradual adaptation, not drastic remodeling, has been the rule. Cambodia's firmly based traditional institutions are likely to survive.

THE QUEST FOR SECURITY

The countries that surround most of Cambodia are among the world's major trouble spots. Laos is struggling to achieve unity and maintain independence. Thailand and both parts of Viet Nam are ancient enemies of Cambodia and are still suspected of aggressive ambition. China's ability to overpower all of southeast Asia is a clear danger. Cambodia is wary.

RELATIONS WITH THE UNITED STATES

The United States has, since 1954, emerged as a new and important influence in Viet Nam, Thailand, and Laos. Cambodian suspicions thus extend to the United States, which has been accused of backing Thai and Vietnamese ambitions against Cambodia. The U.S. is suspected, too, of supporting plots to overthrow the Cambodian government. Such charges have been vigorously denied by the United States.

It is asserted in some quarters that the Viet Cong use Cambodian territory as a sanctuary when pursued by soldiers from South Viet Nam, and as a supply route for materials from North Viet Nam. Cambodia denies these allegations. Crossings—deliberate or accidental—of the Cambodian-Vietnamese border have resulted in the deaths of Cambodians, Vietnamese, and Americans. The situation is fraught with explosive potential.

NEUTRALISM

In the conflict between the Western powers and Communism, Cambodia has chosen a neutral position. It has accepted aid from both sides. Particularly since 1963, Cambodia has moved closer to China, which it sees as the strongest force in Asia today. This seems to reflect a decision to bend with the wind, or set its sails to windward. Cambodia's leaders apprehensively live with the possibility that the east wind will prevail over the west wind, as Mao Tse-tung has predicted.

Supported by China, the Soviet Union, and France, Cambodia has offered many proposals for an international conference to guarantee its security and neutrality. However, the nations involved in the Geneva settlements of 1954 on the Indo-China area, and 1961 on Laos, have not been able to agree on arrangements for such a meeting. For this delay Cambodia blames the United States, which avowedly supports Cambodian independence and neutrality but fears that such a conference would deteriorate into an attack on U.S. policy in Viet Nam.

In 1965, the United States expressed an interest in such a conference, but plans for it collapsed under the weight of wide disagreement among the major countries involved as to who should attend and other pre-conditions. There was also talk of the conference being used

WEIR FISHING ON THE TONLE SAP   Fish traps are used by thousands of the great lake's fishermen. Where channels are narrow, fence-like weirs are built, like that on which the fishermen sit here. The weir forces fish to swim into the opening of a large wooden trap, emptied every few hours. The wooden frame in the foreground marks the location of the trap; men in boats on each side of the frame haul in the hanging ropes, and they raise the trap to the surface.

as a forum in which a settlement of the Vietnamese crisis might be negotiated. This led Cambodia to question the real purpose of the conference and the concern of the United States for Cambodia's needs.

Feelings of resentment over U.S. policy, the border incidents, and continuous radio broadcasts by Cambodian rebels from inside Viet Nam and Thailand were largely responsible for Cambodia's closer association with China. Late in 1963, Cambodia refused further U.S. economic and military aid and recalled its diplomatic mission from Washington. It also recalled its missions from London, Tokyo, and Canberra.

However, there was no break in diplomatic relations with any of these countries. A greatly reduced U.S. diplomatic staff continued to operate in Pnom Penh, though without an Ambassador, since the Cambodian government refused to accept the credentials of the U.S. appointee. In May 1965, however, following the alleged bombing of a Cambodian border village by aircraft from South Viet Nam, Cambodia broke diplomatic relations with the United States. As of the beginning of 1966, neither country had a diplomatic mission in the other. There were signs of even greater tension between the two governments as the intensity of the war in Viet Nam brought military operations closer to the Cambodian border.

DAVID J. STEINBERG

IN BRIEF

AREA	Approximately 70,000 square miles, the size of North Dakota.
TERRAIN	Cambodia is essentially a bowl-shaped plain ringed to a large extent with low, densely forested mountains. The Mekong River and the Tonle Sap, or Great Lake, drain the alluvial central plain. Three-fifths of the land is forest or water; only a fourth of the arable remainder is cultivated.
FLORA	Tropical forest, about half hardwoods. Palm, rubber, coconut, kapok, mango, and other fruit trees, marsh grasses, and spices.
FAUNA	Elephant, buffalo, guar, panther, tiger, leopard, rhinoceros, bear, and many birds, crocodiles and fish.

CLIMATE   Mild, and drier than nearby lands because the southern mountains take some of the rain from the southwest monsoon. Rainfall is about 58 inches a year. Temperature varies from 70°F. to over 90°F., averaging 80°F. The rainy southwest monsoon blows from May to October; the dry northeast monsoon blows from November to April.

CAPITAL   Pnom Penh had an estimated 500,000 inhabitants in 1962.

OTHER CITIES   Battambang, Kompong Chhnang, Kompong Cham, Siem Reap, and Sihanoukville, all but the first with fewer than 25,000 people, are the chief centers.

POPULATION   Almost 5.75 million in the 1962 census. Annual rate of increase is unknown. Density is low, about 81 persons per square mile, and the country could easily absorb another two million.

ETHNIC GROUPS   Khmer, or Cambodians, are the dominant group, comprising over 85 percent of the population. Vietnamese (about seven percent), Chinese (over five percent), Cham-Malays, and scattered hill tribes are the principal minority groups.

LANGUAGES   Cambodian (*Khmer*) is the official language. French, Chinese, Vietnamese, and English predominate among languages used in more populous areas.

RELIGION   Theravada Buddhism is the dominant religion. Christianity, Confucianism, and Islam are found among the minorities, and animism is extensively practiced, often side by side with other beliefs.

DATE OF INDEPENDENCE   On November 9, 1953, national independence was proclaimed, although negotiations with France for complete sovereignty continued until January 1955.

FORM OF GOVERNMENT   Constitutional monarchy. The government is dominated by the Chief of State, Prince Norodom Sihanouk. He has delegated the ceremonial functions of royalty to his mother in order to continue his political functions and his direct leadership. Member of the Colombo Plan and the United Nations.

EDUCATION   In 1962, there were about 615,000 students in over 3,600 primary, secondary, and technical schools. Half a dozen higher institutions had about 1,100 students and there were four teacher-training schools. The Royal Khmer University, established in 1959, has curricula in liberal arts, science, medicine, law, and education. Buddhist monastery schools remain important. Literacy is about 50 percent.

HEALTH FACILITIES

In 1960, there were about 180 doctors, 3 dentists, 127 midwives, and 11 pharmacists. There is considerable dysentery, malaria, tuberculosis, and trachoma. Yaws and other diet-deficiency diseases are common. Cholera, typhus, and leprosy occur, but are not epidemic. Average life expectancy is barely 30 years for a newborn baby. Folk medicines are in general use.

A HALL IN ANGKOR WAT   Khmer artists of the twelfth century created sculptures of classic simplicity and unity. This interior, restored in an Angkor temple, demonstrates the restraint and the artistic discipline achieved by Khmer designers.

CULTURAL FACILITIES

In 1962, there were 11 daily newspapers with a total circulation of about 48,000. Of 159 books published, 122 were first editions. The 40 cinemas had an attendance of 12 million in 1962. There were 32,000 licensed radios and 400 television sets in 1960. Wandering troupes preserve traditional music, legends, and drama, while popular culture is chiefly concerned with improvised lyrics set to traditional music.

CURRENCY AND FINANCE

The *riel*, maintained at an official parity of 7.08 *riels* to one French franc, is officially worth close to 3¢ in U.S. currency. The official rate for imports of nonessentials involves a much higher price for foreign exchange, as does the open market rate. The 1963 government budget provided for 3.84 billion *riels* revenue and 5.6 billion *riels* expenditure. The deficit was to be covered by reserves and foreign aid.

INDUSTRY AND PRODUCTION

In addition to rice, rubber, fish, and timber processing plants, industries include a motor-vehicle assembly plant, cigarette factories, rice mills, paper and textile mills, plywood and cement factories, and a variety of other small-scale projects. The national income, about 14.7 billion *riels* in 1959, is derived chiefly from agriculture and amounts to over $75 per person.

CROPS: Subsistence agriculture is the general occupation. Cash crops used for export include excess rice, rubber, corn, pepper, soybeans, spices, and some forest products, mostly timber. Both rice and rubber crops were excellent in 1963 and 1964, contributing to an improved trade balance.

LIVESTOCK: Chiefly cattle, buffalo, pigs, and poultry.

FISHERIES: With the best freshwater fish resources in Southeast Asia, Cambodia's catch is about 130,000 tons a year. Half of that amount comes from the Tonle Sap, which supports a fishing population of 30,000.

MINING: Very limited, mainly small-scale gold and gem extraction and salt and phosphate production. Mineral resources have, for the most part, not been extensively surveyed.

TRADE

The chief exports are rubber, valued at 720 million *riels* in 1962, rice, 514.5 million *riels*, corn, and timber. Machinery, motor vehicles, chemicals, fuel, textiles, and other manufactured goods are the important imports. The trade deficit was formerly financed largely by U.S. aid, which was canceled by Cambodia in 1963. After that, the deficit was reduced by good crops and by heavier government restriction of imports.

1962: IMPORTS $102,000,000
EXPORTS $ 54,000,000
DEFICIT $ 48,000,000

TRANSPORT   ROAD: Of almost 3,250 miles of road, about two-thirds is hard-surfaced. In 1961, there were an estimated 17,000 motor vehicles, and thousands of motorcycles and similar vehicles.

RAIL: A line about 240 miles long connects the capital with the Thailand border. A railway from Pnom Penh to Sihanoukville was to be completed in 1965.

WATERWAY: About 900 miles of navigable lakes and rivers are the main transport arteries.

AIR: Pnom Penh has the main international airport. There are two flights a week to the small airport at Siem Reap, and Royal Air Cambodge flies to Bangkok, Saigon, and Hong Kong. Cambodia has no national airline.

SEA: The newly built ocean port at Sihanoukville is relieving the country's dependence on shipping up the Mekong from Saigon, Viet Nam. Formerly, all ocean traffic went via ocean-going vessels of up to 7,000 tons, sailing junks, and barges through the Vietnamese capital.

COMMUNI-CATION   In 1962, Cambodia had about 3,500 telephones and limited post and telegraph service. From Pnom Penh, international communication is easier to arrange than internal communication.

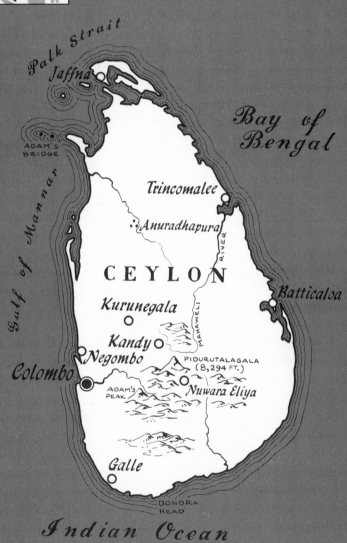

CEYLON

Pearl of Southeast Asia

Lanka, as Ceylon is called by its own people, is a verdant, tropical island with varied landscapes and palm-fringed beaches. Lying close under the southeastern tip of India, it was first colonized by North Indians. They built a flourishing civilization there beginning in the fifth or sixth century B.C. In 1948, after nearly four hundred years of colonial rule, this island nation became an independent dominion in the British Commonwealth of Nations. Ceylon is more prosperous and modern than most other nations of South Asia. But like most of them, it is beset with political, economic, and ethnic tensions.

THE LAND

Ceylon is a small country, about the size of West Virginia. It extends 270 miles from north to south and about 140 miles at its greatest breadth. Although the country lies close to the equator, ocean breezes and high altitudes give most of the island a benign, if somewhat humid, climate. The northern and eastern regions lie in the "Dry Zone." This area is watered by sparse and seasonal rains of the northeast monsoon. The "Wet Zone" encompasses the southwestern and southcentral regions· Here, the land receives abundant rains, primarily from the southwest monsoon.

THE DRY ZONE

The flat and dry Jaffna Peninsula makes up the northernmost tip of Ceylon. This densely populated region has a diversified agriculture. Here rains are supplemented by well-water irrigation for the cultivation of rice, tobacco, and other crops.

The rest of the Dry Zone has undulating plains that rise here and there into rugged hills. Scattered villages are surrounded by forest and jungle. Here the challenge of drought is usually met by irrigation from artificial lakes. Seasonal rains are stored in these lakes for later use in the rice fields. To supplement the rice crops, during the short rainy season, villagers frequently burn off sections of jungle to grow such crops as chillies and corn.

THE WET ZONE

The southcentral region, sometimes called the Kandyan Highlands, is a well-watered region of lushly foliaged mountains. Villagers grow rice in the wet valley; tea and rubber plantations abound on the mountainsides. Many connoisseurs consider the tea grown in the higher elevations to be the world's finest. Rubber plantations are more common in the lower mountains, where there are also widely scattered peasant villages devoted to rice cultivation.

The coastal Low Country extends from north of the capital city of Colombo to beyond Matara, on the southern coast. A region of great urban development, it is also an area of dense village settlement. Coconuts and rice are important village crops. Fishing villages lie along the coast. Fishing is a small-scale enterprise, usually conducted by means of outrigger canoes, catamarans, or hand-hauled shore nets.

WILDLIFE

Herds of wild elephant still roam the forests, as do wild boar, water buffalo, and several species of deer. Monkeys abound. The kabragoya, a giant monitor lizard, sometimes attains a length of over six feet.

A GROWING POPULATION

In 1963, the island had a population of about 10,645,000 persons. Since 1946 the population has been growing at rates between two and a half and three percent each year as a result of natural increase. In that year, the government began an intensive malarial control program which yielded dramatic reduction in death rates. No comparable attention has been paid to programs that might limit births.

Eighty-five percent of all Ceylonese live in rural areas, a proportion which has changed little in recent decades. Density is greatest along the southwest coast and in the northerly Jaffna Peninsula. Village

PADDY FARMERS   *With water buffalo and pronged plows, Ceylonese farmers pre-*
pare their paddy fields for planting rice.

settlements are prevalent throughout the island, although large stretches
of the northern and eastern parts of the island are sparsely settled.

Three ethnic groups—Sinhalese, Ceylon Tamils, and Indian Tamils—comprise over 92 percent of the population. Of these, the Sinhalese are by far the largest, making up about 70 percent of the total
population. Each of these ethnic groups is popularly termed a "race,"
although physical differences between them are minor. In spite of
similarities among these groups, intermarriage is frowned upon and is
uncommon.

THE SINHALESE

The Sinhalese are an easy-going, hospitable, and friendly people.
They are divided into two groups: (1) the Low Country Sinhalese and
(2) the Kandyans of the interior provinces. Cultural differences are
slight. Generally, the Low Country peoples have been more affected by
Western influences. In addition, Low Country Sinhalese are governed
by Roman-Dutch civil law, while the Kandyans retain their ancient traditional legal system in modified form.

STILT FISHERMEN *In the shallow waters off the southwest coast, these fishermen have planted their perches in low water and then wait for the tide to come in. There are many small prongs at the end of the long pole the fisherman holds. He jiggles the pole to catch small fish and shrimp, and then he scoops up his catch into his net. The fish are then stored in the bag which hangs over his shoulder.*

The caste system, which comes from India, is preserved in modified form. Bonds of kinship are revered, but the marital family, rather than an extended family of blood relatives, is the usual household unit. In early days, polyandry was practiced; but this marriage custom is illegal today and rarely found.

The vast majority of Sinhalese are Buddhist. Most of those who are Christian are Roman Catholics. Sinhalese Buddhism is of the Theravada branch, the oldest form of the religion. The Sinhalese have built some of the most sacred shrines of the Buddhist world in Ceylon. The Temple of the Tooth in the hill city of Kandy draws travelers from all parts of the world. The annual *Perahara,* a parade associated with the Temple of the Tooth, is a revered and thrilling event. Scores of elephants, Kandyan nobles in traditional dress, drummers, and dancers join in a festive parade that surpasses all parades.

TAMIL GROUPS

The Ceylon Tamils, who have lived on the island for many generations, are known for their energy and perseverance. They are concentrated in the Jaffna Peninsula and to some extent on the eastern coast of the island. The Tamils are Hindus and maintain a culture similar to the Tamil-speaking people of South India. They retain their traditional civil law, which differs from the Sinhalese legal system.

Although culturally similar to the Ceylon Tamils, the Indian Tamils are a distinct minority. Most live in interior highlands where they form part of the resident labor force that works on tea and rubber plantations. Ceylon has withheld citizenship from all but a few Indian Tamils. Recently an agreement was reached with India for the repatriation of many Indian Tamils.

CHILDREN OF SEAFARING MERCHANTS AND COLONIZERS

In addition to the Sinhalese and Tamils, the population of Ceylon includes three smaller groups—Ceylon Moors, Indian Moors, and Burghers. After the eighth century, Arabs from the Middle East came to trade, and left colonies of Islamic shopkeepers. Augmented by South Indian migrants, this Arab group became what is today known as the Ceylon Moors, a distinct ethnic group bound by the common faith of Islam. The Ceylon Moors speak Tamil, but follow Muslim customs. For example, they do not have a caste system, but they segregate their women.

Like the Ceylon Moors, Indian Moors carefully preserve their separateness within Ceylonese society. Most of them are merchants more recently arrived from South India or Bombay to settle in Colombo.

The Burghers of Ceylon are an exclusive, urban minority with middle class status. They are westernized in dress and custom, speak English, and are frequently Christians of Protestant denominations. Very proud of their Dutch ancestry, they have painstakingly preserved the special identity derived over 200 years ago from the intermarriage between men from the Dutch East India Company and Sinhalese ladies.

The British found the Western-oriented Burghers easy to work with and, as a result, this group has long been disproportionately represented in civil service, the professions, and in white collar occupations. Since independence, Burghers have found life more difficult in Ceylon, and some have emigrated.

LEGENDARY BEGINNINGS

From time immemorial, Ceylon was probably inhabited by a primitive people, ancestors of the Veddahs—a small quasi-tribal group still found in eastern Ceylon.

According to legend, a North Indian prince named Vijaya entered the island about 500 years before the Christian era. He established a great civilization centering on the city of Anuradhapura in the north-central region. Vijaya, or his truly historic counterpart, was the progenitor of the Sinhalese majority. Some of the great structures built at Anuradhapura during those ancient times have been restored; others lie half buried in the jungle growth of many centuries.

INVASION AFTER INVASION

Gradually, the Sinhalese were pressed toward the south and east by successive invasions of Tamil peoples from South India. The Jaffna Peninsula and the forest land north of Anuradhapura became a region of permanent Tamil settlement. Today the Jaffna Peninsula continues to be almost exclusively a Tamil region. The Sinhalese in the remainder of the island preserved their distinctive language of Indo-European origin, and their strong adherence to Buddhism.

With passing centuries, many smaller groups entered the island. Some of these were absorbed either into the Sinhalese or the Tamil societies. A few, like the Ceylon Moors, retained their identity as distinct groups.

EUROPEAN CONQUERORS

At the beginning of the 16th century, the coastal regions of Ceylon were taken by the Portuguese. They introduced Christianity and also developed a lucrative spice trade. After 150 years, the Portuguese were ousted by the Dutch, who, like their European predecessors, ex-

:YLONESE ART   This regal figure appears on a guardstone
an ancient city which was long buried in the jungle. The
·rvings are about three feet high and fifteen inches wide. Finely
tailed and chiseled in hard granite, such works represent the
·est sculpture of ancient Lanka.

ploited the rich Low Country. Both powers retained the feudal system they had found in the island and used it to their own economic advantage.

Although their influence was largely limited to the Low Country and to the Jaffna Peninsula, both the Portuguese and Dutch made substantial impacts on the country. The Portuguese left behind a Roman Catholic religious minority; the Dutch contributed a European legal system that remained as law in the Low Country. No identifiable ethnic group persisted as a result of Portuguese occupation. But the Dutch left the small but significant minority group of mixed Dutch and Sinhalese ancestry, known today as Burghers.

At the end of the 18th century, the British displaced the Dutch and became the first Europeans to conquer the entire island. They soon abandoned the traditional feudal system and established coffee plantations under private ownership in the Kandyan Highlands. After a severe blight, the plantations were shifted from coffee to tea.

The British were unsuccessful in regimenting a Sinhalese work force. To obtain workers, they introduced Tamils from South India as resident plantation laborers, thus creating one of the important ethnic groups found in the island today.

In 1948, after hundreds of years of foreign rule, Ceylon gained its independence. Since then it has been an independent dominion in the British Commonwealth of Nations.

CEYLON'S ECONOMY

Over half of Ceylon's gross national product is accounted for by the growing, transporting, and processing of agricultural products. Major crops are tea, rubber, coconuts, and rice. About 95 percent of Ceylon's foreign exchange earnings derive from the export of tea, rubber, and coconuts. Tea is by far the most valuable crop; about a third of the world's tea is grown in this small island.

Rice is the major crop grown in the villages. But it is not grown in sufficient quantity to supply the island's needs. Whereas plantation production is generally highly organized and efficient, village produc-

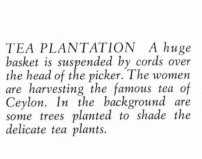

TEA PLANTATION A huge basket is suspended by cords over the head of the picker. The women are harvesting the famous tea of Ceylon. In the background are some trees planted to shade the delicate tea plants.

tion—except in the Jaffna Peninsula—is inefficient. In recent years jungle lands in the north and east have been opened up, at great cost, for colonization and agriculture, especially rice production. It is estimated that 100,000 persons were settled on such colonies between 1945 and 1955. While these lands are not always efficiently operated, they are still highly productive.

In the past, the plantations, especially tea, have been largely under European control. Today ownership is passing into the hands of the Ceylonese. Except for local processing of plantation crops, industrialization has been slow and is still of minor significance in the island's economy.

For centuries Ceylon has been renowned for its gems, particularly its sapphires and rubies. Gemming is currently practiced in the southern highlands, but is not of major economic significance.

TRANSPORTATION AND COMMUNICATION

Ceylon possesses excellent road and communication systems. Nearly 10,000 miles of motorable road, much of it hard surfaced, crisscross the country. There is also a railroad system with nearly 900 miles of line. Postal, telephone, and telegraph facilities are well developed.

Motor trips from the capital city of Colombo are easily made to the ancient city sites in the northcentral region and through the magnificent mountains in the southcentral region. The island is well dotted with government "rest-houses" which provide adequately and inexpensively for the travelers' needs.

SOCIAL SERVICES

Ceylon is relatively developed in modern services and facilities. A socialized medical system brings health services within the reach of all. Elementary schools are generally accessible; enrollments in secondary school are growing. In 1962, 75 percent of all children within the compulsory attendance ages of 5 to 14 were in school. The government-supported University of Ceylon has a diversified curriculum, including a Medical School. Literacy is high. In 1901, only 26 percent of the people could read and write; by 1953 that figure had risen to 65 percent.

Daily newspapers are published in each of the major languages—English, Tamil, and Sinhalese. There are about 140 motion picture theaters in the island.

MAJOR CITIES

Colombo, the capital, set among lush tropical foliage, has a population of over half a million, and constitutes the chief urban center. With its busy harbor, trading community, good hotels, and shopping facilities, it is a modern, cosmopolitan city. There are only four other towns with more than 40,000 people.

The ancient city of Kandy, which overlooks a lovely artificial lake and is rimmed by wooded hills, was once the capital of an interior kingdom. It is the site of the renowned Temple of the Tooth, and constitutes a busy shopping center. The city lies in the mountains of the southcentral area.

GOVERNMENT

The Ceylon Parliament is divided into two houses, a House of Representatives and a Senate. Nearly all members of the House of Representatives are elected on a wide franchise. The Prime Minister, chosen from the majority party, heads the executive branch.

All the functions normal to a modern state are in the hands of various cabinet ministers. The government of the island is highly centralized; but varying degrees of autonomy are given local governments, depending upon the urbanization of the area. A small army and navy are

PERAHARA CELEBRATION   *Gaily caparisoned elephants march in an afternoon ceremony during the seven-day Buddhist holiday in the hill city of Kandy. The devout stand for hours under their black umbrellas to see all of the sacred processions.*

maintained along with an excellent national police force of more than 9,000 men.

The public debt has been increasing in recent years, and economic troubles have led to political tensions. These troubles have been intensified by a rapidly increasing population and by the internal disunities furthered until recently by pro-Sinhalese, pro-Buddhist government policies. In international affairs, however, Ceylon has been quite successful in pursuing a policy of non-alignment.

POLITICAL LIFE

Politics are extremely complicated in Ceylon. The number of political parties fluctuates from time to time. But there are always moderately socialistic groups as well as various Marxist parties, such as Soviet-oriented Communists, Trotskyists, and Peking-oriented Communists.

From 1960 to 1965 the government was headed by Mrs. Sirimavo Bandaranaike whose party, the Sri Lanka Freedom Party, represents a nationalistic, pro-Sinhalese, pro-Buddhist movement with fairly leftist tendencies. In 1964 her government's minority group policies and economic program were so unsuccessful that Mrs. Bandaranaike was forced into a coalition with Trotskyists in an effort to maintain her position.

Before her husband was assassinated by a dissident Buddhist monk in 1959, this convent-educated woman had held no public office in her own right. On her husband's death, she assumed leadership of the Sri Lanka Freedom Party he had founded. Less than a year later, she led her party to electoral victory and won the office her husband had held for three years.

In 1964, with the country on the brink of economic disaster, Mrs. Bandaranaike's government received a vote of "no-confidence" by Parliament. Early in 1965 the Sri Lanka Freedom Party was defeated at the polls by the United National Party under the leadership of Dudley Senanayake. For the third time in the country's short history of independence, Mr. Senanayake became Prime Minister. Mr. Senanayake acted swiftly to reverse the country's trend toward bankruptcy, and to establish more equitable relationships between Sinhalese and Tamils. While reaffirming Ceylon's position of non-alignment, he reversed the trend set by the former government toward closer relationships with the Communist nations. United States economic aid, cut off during Mrs. Bandaranaike's regime, has been re-established and new policies have been created to stimulate the movement of foreign capital into the island.

BRYCE F. RYAN

IN BRIEF

AREA 25,332 square miles, slightly larger than West Virginia.

TERRAIN Ceylon is a pear-shaped island about 270 miles long, separated from India by 40 miles of shallow water. Most of the coast line is sandy beach and lagoon, shaded by palms and protected from surf by offshore coral reefs. In the south, mountains and highlands lie inland from the narrow coastal plain. Many short rivers plunge down to the sea; none is navigable for any great distance.

FLORA Over 3,000 species of flowering plants; ebony, satinwood, and teak in the jungles.

FAUNA The jungle shelters many monkeys, deer, bears, wild boar, snakes, leopards and crocodiles, the giant kabragoya lizard, and the wild elephant.

CLIMATE No recognizable seasons. Mean temperature on the south coast is about 80°F.; at Nuwara Eliya in the highlands, about 60°F. Two monsoons and sea breezes prevent the extremes of heat found in India, but humidity is often high. Rainfall varies from 40 inches a year in some regions to about 200 inches in parts of the southwest hills.

CAPITAL Colombo had almost 511,000 inhabitants in the 1963 census.

OTHER CITIES Jaffna has 94,000 inhabitants; Kandy, 68,000; Galle, 65,000; and Negombo, 47,000.

POPULATION Over 10.6 million people in the 1963 census increased to an estimated 11.2 million in 1965. The annual rate of increase is about 2.7 percent. Density is 418 persons per square mile.

ETHNIC GROUPS The Sinhalese majority numbers over seven million. There are over a million Ceylon Tamils, almost as many Indian Tamils, as well as Moors, Burghers, Malays, and Veddahs.

LANGUAGES Sinhala has been the official language since 1961; Tamil and English are widely used in commerce and education.

RELIGION Theravada Buddhism is practiced by two-thirds of the populace, nearly all of them Sinhalese. Most Tamils are Hindu and most Moors are Muslim. Christians number over 750,000.

SALT MANUFACTURE
In the government-owned salt works, men and women with long-handled tools rake heaps of the salt which have dried.

VILLAGE GIRL

BUDDHIST TEMPLE IN COLOMBO
In architecture, it combines older Sinhalese design with decorative details from European sources.

THE STREETS OF COLOMBO *The minarets of a mosque loom over some small shops in the "Pettah," the oldest shopping area of Colombo.*

DATE OF INDEPENDENCE On February 4, 1948, the *Ceylon Independence Act* came into force; it followed a generation of increasing self-government under the British.

FORM OF GOVERNMENT Parliamentary democracy. A 30-member Senate and a 157-member House of Representatives. A Prime Minister directs the Cabinet. The judiciary is independent. A Governor General is appointed by the British Crown for ceremonial duties. Member of the Commonwealth of Nations and the United Nations.

EDUCATION There were over 2.3 million students in over 9,000 primary and secondary schools in 1962. Ceylon had over 75,000 teachers, with 5,000 more being trained in 26 teachers' colleges. More than 65 percent of the people are literate—the highest literacy rate in South Asia. In 1961, three universities had over 6,000 students and 450 instructors.

HEALTH FACILITIES

There were approximately 2,200 doctors, 190 dentists, 3,000 midwives, and 1,000 pharmacists in 1960. Life expectancy is about 60 years for a newborn baby. Almost seven percent of the national budget is set aside for public health.

CULTURAL FACILITIES

In 1962, 10 daily newspapers had a circulation of 380,000, and seven weeklies had 486,000 circulation. Of the 2,000 or so books published, 1,450 were new, and about 100 were translations. Eight or 10 long films are produced each year and there are over 140 cinemas, 48 of them mobile. The government-operated *Radio Ceylon* broadcasts in Sinhala, Tamil, and English. There is no professional theater, although the people support *Kolam* plays, or masked folk drama, and the famous Kandyan dancers.

CURRENCY AND FINANCE

The Ceylon *rupee* is valued at 2.88 grains of fine gold, or 21¢ in U.S. currency. Government receipts in 1963 were $331.8 million; expenditures, $424.2 million. Social services accounted for $155 million; defense, for $14.29 million.

INDUSTRY AND PRODUCTION

Chiefly rice milling and the processing of tea, rubber, and coconuts. About 85 percent of the people are rural. National income in 1962 was $1.27 billion. Per capita income was close to $130. Cement, salt, and some other basic products are government monopolies. Manufactures include cotton textiles, cloth, steel, fertilizers, tires, shoes, soap, leather, wood products, glass, sugar, cigarettes, and matches.

CROPS: Second largest tea producer, 467 million pounds in 1962, Ceylon provides 30 percent of the world crop. It produces five percent of the world's rubber—102,000 tons in 1962. About 2.5 billion coconuts were harvested, 60 percent for export. Although rice production reached 48 million bushels, Ceylon imports about half of its staple food from Burma or China. Spices, tobacco, and corn are also grown.

LIVESTOCK: Cattle, buffalo, pigs, sheep, and goats. Buffalo are the principal work animals; elephants are used in forestry.

FISHERIES: Fish estimated at 88,600 tons in 1962. Ceylonese eat about 20 pounds of fish a year per person. Pearl fisheries are located in the Gulf of Mannar.

MINING: An important source of high-grade graphite, Ceylon's nine mines exported almost 10,000 tons worth $1.2 million in 1962. Sapphires, rubies, and other precious stones are produced. There are valuable mineral sands on northern beaches which are being exploited by the government, as well as extensive and untouched deposits of iron ore in the southwest.

TRADE

Tea, rubber, and coconut products accounted for 96.7 percent of 1962 exports. Others are cinnamon, cocoa, graphite, and gems. Principal imports were food, fuels, medicine, fertilizers, machinery, cloth, and transport equipment.

1962: IMPORTS $348,516,000
EXPORTS $379,768,000
SURPLUS $ 31,252,000

TRANSPORT

ROAD: Of 18,000 miles of road, 9,000 miles can be used in all weathers. In 1963, the 145,216 motor vehicles included over 83,000 cars, 27,000 trucks, and 18,000 motorcycles.

RAIL: The 898 miles of open railway carry an estimated 50 million passengers and 1.5 million tons of freight each year.

WATERWAY: Canals connect a chain of navigable lakes along the west coast.

AIR: International airports at Colombo and Jaffna are served by Air Ceylon and two foreign lines. Internal service is provided by Air Ceylon.

SEA: The chief ports are Colombo, Galle, and Trincomalee; there are six secondary ports. Colombo handles 85 percent of the shipping; it is one of the largest artificial harbors in the world. In 1962, more than 4,000 ocean-going merchant ships and 3,500 smaller vessels were cleared from Ceylon ports.

COMMUNI-CATION

Post, telegraph, telephone, cable, and radio services are government owned and operated. In 1962, there were 37,000 telephones, 2,000 post offices and 1,000 telegraph offices. Ceylonese owned 397,000 radios.

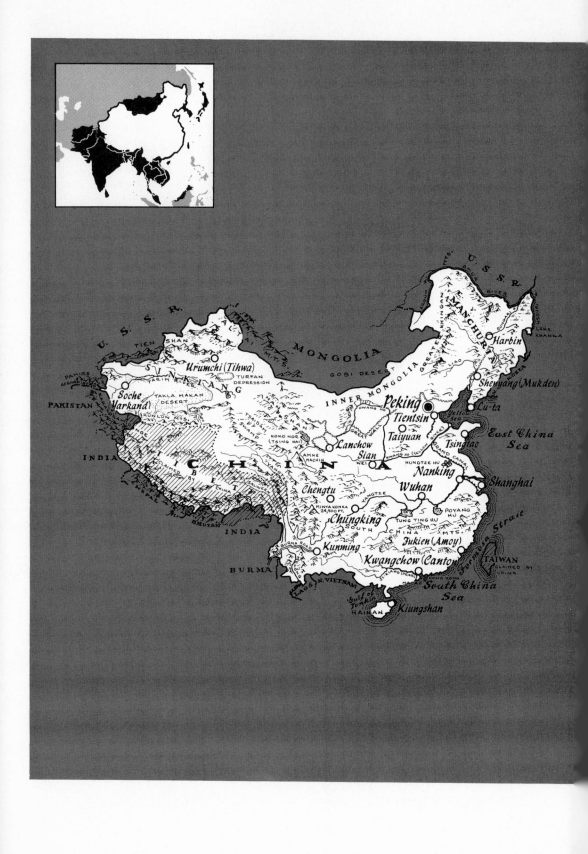

CHINA

Red Colossus in Asia

When, in October 1964, the Chinese Communist Government celebrated its fifteenth year in power, the top leaders had ample reason for satisfaction. During that month, China had exploded its first nuclear device. Such an event reflects the importance and power China has achieved under Mao Tse-tung and his comrades.

At age 56, Mao Tse-tung stood at the Gate of Heavenly Peace in Peking and proclaimed the formation of the Chinese People's Republic. The victory of his Communist Party and his Communist Army was the culmination of almost three decades of warfare since he had helped found the Chinese Communist Party in 1921. When, in 1949, the new ruler of China proclaimed "China has stood up!" he drew applause even from those who opposed his policies, for the days of Chinese humiliation were over. Mao and his cohorts had no doubt that the splendor and power of the "Middle Kingdom" (the Chinese name for China) would be restored.

SWEEPING CHANGES WROUGHT BY COMMUNISM

Fifteen years later, when the 71-year-old Mao stood in the same place in Peking with other top leaders of his Party, no one could deny that his rule had brought about sweeping changes. In 1949, China was divided, war-weary, in economic chaos, rocked with inflation. The nation exercised little power in world councils. In 1964, mainland China was unified as never before in modern times. The Chinese landscape had been changed by the growth of new industry; the people had been brought under discipline; the economy had achieved a fair degree of stability; and China had made its military weight felt around its borders. China was bidding for the leadership of the underdeveloped countries of Asia, Africa, and Latin America; and China was even aspiring to take over the leadership of the world Communist movement.

In Western eyes, of course, all this had been accomplished by deleterious means: the country had been spiritually regimented; the

COALMINERS *Retired after a lifetime of work in the extensive coal mines around Fushun in northeast China, these miners live in a home for the aged. Lodging is free, but they must pay about $6 a month for food out of their pensions, which run from about $13 to $26 a month.*

regime had taken control of all aspects of the economy; Mao had almost become a personality worthy of worship—statues of the leader were to be seen all over and songs celebrating his greatness were sung in schools, in parades, and at meetings.

By the middle of the 1960's, China had become a towering threat to the smaller neighbors around its borders. Worse, China had become a major disturber of peace around the world, as it attempted to export the techniques of guerrilla warfare, terror, and subversion which had helped to bring the Chinese regime into power.

Such a remarkable shift in the internal conditions and world status of China reflected dedication, energy, and ability on the part of the leaders, and also indicated the extent to which a totalitarian regime can build a power position if it is willing to make human sacrifices. For China's new power had been built at the expense of the flight of millions of Chinese to Hong Kong, Taiwan, India, and other lands around the borders of China—including even the Soviet Union. Millions of Chinese had been executed or consigned to camps for "reform through labor service."

EARLY CHINESE HISTORY

Today's leaders are the inheritors of one of the greatest and richest cultural achievements the world has ever known. To begin with, the Chinese have the longest recorded history of any nation—past or present; and Mao reflects his Chinese origins in his world view, in the language he uses, in the despotic institutions he has created, and in his goals.

Chinese civilization dates at least from around 2,000 B.C., when early settlers in the Yellow River valley began to make records. By the time of the Chou Dynasty (1122–221 B.C.), the Chinese had already developed their sophisticated system of writing and had begun to pass along a rich store of philosophy and literature. During the latter half of the Chou Dynasty, such great Chinese philosophers as Confucius (551–479 B.C.) and Lao Tze (fifth century B.C.) and their disciples influenced Chinese thought and institutions.

Warfare and internal division, dating from before the time of Confucius, was ended with the unification of China under a despotic rule by the First Emperor of the Ch'in Dynasty in 221 B.C. This dynasty began a pattern which was to continue down to the present day; a period of harsh unification followed by a season of cultural flowering, followed in turn by invasions by "outer barbarians," then a breakup of internal unity, and once again a restoration of unity by a strong new despot. Thus, following the Ch'in rule, China enjoyed 400 years of cultural achievement under the Han Dynasty (202 B.C. to A.D. 220). A subsequent period of internal division was followed by a despotic re-unification under the Sui (589–617), followed by three centuries of great cultural flowering under the T'ang (618–906). Other great Chinese dynasties followed: the Sung (960–1278), the Ming (1368–1643), and the Ch'ing or Manchu Dynasty (1644–1911). Today's rulers view their own regime within the framework of this long stream of history.

THE CHINESE LANGUAGE

Throughout the ebb and flow of dynastic change, Chinese civilization maintained a remarkable continuity. Many factors enabled Chinese culture to persist; a few deserve special mention because they carry through into the regime of the Chinese Communists.

First, there is the unique Chinese written language. Composed of more than 40,000 different characters (which must be memorized), the Chinese written script has provided unity to the Chinese cultural area (which includes Japan, Korea, and Viet Nam). The works of poets of the T'ang period—and they are among the greatest works of poetry of any culture—were written in the same characters and in the same style as poems written by Mao himself and other poetry published in current Chinese magazines.

Because an adequate working vocabulary for an official requires a knowledge of at least 5,000 characters, and because such a feat of memory requires a modicum of intelligence and a great investment in time, the Chinese written language perpetuated the tradition of rule by a learned élite. Though the spoken language differs widely throughout China—people in the North cannot understand the spoken language of those in the South—the written language has unified the culture.

Although the Communists have simplified the forms of many common characters and have even experimented with a plan for Romanizing the ideographs, they have recently accorded increased attention to tradition and have all but abandoned attempts at major changes.

CHINA'S GEOGRAPHIC ISOLATION

A second factor which enabled the Chinese to develop their unique civilization has been the relative isolation of China from the rest of the world until recent times. The Chinese were, to be sure, influenced by Buddhism from India by way of Central Asia (especially from A.D. 386 to 906), and they were constantly besieged by the nomadic tribes of the north, such as the Mongols who ruled all of China for a century (A.D. 1279–1368); but for the most part, China proved superior to the influence of its neighbors. The "outer barbarians" were judged by the Chinese in terms of the extent to which *they* accepted Chinese customs, institutions, and the interpretations, philosophy, and religion as expounded by the Chinese Emperor. For the Emperor of the Middle Kingdom was the first scholar of the land, and the highest ranking member of its hierarchical and bureaucratic élite.

CULTURAL ACHIEVEMENTS

Another factor which gave staying power to the Chinese culture in its own area was its obviously high level of achievement. China was, through most of the centuries, clearly superior in political organization, population, and power to its smaller neighbors. As the smaller countries paid tribute and homage to the Chinese throne, Chinese faith in their own institutions was reinforced.

Then, too, the Chinese had made significant cultural contributions. When some of the largest libraries in early Renaissance Europe could boast only a few hundred volumes of illuminated parchment, libraries in the cities of China contained tens of thousands of volumes of attractively printed and bound books. Chinese porcelains, from which we get our word "china," have a fragile and artistic beauty which has made them world-renowned collectors' items. Chinese silks have been famous since before the Christian era when the Roman Empire was paying high prices to import them. Tea, lacquerware, fireworks, wall paper, playing cards—all these indicate the high stage of early Chinese civilization.

ROMANIZED ALPHABET Chinese characters must be memorized by everyone who learns to read. A literate Chinese must know about 5,000 different characters to read magazines published in Mainland China today. The government's Committee for Chinese Language Reform has prepared a simplified version for many of the complex characters; these simplified forms are drawn on this blackboard in a Shanghai school room. A phonetic alphabet has also been devised; but the process of introducing it is necessarily slow. So far, the 26-letter Latin alphabet is used only as an aid for pronouncing the characters —not as a replacement of the Chinese "graphs." As in all Chinese classrooms, the photograph of Chairman Mao is placed front and center.

Also, in the fields of art and poetry, the manufacture of paper and the art of printing, and the growing of tea and preparation of food, the Chinese knew they were superior and had little to learn from the outer world.

Today, Chinese opera—a sophisticated and stylized form with lavish costumes—increasingly intrigues Western interest.

If life in China was difficult, the beauties of the Chinese scene offered compensation. The landscape—whether along the rugged terrain over which the Great Wall runs in the north, or along the incredibly steep gorges of the Yangtze River—is beautiful. The countryside has inspired some of the greatest art the world has ever known, Chinese landscape painting.

Because the traditional method of writing the Chinese characters emphasized brushwork, the Chinese have produced outstanding painters in this genre. China has also been famous for many other forms of

art including jade and ivory carving, calligraphy, metal casting, and architecture.

The Chinese pattern of life gave a central role to the family, and put an accent on individual relationships. This, in turn, placed a premium on good manners and on the estimation of decency. Outsiders were also impressed with the traditional Chinese respect for learning and respect for their elders.

ADMINISTRATIVE INSTITUTIONS

Chinese political institutions, closely bound up with the cultural pattern, also provided staying power to the Chinese State. For more than 2,000 years, access to positions of power was related to a system of civil service examinations based on knowledge of the Confucian classics. The affairs of China were run by a great bureaucracy whose members had a vested interest in perpetuating the values which helped them into their positions. What feudalism had existed in China had been abol-

THE GREAT WALL OF CHINA   The most famous monument of China, the Great Wall, was built more than 300 years before the birth of Christ. Rebuilt many times under the reigns of different emperors, the Wall was gradually extended to a length of 1,500 miles. This portion, in the eastern part of the country, is built of earth and faced with stone and brick. Guard towers appear at regular intervals for, in the old days, squads of soldiers patrolled the path along the top. This path at the top is 12 feet wide, the portion of wall at the base is 30 feet wide, and the sloping walls are 25 feet high.

ished with the unification of 221 B.C. Through subsequent periods, land was freely bought or sold. In general, a position in the ruling bureaucracy was the means to wealth rather than vice versa.

Although the State philosophy of Confucianism, with its stress on human values, modified harshness in State administration, the system was highly authoritarian, to the point of being despotic. Corvée labor, invasion of privacy, arbitrary decisions, and high rates of taxation were the rule. In traditional China there were basically two classes: the rulers (the Confucian gentry and the bureaucrats) and the ruled. Though dynasties changed and China was frequently ruled by northern invaders, the core of Confucian scholars continued to provide stability, a solid axle around which the wheel of time turned.

CHINESE SOCIETY

At the base of the pyramid of Chinese society were the Chinese peasants who constituted more than 85 percent of the population. They lived in relatively isolated villages, paying taxes to the representatives of the central government, participating in irrigation and flood prevention works when called upon. Most of the time, they survived at bare subsistence level. Yet even among the peasantry, the basic values of Confucianism were well developed. These tenets included accents on the family, on ancestor worship, on the inferior position of women, and on acceptance of the superior position of those who could read and write.

THE INFLUENCE OF CHINA'S PAST

Mao Tse-tung began his Communist rule within the larger framework of such traditional forces. It was to be expected that he and his colleagues would have a long-range historical perspective.

In the Chinese view, the once-supreme empire began to be subjected to the pressures of the West in the early 1500's. For almost 400 years, the fate of the Far East had been determined in the capitals of Europe. Then, with the emergence of Japan, an uneasy equilibrium was achieved; an Asian nation had asserted itself and had demonstrated that once equipped with the technology of the West, it could achieve almost as much. From that time forward, the world had seen the gradual retreat of Western power from Asia.

The Chinese view themselves as continuing an historical process which the Japanese began. They feel that through their innately superior culture they will prove to be even more successful. This is the background which underlies Mao Tse-tung's insistence that "The East Wind is prevailing over the West Wind." This view, which carries at least implications of revenge of the Eastern powers against the former exploiters from the West, is disturbing to Mao's Soviet comrades, who know that the Chinese think of Czarist Russia as one of the most oppressive of the Western powers during the heyday of imperialism.

STONE BOAT   This marble boat, situated on a lake by the Summer Palace, was built in Peking by the Dowager Empress of China in the latter part of the 19th century. Originally designed as a teahouse, the boat is now used as a public restaurant.

MAY DAY PARADE   Art workers, carrying baskets to indicate their craft, participate in a May Day Parade. They are marching through Peking's central square, T'ien Au Men, the largest plaza in the world. The characters written on the banner in the rear read: "Struggle for Socialism."

COMMUNIST PARTY MEMBER
This well-dressed, stern-looking individual supervises an industrial plant. He is a member of China's emerging class of technologically oriented officials. On the wall behind him are pictures and citations of workers who have distinguished themselves, usually by exceeding their production quotas.

KINDERGARTEN TEACH
Barely in her teens, this girl is ready a worker, teaching m and dancing to the five-year-of a commune near Peking.

NURSERY SCHOOL In China, every mother who works in a factory is given eight weeks of paid leave after her child is born. During pre-school years, the children in this model commune near Peking receive excellent care. The nursery school teacher keeps a close eye on the whirling carousel.

TRANSPORT The stock of draft animals is still insufficient for China's needs. A dozen men at ropes haul this loaded cart. Except for the rubber tires, essentially the same scene could have been recorded when the Great Wall was built.

CHINESE CHESS This is a recreation center in downtown Hankow; similar centers have been opened all over China. A center usually consists of a couple of houses with a stage for opera, an open-air theatre, a tea shop, a refreshment counter, and a game room.

INFLUENCE OF SINOCENTRISM ON PRESENT-DAY CHINA

Such an historical perspective reinforces the present Communist regime's belief in the destiny of their country. The attitude of present-day China reflects the traditional Chinese view that the Middle Kingdom should set the pattern for the rest of the world.

This attitude was reflected in the famous letter which the Manchu Emperor addressed to King George III of England in 1795. Said the ruler in Peking: "Swaying the wide world, I have but one aim in view, namely to maintain a perfect governance and fulfill the duties of the state. . . . Our dynasty's majestic virtue has penetrated unto every country under Heaven. . . . It behooves you, O King, to respect my sentiments and display an even greater devotion and loyalty in the future, so that by perpetual submission to our Throne, you may secure peace and prosperity for your country."

Thus, through the centuries, the Chinese approach to the outside world was China-centered. "Sinocentrism" was bound up in an intellectual isolationism, a conviction of superiority, an attitude of chauvinism and xenophobia. All those who did not accept the Chinese view of life and Chinese customs, and all those who could not read Chinese characters were, from the Chinese point of view, "barbarians" and were so designated.

When, in the 19th century, the Chinese were humiliated by

Western military supremacy, many Chinese scholars opined that as soon as China had learned the sciences of the West—which, of course, they would do better than anyone else including the Westerners themselves—China would once again extend its imperial sway over the whole world. Thus, the Chinese Communist leaders of today are quite convinced that their interpretations of Marxism-Leninism are the only correct interpretations; they lecture the Soviet Communist leaders with the self-confidence of pedagogues.

The Chinese Communist regime of Mao Tse-tung cannot escape its past. This regime views the period starting with the Opium War (1839–1842) as one of imperial decline, leading to the fall of the Manchu Dynasty in 1911. What followed, they believe, was a period of internal dissension and foreign invasion. Finally, a new hero—Mao

CULTURAL PARK IN CANTON

Tse-tung—unified all China, and began to extend China's influence to the whole world. Although the Chinese Nationalists brought about much modernization during 1927 to 1949, the Communists regard this period with contempt. They assert that the regime of Chiang Kai-shek represented a time of oppression and chaos between the collapse of the old China of dynastic times and the creation of the "New China" of Mao Tse-tung.

The comments of a British observer of the Chinese scene written in 1840 are just as valid today as they were during the days of the Manchu Emperor. "After all," he wrote, "what is China but a large and strict school—on an enormous scale, it is true—where neither the youths are allowed to go out, nor other persons to come in. Thus have its inmates no opportunity to learn anything either good or bad, that is prohibited by their master—the emperor."

THE COMMUNIST REGIME

The China of Mao Tse-tung is one of the most thoroughly totalitarian states in world history. The whole structure of the state is subordinated to the Leninist view of a divided world in which there must be continuous struggle until the Communist forces have won total victory. In China today, there is no separation of economic or social or political policies; all measures are subordinated to the over-all goal of building state power. The regime has pushed into the background some of the humanistic values of accommodation which made the old Chinese autocracy bearable. They have given a new direction to Chinese institutions, a thrust which emphasizes the authoritarian past.

Nominally the People's Republic of China operates under a Constitution adopted by the First National People's Congress in 1954. Power is vested in the Congress, which is required to meet every year. When Congress is not in session, power is vested in a Standing Committee.

The head of the People's Republic is Chairman Liu Shao-ch'i; the head of the State Council, or Premier, is Chou En-lai. There are lower level Congresses in the 21 provinces and five autonomous areas into which the People's Republic is divided, and in the more than 1,700 counties or *hsien*.

In actuality, the country is run by the 18-million member Chinese Communist Party. This, in turn, is run by the 18 members (plus six alternate members) of the Political Bureau of the Standing Committee. The Party operates under a Constitution adopted in 1956. So arbitrary is the rule of the top leaders that even the Party Constitution has been violated; it calls for a new Congress every five years, but none has been held since 1956.

Frequently the Party leaders announce new laws without either the formality of a meeting of the Central Committee of the Party or without reference to the formal machinery of the State. The decision to launch the People's Communes in August, 1958, was such an arbitrary decision by the Party leaders; government organs were not involved. The National People's Congress did not meet at all in 1961 or in 1962; and the meetings in the two subsequent years were secret conclaves at which Party spokesmen merely announced policies.

The top leaders are versatile and dedicated first-generation Communists who have worked smoothly together for more than three decades. In addition to Party Chairman Mao Tse-tung, who has retained that position since he assumed it in 1935, other key Party leaders include Liu Shao-ch'i, a fellow Hunanese and a key theoretician; Chou En-lai, the suave, French-trained negotiator; the aged Chu Teh, Mao Tse-tung's comrade-in-arms and the founder of the Chinese Red Army; Teng Hsiao-p'ing, the Secretary-General of the Party and organizational expert; and Lin Piao, the head of the armed forces. In 1965, the average age of the 24 members and alternate members of the Political Bureau was almost 62. The top leaders of the regime are now old men, frozen in their positions of power and convinced of their infallibility.

During 1957, when certain non-Party personages who had been permitted to join the formal government were encouraged to speak up in what became known as the "Hundred Flowers Movement," one of their number commented on the cynical approach of the Communists toward the formal State structure. A member of the Standing Committee of the National People's Congress, he noted, "I always take part in the meetings of the Standing Committee. But the attendance is low, barely the legal quorum. The most frequent absences are the Communist Party members. The fact that Party members do not attend this body, the highest authority in the State, gives us to understand that they have no high esteem for it, that all the real decisions have already been taken in advance by the Party. The assent of the Standing Committee seems to be a mere formality."

The Communist Party has succeeded in making its ideology (Marxism-Leninism and the Thought of Mao Tse-tung) the single, all-pervasive background of life in China today. In line with Mao's decree that there can be neither love nor truth apart from the class struggle, all life is subordinated to the two-camp view of the world. Works of Communist orthodoxy are memorized, much as students and scholars of old used to memorize the Confucian classics. All education is infused with the fervor of the State cult in such a manner as to cause many foreign visitors to comment on the "staggering uniformity" which characterizes China today.

The arbitrary rule by the top leaders has led to secrecy and security consciousness. Outsiders—including Communist leaders from other countries—have been puzzled by developments. After 1960, Peking ceased publishing any statistics on budget, income, or production or even on such aspects of life as population or education. Refugees interviewed by this writer in Hong Kong reported that economists and intellectuals feared to state any but the most general facts because they might be accused of security violations. Ironically enough, economists inside mainland China have complained, at times, that foreigners seem to have a better idea of what is going on in China than they do. The Party leaders have been unwilling to share with the Chinese people their plans or the facts on which such plans might be assessed.

Top Party leaders are themselves surrounded by secrecy. Their whereabouts are not generally known to the Chinese public; they appear in public with their wives only on rare State occasions. Mao lives with his third wife in an unknown location in Peking.

One plan made quite clear, however, has been the subordination of almost everything else to the building of military power. China main-

TEA SELLERS *Elderly women earn a pittance selling tea to passers-by at the Gate of Heavenly Peace in Peking's ancient complex of imperial buildings, called "The Forbidden City." A tiny stool and a tray, mounted on a wide basket, comprise a portable shop.*

tains the largest standing military forces in Asia—more than two and one-half million men. Despite pressing economic problems which include providing an adequate supply of food for the people, the Chinese commitment to developing a nuclear capability has dramatized for the world Peking's determination to move toward great military status, no matter what the economic and human cost.

ADULATION OF MAO

The military buildup is clearly related to the leadership cult built around Mao. He is portrayed as the ever-correct embodiment of Chinese tradition and as the outstanding theoretician of Marxism-Leninism. His works are devoutly quoted and memorized. His beliefs are the single most important factor which gives direction to the Chinese State. Those aspects of his leadership which brought China successfully to power are treated as all-pervasive truths, applicable to all men everywhere.

Several of Mao's basic beliefs deserve enumeration because they help us better to comprehend the policies pursued by the Chinese government. All life must, within the view of his regime, be comprehended as a struggle between opposing forces. This belief aids in extracting maximum effort from the people, helps to keep the country on a war footing, and calls constantly to attention the existence of "enemies" who must be exterminated. Today, in China, the word for struggle, *tou-cheng*, fills the pages of publications. As one of the chief theoretical journals put it in 1960, "Only through struggle can there be hope; only through struggle can there be method; only through struggle can there be victory."

TRUCKER Through the streets of Canton, baskets are transported by yoke. Most of the traffic consists of bicycles and pedicabs; cars and trucks are still rare.

The next tenet is the efficacy of violence for solving problems. The Chinese leaders frequently repeat Mao's statements that "Political power grows out of the barrel of a gun," or "War can only be abolished through war," or "The highest form of revolution is to seize power by armed force, to solve problems by war." Aid for guerrilla activities in Southeast Asia and for revolutionary violence in Africa and Latin America reflects Mao's expressed belief that the world can only be remolded by way of the gun.

BELIEF IN ORGANIZATION AND DISCIPLINE

A third aspect is the belief that "if the masses are organized, anything can be accomplished." Within China, all unofficial forms of human association have been eliminated; individualism has been made the greatest of sins. Mass rallies, mass parades, mass drives, and mass demonstrations—all reflect the almost mystical faith of the Chinese leaders that the great masses of China are an element of strength and that they will prove decisive in history. In 1958 and 1959, Mao organized millions of Chinese to smelt iron in backyard furnaces in the hope that through the mobilization of the energies of the masses he could move China by one "great leap forward" into a modern industrial power. This policy, which proved to be a tragic and wasteful failure, was merely a reflection of his belief in the power of the mobilized masses.

But for the masses to prove decisive, they must be organized; and therefore Mao has placed great emphasis on militant organization as a source of power. All activities in China are highly organized and the population is under severe discipline. This belief in highly disciplined organization was reflected in Mao's creation of the "People's Communes" in 1958, a move which shocked even the thick-skinned Communist leaders of Eastern Europe. These militantly organized groupings of peasant communities regulated all aspects of life including care for children and labor assignments for all adults.

The People's Communes were viewed as a method for replacing loyalty to the family with loyalty to the State. Within a year after the People's Communes had been organized, thousands of refugees

AUTUMN RIVER LANDSCAPE   This painting was done during the middle of the 15th century—a fine example of the Min
Period.

WEN-CH'ANG, THE GOD OF LIT-
ERATURE   This figure was produced
during the K'ang-hsi Period which dates
between 1662 and 1722.

SUNG PERIOD PAINTNG   This picture depicts the Mongols bringing a tribute of horses. It was produced during the
12th century.

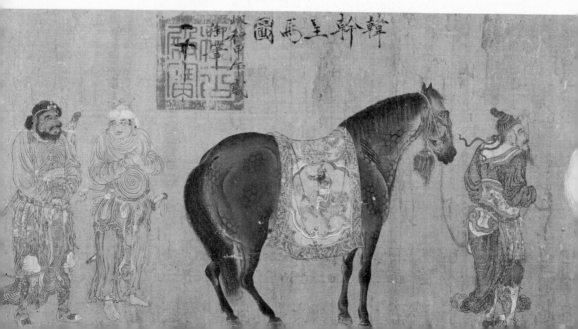

SCULPTURE *An excellent example of the T'ang Period (618-907).*

FIGURE OF SHOU-LAO *Pro-duced during the K'ang-hsi Period (1662-1722).*

ROSE-COLORED VASE *A fine specimen of the Chien-Lung Period (1736-1795).*

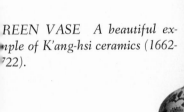

GREEN VASE *A beautiful ex-ample of K'ang-hsi ceramics (1662-1722).*

streamed into Hong Kong, with appalling stories of starvation and agony among the Chinese peasants. Those of us who interviewed refugees in 1959 gasped with disbelief at the stories of dehumanization and the other aspects of the "great leap forward."

But after a little over a year, the Communist leaders had made a tactical retreat, and once again they permitted the peasants to have small individual plots; nevertheless, the basic organizational form of the People's Commune was retained. In 1965, it was reported that 99 percent of peasant households were embraced by the 74,000 People's Communes and that only seven percent of China's limited farmland was given over to private ownership.

Mao's belief that the masses must be organized and disciplined was also reflected in the "Everyone a Soldier" movement, also associated with the "great leap forward." In 1963 and 1964, the Communists were urging the whole population to "learn from the People's Liberation Army" and to view the Army as a model for conduct.

Mao's theories and the actions taken to carry them out in China have, to be sure, provided a unity of control unmatched in China's past. But the human cost has been shocking even to fellow Communists. Many of the Draconian measures have reflected the megalomania of an aging autocrat, ignorant of the realities of the outside world, and increasingly convinced of his infallibility as he listens to songs of praise about himself. When the Communist regime celebrated its fifteenth birthday in 1964, a pageant was produced in Peking, based on the "most popular song in China." Here are the words:

> *The east glows red;*
> *The sun is rising;*
> *On the horizon of China*
> *Appears the great hero Mao Tse-tung—*
> *He is the great savior of the people.*

FOREIGN POLICIES

When the Chinese People's Republic was proclaimed, Mao Tse-tung told the world that the "new China" would "lean to one side," by

SCHOOL BREAK During a recess from back-breaking farm work, a government adult education specialist teaches the workers on a collective farm another few Chinese characters. He is teaching them the simplified versions that have been developed to advance the literacy program. Each of these new characters is composed of less than half as many strokes as are used in the classical counterpart.

which he meant that China would give full support to the Communist camp led by the Soviet Union. At the same time, however, the Chinese leaders began to stake out their claim for leadership of the revolutionary forces in the underdeveloped areas of the world, asserting that the path taken by the Chinese Communist Party to victory in China was the path which should be followed in Asia, Africa, and Latin America. Accent was placed on revolutionary guerrilla violence.

On February 14, 1950, Peking signed a 30-year Treaty of Friendship, Alliance, and Mutual Assistance with Moscow. During the participation of "Chinese people's volunteers" in the Korean War from 1950 to 1953, the two powers worked together in smooth harmony. But following the death of Stalin and beginning with Khrushchev's policies connected with de-Stalinization, the Chinese were increasingly unwilling to play a subordinate role in a Soviet-directed world strategy. They disagreed with Khrushchev's "peaceful co-existence" and resented Soviet policies on a number of other key issues. On their part, the

Soviet leaders began to denounce Chinese international policy.

By 1963, when the leaders of Peking and Moscow were berating each other openly, it appeared that the Soviet Union agreed with Western assessments that China constituted a major threat to world peace. Although issues in dispute between Moscow and Peking were argued in ideological terms—there were, to be sure, some fundamental disagreements on matters of Communist doctrine—the basic clash was over matters of national interest and Communist revolutionary strategy. The Chinese disagreed with Soviet moves toward a detente with the West; they were particularly resentful over the limited Nuclear Test Ban Agreement signed in Moscow in August 1963. From the Soviet point of view, Chinese policies were reckless in their accent on military solutions. Moscow attempted to curb Chinese nuclear ambitions, resented Mao's attempts to unite the colored peoples against the white, deplored the personality cult built around Mao, denounced Chinese plans for hegemony in Asia, disagreed with Chinese aggression against India in 1962, and furthermore charged Peking with violations of the Sino-Soviet border.

For the most part, China's policies have been consistent since the establishment of the Communist regime. Peking has maintained its hostility toward the United States, making quite clear that the price for peace in the Far East is the withdrawal of all American troops and the closing of every base, something the United States could hardly agree to and still remain a faithful ally of Korea, the Philippines, or Taiwan. China has found this policy of implacable hostility toward the United States effective in intimidating smaller countries which are being too friendly to America.

ROAD TO THE MING TOMBS
Lined with stone figures of warriors, this road outside Peking leads to the tombs of the Ming emperors who reigned from 1368 to 1643. These tombs are one of the few places outside the capital Western diplomats are allowed to visit.

China has consistently devoted its resources to assisting guerrilla subversion and violence in the underdeveloped countries. And the Communist regime has consistently reinforced its bid for leadership among the lesser nations by diplomacy and through guided tours in China of foreign dignitaries.

Japan has been a major concern. A full range of diplomatic initiatives and economic pressures have been exerted to persuade the Japanese to renounce their alliance with the United States and to pursue a policy of neutrality.

Peking has wrested control of the Communist parties in Japan, Korea, Viet Nam, and Indonesia away from the pro-Soviet leaders and has exerted political suasion over Burma and Cambodia. Perhaps the major stumbling block in the path of Peking's bid for regional hegemony has been the continued existence of the Republic of China on Taiwan; but the Chinese Communist regime on the mainland has nevertheless established its primacy in the Far East.

Peking has also moved imaginatively to establish contacts, maintaining formal diplomatic relations with more than 50 other countries. Although China is still not a member of the United Nations, Peking makes its weight felt in world councils, and several of the newly independent African states have been increasingly apprehensive over the projection of Mao Tse-tung's strategy of guerrilla violence into that continent. By 1965, it was clear that China had established itself on the world scene as a power of major proportions.

AN AGRICULTURAL LAND

China is the third largest country in the world, after the U.S.S.R. and Canada. Its landscape ranges from the lush semi-tropical monsoon rice paddies in the south to cold and barren deserts in the northwest. According to generous estimates, less than 15 percent of the land in China is arable; over 40 percent of that amount is cultivated under an intensive irrigation which requires constant care. It is not surprising that the major concern of China is scratching a bare existence for the people out of the limited farm plots. A year of unfavorable weather-- inadequate rain or unseasonable floods—can mean starvation for mil-

ICE SKATING On frozen
Pei Hai Lake near Peking,
small boys ice skate after
school. Their home-made
wooden skates are tied to
their boots with string. Bamboo poles, tipped with nails,
help to propel them along
the ice.

lions of Chinese. Over the centuries, the people have been inured to
hardship and have frequently had to turn their faces away from the
suffering of their fellow men.

Because so few areas are fit for cultivation, the Chinese have
crowded into the river valleys. They have become used to lack of privacy. Of necessity, they have come to understand, with a buttressing by
the Confucian philosophy, certain concepts of social responsibility.
Chinese life has been built around the family; there is a deep and intense personal attachment to the clan. It is this overriding loyalty to the
family which has been a problem for any government which has sought
to organize and modernize China. The Communist government, more
than any other, has been able to use modern methods of communication and organization in the rural areas to promote and exact loyalty to
the State, In many respects this has involved a concentrated attack on
the traditional Chinese family and has, in turn, created passive resistance. But, by and large, the regime of Mao Tse-tung has brought revolutionary ideas to the countryside and into the hut of the peasant.

MINORITY PROBLEMS

Another Chinese problem is the existence of minority nationality groups, many of which are antagonistic toward the Han (Chinese) peoples. Most of the western half and the southwestern area of China are peopled by non-Han minority groups, some of them numbering more than a million. These groups resent the constant expansion of the Chinese to the west and south.

Chinese Turkestan or Sinkiang Province contains Kazakh and Uighur tribesmen with close ties to their fellow tribesmen across the Soviet border. The Muslims in northwest China have long been antagonistic toward the Han Chinese as have the Mongols, more of whom live in Chinese territory than in the Mongolian People's Republic.

Mao Tse-tung's regime has applied a carrot-and-stick approach toward the minority nationalities, but anti-Han feelings continue to run high. In Tibet, a revolt againt Han chauvinism in 1959 resulted in the flight of the spiritual leader, the Dalai Lama, to India. The ensuing revolt was put down in such a way as to lead the International Commission of Jurists to charge Peking with attempted genocide. The Tibetan revolt, which still continues to smolder in mountain valleys more than 14,000 feet high, triggered uprisings against the Chinese among the Muslims and the tribesmen of Sinkiang.

The minority nationalities, which Mao concedes occupy more than 60 percent of China's territory, continue to be a threat to stability. It seems likely, therefore, that the regime will attempt to weaken the sense of tribal identity among these peoples, and this may well lead to the elimination of whole groupings.

CHINA'S BURGEONING POPULATION

A census of dubious authenticity was conducted in 1953. Nevertheless, it is clear that the population of China is approaching crisis proportions; by 1965, the population may well have passed 735 million. It is probable that in the decade of the 1960's China will add more people to its already overburdened agricultural base than there are people in all of the United States.

MAO TSE-TUNG *The Chairman of the Communist Party in China emerged from ordinary beginnings. Born in Hunan Province in 1893, he was a Middle School graduate. Later, he worked as a library assistant at Peking University. He went on to write many books and he has also written a number of poems in the classical tradition. An infrequent traveler, Mao has made only two significant visits in his life—both to the U.S.S.R.*

Although the Communists have tried numerous methods to discourage the population growth, including an insistence on late marriage, they admit failure. By 1962, a bad economic year, and despite the increase in textile production, each person was allotted less than two yards of cotton cloth of narrow width for the whole year. Observers commented that the poorer peasants were dressed in patches. Such statistics make all the more tragic the expenditure by the Chinese Communists of scarce resources on military power.

THE CITY OF PEKING

Peking, the capital, was laid out with wide avenues. Its famous palace area was built by the Yung Lo Emperor of the Ming Dynasty in the early 15th century, on the site of a still earlier capital. When the Europeans first visited Peking in the 17th and 18th centuries, they reported that nothing in the world could match the splendors of this city. Under the Communists, many of the traditional palace buildings have been restored. Recently constructed edifices have turned Peking into a resplendent showplace for visiting tourists and dignitaries.

SHANGHAI AND OTHER URBAN CENTERS

Shanghai, the center of Western commerce in China before the Communist takeover, is still the largest city in China. It is the center of the textile industry.

Other important cities include the tri-city area known as Wuhan, the new northwestern science and petroleum center of Lanchow, and such industrial centers in Manchuria as Anshan. But the Chinese themselves frequently claim that the most beautiful city in the world is Hangchow, and Communist leaders frequently go there for their conferences.

PUBLIC HEALTH

With chronic poverty and inadequate diet over the centuries, Chinese villages were vulnerable to frequent epidemics. Infant mortality rates were high; elementary sanitation almost non-existent. The Chinese fertilize their fields with human and animal excrement and, usually, little care is taken in cleaning foods.

However, in recent decades, public health has vastly improved. Much of the impetus for this betterment has come from Western missionaries and educators. Peking Union Medical College, one of the greatest medical centers in the world and the leading research laboratory in parasitology, was established with the assistance of the Rockefeller Foundation and other funds from the United States. Still, China remains subject to serious health hazards, and the chances for continuing improvements are limited by the inadequate diet.

CHOU EN LAI   A skilled diplomat, China's Premier is flexible but unalterably loyal to Mao Tse-Tung. Suave and sophisticated, the Premier was schooled in France. He likes Chinese opera.

FLOATING GENERAL STORE *This weather-beaten old junk, anchored in Canton's Pearl River, sells everything: soft drinks, hair oil, vegetables, etc. Note the modern refrigerator in the front part of the boat.*

LITERACY AND EDUCATION

In the twentieth century, the Chinese have come to accept the concept of mass literacy. Before the Japanese invasion of China in 1937, the Nationalist Government had emphasized education and had experimented with a mass literacy program based on the learning of 1,000 basic characters; but by the end of World War II, less than 20 percent of the Chinese population was literate.

The Communists have continued emphasis on education for all the people. In the 1960's, it was claimed that more than 90 million children were enrolled in primary schools, but the problem remained vast and difficult because of the complex nature of the written language. Today, probably 60 percent of the people can read basic texts and simplified newspapers, but less than one person in 500 is enrolled in an institution of higher learning.

To overcome the educational lag caused by the Confucian view that education should be limited to a qualified élite, the Communists have utilized part-work, part-study school programs, radio, and television in an attempt to provide education for all the people. But the regime has been heavy-handed and has treated education mainly as a means for mass political indoctrination. All communication media are controlled by the Communist Party, which has even attempted to rewrite the classical works of Chinese literature to conform to the Marxist view. Such corruptions have frequently served to alienate the more sophisticated intellectuals and have deprived the Communists of their whole-hearted support.

When, in 1957, Mao felt sufficiently sure of his control to encourage the Chinese to express criticisms, he and his fellow Communists were stunned by the vehemence of the opposition of students and intellectuals to the totalitarian methods used. This period, known as "The Hundred Flowers Campaign," indicated the intensity of resentment over the destruction of some traditional institutions.

FORCED INDUSTRIALIZATION

When Mao's regime came to power in 1949, it faced inflation, disrupted communications, and a state of almost total economic collapse. By 1952, the economy of China had been restored to pre-World War II levels. The Communists were then ready for a Stalin-type forced industrialization under a Five-Year Plan (1953–1957). On the whole, this plan achieved its goals. Despite the chaos caused by the frenetic "great leap forward" of 1958–1960, Communist China had, by the mid-1960's, become a major industrial power.

In line with totalitarian secrecy, since 1960, Peking has released no statistics on production. However, most observers who have visited China have been struck by the industrial progress. China still produces the handicrafts, the silks, and the agricultural products which have constituted her major exports in the past, but now she produces machine tools, automobiles and trucks, bicycles, and heavy electrical equipment. Many such items are exported in limited quantities. By 1965, outside

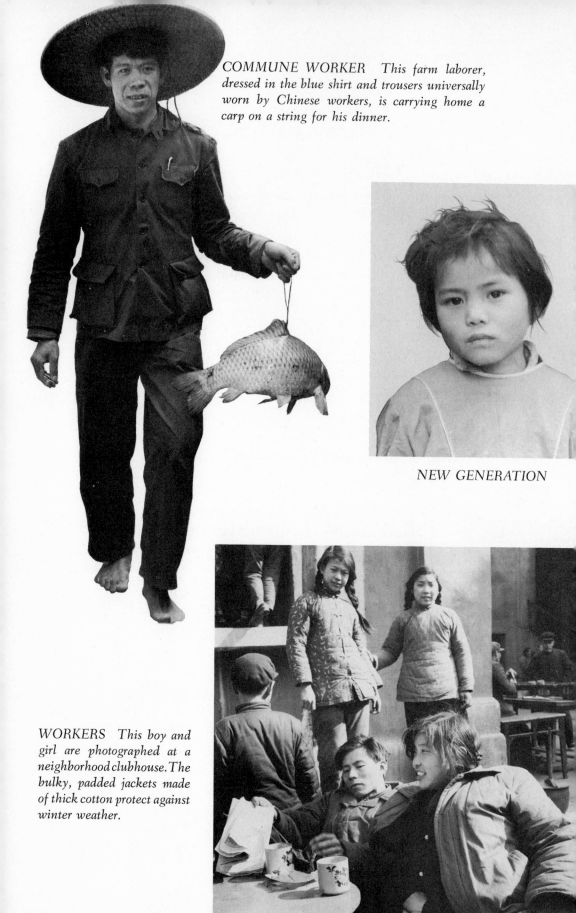

COMMUNE WORKER This farm laborer, dressed in the blue shirt and trousers universally worn by Chinese workers, is carrying home a carp on a string for his dinner.

NEW GENERATION

WORKERS This boy and girl are photographed at a neighborhood clubhouse. The bulky, padded jackets made of thick cotton protect against winter weather.

AFTER SCHOOL HOURS This child dressed in winter garments of padded cotton but lacking gloves, must spend several hours after school waiting at a construction site in Peking for her mother, a laborer. Her mother must work or she will lose her rights to medical care and a pension.

PATRIARCH

SARTORIAL ELEGANCE This woman in Peking apparently enjoys a high social status. Her clothing is cut to the pattern of workers' garments, universal in modern China, but is made of attractive and expensive materials.

experts estimated that China was probably producing more than one and one-half times Japan's steel production of 1941.

After her first two nuclear explosions in 1964 and 1965, it was clear that China had in operation at Lanchow a gaseous diffusion plant for producing U^{235} Despite the expenditure of more than one billion dollars, France had not yet been able to activate such a facility by that time.

Communist China has moved away from a preponderant reliance on agriculture, handicrafts, and light industry. Although there has been a significant growth of heavy industry, there are still major problems. The internal transportation system is inadequate. In 1965, there were only about 22,000 miles of railroad in all of China. Highways are poor, and few are adequately surfaced to carry heavy traffic.

In 1961, the Communist leadership began to realize that there was no instant path to modern industrialization; further progress, it was conceded, would depend upon increased agricultural production. In 1964 and 1965, China began purchasing complete fertilizer factories from Japan and Western Europe, thus changing its direction of trade away from other Communist countries. Peking also devoted increased emphasis to rural electrification and power plants for irrigation.

Most of China's exports continue to be agricultural products, many to the British Crown Colony of Hong Kong, China's biggest trading partner and earner of more than $500 million in foreign exchange for Communist China. China, in turn, has been importing more than five million tons of grain per year, mainly from Australia, Canada, and Argentina, and this has proved a drain on resources. Future progress in industry will depend on the extent to which the regime is able to improve agricultural productivity, and this means a sizable development of a fertilizer industry.

ACHIEVEMENT OF NATIONAL UNITY

There can be no question that the tightly knit Communist leadership has brought a unity and control over all aspects of life in China unequaled in recent centuries. But despite the lavish parades and the great progress shown in displays to visitors, the lives of the people con-

THE GATES OF KUNMING   *This city, capital of Yunnan Province near the Burma border, is one of the most important cities in southwest China. The pagoda-like Chuang Yuan Lou Gate was built during the reign of the Manchus (1644-1911).*

tinue to be characterized by poverty and misery. Per capita income is still about $50 per year.

Like the Confucian gentry before them, the Communist leaders live in relative luxury and possess absolute power. They have forced their people into a stringent discipline which their Marxist-Leninist ideology tells them is necessary for modern industrialization, but they have kept the Chinese isolated from meaningful contact with the outside world. The Chinese masses have been insulated from more humane methods toward modernization and social progress.

Organizational inflexibility and dogmatism have turned the country which once hailed the great humanitarian, Confucius, into a major threat to world peace, an infinitely dangerous threat in the age of nuclear missiles. The outside world can only hope that as the first generation of Communist fanatics fades from the scene, some of the traditional Chinese values of humanity, accommodation, and warmth will replace Mao Tse-tung's doctrine of hate and struggle.

RICHARD LOUIS WALKER

IN BRIEF

AREA

Estimated at 3,284,200 square miles, not including Tibet or Taiwan. China is larger than the continental United States.

TERRAIN

Vast, undeveloped mountain and plateau areas in the interior fall to coastal lowlands. All the great rivers flow east. The Yangtze, 3,200 miles long, and the Hwang Ho, or Yellow River, 2,900 miles, have been the avenues of transport and the centers of civilization, as have the Huai and the Si, or West, rivers.

CLIMATE

Most of the country falls in the north temperate zone. There are desert areas in the west, monsoon tropics in the south, and very cold and windy areas in the north. Typhoons reach the southeast coast during the summer. Parts of the south receive up to 80 inches of rain a year, while parts of the north get only 10 inches.

CAPITAL

Peking. The metropolitan area had an estimated 6.5 million inhabitants in 1963.

OTHER CITIES

Shanghai had almost 10.5 million people in 1963; Mukden, 4.41 million; Tientsin, 2.85 million; Shenyang, 2.41 million; Wuhan, 2.15 million; and Chungking, 2.12 million. Over a million people reside in each of the following cities: Canton, Harbin, Lu-ta, Nanking, Sian, Tsingtao, Chengtu, Taiyuan.

POPULATION

Over 735 million estimated in 1965 in mainland China; estimates of some experts are somewhat lower—there has never been a thorough census. The rate of increase is estimated at 2.2 percent a year. Average population density is 160 persons per square mile; there are more than 1,500 persons per square mile of cultivated land, a figure that indicates serious overpopulation in an agricultural economy.

ETHNIC GROUPS

Han-Chinese constitute the most numerous group and dominate the culture. Groups numbering over a million include the Manchu, Mongol, Korean, Chuang, Uighur, Hui, Yi or Lolo, Tibetan, Miao, and Puyi. Smaller groups are the Kazakh, Lisu, Li, Thai, Hani, Pai, Yao, and Tung. Many smaller, isolated groups exist.

FERTILIZER CAMPAIGN *In 1959, the scarcity of fertilizer led the Chinese government to organize a campaign, complete with awards and citations for workers who
participated. These girls of Hankow are collecting night soil after school hours.*

LANGUAGES Mandarin Chinese is the most extensively used dialect; it is
understood by about two-thirds of the people. Mandarin,
Wu, Hsiang, Hui, Kan, Hakka, Min, Yueh and numerous
local dialects are related but are mutually unintelligible. Over
20 other languages, most of them having several dialects, are
spoken among minority groups. Many of these languages
have no written version. Although users of variant Chinese
dialects cannot speak with each other, they can all read
written Chinese since the characters are translated by the
reader into his own tongue. In 1956, a version of the Latin
alphabet having 30 letters was adopted; it is planned to
gradually replace the use of more than 40,000 Chinese characters.

RELIGION Confucianism, Buddhism, and Taoism are the dominant
faiths. Islam, Christianity, polytheism, animism, and various
folk religions and ancestral cults are followed by minority
groups. For 2,000 years, strong Chinese rulers encouraged

the Confucian ideas most useful to the state and restricted official recognition of all others. The present government has extended this policy, moving toward the complete secularization of society.

DATE OF INDEPENDENCE

On October 1, 1949, the People's Republic of China was inaugurated, superseding the National Republic of China. The People's Republic still recognizes October 10, 1911, when revolt against the Emperor began, as the start of the Chinese Republic.

FORM OF GOVERNMENT

Communist. The National People's Congress is elected for four years and is supposed to meet at least once a year, but actual power rests with the Communist Party of China, which has 18 million members. In 1964, the party's Central Committee was composed of 95 full members and 82 alternates. From the Central Committee, a Politburo of 15 full members and six alternates is made. The first six members of the Politburo are a Standing Committee and hold final authority in all aspects of government. China is not a member of the United Nations.

EDUCATION

In 1958, the last year for which statistics are available, the Chinese government reported 92 million students in 950,000 primary schools, 15 million in 118,000 secondary schools, and 730,000 in 1,400 institutes of higher education. Part-time schools have been used to combat adult illiteracy. Many citizens have been taught the new alphabet. Printed material is scarce.

*EARLY MORNING MARKET
The housewives of Peking line up to purchase noodles and vegetables for the day's dinner from street vendors before going off to their daily work.*

**HEALTH
FACILITIES**

Modern hospitals and doctors are available in large cities. All medical services are integrated in one way or another with other governmental functions. Government teams, successful in stopping epidemics like the bubonic plague, have helped gain acceptance for modern methods, but herb doctors and untrained midwives remain in practice. Life expectancy is a little over 32 years for a newborn baby. Faulty sanitation and nutrition are the basic causes of most deaths, especially among babies and new mothers. Intestinal parasites afflict most of the people; tuberculosis, trachoma, smallpox, malaria, leprosy, and typhus are endemic.

**CULTURAL
FACILITIES**

In 1955, the Chinese government reported 1,954 newspapers, including 392 daily papers, and 288 magazines. The 1958 government figure of 15 million circulation, or one for every 40 persons, is open to question. The most important paper is the *People's Daily (Jen-min jih-pao)*, official organ of the Communist Party. Smaller papers may use news releases only from the New China News Agency *(Hsin-hua She)* or government press officers. Reporters are not to seek news, but must wait for releases to be given them. In 1958, there were 1,386 cinemas, and probably over 6,000 mobile cinemas. About seven million radios were in use in 1959. There were 20 television stations in 1961, and 50,000 television sets in 1962. All art forms, including traditional dramatic and operatic arts, are closely supervised by the government.

**CURRENCY
AND FINANCE**

The *people's yuan,* officially called the People's Bank Dollar, is set at 42¢ in U.S. currency at the official rate. The free market rate fluctuates. The latest published budget, that for 1960, balanced at $29.41 billion. Construction accounted for 61 percent of government expenditure. Defense expenditure supported an army of 2.6 million, a navy of 80,000, and an air force of 75,000 men.

**INDUSTRY AND
PRODUCTION**

The government's efforts toward rapid industrialization can be gauged by the rise in electricity production: 4.3 billion kilowatt hours in 1949 rose to 58.5 billion kwh in 1960. Emphasis is on developing heavy industry. Light industry, except for building materials, cotton cloth, matches, ricemilling, and similar basic necessities, receives little attention. The

BLACK LOLOS *Each wears a traditional long cape and customary topknot. An amulet on the neck is alleged to protect them during war and during the hunt. The brown-skinned Yi or Lolo tribes who live in the hills of Sikang in southwest China are members of a minority group, ethnically and culturally distinct from the majority of Han Chinese. They grow corn and wheat rather than rice; they are organized into clans instead of villages. They follow a form of animism in which every mountain, tree, and stream embodies a spirit; many spirits are evil and cause misfortune. The upper classes are dubbed "Black Lolos;" they are not black-skinned. The lower classes include the "White Lolos"—not Caucasian—and Han Chinese. Although he may tend sheep or goats with propriety, household duties and farming are beneath the dignity of a Black Lolo; for these duties, he uses his slaves—White Lolos.*

KAZAKH WOMAN *Although her teapot is factory-made, this housewife follows a pattern of life scarcely altered in the last thousand years. The Kazakhs are tribes of Turkish origin; they roam the steppes of central Asia with their herds of sheep and horses. The Chinese have been attempting to organize the Kazakhs into collective farms.*

LOLO TRIBESMAN This young man
wears a Chinese shirt over which a
cartridge belt is hung.

LOLO CHILD This little girl lives
in the village of Lanchang in Sikang
Province. The turban-like headdress,
worn by both males and females,
readily distinguishes the Lolos from
the Chinese.

COAL SALVAGE These Hankow school boys, bundled against the winter in bulky clothing of padded cotton, are collecting precious bits of coal. The poster advertises a summer resort for workers.

national income, estimated at $63.84 billion in 1959, indicates a per capita income of approximately $50 a year. However, the government budget is almost half the size of the national income, compared with a government budget roughly one-sixth the size of the U.S. Gross National Product.

CROPS: The Chinese farm intensively, using irrigation, crop rotation, and well-developed horticultural techniques. At the 1953 census, over 86 percent of the population was rural. By 1964, the more than 500 million peasants were formed into 74,000 communes with highly organized living conditions. Rice, wheat, corn, soybeans, and peanuts are the chief subsistence crops. The 1964 grain harvest, a good one, was estimated at about 180 to 200 million tons; nevertheless five million tons of grain had to be imported, mainly from Canada and Argentina.

LIVESTOCK: 1960 estimates were about 44.5 million cattle, 59 million sheep, 180 million pigs, and 7.6 million horses.

FISHERIES: Fish catch in 1959 was reported to be 5.02 million metric tons.

MINING: Coal, gold, iron, copper, lead, zinc, silver, tungsten, mercury, manganese, bauxite, antimony, and tin are mined, chiefly in the west, in significant quantities. An estimated 5.5 million metric tons of crude petroleum was produced in 1959.

TRADE

Much of mainland China's trade is by barter agreement—for example, the rice-for-rubber agreement with Ceylon. Fertilizer and food grains purchased to compensate for poor harvests have accounted for half the imports in recent years. Industrial machinery, automobiles, precision instruments, chemicals, and raw cotton are also imported. Exports include cotton textiles, silk, tea, soybeans, tung oil, egg products, handicrafts, coal, and ores. Mainland China trades with more than 125 countries and regions. By 1965, West Europe and Japan had become major trading partners.

1961 estimates: IMPORTS $1,135,000,000
EXPORTS $1,212,000,000
SURPLUS $ 77,000,000

TRANSPORT

ROAD: There were over 111,000 miles of road in 1957, which the government claimed had been increased to almost 250,000 miles by the end of 1958.

RAIL: Over 21,000 miles of railway were open to traffic in 1964.

WATERWAY: There are about 93,000 miles of inland waterway; almost 25,000 miles are navigable for steamers. Coastal and inland shipping carried about 230 million tons of freight in 1959.

AIR: There are 18 interior air routes connecting Peking with 38 cities. Mainland China is linked to the outside world by air connections with the Soviet Union, Pakistan, Indonesia, Burma, and Cambodia.

SEA: A 1963 estimate gives 502,000 gross tons of ocean-going ships (those over 100 gross tons). Almost 1,200 ships were registered in 1948; most of them remained in Nationalist Chinese control.

COMMUNI-CATION

All services are government controlled. Telegraph service is fairly well-developed. There were 255,000 telephones in 1951; 67,000 post offices in 1958.

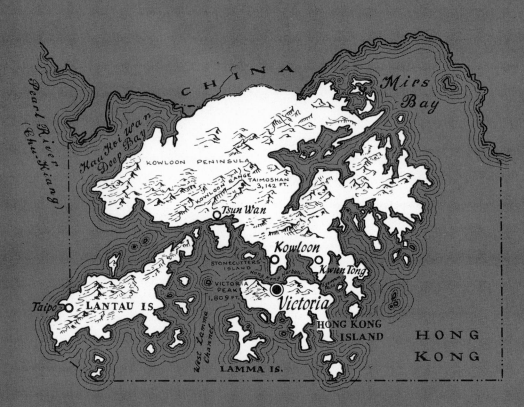

HONG KONG

Miracle of Modernization

*Pearl of the Orient—The Modern Economic Miracle—Shoppers'
Paradise*—such are the epithets commonly applied to Hong Kong today.
When it was founded in 1841, it was scathingly referred to by Lord
Palmerston, then Foreign Secretary, as "a barren rock." Its transformation into an industrialized community of some 3¾ million people in a
little more than a century is one of the outstanding success stories of
modern times. Moreover, the most spectacular growth has occurred in
the last ten years.

ECONOMIC GEOGRAPHY

Hong Kong is a tropical British colony on the southern coast of
China. Its total area of 398 square miles consists of Hong Kong Island,
the tip of the Kowloon Peninsula on the mainland, and the New Territories, lying to the north of Kowloon, which, with some 235 islands,
comprise the bulk of the total area.

The land is hilly, with peaks rising abruptly from the sea to some
3,000 feet. There are heavily eroded granitic ridges at lower levels, and
the coast line is heavily indented.

Over 80 percent of the land is marginal and only 13 percent is
productive. The chief crops are rice and vegetables. Nearly half a million pigs were produced in 1964. But Hong Kong can feed itself for
barely a month from its own resources; thus, 23 percent of its total imports consist of foodstuffs, most of which come from mainland China.

The natural resources are meager—there is some iron ore which is
sent to Japan, and wolframite and graphite are mined.

The climate is monsoonal. From May to September monsoons
from the southwest are hot and humid and temperatures run from 85°F.
to 97°F. Most of the 85 inches of rain which falls annually comes during this period. From October to May the northeast monsoon is usually
dry and cool, but winds from Siberia occasionally send the temperature
down to below 45°F. The typhoon season is from July to October.

ETHNIC COMPOSITION

Hong Kong's main assets are a magnificent natural harbor, and an industrious people. About 99 percent of the people of Hong Kong are Chinese. Most of them come from Kwantung Province. A small group, called egg people, live their lives on board small craft and rarely settle ashore.

Non-Chinese, or foreigners as they are called, number fewer than 50,000. About two-thirds of these are British Commonwealth citizens, and the next largest groups are Americans, Portuguese, and Japanese.

THE TWIN CITIES

The bulk of the people live in the twin cities which lie on each side of the harbor; the city of Victoria on the Island, and Kowloon on the mainland. The name Victoria is rarely heard, Hong Kong being used for both city and Island; Kowloon is used for both the city and the peninsula on which it stands. Ferries ply between the two cities every few minutes. There is a cable railway to the Peak on the Island.

ECONOMIC HISTORY

Before the founding of Hong Kong in 1841, Europeans and Americans who traded at Canton were subjected to most humiliating conditions. They were allowed to reside in Canton during the trading season only, and their families had to be left in Macao. They were forbidden to enter Canton, to ride in sedan chairs, or to study or use the Chinese language.

The British Embassies to Peking could do nothing to alter this situation. The growth of the opium trade, although aided and abetted by Chinese officials, made matters worse. In 1839, the foreign merchants were imprisoned in their houses and were forced to give up all the opium in their possession. A British expedition was sent to demand redress and to seek improved conditions of trade. Hostilities continued until August, 1842, when the Treaty of Nanking was signed. Hong Kong was declared a free port, a status it still retains and which gives it its cosmopolitan character.

After a slow start due to fever and typhoons, Hong Kong became

STREET SCENE   *Characteristic activities are being pursued in this public area of a temple compound which fronts on a lane. An imperturbable black cat luxuriates in the warmth from the water-heating equipment. The little girl is being given a warm bath. Freshly laundered trousers dry against the wall. The sign in the niche says "Heaven bless us" and is a shrine commonly found, no god being honored in particular.*

the headquarters of the chief merchant houses engaged in the entrepôt trade between China and the West. Its boundaries were extended in 1860 by the addition of Kowloon, and in 1898 by the lease for 99 years of the New Territories.

During the Second World War, Hong Kong fell to the Japanese on Christmas Day, 1941, and all Allied civilians were interned. They were finally liberated in August, 1945, after the Japanese defeat.

INFLUX OF REFUGEES

The postwar period brought an astonishing transformation which affected every side of Hong Kong life. The success of the Chinese Communists against the Chinese Nationalists, which led to the setting up of the Chinese People's Republic in 1949, set in train a mass exodus of Chinese to Hong Kong. From the beginning of 1949 to the spring of 1950, more than three-quarters of a million people entered the Colony. Many were genuine political refugees, but most were Chinese from the neighboring Kwantung Province who were attracted by hopes of higher wages and greater security.

GOVERNMENT HOUSING PROJECT *Built to accommodate the multitude of Chinese refugees, these clean and airy one-room apartments are rented for about $2.70 per month. Such projects house over a million people.*

The problem of absorbing this number strained Hong Kong's resources to the limit in the matters of water supply, public services, transport, and schooling. People who had no other homes occupied doorways and rooftops, and squatters' shacks began to cover the hillsides. After more than a century of unrestricted freedom of movement, Hong Kong restricted passage across the frontier.

A disastrous fire on Christmas Day, 1953, in which 53,000 were made homeless, led to the adoption of a resettlement program. Seven-story blocks were built providing single-room accommodations at the cheap price of $2.70 per month. In addition, a Government Housing Authority was set up to provide housing for white collar workers. In ten years over 800,000 people were housed by the government.

However, illegal immigration has continued, and in 1962 over 200,000 succeeded in a mass attempt to cross the frontier. As a result, the number awaiting resettlement shows little reduction from 1954 when the housing scheme began.

Hong Kong's "Problem of People" did, however, have one advantage—it brought to the city an abundant supply of industrious workers. Some of the refugees from Shanghai even brought industrial techniques. There followed a rapid expansion of industry, which provided employment to the newcomers and helped in the policy of integrating them into the community. Textiles, plastics, shipbuilding, rattan furniture, and garment-making became important industries. Soon, even the industrially advanced nations had to protect their own textile industries against the competition from Hong Kong.

NEW INDUSTRIES

The entrepôt trade declined as Hong Kong became rapidly industrialized. Oysters had been farmed in local waters for 700 years, and an interesting recent experiment was the creation of the cultured pearl industry at the island of Kat O in Mirs Bay. New industries, such as the manufacture of television sets and transistor radios, sprang up; and the search for new products and new markets goes on. In 1963, 90 percent of its industrial production was exported. The United States was the Colony's best customer, taking 25 percent of the total exports.

SHIPPING AND AIRLINES

The Harbor remains a great economic asset, since not only are most products exported, but, in the absence of natural resources, all raw materials have to be imported. Forty important shipping lines link Hong Kong with all parts of the world. During 1964, an average of 17 ocean-going vessels entered the port every day throughout the year.

Hong Kong's air communications are abreast of the jet age, with a modern airport at Kai Tak handling as many as 5,000 passengers in a day.

TOURISM

Hong Kong is a tourists' heaven. Some 300,000 tourists come annually and find modern hotels, a shopping paradise, and the exotic life of an oriental people. In the New Territories, a traveler can get a glimpse of the old traditional China. In the city, a tourist can get a suit made overnight, to his own measurements. The streets of Hong Kong are crowded, as if the people were on a perpetual shopping spree. There are floating restaurants at Aberdeen which are world famous. Generally, the cuisine in Hong Kong is considered to be of surpassing excellence.

POLITICAL SETUP

Hong Kong is a British Crown Colony, and the Parliament at Westminster in London is responsible for its defense and administration. The British Governor is advised by an Executive Council of 12, consisting of six senior officials and six residents chosen from among prominent members of the community. Of the latter, in 1964, two were British, two Chinese one Indian, and one Portuguese.

The Legislative Council has 12 official members, and 13 unofficial members who are also prominent residents of the Colony. In 1964, these consisted of three British, one Indian, and nine Chinese.

HONG KONG STREET   Each of the hundreds of shop signs indicates a separ *business. Many of the people wear western clothes, but the man who has adapted* *hoe as a carrying pole represents the old style Chinese costume.*

WATERFRONT *Gleaming skyscrapers rise in the commercial district. Back of the docks looms the dome of the City Hall. Close by are theaters, a fine restaurant, an art gallery, libraries, a museum, and a ballroom. Directly behind this area is the 26-story Hong Kong Hilton. The massive structure in the center is the Mandarin Hotel. The busy little boat is a passenger launch—known as a walla-walla.*

An Urban Council has six official members and 20 unofficials (i.e., local residents), of whom ten are elected by a limited franchise and ten are nominated by the Governor. The Urban Council controls such important services as street cleaning, resettlement of refugees, environmental hygiene, markets, the Housing Authority, library services, etc.

Recruitment to the Government Service is by examination, and qualified local candidates are preferred. Hong Kong, in fact, enjoys virtual financial and administrative autonomy. The preponderance of Chinese on the Finance Committee of the Legislative Council ensures that Government policy will be acceptable.

EDUCATION

The need for educational facilities is especially important because in 1964 over 40 percent of the population was below the age of 15. Education is as yet neither free nor compulsory, but most children attend school, the main exception being the boat people. In the 1961 census, the literacy rate was found to be 75 percent.

Education in Hong Kong follows a British pattern. Primary education is conducted in Chinese except in the few schools that have European and American children. At the secondary level, Anglo-Chinese schools, run chiefly by the Government and the missionary bodies, use English. Further education of a vocational nature is provided in the Technical College. The University of Hong Kong was founded in 1912 and included the Medical College founded previously. In 1963, the Chinese University of Hong Kong was set up, combining Chung Chi College, New Asia College, and United College on a federal basis. The standards are quite high, and enable students to read for higher degrees in British and American universities.

CHINESE CUSTOMS AND FESTIVALS

Hong Kong is predominantly Chinese and when it became a British Colony, the British promised to respect Chinese law and custom. Thus it is that the institution of concubinage survives in Hong Kong, though it has been abolished in the two Chinas.

Many colorful Chinese festivals are observed in Hong Kong. The

CRAFTSMAN   The creation of wooden chests such as this requires artistry. This worker, with his finished screens and panels, is typical of the Hong Kong artisan who in small space and with few resources turns out the products from which the community derives much of its income.

FISHING JUNKS *A power-driven boat runs alongside a traditional sailing craft. The independent businessman in the modernized vessel negotiated a government loan with which to buy his.engines. Government support has quadrupled Hong Kong's fishing production since 1946. The picturesque junks are rapidly disappearing from the colony's waters; today, more than half the 10,000 fishing vessels in these parts are powered.*

Chinese Lunar New Year festival occurs at the end of January or the early part of February, and the New Year's prosperity is ensured by a deafening roar of firecrackers lasting 48 hours or more, designed to frighten away evil spirits.

The Ching Ming Festival is held in Spring when visits are paid to the graves of the family ancestors with gifts of food, and the graves are reverently tended, a process referred to as "sweeping the graves." The Chinese believe that ancestors can influence the family fortune and, in return, expect a measure of devotion.

During the Dragon Boat Festival held on the fifth day. of the fifth month (in June) boats from 50 to 100 feet long, paddled by some 50 or more men, race vigorously to the beat of a drum. The festival commemorates the death of a famous statesman, Wat Yun, who was devoted to the poor and who drowned himself because he could not eliminate poverty.

The Moon Festival, held on the eighth day of the eighth moon, celebrates the moon goddess' birthday, and moon cakes are eaten.

One of the most colorful festivals is that held in June in honor of Tin Hau (Queen of Heaven), who has in her special care the protection of fishermen and others who live or work on the sea. Hundreds of gaily decorated junks and. sampans go to the chief Tin Hau temple at Joss House Bay near the Island, and make their offerings in a spectacular display.

THE FUTURE

What of the future? There seems to be no let up of the industrial boom. The population will certainly continue to rise as quickly in the future as it has in the past. Even the natural increase is already about 100,000 a year. Much depends on the policies of neighboring Communist China and on the reaction of the West.

GEORGE B. ENDACOTT

IN BRIEF

AREA 398 square miles. About a third the size of Rhode Island.

TERRAIN Hilly and rocky, with many deep bays and small islands, and the best natural harbor in the Far East. The city lies on the slopes of Victoria Peak. Only a fifth of the area is flat enough for cultivation.

FLORA AND FAUNA Same as that of the Chinese mainland. Extensive urbanization is restricting wild animal and plant life but barking deer, Chinese ferret-badger, Chinese porcupine, many snakes, and over 70 species of native orchid are found.

CLIMATE Subtropical, with wet summers and dry winters. About 85 inches of rain fall each year. Average annual temperature is 72°F. Typhoons usually occur between June and October.

CAPITAL Victoria, on Hong Kong Island, has about 1.1 million inhabitants.

OTHER CITIES Kowloon, across the harbor from Victoria, has a population of 860,000.

POPULATION 3.13 million in the 1961 census, increased to 3.5 million in 1963. Annual rate of increase is about three percent. Density is one of the highest in the world: 2.5 million people live in 36 square miles of urban area.

ETHNIC GROUPS Over 98 percent Chinese, chiefly of Cantonese or Kwantung Province origin. The remainder are foreign nationals — British, American, etc.

LADDER STREETS   *Though motor roads now wind up Hong Kong's steep ridges, these old streets with hundreds of steps serve many neighborhoods.*

TAO-SHIH This Taoist holy man is vested with the responsibility of leading his people in prayer and in ceremonies of penitence.

RICKSHAWS These ancient vehicles are still used for short trips in Hong Kong's central district, especially by footsore tourists. The City Hall and some of the great hotels are within a block or two of this scene. The large building is the headquarters of the Hong Kong Bank Group. There is a two-story garage on the left, filled with parked cars. Because of the hard labor and scanty return for the worker, the continuance of the rickshaw has been discouraged by most governments in Asia. The earnings of Hong Kong's rickshawmen, who remain mostly as a tourist show, average $2.50 per day.

LANGUAGES   Cantonese is the lingua franca, although many other Chinese dialects are in use. English is spoken by 10 percent of the populace.

RELIGION   Confucianism and Buddhism predominate. Taoism, Hinduism, Islam, and Christianity are also practiced.

DATE OF INDEPENDENCE   Hong Kong Island was first ceded to Britain in 1842. Although largely self-governing, it remains a British Crown Colony.

FORM OF GOVERNMENT   Limited autonomy. A Governor, appointed by the British Crown, is responsible to the British Parliament. An appointed Executive Council aids in administration; an appointed Legislative Council advises on legislation. In practice, the local appointees reflect local needs and opinions.

EDUCATION   In 1963, there were approximately 810,000 students in over 2,100 primary and secondary schools, staffed by some 18,600 teachers. Three teachers' colleges had an enrollment of almost 1,000 students. The University was attended by 1,750 students, and had 375 teachers. The Chinese University of Hong Kong was established in 1963. Over 65 percent of the people are literate.

HEALTH FACILITIES   In 1961, there were 1,165 doctors, 400 dentists, 1,840 midwives, and 95 pharmacists. Life expectancy for a newborn child is about 67 years. Health conditions are improving rapidly. Over eight percent of the 1963 budget went for health facilities. A School Health Service and a School Medical Service are subsidized by the government.

CULTURAL FACILITIES   In 1962, there were 44 daily newspapers with a total circulation of over 770,000. In the same year, over 270 films were made, and the 80 cinemas had an attendance of almost 74 million—equivalent to everyone seeing 21 films. Three radio and two television networks broadcast in English and Chinese. Library service, theater, and concerts are generally accessible.

CURRENCY AND FINANCE   The Hong Kong dollar is linked to the sterling and equals 2.4 grains of fine gold or 17.5¢ in U.S. currency. In 1963, the colony had revenues of U.S. $218.5 million, expenditures of $194.1 million, and a surplus of $24.4 million. The budget for 1964 allocated 45 percent of expenditures to public works.

THE FLOATING PEOPLE *This crowded craft is anchored among a colony of junks in a typhoon-safe harborage off Kowloon. This small boat is home to a family of the water people. Centuries ago, their ancestors, tribal peoples of South China, were condemned to a life on the water by their Han Chinese conquerors. In 1730, they were allowed to live ashore, close to the sea or river, but they were not allowed to take the examinations leading to state office, and they were forbidden to intermarry with Chinese.*

INDUSTRY AND PRODUCTION

Manufacturing and commerce through the free port accounted for most of the national income, estimated at $1.5 billion in 1963. Average per capita income is about $400 a year, one of the highest in Asia. The economy is believed to be growing at a rate of 10 percent per year. Over 8,300 industrial undertakings employed almost 355,000 workers in 1963. Textiles employ 42 percent of the industrial workers and account for 52 percent of total exports.

CROPS: Intensive farming on about 13.7 percent of the land area provides rice, fruit, vegetables, and animal feed sufficient to the colony's needs for one month of the year.

SAMPAN   *Two Chinese women briskly scull their boat across the waters of Kowloon Peninsula. In a windless morning, the sail does little good.*

LIVESTOCK: Chiefly pigs and poultry for local consumption.

FISHERIES: Ocean catch, valued at almost $12 million in 1963, supports 80,000 people and 10,000 fishing junks. Oyster farming and pearl culture are practiced. Fish ponds, mainly producing grey mullet, cover 1,360 acres.

MINING: Mineral production is of limited importance. Iron ore, wolframite, graphite, kaolin clay, feldspar, and quartz production was worth a little over $1 million in 1963.

TRADE

Chief exports are manufactured goods and textiles; imports are largely foods, fuels, and raw materials. The apparent trade deficit is offset by income from exchange, shipping, and insurance transactions, tourism, new investment, etc.

1963:	IMPORTS	$1,297,100,000
	EXPORTS	$ 873,500,000
	DEFICIT	$ 423,600,000

TRANSPORT

ROAD: Of 524 miles of road, 192 miles are on Hong Kong Island. The 73,000 motor vehicles registered in 1964 included 818 public and private rickshaws.

RAIL: An electric street car line 20 miles long, a funicular railway to the Peak on Hong Kong Island, and a 22-mile spur line connecting with the Chinese railways carried over 200 million passengers in 1963.

WATERWAY: In 1963, two large ferry companies transported over 170 million passengers across the harbor and to the islands. Several hundred junks and lighters are in use.

AIR: During 1962–63, over 8,000 aircraft brought almost 300,000 passengers on international flights to the Hong Kong airport.

SEA: The excellent natural harbor accounts for the city's existence and prosperity. Almost 8,000 vessels of over 60 tons net entered the harbor in 1963, discharging 8.1 million tons of commercial cargo and loading 2.2 million tons.

COMMUNI-CATION

There were 35 post offices, 165,000 telephones, over 53,000 television sets, and about 500,000 radios in use in 1963. There are three radio stations and two television wire services.

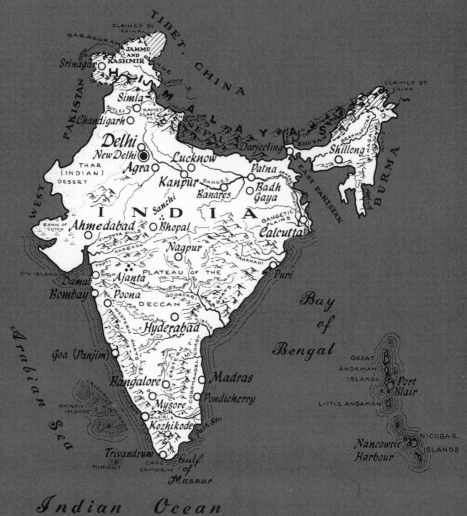

INDIA

The World's Largest Democracy

Known to its inhabitants as Bharat, India can trace its history back to 5000 B.C. Today, with a population of 471 million, it is the second most populous nation in the world. At the present rate of increase, India will have 800 million people by the year 2000.

Except for Japan, India is the only nation in Asia which has a democratic, Western-type political system—and this in spite of the fact that over 70 percent of the people are illiterate.

A VAST TERRITORY

India is separated in the north from the rest of Asia by mountains, and otherwise surrounded by seas.

In the past, the Himalayas served as a formidable barrier against invasion by China from the north. The high altitudes of the Himalayas also limited travel. Only a few passes could be crossed. Today, the airplane has ended India's apartness; and now, overland enemy attack is possible—witness Peking's invasion in 1962.

Below the Himalayas lies the Indo-Gangetic plain, formed by the basins of three distinct river systems—the Indus, the Ganges, and the Brahmaputra, all fed by Himalayan snows. Fifteen hundred miles long and 150 to 200 miles wide, this plain is one of the world's most densely populated areas. The exceptionally fertile soil of the Ganges River banks has drawn 66 percent of the country's population to this area.

THE SACRED GANGES

The Ganges, one of the greatest rivers in the world, is regarded by Hindus as sacred. Along its banks stands the holy city of Benares, as sacred to the Hindu as Mecca is to the Muslim. When Prime Minister Jawaharlal Nehru, an avowed agnostic, died in 1964, he asked in his testament that a handful of his ashes be thrown into the river at Allahabad, his native city. "I have no religious sentiment in the matter," he wrote, but "I have been attached" to the Ganges "ever since my

childhood and, as I have grown older, this attachment has also grown...
The Ganges," he went on, "is the river of India, beloved of her people,
round which are intertwined her racial memories, her hopes and fears,
her songs of triumph, her victories, and her defeats. She has been a
symbol of India's age-long culture and civilization, ever-changing, ever-
flowing, and yet ever the same Ganges."

THE PENINSULAR PLATEAU

South of the Indo-Gangetic plain lies the Peninsular plateau, with
mountain and hill ranges varying from 1,500 to 4,000 feet in height.
According to the great Indian epic, *Ramayana*, which tells about the
tribulations of a celebrated prince, Rama, and his beloved wife, Sita,
vast, thick forests once covered this plateau. These forests were indis-
criminately cut down for fuel. Today, in the absence of wood, Indian
villages must resort to the use of cow-dung for fuel. Only in recent years
has the Indian government started reforestation of this tree-denuded
plateau.

Unlike the rivers of the Indo-Gangetic plain, which are fed by
mountain snows, the rivers of the Peninsula are fed by rains which
come during the brief season of the monsoon, usually in July and
August. During this period, the rivers often overflow, causing disastrous
floods. By contrast, in the dry season drought often increases the misery
of the population by curtailing the crops of wheat and rice, the two
staples of India's diet. A British administrator in India once said that the
budget of British India—the cost of governing the country—was "determined by the monsoon."

NATURAL RESOURCES AND FOOD SHORTAGES

India is rich in coal, lignite, iron ore, manganese, bauxite, and
mica, but India's resources may not prove adequate to meet even the
modest needs of its large, and rapidly expanding, population. Oil deposits are still at the stage of exploration. India also exports iron ore to
Japan, in return for Japanese manufactured goods.

As of 1965, India's main shortage was not raw materials for its as yet
limited industrial development, but grains—wheat for the population

STREET SCHOOL *Carefully washed and brushed Hindu children are collected in a Calcutta street to learn reading and writing in a government school.*

of the north and of central India, and rice for the people of the south.

The chief cause for the shortage of basic foods is the rapid growth of population. Moreover, the 1950 Constitution assigned control over land not to the Central Government but to each of the 16 states which comprise the Indian Union. Thus, the states which produce the bulk of wheat and rice have on occasion—as in the serious food crisis of 1964—held back their supplies from the less productive states, in the hope of obtaining better prices. Famine in food-deficient areas was prevented only by the shipment of six million tons of food by the United States and the rationing of grains in India's principal cities.

Another reason for India's recurring food difficulties is that the Hindus are for the most part opposed to the use of meat. They hold that it is wrong to kill and eat animals, and regard the cow as sacred. This ancient belief was reinforced by Buddhism, founded by Gautama Buddha. Born in 563 B.C., the son of a princely family, Buddha preached against the killing of man or beast. Today, cows are often left to wander untended through city streets, where they become a menace to traffic. Although the custom of vegetarianism has some merit in a tropical climate, it deprives growing children of needed proteins, particularly when milk is not available.

THE PROBLEM OF OVERPOPULATION

India's greatest problem is its rapidly expanding population. Unless India can stabilize its population within the next two decades, the country will be confronted with the terrifying task of feeding, clothing, housing, and educating more than twice its present citizenry. Until the late 19th century, India's population was relatively stable. Wars, infanticide, the custom of burning a widow on her late husband's funeral pyre, and a wide range of diseases, regularly took a heavy toll of lives. In 1901, the population was about 240 million; it remained at that figure until 1931.

INDIA INTERNATIONAL CENTRE *This center, the largest in Asia, was inaugurated in New Delhi in 1962 to serve as a meeting place for scholars and cultural leaders of all nations.*

BOMBAY DANCERS *Clashing sticks together as they leap, men from Saurashtra, Bombay, perform a dance known as Dandia Ras.*

However, the public health measures of the British brought about a rapid growth of population both through lessening of infant mortality and greater life expectancy. In 1965, the population rose to 480 million —about twice what it was some 30 years earlier.

Actually, since the 1901 census, the birth rate has declined from 48 per thousand to 41 per thousand; but the death rate has declined still more sharply, and is now 19 per thousand. Thus, India acquires 11 million new citizens a year. The current increase in India's population is 2.3 percent a year, one of the highest rates in the world. If India's population could have been stabilized at its 1951 level, it is estimated that the income of the average Indian family would have increased by about four percent a year—more than double what it actually has been.

The country's two major faiths—Hinduism and Islam—have no objections to population control, although the Catholics, a minority group centered in the Bombay area and the former Portuguese colony of Goa, oppose birth control measures. The government has taken steps to limit births through instruction of women in the use of inexpensive, easily usable contraceptives, and through the voluntary sterilization of men after the birth of three children.

So far, these efforts, applied over a vast country where medical facilities are still very limited, have proved inadequate. The government has recognized that a crash program is urgently required to deal with this Number One problem. It is realized that unless the population can be stabilized, the country's natural resources will prove inadequate to sustain its inhabitants—even at the present low standard of living.

In 1965, India requested the United Nations to send a five-member team to advise about ways of gaining greater acceptance of family planning by village dwellers. (The team was also to assist in planning programs in the related fields of health, education, and the status of women.)

In the spring of 1965, the government announced the introduction of a greatly intensified program of birth control, based primarily on a newly developed low-cost device, the plastic interuterine Lippes loop. In the campaign for birth control, thousands of doctors and lay assistants are now being recruited in teaching centers throughout India.

INDIA'S POPULATION

As of 1951, infants and young children up to 14 constituted 38.3 percent of the total population; young adults from 15 to 34, 33 percent; middle-aged men and women from 35 to 54, 20.4; and elderly persons 55 and over, 8.3. The predominance of young people in the population means that facilities for education, housing, and new jobs are increasingly strained. At the same time, the rise in life expectancy, from an average of under 30 to an average of 47 in the 1950's, also means that job and housing prospects will be in increasingly short supply, unless India succeeds in greatly expanding its economic development.

India is a Union composed of 16 states and a number of Union Territories.

The majority of the population—82 percent as of 1961—live in over 580,000 villages. However, since India achieved independence from British rule in 1947, and started on a program of industrialization, many villagers have moved to urban centers in search of work. Also, Hindu refugees from areas which upon partition became part of the new state of Pakistan have flocked to the cities. As a result, India's urban centers have grown rapidly since 1947. By 1965, Greater Bombay had seen a doubling of its population, now estimated at four million; Calcutta has close to three million.

Although India is surrounded by water, the Indians in the past were not seafarers, nor did they engage in fishing. The principal reason for this was that, according to Hindu religious concepts, travel and resi-

SHORE TEMPLE *Perched at the ocean's edge at Mahabali-puram, near Madras, this shrine, built more than 1,300 years ago, was carved in one piece from a granite hillock. It represents one of the finest examples of Pallava art, which preserved elements of pre-historic Dravidian culture.*

dence abroad polluted the traveler. On his return, he would have to undergo an elaborate rite of purification which included drinking the urine of the sacred cow.

Today, India has undertaken to develop its fisheries, and has received aid for this purpose from Norway, which raised funds through public contribution to supply India with fishing boats, equipment, and technical assistance.

A MANY-TONGUED NATION

India is multilingual to an extraordinary degree; only in the U.S.S.R. are so many languages spoken. The 1951 census listed a total of 845 tongues spoken in the country.

The 1950 Constitution specified 14 major languages. Three of these—Hindu and Hindustani (based on ancient Sanskrit and spoken by Hindus of the north) and Urdu (spoken by Muslims) are used by 180 million people, or better than one-third of the population.

Tamil is used in South India by 30 million; Telegu, also in the South, by over 30 million; Bengali in West Bengal by over 20 million. Every language has its own well-known literary works. For example, there is a rich literature written in Bengali which includes the works of the poet and dramatist, Rabindranath Tagore. It is interesting to note that as of 1951 Sanskrit was spoken by only some 550,000 people.

The government has had fears that this multiplicity of languages would hamper unification of the country, and announced that every child, in addition to his native tongue, would have to learn Hindi, which in January, 1965, became the official language of the country.

The future of English was the subject of prolonged, violent debate. Some nationalists demanded that the use of English be abandoned, and that all education and business be conducted in an Indian language. Others pointed out that the exclusion of English would make it difficult for Indians to share in the scientific and cultural developments of the Western world, and would hamper the nation's participation in the work of international organizations. It was eventually decided to continue the teaching and use of English at advanced levels in schools. Starting in January, 1965, English was to be used as an "associate" language.

An even more painful controversy arose about the use of Hindi as the official language. Hindustani, from which Hindi is derived, has been used only in northern India, while Tamil and other languages have been used in the south. The people of Madras State were incensed at the imposition by the people of the north of its language on the people of the south. In the area known as Tamilnad, which has an old and rich culture, and where Tamil is in widespread use, many resorted to violent and non-violent resistance. As a result, the Central Government subsequently announced that Hindi would be introduced only gradually in non-Hindi-speaking areas, and that English would remain in use indefinitely as an official language. This decision, in turn, aroused the opposition of Hindi-speaking people, among them some prominent political leaders.

The emotions caused by this controversy over language may be understood if we remember that India is composed of many large areas, comparable to nations, each with its own history, language, and literature. West Bengal, for example, has 45 million people, a population comparable to that of France or Italy.

RELIGIOUS TOLERANCE

Hinduism, the religion of 85 percent of India's inhabitants, has displayed, over the centuries, a capacity to absorb the concepts and practices of other faiths. Dr. Sarvepalli Radakrishnan, President of India and a world-renowned Hindu philosopher, commenting on the tendency of Americans to view ideologies in terms of black and white, has asked: "Why this *or* that? Why not this *and* that?"

Over the ages, Hinduism absorbed Buddhism which represented an attempt to reform Hindu concepts and practices. This development was comparable to what might have happened in the West if Catholicism in the 16th century had absorbed Protestantism and reduced it to a minor faith, as Buddhism is today in India, with less than one percent of the population listed as Buddhists.

Mahatma Gandhi, a devout Hindu, found inspiration in Christianity, particularly in the Sermon on the Mount. Even Islam, which at certain periods of history and in certain countries has appeared as an exclusivist and even harsh religion bent on converting infidels by either persuasion or holy war, has developed a mellow character in India. When, in 1947, some 60 million of their co-religionists founded the independent state of Pakistan, 45 million Muslims chose to remain in

India and now live at peace with the Hindus.

Religious freedom is enjoyed by all minority groups, including the Christians, who are mostly Catholics centered in Goa, Bombay, and Kerala. The respect of India's people for all faiths was strikingly demonstrated by the enthusiastic welcome given to Pope Paul VI when, in 1964, he came to Bombay for the Eucharistic Congress and was warmly

ELECTIONEERING IN DELHI
Crowds gather in the narrow streets of Old Delhi to hear speeches by candidates for Parliament. The first-aid auto is present to cope with any injuries resulting from over-enthusiasm among the crowds. The sign is written in Urdu, the language spoken by Muslims.

greeted by Hindu and Muslim as well as Christian leaders. India's religious tolerance even includes non-believers. Indians not only tolerated, but revered, Jawaharlal Nehru, an avowed agnostic, who became the leader of the ruling Congress Party and a highly popular Prime Minister.

THE SIKHS

Though less than two percent of India's population, the Sikhs have played a significant role in the life of India. The group was founded in the 16th century by the *Guru* or prophet, Nanak, who sought to abolish caste distinctions and to bring Hindus and Muslims together into a single religious fold.

The Mogul Emperor Akbar (1556–1605), a Muslim famed for his tolerance, had befriended the Sikhs and had permitted them to build their Golden Temple at Amritsar. However, his successors persecuted the Sikhs, and as a result, this sect, originally a peaceful group, transformed themselves for self-defense into a military brotherhood. In time, they became famous for their prowess· During Britain's rule in India, Sikh recruits were highly prized by the British and in two world wars Sikh soldiers impressed the world by their bravery.

The tenth and last Guru, Govind Singh (1675–1708), was the real founder of Sikh power which was centered in the Punjab. At his command, Sikhs bound themselves to abstain from wine, tobacco, and drugs. All who were admitted to the brotherhood were dubbed *Singh* or lion. Sikh men have traditionally worn their hair long; a Sikh piles his hair on top of his head under a colorful turban. In recent years, however, young men have increasingly sought to have their hair trimmed in the modern manner.

The Sikhs are generally very lively and able people. Many of their leaders hold high office in the government of India, notably Swaran Singh, who was Foreign Minister in the Shastri Cabinet.

DANCERS   Professional actors from Kerala state demonstrate the Kaliyattam Dance during the Republic Day celebrations in New Delhi, displaying images of Hindu gods and goddesses. The figure in the center portrays the elephant-headed god of jollity, Ganesha.

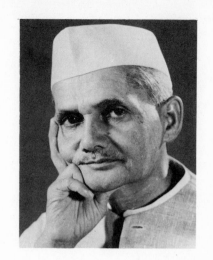

LAL BAHADUR SHASTRI Leader of the Congress Party and Prime Minister of India since the death of Nehru, the 62-year-old former teacher was known as a devout, ascetic Hindu. He died in January of 1966 in the city of Tashkent of the Soviet Union almost immediately after the signing of an accord with Ayub Khan of Pakistan. This accord, engineered by Premier Kosygin of the U.S.S.R. put an end to hostilities between Pakistan and India.

THE JAINS

Another once significant religious group is that of the Jains, founded in the sixth century B.C. The Jains enforce strict observance of certain Hindu customs and lay particular stress on not killing any living thing. In order to observe this tenet scrupulously, a religious Jain would not breathe deeply for fear that he might inadvertently swallow, and thus kill, an insect. The more affluent of this sect have been known to hire a sweeper to walk before them and carefully sweep the ground so that the Jain might avoid treading on a bug and thus inadvertently commit the sin of killing.

About 1,000 A.D., the Jains went into decline. Today, they no longer play a significant role in India. In 1961, the number of Jains constituted less than one-half of one percent of the population.

NATIONAL UNITY

Thus, while India remains a land of many languages and many faiths, this diversity does not endanger national unity. Today this unity becomes increasingly evident as economic and social changes brought about by industrialization accelerate population mobility. Villagers move to urban centers in search of jobs; large national projects, notably construction of dams, new opportunities for education, and so on cause an increasing number of people to leave their birthplace for some other state where they are confronted by different customs and different languages—and manage to get along peacefully with their new neighbors.

CASTE AND CLASS

This growing mobility is beginning to alter the pattern of life in ancient villages. Many villagers now own bicycles, use rural buses, and work full or part-time in newly built small factories. This co-mingling is also affecting the caste system of India, once strictly defined and rigidly enforced.

The Indian caste system seems very strange to Americans because there has been no comparable institution in our history. The system, which goes back to the early days of India's history, consists of four main castes: priests, or *Brahmins;* kings, princes, and warriors, or *Kshatriyas;* landowners and merchants, or *Vaishyas;* peasants and (in recent times) factory workers, or *Sudras.*

This four-caste system, similar to that of medieval Europe, exists in one form or another in all underdeveloped agrarian societies—which is what India still remains in large part.

THE OUTCASTES

The unusual feature of the Indian social system is the existence of outcastes—people not included in the four castes. In the past the outcastes were compelled to earn a living by doing all the menial jobs which other castes regard as unclean—either literally unclean, or unclean in terms of religious beliefs. Outcastes served as scavengers and street cleaners, washed dirty clothes, and cured the hides of animals.

Because they were considered unclean, it was ruled that they should never come in contact with "clean" people. They were not permitted to enter Hindu temples, to drink water from wells used by Hindus, to prepare food for caste Hindus, to serve water to them, to associate with them in any way. An outcaste could not even cross the path of a caste member. To avert such a misfortune, an outcaste used to wear a bell which warned the caste Hindu of his approach, to avoid an accidental encounter. In the past a caste Hindu went thirsty or hungry rather than accept water or food from the "unclean" hands of an outcaste.

The only analogous situation in the West was the role assigned to the Jews in the Middle Ages. At that time the Jews were not allowed

NATIONAL ELECTION 1962 *In this election, the largest ever held anywhere in the world, 210 million people were eligible to vote. Some 240,000 polling stations used 700 tons of paper ballots in nearly 20 days of the election. During the campaign, streets like this in Calcutta were thronged with people. Campaign signs, strung above the street, are written in Bengali and in Hindi.*

to own land, were restricted to certain occupations, were often confined to certain locations, and were often reviled. Even as late as the 20th century, Jews were frequently barred from certain educational institutions. Another comparable example, familiar to us in the United States, has been the denial of full citizenship to Negroes, their exclusion from many public places, including educational institutions, and their job confinement in many areas to the most menial tasks.

Actually, the caste system and the institution of the outcastes are believed to have been based on differences in color. The Hindu word for caste is *varna* or color. It is believed that the early inhabitants of

MAHATMA GANDHI *Born in 1869 and trained as a lawyer, Gandhi developed his philosophy of non-violent resistance as a young man while opposing British rule in South Africa. Until he was assassinated in 1948, his person and his philosophy were the symbolic incarnation of India's national consciousness.*

India—the aborigines now found only in some border areas—were black. The Dravidians, who live in South India, are much darker than the relatively fair-skinned Aryans, who invaded India from Central Asia. It is possible that the lighter-colored peoples initiated the caste system to force peoples of dark color to perform the less desirable tasks.

Today, the caste system with its 60 million outcastes (also called Scheduled Castes and Untouchables) is gradually changing. The strict differences between the four castes, which reflected the rigidity of a social order unchanged for millenia, are being erased. Today, men and women are increasingly elected to office or appointed to jobs on the basis of their personal qualifications, without regard to their caste affiliation. For example, Nehru was a Brahmin; Gandhi was a Vaishya; Prime Minister Lal Bahadur Shastri was a Vaishya; Kumaraswami Kamaraj, president of the Congress Party, came from a Sudra family.

As for the outcastes, the 1950 Constitution provides for the abolition of "untouchability" and forbids its practice in any form. It calls for the "removal of any disability, liability, restriction or condition with regard to access to shops, public restaurants, hotels and places of public entertainment, the use of wells, tanks, bathing ghats, roads, and places of public resort maintained wholly or partly out of State funds or dedicated to the use of the general public." (Tanks are pools.)

Former outcastes are now assured the right to practice any profession and carry on any occupation, trade, or business; and they can attend any educational institution supported by State funds. To assure the upgrading of their position, the outcastes have been granted special representation in Parliament and in State Legislatures for a period of 20 years.

SOCIAL REVOLUTION

In short, as a result of far-reaching economic changes due to industrialization and to land reform, India is in the midst of a profound social revolution. As one perceptive Indian observer has pointed out, it is impossible to maintain untouchability in a village bus crowded to the roof with villagers traveling to take their produce to market or to work in nearby small factories. This is not to say that India, in the 18 years since it achieved independence, has solved the problems created by the thousand-year-old system of castes and outcastes. As we know from our experience with our Negro fellow-citizens, such a far-reaching change cannot come overnight.

THE GREAT STUPA OF SANCHI   This massive, intricately carved dome consists of solid sandstone with a diameter of 120 feet. A stupa is the central part of an open-air shrine, built to honor the Buddha. Relics of the Buddha would be placed in a small casket, often of carved crystal, and then sealed up in the central chamber. Sanchi's Great Stupa was enlarged to its present size about 200 years before Christ, at which time it was faced with masonry. This complex strongly influenced Hindu and Buddhist art during the succeeding centuries. The main form of reverence to the relics was a ceremonial, clockwise walk around the path built near the base of the dome.

ROLE OF EDUCATION

The pace of social, as well as economic, change will be determined to a considerable extent by the expansion of educational opportunities. In India, education is primarily the responsibility of the state governments. The Union government concerns itself primarily with coordinating educational facilities, determining standards of higher education, and planning research and technical education. The Union government also administers four universities—Aligarh (Muslim), Benares, Delhi, and Visva Bharati. Other universities are operated by the states or by municipalities.

The basic problem of educators is to increase literacy as rapidly as possible. As of 1961, only 24 percent of the population was literate. Some 34 percent of men could read and write, and only about 13 percent of women.

At the elementary level an activity-centered curriculum is offered; learning is correlated with the actual environment. Spinning, weaving, gardening, carpentry, leather work, domestic crafts, pottery, and elementary engineering are taught.

Post-secondary schools include 1,900 colleges and 46 universities.

RADIO, TELEVISION, AND PRESS

India has developed a wide range of information media. The All-India Radio (AIR) has a network of 31 stations. Broadcasts are devoted to music, discussions, dramas, news, and educational programs for schools.

Mrs. Indira Gandhi, daughter of the late Prime Minister Nehru, was appointed Minister of Press and Information in 1964. She hoped to expand the educational facilities of AIR and to introduce educational television. Television programs were inaugurated in 1959 in New Delhi. At present, these programs can be seen only within a range of 25 miles and are designed only for community viewing.

The press enjoys freedom of news coverage and expression. As of 1962, there were over 8,000 newspapers and periodicals in India, including 457 daily newspapers. English is the language of 1,698 newspapers, or 20.4 percent of the total number, while 1,575 newspapers or

19 percent are printed in Hindi. Newspapers are also published in other major languages—Urdu, Bengali, Gujarati, Marathi, and Tamil.

India is producing many notable films, both in English and in various Indian languages. Three hundred and seven films were produced in 1962. The Films Division of the Union Ministry of Information and Broadcasting has produced newsreels (742 by the end of 1962) and short films (624 in the same period) in 12 Indian languages and in English. These films are circulated in rural areas by vans.

POLITICAL HISTORY

India is a democratic Republic, a Union of States. Its Constitution came into force on January 26, 1950, which has become a national holiday called Republic Day.

It is, perhaps, surprising that a nation which achieved independence from colonial rule only in 1947 has successfully established democratic institutions in spite of political tensions and severe economic and social problems.

However, a study of early Indian history reveals influences that provided valuable preparation for modern democracy. The political and administrative ideals of both Hindus and Muslims at peak periods of India's history, under three dynasties—the Maurya dynasty, notably Emperor Asoka (322–185 b.c.), the Gupta dynasty (320–450 a.d.), and the reign of the Moghul ruler Akbar (1556–1605)—displayed a quality of statesmanship, a concern for cultural values, and a spirit of reconciliation between conflicting faiths and ideas that were then well in advance of any Western nation. For example, the Emperor Asoka constantly stressed the duties of governors to improve the welfare of the people. During his reign, education became widespread.

GOVERNMENT BUILDINGS In this New Delhi square stand the Ministry of Railways and the Secretariat.

NAGA WARRIOR This man wears the ceremonial garments of his tribe, the Ao Naga of the hills near Burma. His shield is of buffalo hide. The feathers in his hat come from the hornbill. The shape of his dah, bared at salute, indicates his tribe.

LADAKHI TEENAGERS This young girl and were part of the crew which helped the Indian Ar build roads through the high Himalayas at the time the Chinese invasion.

BEGGAR He is one of the many Indians in Calcutta for whom no employment is available.

HER AND SON Dressed
ly against the chill of her valley
in the Himalaya, this Kashmiri
n wears the heavy earrings com-
among her people. Her robe is
ose, wide-sleeved pharan which,
stom, is always maroon. Her lit-
oy is wearing a cap of Persian

NISU TRIBESMAN Notice the elaborate hairdo, the cloth
and needle ornament around his topknot, the dangling earrings,
and the chain-like beads around his neck. His garments are made
out of two cotton sheets. The handle is that of a Pong dagger.

LAMAS Most of the people of
Ladakh, a land high in the Himalayas, follow the Mahayana
Buddhism of Tibet. As part of
the prayer ceremony, three of
the priests crash their cymbals
together.

The Muslims believed in the equality of man, and judged people not by the group or station into which they were born, but on the basis of their own individual skills. Under Akbar, Muslim law, based on the Koran, was at that time in certain respects more advanced than Indian law.

While the British have been criticized for many of their colonial practices, they made major contributions to the democratization of India. They introduced order and security in the areas over which they had control. These areas were known collectively as British India (as distinguished from over 500 princely states which remained independent), and the colonial power introduced British law which guaranteed equal treatment for all individuals, irrespective of color, race, or religion. Moreover, in contrast to the Dutch in Indonesia and the French

TAJ MAHAL Renowned as the most beautiful building in the world, the Taj is a white marble mausoleum which took 20 years to erect. It was built at Agra between 1623 and 1653 by the Emperor Shah Jahan to honor the memory of his favorite wife, Mumtaz-i-Mahal.

in Indo-China, the British gave the opportunity to a small but significant number of Indians to be trained for civil service under their supervision, both in India and at English universities. These individuals were then entrusted with high-level jobs. Thus a select group was prepared for the administrative tasks to be performed when the country became independent.

But what the British refused to do, until after World War II, was to give the Indians the thing they wanted most—political independence. The struggle for independence, started in 1885 with the establishment of the Indian National Congress, was waged with increasing fervor. Yet, except for a few incidents, notably the Amritsar massacre, this campaign was waged by peaceful means, without resort to violence. This was largely due to the leadership of Gandhi.

MOHANDAS GANDHI

Mohandas K. Gandhi was born in 1869, in Gujarat in northwest India, of a family who had once been merchants. His father was an adviser to the royal family of a small Gujarat kingdom.

During his childhood, Gandhi had learned from his mother the importance of *ahimsa*, or non-violence, which means that one should not kill or harm any living thing, for whatever reason. He also found inspiration in the doctrine of *satyagraha*, which he defined as "the force which is born of truth and love." These two doctrines became the basis of Gandhi's philosophy. By these tenets, he fashioned his personal life and his political doctrine.

After receiving a good education in India, Gandhi studied law in Britain for three years. Following a two-year stay in India, he went to the Union of South Africa, where many Indians had settled. There he practiced law for a quarter of a century. During that period, he devoted his efforts to defending the rights of Indian settlers who, in his opinion, were being unfairly treated by the ruling white government dominated by Boers, settlers of Dutch descent.

Upon his return to India in 1919, Gandhi was welcomed by many Indians as the leader who could free India from British rule. Jawaharlal Nehru, who became India's first Prime Minister, was his closest and most devoted associate. Speaking of Gandhi's return, Nehru wrote: "We did not quite know what to make of him, but we were thrilled. . . . Behind the language of peace and friendship, there was power and the quivering shadow of action and determination not to submit to a wrong."

Gandhi gave up Western-style clothing and instead wore the *dhoti,* or loin cloth. He walked all over India, urging villagers to join him in demanding the end of British rule. At the same time, while he was a devout Hindu, he deplored the treatment of the untouchables, and called them *harijans,* or children of God. He found inspiration in all faiths, notably Christianity, particularly in Jesus' Sermon on the Mount.

The Indians, inspired by his call to action, called him *Mahatma,* the Sanskrit term for "great soul," a title given to honored religious leaders. He was also addressed as *Bapudi* (honored father) and with a similarly affectionate suffix, *Gandhiji.*

It was Gandhi's profound conviction that the Indians could bring the British to leave India by two policies: (one) by not fighting them— the policy of non-violence, and (two) by non-cooperation. He demanded not only self-rule for Indians (*swaraj*) but also the possibility for Indians to manufacture their own goods, especially cloth (*swadeshi*), so that they need not be forced to import British-made cloth. Thus Gandhi's struggle also had an economic objective·

Time and again Gandhi defied the British government by fasting. The colonial power was afraid that if Gandhi died during a fasting protest, the entire continent would rise up in revolt. Time and again the British gave way to Gandhi's particular form of pressure. During the struggle, Gandhi was jailed many times, but after the end of World War II, the British, seeing the handwriting on the wall, voluntarily departed from India. Indian independence was proclaimed on August 15, 1947. Gandhi, with non-violence and non-cooperation, had won.

In 1948, Mohandas Gandhi was assassinated by a fanatical Hindu who opposed Gandhi's efforts to develop a rapprochement between the Hindus and Muslims, who clashed sharply with each other after independence was declared.

DIET IMPROVEMENT In 1962, with the help of United Nations agencies, the Indian government began an expanded Nutrition Program. The theory was that if children were taught to grow valuable vegetables, such as beans, tomatoes, and cauliflower, nutrition would improve. These children in the eastern state of Orissa have each been assigned a small plot in the school garden.

THE AFTERMATH OF INDEPENDENCE

Gandhi's historic success was darkened by the grievous event of fratricidal strife between Muslim and Hindu. While the British had departed peacefully, the Muslims, under the leadership of Mahomed Ali Jinnah, feared that they would become second-grade citizens in independent India where the Hindus constituted such a large majority. When Hindu-Muslim negotiations about an independent India failed, Jinnah and his followers insisted on the partition of the subcontinent into two states—India, predominantly Hindu, and Pakistan, predominantly Muslim. As a result, Pakistan now consists of two wings— West and East—separated by a thousand miles.

MADRAS CLOTH For generations, the city of Madras has been famous for its richly textured cotton fabrics. These weavers are working on a length of cotton which will become a sari. Several families in the Saidapet district of this city have formed a marketing cooperative which handles the products of their nine looms. The symbol on the ground is a good omen sign.

of Indian territory. The partition engendered a violent struggle between Muslim and Hindu, with many acts of cruelty on both sides, and a loss of life estimated at around half a million people. The flight of refugees from one sector to the other wrenched the social fabric of the country, and constituted a grim chapter in the history of India, leaving a dark imprint on relations between the two states, India and Pakistan, which still deeply affects their relationship.

In India, the fear that Muslims would be treated unfairly proved to be unfounded. For example, in the Shastri government the Vice President of the Union was Dr. Zakir Hussain, a Muslim, and the Minister of Education was M. C. Chagla, former Ambassador to the United States. Moreover, this key post of education has so far been occupied by a Muslim—a situation best understandable to us if we could visualize a Catholic as Minister of Education in the United States.

JAWAHARLAL NEHRU

Fortunately for India, a peaceful succession in power had been assured by Gandhi's own choice of Nehru. From the time of independence until his death in 1964, Nehru served both as president of India's ruling political group, the Congress Party, and as Prime Minister.

Nehru was born in Allahabad in 1889, the only son of a wealthy Kashmiri Brahmin. While Nehru's father was conservative in politics, he became deeply attached to Gandhi, and he and his entire family worked closely with the Mahatma in the struggle for independence. (Motilal Nehru, his son Jawaharlal, and Gandhi were known irreverently as the Father, the Son, and the Holy Ghost.)

Following the practice of many wealthy families, Nehru's parents sent him to Britain for his schooling. He studied at Harrow, and then at Cambridge University, after which he studied law. In 1912, he was called to the bar.

Upon his return to India, Nehru became a member of the All-India Congress Committee. By 1923, he rose to the office of general secretary. Inspired by Gandhi's ideas, he became president of the Indian National Congress, and on a number of occasions was jailed by the

JAWARHARLAL NEHRU India's Prime Minister from 1947 until his death in 1964, Nehru was the main architect of modern Indian government. Born in 1889, he was educated at Harrow and at Cambridge, and was admitted to the bar in London's Inner Temple in 1912. Shortly after returning to India, he joined Gandhi in the non-violent battle for Indian independence.

British for his anti-British activities. During one of his jail terms, he wrote a long book, *Glimpses of World History*, addressed to his daughter and only child, Indira (Mrs. Indira Gandhi), who in later years became his close assistant and confidante. After his death, she was appointed Minister of Press and Information in the Shastri government.

Some critics contend that Mr. Nehru, as president of the Indian National Congress, displayed intransigence about some of the demands of Muslim leaders for clarification of the role they would play in independent India, and thus was at least partly responsible for the campaign for partition. Some believe that his opposition to the inclusion of Kashmir, the birthplace of his ancestors, into Pakistan, thwarted reconciliation after 1947. However, throughout his term as Prime Minister, Nehru displayed admiration for the Muslims and concern for their success and well-being.

The author of many books, among them *The Discovery of India* and *Toward Freedom*, a brilliant orator who held Indian audiences of villagers and workers, as well as intellectuals, enthralled, Nehru was a statesman with a world view. He was an aristocrat who believed fervently in the need for economic change and social progress. Though often called a Socialist, he was opposed to communism within India. In a country deeply committed to a wide range of ancient faiths, Nehru never hesitated to say that he was an agnostic; among a people who had just achieved nationhood, Nehru emphasized the need for an international outlook; and far from stressing his Indian origins, he confessed that he found himself constantly torn between the ideas of East and West, finding inspiration not only in the thinkers of his own land, but in those of the rest of the world. This writer considers Nehru one of the outstanding figures of the 20th century.

THE GOVERNMENT STRUCTURE

The Union Executive consists of the President, the Vice-President, and the Council of Ministers, with the Prime Minister at its head. The President is elected by an Electoral College consisting of the elected members of both Houses of Parliament and of the Legislative Assemblies of the States. He serves for a term of five years, and is eligible for re-election. The President appoints the Prime Minister and the other ministers. In 1965, the President was a noted Hindu philosopher, Dr. Radakrishnan, who had previously served as Vice-President.

From 1947 until his death in 1964, Mr. Nehru served as Prime Minister. He also held the ministry posts of External Affairs and Atomic Energy, and headed the Planning Commission. He was succeeded as Prime Minister by Lal Bahadur Shastri, a small, soft-spoken man of simple tastes who had been a teacher and had served in Mr. Nehru's Cabinet as Minister of Home Affairs. In this post he had acquired the reputation of being an able conciliator.

India has a form of central government modeled on that of Britain. The Parliament consists of two houses—the Council of States (*Rajya Sabha*), the equivalent of Britain's House of Lords, and the House of the People (*Lok Sabha*), the equivalent of Britain's House of Commons.

The Council of States is composed of not more than 250 members, of whom 12 are nominated by the President for distinguished contributions to the nation, and the rest are elected by the elected members of the Legislative Assembly of each State, in accordance with the system of proportional representation.

The House of the People consists of not more than 500 members directly elected from territorial constituencies in the States. The representative of the State of Kashmir is appointed by the President, on the recommendation of the Legislature of that State. The number of seats for each State is allocated so as to allow for proportional representation.

POLITICAL PARTIES

India, since independence, has been in the unusual position of having had what looks like one-party rule, although all political parties operate freely in national elections. This situation came about because the Indian National Congress attracted all opponents of Britain, whatever their political views—from old-line conservatives and reactionary orthodox Hindus to the most advanced Socialists. The one notable exception to this national consensus were the Communists, who remained outside the struggle for independence, and actually supported Britain in World War II because British participation, in their view, was important for defense of the U.S.S.R.

After independence, the National Congress was reorganized into the Congress Party. Reactionary Hindu groups soon formed their own small parties of the Right, Jan Singh and Mahasabha. It was a member of Mahasabha who assassinated Gandhi because of his efforts to protect Muslims in independent India.

The Socialists' outstanding leaders have been Asoka Mehta—theoretician of the Socialist Party, an economist who is now chairman of the Planning Commission—and Jayaprakash Narayan, an idealist educated at the University of Wisconsin, who withdrew from the Congress Party in the 1950's because he felt it was dominated by conservatives. However, the Socialist Party (now called the Praja—that is, Peasants' and Workers' Socialist-Party) has little influence because its leading figures either serve in the government—notably Asoka Mehta—or remain outside the political struggle—notably Narayan. The Congress Party itself, although it has many business leaders among its members, follows a moderate Socialist policy.

The Communists, who are a small minority in the House of the People, have been hampered by three factors. First, the Socialist policies of the ruling Congress Party leave little room for leftist groups; second, the Communists themselves are split into three groups—pro-Indian, pro-Russian, and pro-Chinese, the last now being the most important. And

CALCUTTA SLUMS *Families like this sleep in tiny shacks of straw matting in the alleys behind modern buildings. Cooking, mending, eating, and almost all other family activities are carried on in the street.*

VILLAGE SCHOOL *These buildings in Kerala are merely roofs supported on cement pillars; nevertheless, they are adequate for the climate. The school was built by the villagers and is supported by the parents.*

TROPICAL VILLAGE Laden with food and grain, a pirogue is poled up the River Kosi in the swampy area near the border of Nepal. The thatched houses are constructed largely of bamboo.

THE GOLDEN TEMPLE Built in the architectural style brought to India by the Moghul rulers, this temple in Amritsar is the center of the Sikh faith. The city was founded in 1574 by Ram Das, a Sikh leader.

third, China's invasion of India in 1962 aroused profound resentment against communism. However, Communists have won some successes in states which have been beset by economic and social problems—notably the State of Kerala where the government was briefly headed by a Communist Chief Minister.

Recently, a moderate conservative party—Swatantra (Freedom) Party—has been formed, but has so far attracted little voter support. The Congress Party has succeeded in winning close to 50 percent of the national vote in all three general elections that have been held since independence, despite increasing talk of the need for its reinvigoration.

ECONOMIC DEVELOPMENT

India's economy is still dominated by a primitive agriculture. Nearly half of the country's national income (46.8 percent) is derived from agriculture and allied occupations, in which nearly three-fourths of its working force are engaged.

Since independence, it has been the task of the National Planning Commission, first headed by the late Prime Minister Nehru, to increase agricultural productivity and at the same time to accelerate the pace of industrialization. Government investment in the economy has been rising year by year. By the end of the Second Five-Year Plan in 1961, it amounted to 11 percent of the national income.

The increase in national income has been modest, and so far has not reached the projected rate envisaged by the Five-Year Plans. Also modest has been the rise in the average per capita annual income from about $54 to $69 (as compared with $2,500 in the United States, and $300 in the U.S.S.R.).

The economy of India is neither entirely controlled by the State, as in the U.S.S.R. and Communist China, nor entirely controlled by private owners. About 90 percent of the net domestic output derives from private enterprise, and the balance from state-controlled organizations and from enterprises in which both government and private owners participate.

According to 1959 figures, 33 percent of the population is employed in urban areas, and 42.7 percent in the rural areas.

LAND REFORM

Of India's total geographic area of 326.3 million hectares (a hectare equals 2.47 acres), somewhat over 40 percent is cultivated. Fallow lands and cultivable wastes total an additional 44.3 million hectares. It is difficult to expand production because most of the land not under cultivation is located in areas of low rainfall or in hilly country where a certain proportion of it has to be kept fallow every year. Large areas consist of marginal lands of low productivity; others can be reclaimed only at very high cost.

In the 1950's it was estimated that 40 million villagers and their families were without land, working either as tenants or laborers for landowners. Others worked at various non-agricultural jobs—often on a temporary basis—with the result that underemployment and limited seasonal employment were widespread. Among those who owned land, the majority had only between one and five acres, not enough for efficient cultivation. As of 1958, 25 percent of village families owned 84 percent of the land.

The first important reform measures taken by the Indian government were: (1) to abolish a wide range of complicated, semi-feudal relationships between tenants and landless workers on the one hand, and landowners on the other; (2) to assure security of ownership for those who already owned land; (3) to limit the maximum amount of land to be owned by any one landowner. Land above that maximum was bought from owners by the State and redistributed among landless villagers.

This far-reaching land reform program has, however, been seriously hampered by three problems. First, under the Constitution, land is under the control, not of the Union government, but of the several States, each of which has its own land laws. As a result, ceilings set for maximum land ownership have varied from State to State. (Minimum figures vary from 18 to 25 or 30 acres, and maximum figures from 60 to 250 acres.) Second, the government has not had the funds to pay adequate compensation for land that might be taken over for redistribution. And third, even when land redistribution has been effected, the new owners, formerly landless, do not have the capital, tools, and draft animals to develop the land they receive. Many experts contend that some form of consolidation of small plots awarded to the landless must be effected, possibly through the formation of cooperative farms.

In an effort to ease some of these difficult problems, the venerable Sanskrit scholar, Acharya Vinoba Bhave, a devoted disciple of Gandhi and leader of the Bhoodan movement, has urged landowners to surrender some of their land voluntarily as a gift to the landless, and urban dwellers to contribute funds for the purchase of fertilizer, tools, and draft animals for use by the former landless. The inspiring presence of Vinoba Bhave, known as "The Walking Saint" because he goes on foot from village to village, has brought about the gift of a million or so acres of land, but critics have claimed that much of it was stony unproductive.

Another movement called *Gramdan*, or donations of entire villages, seeks to have land transferred to a village community as a whole, rather than to individual owners. Some experts believe that the wisest policy would be to assemble plots into large areas so that land could be efficiently cultivated with the aid of modern machinery, seeds, fertilizer, insecticides, and adequate irrigation facilities; and at the same time to shift surplus farm workers to work in industries located in the vicinity of villages.

VILLAGE AND TOWN LIFE

Meanwhile, life both in villages and in the slum areas of big cities remains difficult. In 1957, about 73 percent of the households in rural areas and 76 percent of the households in urban areas had no more than two rooms each; many had only one room. About 69 percent of the rural households used drinking water drawn from tanks and ponds; tap water was almost unknown. A constructed latrine was used by only three percent of rural households.

In the big cities—Calcutta, Bombay, Delhi, and Madras—92 percent of households obtained their drinking water from municipal taps. In the urban sector, 44 percent of the households did not use a con-

structed latrine, about 37 percent used a common latrine, and only 19
percent of the households had a private latrine.

LITERACY PROGRAM   *Lacking school rooms, the people of Samana
Bahu, a small village, learn their letters on a whitewashed wall near the
village well. The letters are in Hindi, India's national language.*

Efforts to improve conditions in rural areas are centered in the
Community Development Program, launched in 1952, a program designed to serve India's 580,000 villages, and administered through
specially trained workers. The aims of the program are to improve agriculture, roads, sanitation, and housing, and to develop cottage and small-
scale industries.

India's large cities have found many of their districts turned into vast slums by the influx of refugees from Pakistan. Authorities are dismayed at the prospect of providing shelter, potable water, sewage facilities, buses, and schools for so many newcomers. Because of this fantastic overcrowding (comparable conditions can be found in Hong Kong, Singapore, Cairo, and Rio de Janeiro), urban planners are feverishly trying to construct new housing.

Meanwhile, foreigners are startled to see men, women, and children sleeping in the streets. However, this practice is due, in many cases, not to lack of shelter, but simply to the Indian preference for sleeping outdoors, particularly on a hot, steamy night. In even a smaller, relatively uncrowded city, inhabitants who do have homes will bring their beds out, either on terraces or on the pavement, to enjoy a breath of fresh air.

NEW DELHI

Within India, there are some 580,000 villages; here, in the second half of the 20th century, people still live under the most primitive conditions. In contrast, India's principal cities—New Delhi, Bombay, and Calcutta—offer many of the amenities of the Western world.

Delhi, the capital of India, consists of two sectors, the Old and the New. Over the centuries, this city has served as capital for the Hindu, the Muslim, and the British Empires. Situated on the Jumna River, Delhi is the communication center of India. The old section of the city, once a fortress of the Moghul Empire, is surrounded by a wall of red sandstone 75 feet high. The enclosed area is known as the Red Fort, and serves as the site of parades held on important national holidays. From a platform on the walls of the fort, Nehru and his successor, Shastri, have addressed the Indian masses. There are many old mosques and temples in this neighborhood. Chandni Chauk, which means Silver Street, is famous for its jewelry wrought of gold and silver, and for the many brass artifacts which are sold there.

New Delhi was built in 1912 by the British. Here are located the two houses of Parliament, the principal ministries, and many other government buildings, as well as foreign embassies. The city is notable for its wide avenues, and the profusion of private gardens and public parks.

VILLAGE COMMUNITY *The sari-clad women of Faridabad in Punjab gather around the village stand-pipe with their water jars. They are expert at carrying piles of jars balanced on their heads. The woman stooping to fill her brass jar has a small circular mat on her head on which to balance the jar.*

BOMBAY

With a population of more than four million, Bombay is India's largest city. Through its harbor most of the trade of India passes.

With its magnificent sea-front villas, modern apartment houses and large hotels, its excellent European-style restaurants, its attractive shops full of tempting silks and cottons, jewelry, and other luxury articles, and with its lively intellectual life, Bombay has achieved something of the atmosphere of Paris, although it resembles, to a large extent, a Mediterranean port.

CALCUTTA

Calcutta was built by the British at the end of the 17th century to facilitate the trade of the East India Company. Situated on the Hooghly River, a tributary of the Ganges, Calcutta serves as a transportation center and a busy seaport. It is the center of India's industrial region. Calcutta proper has a population of three million, but in the greater metropolitan area there reside an estimated six million people, a figure expected to rise to ten or even eleven million within the next few years.

As in other developing nations, an urban center such as this, with its glamorous, fine residential area, and its busy commercial districts, exerts a powerful attraction for the inhabitants of villages, particularly for the youth, who want to break out of the restrictions of traditional life, and seek to find new work, broader horizons, and greater amusement in the city. The magnet of the hustle and the bustle, the neon lights, and the movie theaters, as well as the even more powerful attraction of economic advancement, lure thousands upon thousands each year to Calcutta and Bombay. Most often, men come in search of jobs, leaving their families at home in the villages. These newcomers crowd into the cities, originally designed for a much smaller population. The influx strains transportation, housing, and school facilities to the breaking point· The municipal governments of India, as in other developing nations, are hard pressed to maintain reasonably decent standards of public health and habitation.

STONE CARVING   Ten-feet high, this is the most perfect of the 12 chariot wheels of the Sun Temple at Konarak. Note the line of marching elephants directly beneath the wheel. Each of the small medallions on the spokes represents a scene important in Hindu theology.

These grave problems are further compounded whenever Hindu refugees from Pakistan stream into India, as they do from time to time, either by their own volition or driven to leave the neighboring country because of exactions of the Pakistan government. This has proved particularly onerous for Calcutta, to which refugees from East Pakistan (formerly East Bengal) turn in the first instance, often refusing to resettle in other less crowded areas of the country where their native tongue, Bengali, is not spoken.

FINANCE

Power to raise and disburse public funds was divided under the Constitution between the Central Government and the States.

Currency was issued under the decimal system for the first time on July 2, 1962. The *rupee* has an approximate value of 20 cents; a dollar corresponds approximately to five rupees.

As of 1965, although India has been financing 90 percent of its economic development out of its own resources, substantial financial aid comes from the United States, Britain, France, and West Germany, as well as from the U.S.S.R. Steel mills were built by the British (Durgapur), the Germans (Rourkela), and the Russians (Bhilai); in early 1965, the Russians undertook to build a second steel mill, at Bokaro.

The India Consortium, in which the United States, Britain, France, West Germany, and Japan participate, has been aiding India's industrialization. Moreover, the United States has been supplying food (mostly wheat) to India, for which New Delhi pays in rupees, which are then loaned as counterpart funds to India by Washington for investment in mutually agreed upon development projects. Private United States organizations, notably the Rockefeller and Ford Foundations, also give various kinds of aid to India.

United States government aid, estimated in 1965 at over six billion dollars, is given in the form of grants, long-term loans, services of American technicians, and training for Indian nationals in American educational institutions. U.S.S.R. aid, estimated in 1965 at over one billion dollars, is given in the form of credits and outright grants, as well as services of technicians, for example in the construction of steel mills.

FOREIGN POLICY

The foreign policy of India has often been described in the United States as "neutralism." Mr. Nehru and other Indian leaders, however, described their policy as "non-alignment." India has tried to maintain an independent course in world affairs, and not become aligned with

STREET SCENE *This street is typical of the overcrowded suburbs of Delhi. Peddlers hawk their wares, children scream from the ride resembling a ferris wheel, and lines of wash dangle on the balconies.*

either the U.S.S.R. or the United States. This policy has not prevented India from joining the British Commonwealth. Nor has non-alignment prevented India from accepting military aid in the form of planes, arms, and technical assistance from both blocs, after the country had been attacked by Peking in 1962. While India has undertaken no military commitments to either of the great-power blocs, it has demonstrated its commitment to the United Nations by providing troops and materials for U.N. peacekeeping operations in the Gaza Strip and in the Congo.

India is aware that, with a relatively small army of some 500,000 men as yet inadequately equipped with modern arms, it would be no match for its powerful Asian neighbor, Communist China. After Peking's 1962 attack, some Indian critics of non-alignment urged that India enter into a military alliance with either the United States or with the U.S.S.R.—or preferably with both, but the Indian government rejected this policy.

INDIA'S NATIONAL INTERESTS

As of 1965, India had four major national interests. The first, and in the opinion of the Shastri government the most important, was to improve relations with all the states along its borders, particularly with those nations where a considerable number of Indians have been settled for years, or even centuries. The new Foreign Minister Sardar Swaran Singh (Mr. Nehru, it will be recalled, was his own Foreign Minister) therefore made it his first order of business to pay friendly visits to Nepal in the Himalayas, through which the Chinese might seek to penetrate India, and to Burma and Ceylon, which have within their borders many Indian settlers whose economic and/or linguistic rights have been endangered by the legislation of these countries. As a result of these visits, India's relations with its neighbors have improved. However, it is expected that ultimately New Delhi will have to accept the return of some 600,000 Indians who can no longer hope to live and work satisfactorily in Burma and Ceylon.

A somewhat comparable problem exists in Kenya, in Tanganyika, and in Uganda. In these countries, Indians have been settled for three or four generations, are in control of trade, and are now being challenged by Africans eager, in their turn, to become traders.

KASHMIR

India's second major national interest is to improve its relations with Pakistan. In spite of the violence which marked the partition of the subcontinent in 1950, India and Pakistan have peacefully settled the problems of refugees, as well as the complex issue of division of irrigation canals in the Indus River Basin.

The thorniest problem in Indo-Pakistan relations is that of Kashmir, an area which borders on both countries and was incorporated into India at the time of partition. Kashmir's four-million population consists of 77.11 percent Muslims concentrated in the Vale, 20.12 percent Hindus, and a relatively small number of Buddhists (concentrated in Ladakh in the North) and Sikhs. Mr. Nehru, a Kashmiri Brahmin, strongly resisted Pakistan's demand for a plebiscite in Kashmir. The Indian government regards Kashmir (except for the western section seized by Pakistani forces in 1947 and known as Azad, or Free Kashmir) as a State of the Indian Union. But some Kashmiri leaders demand that Kashmir be divided between Pakistan. and India along religious lines, or be made an independent State. A number of Indians, notably the Socialist, Jayaprakash Narayan, would be ready to give up the entire state for the sake of improved relations with Pakistan which, they fear, may otherwise support Peking against New Delhi. The India-Pakistan armed clash of 1965 was directly due to Pakistan's demand for a Kashmir plebiscite.

The average Indian ordinarily feels little or no resentment against Pakistan, except when Pakistanis act unfairly toward Hindus within their borders. This was the case in East Pakistan bordering on West Bengal, an area from which many refugees fled to India in recent

AT THE BURNING GHATS The waters of the holy Ganges are alleged to wash the bather free of his sins. These men, at a cremation site on the banks, are carrying water with which to wash the deceased free of sin before his cremation.

years. Far more emotion has been aroused among Indians by China's invasion, and by fear that the Chinese might apply further pressure in the future, particularly since they now have a nuclear bomb. Demands that India, too, should begin to produce nuclear bombs have been made by some politicians and editorial writers, but this proposal was resisted by the Shastri government.

INDIA BETWEEN EAST AND WEST

India's third important interest is to maintain friendly relations with both West and East, with Washington and Moscow, so as to assure a continued flow of economic aid and of military aid, particularly in case of renewed pressure by Peking.

The fourth major facet of India's foreign policy is active participation in the United Nations and in the Specialized Agencies. India receives substantial aid from the World Bank, the International Monetary Fund (IMF), the U.N. Technical Assistance Program, the International Development Association (IDA), and the U.N. Special Fund Aid is also obtained under the Colombo Plan, organized by the Commonwealth nations, in which the United States participates.

In the U.N., India is seeking to strengthen its relations with the Asian-African bloc of which it had once been a leader until its position seriously declined, first as a result of China's invasion, and then as a result of tension between Indians and Africans in the new nations of East Africa.

PEDICAB   A rickshaw coolie pushes his pedicab up to speed before leaping onto the bicycle seat. The pedicab is a rickshaw with a bicycle attached in front; it provides all the pleasures of leisurely travel with less expense in human energy.

SIKH PILGRIM A pilgrim from the Punjab washes his feet before entering the Golden Temple, the most sacred shrine of the Sikhs.

LITERATURE

Westerners who want to know how people live in India today and what Indians in various walks of life think, should turn to the novels, poems, and plays of modern writers. One of India's most distinguished writers is Rabindranath Tagore. His *Collected Poems and Plays* and his small book on *Nationalism* show the wide range of Tagore's interests.

For a picture of life in India's teeming cities and ancient villages, the novels of Mulk Anand (particularly *Coolie* and *Untouchable*) should be read, as well as the remarkably interesting novels of the witty R. K. Narayan: *The Financial Expert, The Man-Eater of Malgudi*, and *The Guide*. His most recent book is *Gods, Demons and Others* (New York, Viking, 1964). K. Markandaya, in *Nectar in a Sieve*, gives a remarkable picture of village life.

For an Indian's impressions of modern India, the following books are of particular interest: Santha Rama Rau, *Home to India* and *This is India*; Nirad Chaudhuri, *The Autobiography of an Unknown Indian*; and Ved Mehta, *Face to Face*.

Among the ancient literary treasures of India, one which has served as a source of drama and poetry throughout the ages is the *Mahabharata* or great epic of Bharat (the ancient name of India), a folk legend about the struggle between rival clans over succession to a throne in the Upper Ganges Valley.

254   THE NATIONS OF ASIA

The great epic poem *Ramayana* is responsible for the tradition of regarding the monkey as sacred. It tells the story of the struggles of Prince Rama who, driven into exile by his brothers, fought against Ravana, the King of Demons living in Lanka (Ceylon) to free his captured wife, the beautiful Sita. Rama finally rescues Sita with the aid of the King of the Monkeys—a good deed which has caused Indians even in modern times to forbear from killing monkeys, no matter how much food these animals may purloin. A remarkable fresco in a Bangkok temple depicts scenes from the *Ramayana,* including the final triumphal return of Rama to the capital of his country with the rescued Sita, and shows the King of the Monkeys in a prominent position at the festive ceremony.

The most famous Indian dramatist remains Kalidasa, who flourished in the Golden Age of the Gupta dynasty in the fifth century A.D. His best-known plays, *Sakuntala* and *The Little Clay Cart,* continue to be very popular. Kalidasa has often been described, as a dramatist, as "The Indian Shakespeare," and as a lyrical poet has been compared with Shelley and other British lyricists.

THE ARTS

India has a long and venerable history of art and architecture. Among its architectural treasures, the most famous is the Taj Mahal at Agra, a world-renowned white marble memorial built in the 1600's by the Muslim ruler Shah Jahan in honor of his beloved wife, Mumtaz-i-Mahal; it is the most striking example of Indo-Muslim architecture. Other notable examples are the 16th century palace of Mogul Emperor Akbar at Fatepur Sikri near Agra, and the Red Fort, the tomb of Humayun, and the Mahatma Gandi memorial, all in New Delhi.

Some notable ancient works are the paintings on the inner walls and ceilings in the Buddhist caves at Ajanta, probably executed in the second or third century A.D. and the Ellora temples, both near Hyderabad; the palaces and the collection of beautiful Moghul miniature paintings in Jaipur; the column at Sarnath commemorating the spot where Buddha preached his first sermon, one of the many columns erected by Emperor Asoka in the third century B.C.; the *stupas* or burial mounds built in honor of Buddha at Sanchi; the Hindu temples of Benares, the sacred city of the Hindus, picturesquely built on the banks of the Ganges; and sculptures in the temples of Orissa State.

India is also famous for its music, which is closely associated with the drama and the dance. Indian music, called *ragas* (*rag* means color, emotion, or passion), is played on stringed instruments such as the *vina,* the *setar,* and the *saranji;* and on percussion instruments which include the *ghauta* or hand bell, tinkling cymbals, clashing cymbals, *ghari* (circular or triangular bronze discs), the *ghata* (pottery jar), the *tabla,* and the *damya.* Indian musicians sit cross-legged on the floor, and as a recital proceeds, they throw themselves with mounting passion into the music, nodding vigorously at each other and stirring each other to greater and greater heights of excitement, in which the audience joins.

The modern drama and dance, and even the motion picture, are for the most part based on religious and heroic legends. Dramatic acting is often done in pantomime and dance, accompanied by instrumental and vocal music.

BUDDHIST SCULPTURE   *Here is a portion of the curved architraves of the north gateway at Sanchi.*

RICE FARMERS *Farm laborers from Bengal relax on a stack of rice straw.*

HOLIDAYS: RELIGIOUS AND CIVIL

The most popular holidays in India are Dussehra and Divali, both of which take place in the autumn. Dussehra recalls the time when the evil King Ravana, who had captured Sita, was slain by Rama. Divali celebrates the return home of Rama and Sita after 14 years in exile. These holidays, which come in October, involve a festival of lights burning in homes and in public buildings, and the message is that light shall win over darkness, and good shall triumph over evil.

Another gay holiday is Holi, which ushers in spring. On this occasion, amidst much laughter, colored water is gaily thrown at whoever passes by. Everyone does this, particularly the children.

The two most important national holidays are Independence Day, August 15, which marks the date when, in 1947, India became independent of British rule; and Republic Day, January 26, which commemorates the date in 1950 when the Indian Constitution was proclaimed.

The birthday of Mahatma Gandhi, born in 1869, is celebrated on October 2, with special ceremonies held on the grounds of his beautiful memorial in New Delhi.

VERA MICHELES DEAN

IN BRIEF

AREA 1,261,597 square miles, about one-third the size of the U.S.

TERRAIN Three major topographic regions. The High Himalaya mountain region lies in the north and in Kashmir. The Indo-Gangetic plain, formed by the basins of the Indus, Ganges, and Brahmaputra rivers, is the most fertile and heavily populated region. The Deccan Plateau, which covers most of the triangular southern peninsula, is bounded by the Eastern Ghats and the Western Ghats, low mountains which fall to narrow coastal plains. Fertile river valley regions are created by streams flowing down from the Deccan.

FLORA Tropical rain forests include broadleaf evergreen, bamboo, and scrub or brush jungle. Temperate forests are primarily composed of oak, chestnut, and evergreen, with many climbers and parasitic plants. Tidal forests of the Ganges delta region—the Sundarbans—are composed of the *Sundri* tree, the mangrove, and the palm, including both the coconut and the areca palm.

FAUNA Lion, tiger, hyena, elephant, cheetah, jackal, deer, and monkey. Snakes and birds.

CLIMATE Varies from sub-arctic in the Himalayas to tropical in the plains. Weather is dominated by monsoons. November to February is cool and dry; April to June is hot and dry; June to September is hot and rainy. In Delhi, temperatures reach 120°F. during April, May, and June.

CAPITAL New Delhi. Estimated population of 300,000 is included with that of Delhi in census reports.

OTHER CITIES In the 1961 census, Bombay had over 4.15 million people; Calcutta, 2.93 million; Delhi, 2.06 million; Madras, 1.73 million; Ahmedabad, 1.15 million; and Hyderabad, 1.2 million. Cities with over 350,000 people included Agra, Amritsar, Allahabad, Bangalore, Howrah, Indore, Jaipur, Kanpur, Lucknow, Madurai, Nagpur, Patna, Poona, and Varanasi.

POPULATION 471 million estimated in 1965. Density is about 380 persons per square mile. Annual rate of increase is 2.3 percent.

KONARAK SCULPTURE *In contrast to its lavishly sculptured exterior, the interior of the Konarak temple is unadorned. But in the court there are many large sculptures of great strength and beauty, many like this erotic Maithuna figure.*

ETHNIC GROUPS Ethnic distinctions have largely broken down; linguistic and some cultural distinctions remain prominent. Caste divisions may reflect ancient ethnic groupings. In general, Indians of Dravidian descent live in the south, and those of Indo-European descent in the north. Some mountain groups, such as the Ladakhis, are of Tibetan origin. Numerous enclaves of hill and forest people, such as the Naga tribes, are related to groups in Burma and other areas of Southeast Asia.

LANGUAGES The official language is Hindi, written in the Devanagari script, but English can be used for all official purposes until 1975. There is considerable controversy, sometimes violent, over the determination of the government to give priority to Hindi. Hindi is understood by about 40 percent of the population. Of the 845 known languages and dialects in use, 14 are recognized in the Constitution: Assamese, Bengali, Gujarati, Hindustani, Kannada, Kashmiri, Malayalam, Marathi, Oriya, Punjabi, Sanskrit, Tamil, Telegu, and Urdu.

RELIGIONS In 1961, there were about 366.5 million Hindus, 7.85 million Sikhs, 2.03 million Jains, 3.25 million Buddhists, 46.94 million Muslims, and 10.73 million Christians. Animist faiths are followed by tribal groups which comprise less than one percent of the population.

DATE OF INDEPENDENCE On August 15, 1947, British rule ended with partition of India into the Indian Union and Pakistan.

FORM OF GOVERNMENT   Federal Republic. India is a union of states, with sixteen states and nine territories. The President of the Republic is elected for a five-year term by a college made up of all elected members of Parliament and of the state legislatures. Two houses of Parliament include the *Rajya Sabha,* or Council of States, and the *Lok Sabha,* or House of the People. The upper house, *Rajya Sabha,* is indirectly elected by members of state legislatures; it has a maximum of 250 members. The lower house, *Lok Sabha,* is composed of 500 members, who are directly elected by people of both the states and the territories. The Prime Minister and members of the Cabinet are appointed by the President and are responsible to the Parliament. The judiciary is independent. Elections must be held every five years, but can be called earlier on a parliamentary vote of no confidence. India is a member of the United Nations and of numerous international organizations.

EDUCATION   In 1961, nearly 27 million students were enrolled in almost 335,000 primary schools staffed by over 700,000 teachers. Over 71,000 secondary and vocational schools enrolled 18.4 million students with 625,000 teachers. Almost 100,000 were enrolled in teacher-training institutions. Some 46 universities and over 1,900 colleges with about 70,000 instructors enrolled 977,000 students. About 10,000 students attended foreign universities. Four of India's universities are administered by the central government; the remainder are controlled by state or municipal governments. In 1961, only 24 percent of the people were literate.

SUGAR CANE MILL A typical slum scene near New Delhi. The large machine is a sugar cane mill. The squatting man is feeding the cane between the cylinders which crush the stalks and extract the juice. The bullock, driven by two small boys, walks in a circle pulling the heavy lever which turns the cylinders. A cow, a sacred animal in India, is wandering freely among the people.

**HEALTH
FACILITIES**

By 1960, there were close to 85,000 doctors, 3,600 dentists, and 40,000 pharmacists. There were also some 145,000 practitioners of Ayurvedic and Unani medicine, systems based on very ancient religious writings. The country still has a shortage of medical and public health nurses in the villages. In 1961, there were almost 12,000 hospitals and dispensaries and 33,000 nurses. Diseases such as malaria, tuberculosis, leprosy, and typhoid fever remain serious problems, as do conditions caused by inadequate diet and sanitation.

**CULTURAL
FACILITIES**

In 1962, there were over 8,000 newspapers and periodicals, including 457 daily newspapers with a circulation of close to six million. Over 20 percent of the periodicals use English; about 19 percent use Hindi, with significant numbers appearing in Urdu, Bengali, Gujarati, Marathi, and Tamil. Over 11,000 books were published in 1962, including more than 750 translations of literary and scientific works from English and other European languages. There were 319 long films produced for showing in 3,650 cinemas and almost 1,400 mobile film units. All-India Radio broadcasts to well over three million radios via a 31-station network. Television, still in an experimental stage, is in operation at New Delhi. Scientific and historical research is aided by the government, with most publications appearing in English or Hindi. Literary arts thrive in many languages, notably Bengali. Film art and music are especially popular.

**CURRENCY
AND FINANCE**

The Indian *rupee* is valued at 0.186621 gram of fine gold, or 20¢ in U.S. currency. In 1964, national revenue, including foreign aid, was $3.89 billion; expenditures were slightly greater than revenue. Total revenue and expenditures of the several states balanced at about $2.85 billion.

**INDUSTRY AND
PRODUCTION**

Approximately 70 percent of the people are farmers or farm laborers living in 580,000 small villages, and nearly half of the national income is derived from agriculture. Estimated national income was over $30.7 billion in 1961; it was increasing by 2.5 percent per year in the first years of the 1961–65 Five-Year Plan. Per capita income was $69 in 1962, with the rise in national income almost totally offset by population increase. After agriculture, the most important industry is weaving cotton cloth, followed by silk rearing, silk weaving, shawl and carpet making, wood carving, and metal working. Over 9,000 factories process foods, lumber, jute, and hides; make cement, glass, ceramics, cotton and woolen textiles; or manufacture chemicals, aluminum, copper, brass, iron and steel, bicycles, or electrical machinery. Steel capacity is about 10 million tons a year. Production of petroleum products is close to 2 billion gallons a year. By 1963, electric power from over 5,000 generating plants was close to 20 million kilowatts. Two nuclear reactors are in operation.

CROPS: Rice, wheat, sugar cane, oil seeds, peanuts, cotton, jute, tea, coffee, rubber, and opium are the principal products. Only China has more irrigated farmland than India; 60.2 million acres are irrigated by 67,000 miles of canals.

LIVESTOCK: In 1961, there were 175.7 million cattle, 51.1 million water buffalo, 40.3 million sheep, 60.8 million goats, 1.4 million horses, and 116.9 million poultry.

FISHERIES: The 1962 catch was almost 974,000 metric tons.

MINING: In 1962, mineral production was valued at about $392.7 million, with coal accounting for almost three-fourths of that amount. India's excellent mineral resources include especially plentiful reserves of oil, coal, lignite, manganese, bauxite, mica, and the thorium and monazite sands used in nuclear power production.

TRADE   Because of the severe trade imbalance, India buys heavily from countries offering special financing or aid, restricts imports stringently, and arranges barter agreements whenever possible. Tea is the chief export, amounting to 25 percent of the total. Agricultural commodities, jute and cotton fabrics, minerals, leather, gums, and resins are next in importance. Imports are chiefly construction and industrial machinery, petroleum products, chemicals, and fertilizers.

1962:	IMPORTS	$2,254,000,000
	EXPORTS	$1,447,000,000
	DEFICIT	$ 807,000,000

TENZING NORGAY This is the Sherpa mountaineer who guided the first successful expedition to conquer Mount Everest.

MEN OF THE HIGH HIMALAYA
Three men of Hemis Gumpa in Ladakh are dressed very much as their contemporaries in Tibet. They share most of the Tibetan way of life. On the hill stands a chorten, a Buddhist shrine.

MISHMI FAMILY The Mishmi are a tribal people renowned for their courage; they tenaciously cling to their own primitive ways. This Mishmi warrior, armed with a wicker shield, wooden spear, and a dah, is seated with wife and child. These men stood up against Chinese troops when the northeast frontier was penetrated by Communist invaders in 1962.

WATERING PLACE   A large portion of Calcutta's slum dwellers wash their clothes and themselves at street pumps like this, which may serve over 100 families.

TRANSPORT

ROAD: In 1961, there were 735,000 miles of road, about 441,000 miles of it surfaced. Some 15,000 miles of national highway were the main arteries of communication. More than 675,000 motor vehicles included about 260,000 private cars, 31,500 jeeps, 90,000 motorcycles, 6,300 auto-rickshaws, 22,000 taxicabs, 57,000 buses, and 171,000 trucks.

RAILROAD: The government-owned railway system maintains almost 35,000 miles of track, almost half of it broad gauge. There were about 1.7 billion passengers during 1962.

AIR: Two government-owned corporations carried 1.13 million passengers and over 75 million tons of cargo during 1962. Some 205 aircraft were in service. Air India International operates long-distance international flights; Indian Airlines Corporation flies to neighboring countries and provides internal service to 82 airports. There are international jet airports at Bombay, Delhi, and Calcutta.

SEA: Calcutta, Bombay, and Madras are the chief ports. There is one government-owned shipyard, with a second under construction. In 1963, there were 193 ships of 150 gross tons or more flying the Indian flag; over half were engaged in coastal rather than in international trade.

COMMUNICA-TION

Telephone, post, radio, and telegraph services are government owned and operated. In 1962, there were 521,000 telephones and over three million radios in use. There are 31 radio stations.

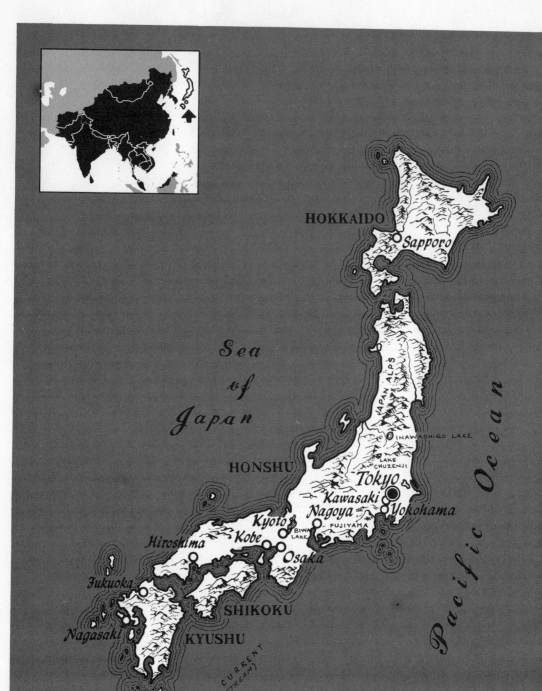

HOKKAIDO

Sapporo

Sea
of
Japan

HONSHU

JAPAN ALPS

INAWASHIRO LAKE

LAKE
CHUZENJI

Tokyo
Kawasaki
Nagoya   Yokohama
FUJIYAMA

Kyoto
Hiroshima   Kobe   BIWA
LAKE
Osaka

Fukuoka

SHIKOKU

Nagasaki   KYUSHU

JAPAN CURRENT
(BLACK STREAM)

Pacific Ocean

JAPAN

Industrial Giant of Asia

Japan, the most highly industrialized and Westernized nation in Asia, stands today as a symbol of progress, giving irrefutable proof that a non-Western nation can, without embracing Communism, achieve as high a degree of economic development as the advanced nations of the West.

After the end of World War II, Japan was so utterly defeated and exhausted that it appeared that she was forever finished as a great power. Yet within less than a decade, not only did she make an astonishingly speedy recovery, but she achieved a rate of economic growth that has startled the world. Today, Japan has once again become a major industrial nation.

CLIMATE AND NATURAL BEAUTY

Anchored off the northeast coast of the Asiatic continent, Japan's four main islands and the 3,325 smaller islands extend over a distance of 1,200 miles. With an area of approximately 142,500 square miles, Japan is approximately the size of Montana. This represents a shrinkage of 40 percent in area since before World War II.

Nature has generously endowed the country with beautiful scenery and abundant rainfall, but has been niggardly with natural resources. Of volcanic origin, the country is mountainous. There are no large plains. The soil is infertile. Only 16 percent of the land is arable; and every year, valuable land is being taken up for the building of homes and factories.

Most of Japan enjoys a temperate climate; the warm Japan Current and the seasonal winds exert a moderating influence. Extending over the same latitudinal spread as Maine to Georgia, Japan enjoys a similar range of climate.

Abundant rainfall accounts for a very high humidity, especially during the summertime; but the mist and haze which veil the landscape in the spring have added an especially delicate and esthetic touch to

Japanese painting and poetry.

Mt. Fuji symbolizes Japan. This beautifully symmetrical extinct volcano rises in solitary splendor on a flat plain to a height of 12,395 feet. For centuries, the Japanese have reveled in the majestic beauty of Mt. Fuji. Enraptured poets have written ecstatic verses about beloved Fujiyama, while painters have captured the sacred mountain in all its varying moods.

The whole Japanese archipelago is in the earthquake belt, with scores of active volcanoes, making it a veritable seismographic laboratory. Because there are some 1,500 earthquakes a year, in the past buildings were restricted to 200 feet in height. However, since the war, improved techniques have brought about the lifting of these restrictions and a 17-story hotel was built in Tokyo for the 1964 Olympics. Today, much taller buildings are under construction.

Few places in Japan are far removed from the mountains or the sea. Consequently, people take readily to mountain-climbing, hiking, skiing, swimming, and sailing. Rivers, however, are small and short, the longest—the Shinano River—being only about 230 miles. There are a few lakes. The largest and best known is Lake Biwa near Kyoto. The Inland Sea, nearly enclosed by the three islands of Honshu, Kyushu, and Shikoku, is more like a huge lake; it is one of the most beautiful scenic spots in the world. Japan's long shoreline of roughly 17,000 miles of coast, with its deep indentations, provides beautiful promontories, numerous inlets, and fine harbors.

FLORA AND FAUNA

Luxuriant growth covering the mountainous slopes adds to the beauty of the landscape. Everywhere, even in the middle of paddy fields,.there are wooded areas marking village shrines.

The forests provide timber, charcoal, wood pulp, and edibles such as nuts, fruits, bamboo shoots, and mushrooms.

Flowering plum and cherry are highly prized. Cherry blossoms have always been cherished as a symbol of Japanese courage and loyalty. Maple, chrysanthemum, wisteria, iris, azalea, and peony also rank high as objects of esthetic appreciation.

FUJIYAMA   Japan's sacred mountain, visible here through a screen of cherry blossoms, is seen from Mito-hama Beach.

Japan is free of dangerous beasts; only the wolf, the wild boar, and a few poisonous snakes have been natural enemies to man. Birds of all sorts thrive in Japan—herons, hawks, owls, crows, cuckoos, nightingales, warblers, and sparrows; song birds in particular are greatly prized.

A CULTURALLY UNIFIED NATION

Culturally homogeneous to a degree hardly matched anywhere, the Japanese have developed a strong sense of national solidarity—even

kinship. Although in origin heterogeneous, cultural assimilation over a period of nearly 2,000 years has completely obliterated original ethnic differences, even though differing physical types can still be quite easily identified.

Japanese belongs to the Ural-Altaic family of languages and is related to Finnish, Hungarian, Mongolian, Korean, and Okinawan. The written language is a mixture of Chinese ideographs and a syllabary devised by the Japanese in the eighth and ninth centuries.

After a period of imitating Chinese prose and poetry, the Japanese developed their own literature. The *Tale of Genji*, a realistic novel of the early 11th century written by Lady Murasaki, antedates Chaucer by two centuries; this work is older than anything of its genre in Western or Chinese literature. Since the 19th century, Japanese letters have fallen strongly under Western influence.

POPULATION

With a population of close to 100 million, Japan is the seventh most populous country in the world. In land area, it ranks about fiftieth. Density is very heavy, with 682 persons per square mile. There are 4,266 persons per arable square mile, which makes Japan one of the most heavily populated countries in the world. With a birth rate of 17 per 1,000 and a death rate of 7 per 1,000, Japan increases its population each year by approximately one million.

Until the 20th century, Japan's population was predominantly rural. Then, rapid industrialization accelerated urbanization. Yet in the 1950's, 65 percent of the people were still living in the country. In the 1960's, a reversal took place; today, 65 percent of the population is urban.

There are now seven cities which have more than a million in population. Twenty percent of Japan lives in these seven cities. Tokyo, the world's largest metropolis, boasts more than 10 million people. Osaka, the leading commercial and industrial center, has more than

NTH CENTURY PAGODA   Daigoji Temple in Kyoto was built in 951 at the nmand of the Emperor Murakami. The nine metal rings on the peak of this five-ried edifice constitute a stylized symbol which portrays the tiered umbrella indicative royalty.

three million; Nagoya, the city of modern industry, over one and a half million; Yokohama, the largest port, almost a million and a half; Kyoto, the ancient capital, a million and a quarter; Kobe, the leading Asian trade port, and Kita-Kyushu, the nation's largest steel-producing center, slightly over one million. In all, there are 560 cities in Japan with a population in excess of 30,000; of these, 115 are cities of 100,000 or more, and 45 are cities of 200,000 or more.

RELIGIOUS AFFILIATIONS

Religion has always been a pervasive force in Japanese life, even though the people's religiosity may not be apparent. The three main religions are Shinto, Buddhism, and Christianity. There are no Hindus, Jews, or Muslims among the Japanese.

Traditionally, there have been three distinct aspects of Shinto: State Shinto, sectarian Shinto, and popular Shinto. State Shinto was set up by the Meiji government in 1868 as a means of achieving nationalism. Every Japanese automatically became a State Shintoist even though he was a member of a regular Shinto, Buddhist, or Christian church.

Sectarian Shinto, with a total membership of over 25 million, consists of more than 20 sects. Each of these sects was founded by a spiritual leader to meet the special needs of his followers; each sect constitutes an exclusive church.

Popular Shinto operates on a local level; it has its own shrines and tutelary deities. These local shrines are the scene of all sorts of parochial celebrations and festivals.

In Japanese religious life, Shinto and Buddhism play different roles. Temporal matters, the celebration of auspicious occasions such as birthdays and harvest festivals, and general village festivities are handled by Shinto shrines. Grave rituals, especially those relating to the after life—funerals, memorial services, and the propitiation of the spirits of the dead—fall under Buddhist auspices.

Buddhism, first introduced in the sixth century from Korea, today claims more than 65 million followers. The Shin sect has the largest following; but the Zen sect has left the greatest imprint on Japanese culture and on everyday life, too. The tea ceremony, the arrangement of flowers, residential and garden architecture, painting, poetry, and many other aspects of Japanese life developed under Zen influence.

Christianity, introduced in 1549 by the Jesuit, Francis Xavier, gained some 150,000 converts during its first three decades of missionary activity. Proselytization was completely banned in the 17th century. For the next two centuries, Christianity survived underground. Today, Japanese Christians total approximately 850,000, less than one percent of the population. There are more Protestants than Roman Catholics, the former comprising little over 50 percent.

SOCIAL STRUCTURE

At present, Japan is the only Asian country with a large middle class. In a survey conducted in 1961, 76 percent of those polled identified themselves as belonging to the middle class.

In spite of the change in its legal status, the family remains the basic unit of Japanese society. Even though parental authority is no longer what it used to be, family influence is by no means negligible. Primogeniture is gone; the legal position of women has been enhanced. Although freedom of choice in the selection of a spouse is guaranteed by the Constitution, marriages are still arranged by go-betweens. Proper family background is still enormously important in securing a desirable marriage or a successful career.

Kinship organizations, as such, no longer exist; but the right kind of family ties continues to be of decisive importance in insuring success socially, economically, and politically. Status consciousness remains strong.

Since the end of World War II, the businessman enjoys greater prestige than ever, while the intellectuals and academicians have suffered a decline in prestige. However, as the result of defeat in the last war and the subsequent demilitarization imposed by the Constitution, it is the army and its personnel who have suffered the greatest loss of status.

Since the end of the war, Japan has become extensively Westernized in its tastes; this applies to food, clothing, housing, art, music, litera-

KABUKI THEATER   Built in 1958, this playhouse in Osaka is patterned after the Momoyama architectural style (14th to 16th centuries). The edifice is of steel and concrete construction; the roof is covered with copper plate.

FISHERMAN   This gloved fisherman has just pulled a giant crab out of his net. He works from a small boat, one of a fleet centering around a mother ship that has facilities for refrigerating, processing, and canning the catch at sea.

BUDDHIST SHRINE
The Byodoin Temple at Uji was built in 1053 by the Fujiwara family.

SACRED DEER   Some 600 sacred deer are at large in the vast park of Kasuga Shrine, located in Nara not far from Osaka. Every year, the deer are rounded up by game-keepers wearing happi coats. Temple priests offer ceremonial prayers for the well-being and increase of the herd. The stags are lassoed and carried to the de-horning mat. This stag's head will be placed on the small pillow and his horns will be neatly removed with an ordinary hand-saw. The process is painless. The antlers are dedicated on an altar by the priest. When the hornless stags return to the herd, they soon abandon their habit of fighting. They become monogamous, settling down with a single doe instead of battling the other stags to gain control of the females of the herd.

ture, and social life. The increasing use of electrical appliances and electronic devices such as stoves, refrigerators, washing machines, vacuum cleaners, blenders, toasters, radio and television sets, record players, and tape recorders not only evidences affluence but reflects new tastes.

Apartment house communities have appeared on the periphery of large cities. Westernization of the pattern of life has resulted in the weakening of traditional social ties and the strengthening of the position of the individual.

EDUCATION AND LITERACY

Japan has one of the highest literacy rates in the world—something like 98 percent, which puts her among the leading half dozen nations. Compulsory education up to nine years of age keeps 99 percent of the children in school. It is this high literacy rate which has enabled the nation to become one of the world's leaders in industry and trade. Faced with the stringent demands of a highly industrialized society, the Ministry of Education anticipates the extension of the compulsory education requirement to a total of 12 years.

Education is one of the most effective methods of achieving status in Japan. A university degree, especially one from the University of Tokyo, is a passport to, if not a guarantee of, a good position, a desirable marriage, and a successful career. Education can indeed more than compensate for the lack of wealth or family background.

The shortage of manpower created by the rapid expansion of industries has forced the government to establish additional technical schools and to expand the engineering departments of the universities to turn out more engineers and technicians. Mass communication media have been developed to a point where they are easily the equal of those of the Western nations. A half dozen daily newspapers with a national circulation are published in Tokyo.

Japan publishes more books than any other Asian country: Tokyo is the publishing center of the Orient. Journals and magazines, both scholarly and popular, run into the hundreds. To satisfy a voracious reading public, the leading dailies in Tokyo publish weekly magazines, not as supplements—but as separate publications.

DOWNTOWN KYOTO *This is one of the many shopping streets of Kyoto, the ancient capital of Japan, known for its old and beautiful temples. The lanterns over-head advertise an afternoon dance performance by student geisha girls.*

JAPANESE ARTS

Sensitive awareness of nature is the basis of Japanese art. This traditional approach to art has survived the onslaught of modernization that has influenced Japanese taste in the past hundred years. The emphasis on the traditional appears particularly in the art of the woodblock print, which first flourished in the 18th and 19th centuries. Since the end of World War II, there has been a strong revival in woodblock printing. The medium remains much the same today as it was in early days, but the subjects nowadays have become untraditional and even international.

In painting, the traditional is waging a struggle for survival against great odds. Western forms and techniques are gaining ground with new styles such as abstract painting. In sculpture, Westernization has almost taken over completely.

Japanese architecture reflects the durability of the traditional, which is being used to produce a new style designed to meet modern requirements. Japanese influence on home architecture and landscaping throughout the world, and especially in the United States, has been conspicuous.

In the art of gardens and landscaping, the Japanese have created unique forms. Outstanding examples are the Katsura Imperial Villa, the Shugakuin Villa, the moss garden of the "Moss Temple," and the highly sophisticated sand and rock garden of Ryoanji Temple, all in Kyoto.

Native Japanese music has been mainly theatrical or incidental music employed to give atmosphere and to enhance the meaning of a dance or a story. As such, it is perhaps the most highly refined theatrical music in the world. But the introduction of Western music in the late

DRY LANDSCAPE The garden this 14th century Zen-Buddhist shr the Daitokuji Temple in Kyoto, typical example of the Japanese landscape. Built by a priest in the century, the spread of raked, white s represents the sea and rocks, and c fully trimmed trees represent the sa and the mountains.

19th century has had an important impact on present-day Japanese music.

Eclecticism has been quite noticeable among Japanese composers, who make use of traditional Japanese elements derived from dance music, drama, and ancient court music. Symphonies have been composed and performed by the Japanese. In Tokyo alone there are five flourishing symphony orchestras. In addition, choral singing has spread, and glee clubs have become so popular that the visits of the Harvard and Yale Glee Clubs were memorable events for Japanese music lovers.

Kabuki drama is internationally known and appreciated. It is drama with three component parts—music, dance, and acting. Even more classical is the *Noh* drama, which goes back some five centuries. Along with these traditional forms, Western-style drama also flourishes in Japan.

The Japanese have adapted Western opera and musical shows to their own themes and tastes. For example, Puccini's *Madama Butterfly* has been adapted to the puppet theater. Musical comedies have become immensely popular, thanks to the Takarazuka Theater which has been staging thrilling extravaganzas. An all-Japanese cast put on *My Fair Lady* in Tokyo, and it was a big hit. Only recently, *Hello Dolly*, featuring Mary Martin, was a sensation in Tokyo.

TELEVISION AND THE CINEMA

Japan is second only to the United States in the number of radio and television sets in use. Radio stations are numerous; their programs offer a rich variety including broadcasts in foreign languages, high school subjects, and adult education programs. Television has become big business in the last 10 years and is booming.

Japan's motion picture industry leads the world in the number of films produced. It has achieved a world-wide reputation through production of such prize-winning films as *Rashomon, Gate of Hell, The Seven Samurai* (Magnificent Seven), and *Woman of the Dunes*.

No restriction of any kind is placed on freedom of speech in films or in the press.

THE ROYAL FAMILY *In a sitting room in the Imperial Palace in Tokyo during 1964, Japan's royal family gathers for a photograph. Prince Hiro, the young son of the Crown Prince, wears "tabi," the heavy socks with a separate compartment for the large toe designed to accommodate sandal thongs. Around him are his elders, the Empress Nagako, Emperor Hirohito, Crown Prince Akihito, Crown Princess Michiko, and Prince Yoshi, the Emperor's second son. The Crown Princess was the first commoner ever to marry into the imperial family.*

HEALTH AND LIFE EXPECTANCY

Sanitation in Japan is on a par with that in the advanced Western nations. Japan is the only country in Asia where it is possible to drink tap water without risk of catching a contagious disease. There are no epidemic outbreaks of dysentery, malaria, typhoid fever, cholera, typhus, or yellow fever, still so common to much of Asia.

Life expectancy has risen to 67.2 years for males and 72.3 years for females, putting Japan among the world's highest 10 countries in this respect. The birth control program has been a success, and the birth rate has dropped to an unprecedented low of 17 per thousand.

ECONOMIC FACTORS

The main sources of national livelihood are agriculture, fisheries, manufacturing, and processing.

The salient fact of the Japanese economy is the absence of raw materials. Japan's mineral resources are negligible—entirely inadequate for her industrial requirements. She has only sulfur in abundance, a limited supply of low-grade coal, very little oil, no iron ore, no zinc, no lead, and no bauxite, tungsten, mercury, or chromium. She has but a token supply of copper, silver, and gold. Nearly all raw materials have to be imported to keep her industries supplied.

Despite this basic deficiency, Japan has achieved a commanding position as an industrial power. In crude steel production and petroleum refining, she ranks third in the world, following the United States and the Soviet Union. In shipbuilding, she has led the world since 1956, supplying 45 percent of the world tonnage in 1964. In automobile production she now ranks fourth.

In several areas of industrial technology, Japan has overtaken the West and is now exporting her own inventions. Outstanding examples are the Esaki tunnel diode widely used in electronic devices, and an improved memory system for computers designed to work 10 times faster than those previously used. In railroading and shipbuilding technology, she is in the forefront of the industrial nations. She leads the world in the production of cameras, bicycles, motorcycles, transistorized radio and television receiving sets, and electron microscopes. In the production of electronic computers, regular television and radio receiving sets, and motor trucks, she ranks second only to the United States.

Japan must literally trade or perish, for trade is the life blood of the nation. Unless she sells the products of her factories, she cannot buy the raw materials required for her industries. It is an imperative of her very survival that she have access to the world's markets as well as to the sources of raw materials.

Japan's most important trade partner is the United States, with a total volume of over $3.5 billion a year.

For a fuel-scarce economy like Japan's, power development is a major problem. Finding energy sources has become a national obsession. Although thermal and hydroelectric power plants are used throughout the country, both industry and the government are vigorously pushing the development of atomic power for industrial use. The Institute of Nuclear Research and Development at Tokai village, some 90 miles from Tokyo, is Japan's counterpart of America's Oak Ridge.

Unexpected growth in industry has brought about an acute labor shortage that was not fully anticipated. This has enabled automation in industry to proceed at a rapid pace, without the opposition of labor.

The labor movement, promoted under the aegis of the U.S. occupation authorities, has come of age. Today, membership in the labor unions is approximately nine and a half million. The largest and best-known group is the General Council of Labor Unions; it has over four million members.

AGRICULTURE AND FISHING

Until the end of the war, approximately 48 out of 100 Japanese depended on agriculture for a livelihood. Today, this figure has dropped to 26. As mechanization is accelerated, the percentage of people employed in agriculture decreases. No less than 65 percent of Japanese farm households are using motorized equipment. Intensive mechanized cultivation is yielding spectacular results. Rice production has been breaking records year after year, with the result that there is no longer the need to import rice.

The average holding of two and a half acres per farm family has remained unchanged; but as a result of the land reform instituted by

MARUNOUCHI DISTRICT   *These modern buildings are in the commercial center of Tokyo. The large square is called the Tokyo Station Plaza, and the Tokyo Station itself is to be seen in the lower right-hand corner.*

NIGHT-TIME NEONS Every sign represents a separate bar on this street in downtown Tokyo.

the U. S. occupation authorities, more than 80 percent of the farmers now own the land they cultivate.

Silk, once the great cash crop, is no longer an important factor in the farm economy. Perhaps the most important of the common vegetables grown is the giant radish or *daikon,* truly a versatile vegetable which the Japanese eat fresh, cooked, dehydrated, or pickled.

Fish has always been an important part of the national diet. Today, the per capita consumption of marine products is the highest in the world.

A unique product of Japan is the cultured pearl, the result of Japanese technique. The most famous pearl farm, visited by thousands of tourists, is located at the entrance to Ise Bay on the southeastern coast of Honshu. Interestingly, the entire operation depends completely on the skill and stamina of the women divers.

SUMO CEREMONIAL A w
tler who has won his bout crouc
to receive the prize. Packets of mor
done up in rice paper and ribbons,
delivered to the winner on a woo
fan by the chief referee. Onos
Shikimori, the referee shown here,
been famous for 60 years. He is kno
for his flowing white beard, his ex
lent announcer's voice, and the gr
ful manipulations of his fan.
kimono is embroidered in gold
black, and he wears the buckram
of a Buddhist priest, traditional
all Sumo arbiters.

BULLFIGHT ON SHIKOKU Bullfights
are staged in rural communities near the shores
of the Inland Sea, but no blood is shed, for in
Japan the bulls fight each other—men do not
fight bulls. That bull which is still willing to
fight after smashing his head against the other
bull's head for half an hour is declared the
winner. Usually, one of the bulls finally gets
discouraged and runs off despite encouragement from his owner and bystanders who have
placed bets on his endurance.

SHORE RESORT On
the seacoast of Honshu,
not far from crowded To-
kyo, Oiso Long Beach is
a popular summer retreat.
Here bathers relax under
square umbrellas around a
swimming pool that over-
looks the sea.

RODEO   *Every year, Noma Oi Matsuri, the Wild Horsebreaking Festival, is held on a plain near Soma in central Honshu. The villages of the district are famous for their splendid horses and skilled horsemen. During the festival, they re-enact a feudal mustering. Wearing the knightly armor of the Samurai, they gather as they would have gathered centuries ago, if called to duty by the lord of the fief. Boys in Samurai armor are used as couriers.*

BASEBALL   *Many boys would like to play in the Japanese big leagues. This youngster, in the courtyard of his pleasant home, has improvised a bat, but is the proud possessor of a regulation glove.*

SUMO BOUT   *Gigantic wrestlers, their hair pulled back into a topknot, wait for the referee to signal the fight's commencement. In this sport, which dates back almost 2000 years, every gesture follows a formal pattern set by tradition.*

RAILROAD AND HIGHWAY SYSTEMS

Japan's rail transportation, which had its beginnings in the 1870's, is one of the most efficiently run systems in the world. The National Railway Corporation operates more than 12,740 miles of road. Private railways, totaling more than 4,650 miles, do not compete with the National Railways, but rather serve as feeders and interurban carriers. A number of these lines own the department stores at their terminals, engage in a real estate business which promotes housing developments along their routes, operate resort hotels and travel agencies, and conduct tours.

With the recent advent of super highways, the traffic pattern is undergoing rapid change. Motor transport is beginning to encroach upon the long-standing primacy of the railroads.

Subway systems operate in Tokyo and Osaka. Nagoya is slated to have an underground by 1985.

GOVERNMENTAL ORGANIZATION

The new postwar Constitution, which went into effect on May 3, 1947, vests sovereignty in the people and makes the popularly elected Diet the highest organ of state power and the sole law-making body. The bicameral legislature consists of the 250-member upper chamber called the House of Councillors and a 467-member House of Representatives. One hundred members of the House of Councillors are elected from the nation at large, while 150 represent the constituents of the election districts. All serve for a term of six years. The members of the House of Representatives are elected for four years; but, unlike the upper chamber, the lower house is subject to dissolution by the government.

Under the old Meiji Constitution, the Emperor was the head of state at the very apex of the political structure. It was from him that all political power flowed. Under the present Constitution, he is "the symbol of State and the unity of the people"; he only performs ceremonial functions. This makes the Cabinet, headed by the Prime Minister, the important executive organ. The Prime Minister, who must be a Diet

THE MARRIED ROCKS OF FUTAMIGAURA
Off the Ise Peninsula near Nagoya, Shinto priests married the "male" rock to the small "female" rock many years ago, joining them together with ropes of rice straw in an ancient religious ceremony. They also erected a shrine on the larger rock. The family name given to the couple is Meotoshima. Every summer, thousands of Japanese set out on a pilgrimage, visiting the rocks at dawn to view the sun rising exactly between the rocks. Such a pilgrimage is alleged to guarantee happiness for the ensuing year.

member as well as president of the majority party, is elected by the whole Diet. Constitutionally, at least one-half of the Cabinet members must have seats in the Diet. In spite of the constitutional provision that the Diet is the highest organ of state power, in practice, it is the Cabinet which initiates the legislative program, administers the laws, manages foreign affairs, decides fiscal and financial policies, prepares the budget, and isuues orders and instructions to administrative officials. The Prime Minister's Office is the nerve center for the planning and administration of national affairs.

The independence of the judiciary is firmly established by the Constitution. The Chief Judge of the Supreme Court occupies a rank equivalent to that of the Prime Minister. Introduced after the end of the war, the doctrine of judicial review gives the Supreme Court the power to declare laws and administrative acts unconstitutional. The composition of the 15-member Supreme Court calls for 10 legal experts of more than 20 years' professional standing, but allows for five learned personages who need not be jurists.

ASAKUSA DISTRICT This is Tokyo's street of theatres in the heart of the capital's amusement center. The many signs proclaim titles of motion picture films being shown, some of which are of Western origin.

RENUNCIATION OF WAR

The unique feature of the Japanese Constitution is the renunciation of war as a right of a sovereign nation. The use of force, as a means of settling international disputes, has been disavowed. Land, sea, air forces, and all war-making potentials have been abandoned along with the right of belligerency. However, the right of self defense is acknowledged, and "self defense forces" of some 250,000 troops are maintained. The actual defense of Japan against external aggression is a responsibility undertaken by the United States. As a result of Japan's exposure to the atomic bomb, there is powerful resistance to rearmament, and to nuclear testing by any nation.

THE CONSERVATIVE LIBERAL DEMOCRATIC PARTY

Political parties in Japan date back to 1881, making them the oldest in Asia. The conservative Liberal Democratic Party, resulting from the merger of two conservative parties in 1955, has been in power without interruption since the end of World War II. It is supported largely by big business, and pursues policies favorable to the business community. In domestic policy it stands for the healthy growth of economy and greater government spending in the public sector. In foreign policy it maintains close cooperation and collaboration with the United States and pursues an anti-Communist policy. The Liberal Democratic Party is headed by Prime Minister Eisaku Sato.

The Prime Minister was born in 1901. He is the younger brother of two-time Prime Minister Nobusuke Kishi. He became Secretary General of the Liberal Party in 1950 and won the premiership in 1964, succeeding Prime Minister Ikeda who resigned because of ill health.

JAPAN SOCIALIST PARTY

The Japan Socialist Party, which ranks second in the Diet, is the party of the working classes. It is supported by the powerful General Council of Labor Unions, and is strongly anti-big-business. Although it is gaining strength, it has not yet been able to provide effective opposition to the conservative party. This party favors complete disarmament, a neutral Japan, and a ban on nuclear weapons. It adamantly opposes any change in the Constitution.

SOCIAL DEMOCRATIC PARTY

The Social Democratic Party, which broke off from the more leftist Japan Socialist Party, is actually closer to the conservative party than to the Japan Socialist Party. This party is opposed to any change in the Constitution. Like the Japan Socialist Party, the Social Democratic

Party would like to see possession of nuclear bombs banned completely, and advocates world disarmament.

THE SOKA GAKKAI

An organization which has made inroads into Japanese politics in a sensational way is the *Soka Gakkai* (Value-Creating Society). A well-organized and disciplined lay Buddhist group, it has some 15 million adherents recruited mainly from the lower middle class and from the urban poor. As a middle-class party with strong evangelical drive, it aims to establish a new system loosely translated as "new socialism."

The group stresses firm establishment of parliamentary democracy, a welfare state, and elimination of corruption. It opposes any change in the Constitution, and opposes the use of nuclear weapons. To achieve these goals, in 1964 the *Soka Gakkai* launched the *Komeito* (Clean Government Party). This party won 11 new seats in the House of Councillors election of 1965 to become the third-ranking party in the upper house.

INTERNATIONAL AFFILIATIONS

Twenty years after World War II, Japan has finally come out of the shadow of defeat. She is a member of the United Nations, and acts within the framework and spirit of the Charter. She participates in all the U.N. agencies and is a member of the Colombo Plan, International Monetary Fund, World Bank, General Agreement on Tariff and Trade, and the Organization for Economic Cooperation and Development. She is bound with the United States by the United States–Japan Security Treaty.

Japan dispenses an impressive amount of technical assistance to the developing nations of Asia, the Middle East, Africa, and Latin America. Japan is solidly committed to the Free World, but also feels close to the Afro-Asian group of nations, with sympathy and understanding of their hopes, fears, and aspirations. In her fervent desire for world peace, Japan earnestly wants to become an effective mediator between East and West to help resolve such conflicts as threaten to precipitate a nuclear holocaust.

AINU CHIEF *In northern Hokkaido, the Ainu, the aboriginal inhabitants of Japan, still retain vestiges of their ancient dress and customs. This Ainu Chief and his wife have come to see a bronze monument erected in honor of 15 Karafuto sled-dogs. These Japanese huskies, bred on icy Hokkaido, had been abandoned during an emergency that ended an Antarctic expedition.*

TOKYO

With a population of more than 10 million, Tokyo is the world's largest metropolis.

The city sprawls over a huge area and is dotted with numerous parks and gardens. Only recently have high-rise buildings become common. Downtown Tokyo is every bit as modern as Washington, D. C. or London. It has a network of subways that include the largest subway station in the world. It also boasts the largest office building, bowling alley, and busiest railway station in Asia. Traffic congestion and noise have become a serious problem because of the rapid increase in automobiles in the narrow streets. Unlike American cities, there has been no zoning in Tokyo.

OSAKA

The second largest city in Japan, Osaka has a population of three million. Founded in the fourth century A.D., it is the oldest port and financial center of the nation. Osaka Castle, originally built in the 16th century, is a prominent landmark. Osaka is also noted for its numerous canals.

KYOTO

This city served as the nation's capital for more than ten centuries, from 794 to 1868. It is the only large city that has managed to preserve the charm, elegance, and quiet refinement of old Japan. In the center of

Kyoto, the original capital as it was laid out in the eighth century is preserved to this day. It has a population of 1,400,000 and ranks fifth in size among Japan's cities.

Primarily a religious and cultural center, Kyoto is the headquarters of many Buddhist sects. It has escaped industrialization and remains a city of craft industries, producing porcelain, bamboo, cloisonné, bronze wares, and silk textiles. Its *Gion* festival is one of the highlights of the city, with geisha girls participating in the dancing.

The old Imperial Palace, a beautiful monument of early days, is located here. Other famous landmarks include the Katsura Imperial Villa and the Shugakuin Villa, both known for their exquisite landscaping. Ryoanji, a Buddhist temple, is famed for its sand and rock garden; while Saihoji, another Buddhist temple, is noted for its beautiful moss garden. Art treasures abound in this old capital.

OTHER CITIES

Japan's three other major cities are Nagoya, Yokohama, and Kobe. Nagoya, the third largest city, has a population of almost two million. It is much older than Tokyo and serves as the industrial and commercial metropolis of central Japan.

EISAKU SATO   The current Prime Minister was born in Yamaguchi prefecture. He is a graduate of Tokyo Imperial University, and entered government service immediately upon graduation. He held important positions in the Conservative Party, and served as minister in several post-War cabinets. He is the younger brother of former Premier Kishi. Sato assumed office in 1964.

Yokohama was just a quiet fishing village until 1858 when the first commercial treaty was signed with the United States. Since then it has become the chief port for trans-Pacific trade.

Kobe came into existence in the 1860's. It is the chief port for trade with Asian countries and Europe.

CHITOSHI YANAGA

CHILDREN OF AOMORI   *Gaily costumed children of this city on the northern coast of Honshu pull the float which is their contribution to the traditional celebration of the rice harvest. The figures on the float are from a Japanese legend which tells about an evil man about to receive his just deserts from a good man. The sign on the front names the two persons who were responsible for its construction.*

IN BRIEF

AREA
142,726 square miles; slightly smaller than Montana.

TERRAIN
The four main islands—Honshu, Kyushu, Hokkaido, and Shikoku—with numerous smaller islands and islets extend in a 1,200-mile curve off the northeast coast of Asia. Numerous earthquakes have created great variety in surface features. The islands are volcanic and rocky, with sharply indented coast lines. Fertile land is limited; there are several small alluvial lowland areas. Rivers are short, falling steeply at many places on the way to the sea; they provide excellent power potential but none is navigable. About 500 volcanoes, some still active, form the highest ranges. Asama, Aso, Kirishima, and Mihara are active; but the extinct volcano, Fujiyama, is the highest point (12,395 feet), and is famous for its beauty and its symbolic significance to the Japanese.

FLORA
Forest cover is over half subtropical, a mixture of broadleaf evergreens and conifers. Temperate forests are largely oak, maple, and elm. Flowering azalea, plum, cherry, and chrysanthemum are famous.

FAUNA
Bear, fox, wolf, deer, rabbit, squirrel, bats, one species of monkey, and many varieties of bird. Reptile species are few, although there are two varieties of venomous snakes.

CLIMATE
Mild and temperate, except on the northern island, Hokkaido, where the climate is much like that of Maine. Rainfall is abundant; most of the precipitation occurs during May and June. Moderated by the warm Japan Current, the average yearly temperature is close to 72°F., with summer temperatures up to 90°F.

CAPITAL
Tokyo, with about 10.17 million inhabitants in 1962.

OTHER CITIES
Osaka, 3.11 million; Nagoya, 1.66 million; Yokohama, 1.46 million; Kyoto, 1.3 million; Kobe, 1.15 million. Some 32 cities with more than 200,000 inhabitants include Kita-Kyushu, Fukuoka, Kawasaki, Sapporo, Hiroshima, Nagasaki, and Kagoshima.

COUNTRYWOMEN *On a stream too shallow for oars, these peasants, wearing hats of rice straw, pole the boat which carries their products to market. Such costumes are common on the farms.*

MODERN TRANSPORT
The new express Tokaido Rail Line is running across the Meishin Super Highway, a thruway between Magoya and Kobe. The train roaring over the trestle averages 155 miles per hour. Of very recent design, it is called the Hikari, which means "light."

FESTIVAL OF THE LOVER STARS
Sendai, on the east coast of Honshu Island, is famous for its paper decorations. No other town in Japan creates such elaborate ornaments for its festivals. According to fable, Aquila and Vega are in love. Because they live on opposite sides of the Milky Way, they are able to meet only once a year, on the 7th day of the 7th month. Here, crowds gather on the main street to celebrate the yearly meeting of the astral pair.

EW YEAR RECESS   On January 4th, the long New Year holiday ends and workers urn to their offices. Many young secretaries wear the traditional kimono to work on s one day when wishes for the New Year are exchanged.

POPULATION   98.5 million estimated in late 1964. Density is about 682 per square mile, or 4,266 per square mile of arable land. Annual rate of increase is 0.9 percent.

ETHNIC GROUPS   Original ethnic differences have disappeared due to assimilation and resulting cultural and linguistic homogeneity. Only the Ainu of the north retain mere vestiges of their former distinctive customs.

LANGUAGES   Japanese is universally spoken; it is a Ural-Altaic tongue related to Finnish, Hungarian, Okinawan, and Korean, and is written in a mixture of Chinese characters and a syllabary, *kana,* devised a thousand years ago by the Japanese. English, a compulsory subject during junior high school and later school years, is the most commonly used foreign language.

RELIGION   The indigenous faith, Shinto, has about 38 million adherents in a variety of sects; since 1945 it has received no state support. Religious teachings are forbidden in the public schools; freedom of religion is guaranteed. The usual faith is a combination of Shinto and Buddhism—there are about 65 million Buddhists. Christians, two-thirds of whom are Protestants, number about 850,000.

DATE OF INDEPENDENCE   On May 3, 1947, the present constitution came into force. On April 28, 1952, the peace treaty ending World War II came into force and Japan regained its sovereignty.

FORM OF GOVERNMENT   Constitutional monarchy. The duties of the Emperor are ceremonial. Executive power rests with the Prime Minister, who must be a civilian, and his Cabinet. The Prime Minister is elected by and is responsible to the Diet, which exercises legislative power. The Diet includes a 467-member House of Representatives, directly elected for four years by citizens over 20, and a 250-member House of Councillors, half of whom are elected every three years. The House of Councillors is directly elected; 100 members are elected from the nation at large, the remainder from the prefectures. Local government in the prefectures is wholly elective. The judiciary is independent, and the police are controlled by the central government. The constitution renounces war as an instrument of national policy and, instead of conventional military forces, the country has limited "Self-Defense Forces." Japan is a member of the United Nations.

EDUCATION

In 1961, there were over 26,700 primary schools, with 349,000 teachers and 11.81 million pupils; over 12,000 junior high schools, with 231,600 teachers and 6.92 million pupils; 3,600 high schools, with 134,400 teachers and 3.12 million students; 290 junior colleges, with 6,750 teachers and 93,400 students. Over 70 institutions of university rank included six large national universities. The 250 colleges and universities had over 45,000 instructors and 670,000 students. The first nine years of school are compulsory; over 99 percent of school-age children are in school. More than 98 percent of the people are literate.

HEALTH FACILITIES

In 1960, there were almost 100,000 doctors, 32,250 dentists, 52,400 midwives, and 58,400 pharmacists. Nearly 6,100 hospitals with 500,000 beds included 500 mental hospitals, 600 tuberculosis hospitals, and 14 leprosy hospitals. Life expectancy is approximately 70 years for a newborn child. Health conditions are on a par with those of other advanced nations; there are no uncontrolled endemic or epidemic diseases. About 90 percent of the population is covered by various forms of government health insurance.

CULTURAL FACILITIES

In 1961, there were 157 daily newspapers, over a third with both morning and evening editions; total circulation was 39.14 million, indicating that over two-fifths of the people buy a paper every day. Over half of the 22,000 books published in 1962 were first editions; about 1,200 translations, close to half from English, were printed. In 1962, the thriving film industry released 650 films for showing in over 6,700 cinemas with a yearly attendance of 662.3 million. One person in five owned a radio; one in eight owned a television set. Television programs in color have been broadcast since 1960. Traditional and indigenous arts, such as *Noh* plays and *Kabuki* drama have felt the impact of new media but receive considerable support from the intellectual community.

CURRENCY AND FINANCE

The *yen* is valued at 0.00246853 grams of fine gold, or 28¢ in U.S. currency; 360 *yen* equal $1.00. The national budget

SAKURAJIMA RADISHES—A farmer, and the young girls who help him, harvest the giant, white radishes which grow only in the neighborhood of Sakurajima Island in southern Kyushu. These radishes will be cut up and pickled. Four of these monsters will be as much as a girl can carry on the A-frame strapped to her back.

RICE FIELD This young girl is a farm worker in the Murayama district. The long, fingerless gloves are protection both from scratchy stalks and sunlight. The Japanese woman has always been careful to protect herself from a coarse suntan just as the Western woman has been eager to acquire a light sunburn.

NOBLEMAN'S VILLA *Suizenji Garden in Kumamoto, Kyushu was planned for the Hosokawa family in the 17th century. With its miniature hills and islet-filled lake, it is designed to afford a pleasing vista from every angle of the grounds.*

for fiscal 1964 was expected to balance at close to $8.26 billion.

INDUSTRY AND PRODUCTION

One of the greatest manufacturing nations in the world, Japan had a national income of over $42.83 billion in 1962. The Gross National Product is estimated to be between $65 and $70 billion. In 1960, some nine million workers were employed in over 553,000 manufacturing industries, almost two million were employed in construction industries, and over 500,000 worked in 10,000 mines. Textiles, iron and steel, and chemicals are the three primary industries. In 1962, production included 1.21 million metric tons of iron, 27.55 million metric tons of steel, 28.79 million metric tons of cement, 69,000 metric tons of synthetic rubber, and 1.15 billion metric tons of fertilizer. Japan is the world's largest shipbuilding nation; 2.18 million gross registered tons of shipping were launched in 1962. Production of machinery and electronic equipment is increasing rapidly; in 1962, over 1.12 million motor vehicles, 15.48 million radios, 4.89 million television sets, about 2 million cameras, and computers and automation equipment were produced. Electric power production was 140.38 million kilowatt hours.

CROPS: Rice is grown on over half of the arable land; modern agricultural machinery and techniques have succeeded in making the crop—16.26 million metric tons in 1962—sufficient for internal consumption. Other important crops are wheat, corn, barley, oats, peanuts, soybeans, sweet potatoes, tea, sugar beets, fruit, and tobacco.

LIVESTOCK: In 1962, there were one million dairy cattle, 2.3 million draft cattle, 4.03 million pigs, 504,000 sheep, 547,000 horses, and 498,000 goats.

FISHERIES: Japan is the world's greatest fishing nation. The 1962 catch included 6.86 million metric tons of fish and 124,000 metric tons of whale and sperm oil from 14,000 whales.

MINING: Coal, lignite, natural gas, petroleum, copper, manganese, and sulfur are among the mineral products. The sparse mineral resources are carefully exploited.

TRADE

Japan's chief imports are wheat, sugar, raw cotton and wool, petroleum, iron ore, coal, lumber, crude rubber, and soybeans. Principal exports are cotton and rayon fabrics, clothing, iron and steel, fish, ships, fertilizers, textile machinery, and toys. Japan imports raw materials, manufactures or refines them, and exports them. The United States is the largest customer. An apparent trade imbalance is partially offset by tourism, services, and other intangible exports.

HIROSHIMA   The f
atomic bomb was explodec
August 5, 1945. This st
was once one of the m
streets of the city.

HOKKAIDO FARM HOUSE   *A family gathers around its sunken cooking fire for dinner. The coal-burning stove and solid construction of the house are required by the harsh climate of this northernmost island.*

1963: IMPORTS $6,736,000,000
EXPORTS $5,447,000,000
DEFICIT $1,189,000,000

TRANSPORT

ROAD: In 1961, there were 91,300 miles of road, very little of it paved. In 1962, some 743,000 cars and 1.79 million commercial vehicles were in use.

RAILROAD: Almost 16,800 miles of railway carried 5.3 billion passengers and 206.4 million tons of freight in 1961.

SEA: Yokohama is the largest port. In 1962, over 3,000 ships of 100 gross tons or more flew the Japanese flag. They included 110 passenger ships, almost 2,000 cargo ships, and 900 oil tankers; however, the fleet could accommodate only 41 percent of the country's commerce.

AIR: Japan Airlines and All Nippon Airlines serve America, Asia, and Europe. Most of the large international lines fly to Japan. In 1961, Japanese planes carried 1.87 million passengers on internal flights and 165,000 on international flights.

COMMUNI-CATION

Postal service is excellent. Telephone, radio, radio-telephone, telegraph, and television services are not government-operated, but are fully modern. Some 7.36 million telephones were in use in 1963.

LAOS

Tinderbox of Southeast Asia

Of all the new nations of Southeast Asia, Laos is the country most bound by traditional influences. It is also the least developed economically. Independent for just about a decade, Laos has made but little progress.

With an area just about the size of the states of Kentucky and Louisiana combined, Laos has a population of about two million people. About 90 percent of the population is engaged in subsistence farming. Rice, the staple diet and main crop, is cultivated extensively in the river valleys, and is also grown by the tribes of the highlands.

The climate is tropical, and wild life abounds. The leopard, the tiger, and the cobra are at home here. Elephants are domesticated as draft animals, and by law become the property of the King.

ART AND CULTURE

Recent archaeological discoveries, dating from the Paleolithic, the Neolithic, and the Bronze Ages suggest that in the earliest times Laos was inhabited by an Indonesian people. The Lao culture of historic times is, however, closely linked to Buddhism and to Thai art. Statues of Buddha, wrought in an antique Thai style of ancient Aynthia, have been found both in bronze and in wood. Although its sculpture is not outstandingly creative, Laotian architecture combines original forms with those of India, Thailand, and Cambodia, to form a truly superb style.

ETHNIC MINORITIES

The Lao make up about half the population and form the political and social élite of the country. They are part of the greater Thai family of peoples who originated in South China but are today dispersed throughout the northern ring of Southeast Asia. Most of the Lao settled in the plains and valleys of the Mekong River. In recent years,

303

the Lao élite began to move to growing urban communities, causing a breakdown of the traditional village structure.

Some 300,000 Kha of Indonesian origin dwell in the southern highlands, and are grouped into some 60 different tribes. In the 19th century, the Meo and the Yao moved from China into Laos. The Black Thai, the White Thai, and Red Thai, distinguished by the color of their clothing, inhabit the river valleys of the north. In the process of national development, the integration and involvement of these minor-

ROYAL FUNERAL   *Sisavang Vong, the well-loved king who led Laos to independence, died in 1960. Here, his uniformed palace guards draw the gilded "dragon ship" bier toward the gilded and curtained pyre, which will be burned once the king's remains have been ceremonially placed under the elaborate canopy. A broad, white ribbon is held by the procession's leader, but the dragon ship is actually pulled along by stout ropes tugged by guards. The seven-tiered umbrellas around the edge of the pyre and at the peak of the pyre's tower are symbols of royalty. A similar symbol is carved at the top of the bier.*

ity groups remain a fundamental task for any Laotian government. Discontent is rife among the numerous Kha, whom the Lao regard as little more than slaves. Today, because of lack of national cohesion and political stability, Laos is one of the softest spots on the political map of Asia—a land caught in the throes of the Cold War.

HISTORY OF LAOS

Until the 13th century, Laos belonged to the kingdom of Cambodia and was part of the Indo-Khmer civilization. The territory was later taken over in the 13th century by the Thai kingdom of Sukhotai. In the middle of the 14th century, Sukhotai weakened, and this permitted the formation of an independent state known as Lan Xang, the "Kingdom of a Million Elephants."

In its golden period (14th to 16th centuries), Lan Xang extended from China into northern Thailand. But interfamilial quarrels and unrelenting pressures from the adjoining kingdoms of Burma, Thailand, and Viet Nam combined to bring about the disintegration of Lan Xang in the 17th century. Since then, the reconstruction of a viable Laos state has proved to be an incredibly difficult task.

ERA OF FRENCH CONTROL

Up until the 19th century, Laos had little significant contact with the western world. In the 1880's, France intervened between Viet Nam and Thailand to settle a conflict for control of Laos. At that time, the French were administering a part of Laos as a colony. As a result of such intervention, the French granted protectorate status to the area governed by the royal Laotian house situated at Luang Prabang. France's aim was to preserve Laos as a closed, underdeveloped territory which would serve as a buffer between Thailand and British Burma.

INDEPENDENCE AND THE TASK OF NATIONAL UNIFICATION

In 1954, as part of the settlement of the Indo-China War, the Geneva Conference bestowed independence on Laos. All but two Laotian provinces came under the control of the King. These two provinces, which bordered North Viet Nam—Phong Saly and Sam Neua—were left in the hands of the Pathet Lao—the North Vietnamese guerrilla forces.

King Sisavong Vong, the ruling monarch, inherited two particularly formidable tasks. He needed to consolidate his nation and to establish hegemony over all the minority peoples. Among these were some groups which were nearly as numerous as the Lao. The King also was obliged to solve the problem of the Pathet Lao (the Lao national movement).

THE PATHET LAO AND THE VIETNAMESE COMMUNISTS

Dealing with the Pathet Lao proved most difficult. The Pathet Lao had been created by the Vietnamese Communists in 1945 as a Laotian appendage of the guerrilla army which fought to expel the French forces from Indo-China. When independence was granted to Laos in Geneva, the Pathet Lao refused to give up the territory it then held. The organizer of the Pathet Lao and its initial leader was Prince Souvanouvong, a Laotian who had been educated in Paris and who had resided in Hanoi.

From the very outset, the government was divided on how to cope

RURAL VILLAGE This Lao settlement in the valley of the Nam Ou River is characteristic. Built on stilts for protection against rising waters during the rainy season, these houses, with their thin, woven bamboo walls and high, thatched roofs, are typical in this sub-tropical climate. Dogs, chickens, and pigs wander freely about the village area.

HIS MAJESTY SRI SAVANG VATTHANA The present king assumed royal duties during the final illness of his father, King Sisavang Vong. He became king in November, 1959.

with the Pathet Lao. A right-wing faction favored alliance with the United States. This group argued that such an alliance would be the best way to obtain the military and economic assistance required to overcome Pathet Lao—North Vietnamese influence and power. In 1964, the same line was urged by a strong military group.

A center faction favored accommodation with the Pathet Lao, and supported a neutral stance in the Cold War. The main proponent of this position was Prince Souvannaphouma who, in 1954 as premier, made the first of what was to become a series of efforts to form a coalition government with Pathet Lao participation. However, the conciliatory policies of the Prince were repeatedly undermined by Pathet Lao duplicity, as well as by the opposition of the United States embassy in Vientiane. The United States frequently by-passed the Prince's government to directly supply royal army units with payments and supplies.

UNITED STATES INTERVENTION

In 1962, the United States suddenly shifted its policy. At a second Geneva Conference, the United States agreed to the neutralization of Laos and the consolidation of a center force under the leadership of Prince Souvannaphouma. However, a split in the ranks of the neutralist military forces tore away Souvannaphouma's base of power, and permitted the resurgence of rival Pathet Lao and right-wing factions.

Since 1960, a build-up of the Pathet Lao forces by the Soviet

Union and by other Communist countries has enabled the Pathet Lao to gain control over nearly two-thirds of the territory of Laos, and to move dangerously close to the strategic Mekong River. In 1964, the United States air power was brought into play. At first, the United States flew only reconnaissance missions over Pathet Lao territory; but later, troops and enemy bases situated on the strategic Plain of Jars and near the South Vietnamese border were attacked.

GEOGRAPHY AND THE ECONOMY

The country is completely landlocked. There are no railways, and but few highways. Because of this poor development of transportation facilities, the Mekong River functions as the main route of communication, wherever that stream is free of obstructing rapids. All important towns in Laos lie along this river. The Plain of Jars, an ancient site of urn burials, controls trade from South Viet Nam into the central valley of the Mekong. In the north, the vital valleys of Nam Ngoua and Nam Hou connect Laos with the Dien Bien Phu plain in North Viet Nam.

Control over these two northern valleys by the Pathet Lao spelled victory to the Communists in 1954. It was France's attempt to defend upper Laos against Pathet Lao–Vietnamese infiltration that led her into the military trap at Dien Bien Phu which brought about the collapse of the French forces in Indo-China.

VIENTIANE AND LUANG PRABANG

Vientiane, the ancient capital of the kingdom of Lan Xang, flourished from the 14th century until sacked by the Siamese early in the 19th century. The site was rebuilt by the French on the bank of the

BUDDHIST MONKS   It is six o'clock in the morning, and the monks are leaving their wat to beg their food for the day. The bump under each saffron robe is a begging bowl which will be generously filled by the town's housewives. These men have already been at their prayers for two hours. According to the rules of their life, they may not eat after midday. Many men seek monastic peace in this unsettled land.

Mekong River. Today, the city has 150,000 inhabitants. Since most of its ancient pagodas are in ruins, this town has few attractions.

Luang Prabang, a considerable distance upstream from Vientiane on the Mekong River, is a town of about 25,000 people. Long a religious and dynastic capital, it was little affected by the period of French control. It lies crowded on a hilly peninsula, dominated by a sacred mountain of limestone. Thatched houses, set on piles, are hidden in gardens of palm trees and banana trees.

ROY JUMPER

NEW YEAR'S CELEBRATION
In a carved and gilded palanquin, the chief lama of Vientiane is carried through the streets on the shoulders of citizens. The Festival of the New Year lasts for three days. As in customary in the yearly Buddhist rite of purification, people are throwing water at each other and dancing in the streets. The chief lama, shown wearing a soaking wet robe and a stoic expression, is a favorite target of the water-throwers.

IN BRIEF

AREA

91,428 square miles, about the size of Oregon. Landlocked.

TERRAIN

Mountainous, with peaks of over 9,000 feet. The Viet Nam Cordillera from the eastern frontier. Two-thirds of the country is densely forested. The centers of settlement and cultivation are in the deep river valleys of the Mekong and its tributaries.

FLORA

Tropical rain forests composed chiefly of evergreens and trees ranging from 80 to 100 feet in height. Also lianas, parasitic vines, orchids. Plateau ground cover is a coarse grass, *tranh,* which stands six feet high.

FAUNA

Elephant, leopard, tiger, cobra, lizard, small crocodile, and birds.

CLIMATE

Two main seasons created by monsoons. The southwest monsoon brings rain from May to October which averages 12 inches a month. The northwest monsoon blows dry and cool from November to April. Temperatures are never extreme, ranging from tropical in the south to subtropical in the northern mountains.

CAPITALS

Vientiane is the administrative capital, with about 150,000 inhabitants. Luang Prabang is the royal capital, with some 25,000 people.

OTHER CITIES

Savannakhet, Pakse, Bassac, Xieng Khouang, Thakhet are administrative centers and market towns.

POPULATION

Around 2.2 million by 1962 estimates. No census has ever been taken. Density is about 19 persons per square mile. Annual rate of increase is estimated as high as 2.5 percent.

ETHNIC GROUPS

The dominant Lao occupy the fertile areas. About a sixth of the people belong to the so-called Black, White, or Red Thai tribes, ethnically related to the Lao. Unrelated Kha tribes comprise a fourth of the population. Meo, Yao, and other small tribes of Chinese origin occupy the northern hills. About 50,000 Chinese and Vietnamese live in the towns.

LANGUAGES   Lao is the official language. French is used by many officials and in towns. Thai, Mon-Khmer, and tribal tongues are in limited use.

RELIGION   Theravada Buddhism is the state religion. Tribal peoples follow Buddhism, animism, primitive Brahmanism, and ancestor worship.

DATE OF INDEPENDENCE   In October 1953, Laos became a fully sovereign state through a treaty ending French rule.

FORM OF GOVERNMENT   Constitutional monarchy. The King is Head of State and supreme religious authority. He appoints the Prime Minister, who is assisted by a Council of Ministers. The legislative body is a National Assembly, elected every five years by universal suffrage. In practice, most governments have been formed as a result of *coups d'état* or plots.

EDUCATION   In 1960, about 103,000 students were enrolled in primary, secondary, and technical schools. An estimated 20 percent of the population is literate.

GENERAL KONG LE   A politically unkown captain in a paratroop battalion in 1960, Kong Le led a coup d'état that brought down the rightist government of the day and reinstated neutralist leaders. Kong Le, now a general, is one of the first individuals of the Kha ancestry to reach a position of influence in Laotian national affairs.

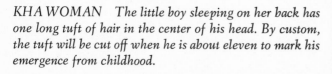

KHA WOMAN   The little boy sleeping on her back has one long tuft of hair in the center of his head. By custom, the tuft will be cut off when he is about eleven to mark his emergence from childhood.

LAOTIAN LEADERS *Here are the famous "three princes" who have dominated Laotian politics since independence. In the center is Prince Souvannaphouma, the neutralist member of the trio who has served repeatedly as premier. On the left is the conservative Boun Oum, Prince of Champassak. On the right is the radical Prince Souvanouvong, leader of the Pathet Lao. They are shown here at a 1964 meeting.*

HEALTH FACILITIES

In 1960, there were about 40 doctors, 4 dentists, 6 midwives, and 6 pharmacists concentrated largely in urban areas. Malaria and intestinal parasites are endemic. Tuberculosis, yaws and other diet-deficiency diseases are frequent. Life expectancy at birth is estimated at 30 years.

CULTURAL FACILITIES

There are about 20 newspapers, mostly mimeographed sheets. The government paper, *Lao Presse,* is printed in two languages; it has a daily circulation of 160 in French, 2,000 in Lao. There are six radio stations, about 5,000 radios, and a few cinemas near Vientiane. Improvised ballads of traveling folk singers are the chief news source, and the focus of popular culture.

CURRENCY AND FiNANCE

The *kip,* officially valued at 240 to $1.00 of U.S. currency, is in process of inflation, and may be worth half or a third of that figure. The government budget for fiscal 1963 expected revenues of about $5 million and expenditures of over $19 million.

INDUSTRY AND PRODUCTION

A tobacco factory is the only substantial industrial enterprise. There are a few sawmills, brick works, and rice mills. Skilled and semi-skilled labor is almost unavailable. Handicrafts include silk-weaving, leather goods, and silver work.

CROPS: Chief crop is rice, averaging 520,000 tons a year. Other crops include corn, tobacco, citrus fruits, tea, coffee, potatoes, cardamom, and cinchona. Opium is the most important cash crop of the hill tribes, with an estimated 65 tons produced each year. Stick lac, benzoin, and teakwood are the chief forest products.

MONASTERY SCHOOL *Laotian monks learn English from a fellow monk. During the course of the morning, they will also attend lessons in Laotian and in typing.*

VIENTIANE *Here is a typical street of the administrative capital.*

LIVESTOCK: Mostly cattle, buffalo, and pigs. Elephants are used in forestry.

FISHERIES: Quantities of fish for local consumption are taken from the Mekong and its tributaries.

MINING: One small tin mine is in operation. Extremely rich deposits of iron ore remain undeveloped.

TRADE
The least active of all the Indo-Chinese states in international trade, Laos imports food, textiles, machinery, and metal products. Chief exports are teakwood, coffee, and tin. Imports come mostly from Thailand, the United States, and France. The trade deficit is largely covered by foreign aid.

1962: IMPORTS $24,000,000
EXPORTS $ 1,000,000
DEFICIT $23,000,000

TRANSPORT
ROAD: In 1961 there were over 1,700 miles of road, of which about 270 miles were asphalted. The remainder are usable only in the dry season. In 1961 there were about 5,000 private cars and about 1,750 trucks and buses.

RAILROAD: There are no railroads.

WATERWAY: The Mekong River and its tributaries carry small boats used for freight, but the waterways are broken by rapids and falls, so that extensive transshipping is required.

AIR: In 1960 there were four airports and 19 airstrips. Royal Air Lao and Air Viet Nam service internal Laos and Saigon.

COMMUNI-CATION
There were about 850 telephones, 6 radio stations, and 25 post offices in 1962. Communications are primitive.

SHOPPING TRIP Wearing the traditional silk-scarf headdress, three Lao women return from early morning market, each with a full basket of vegetables on the arm and a fat duck in hand. This road, busy with trucks, cars, pedicabs, bicycles, and bulldozer, is near the National Assembly building in Vientiane.

CHINA

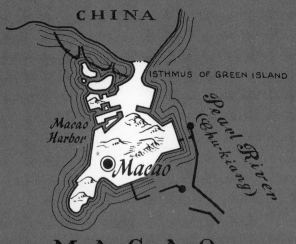

ISTHMUS OF GREEN ISLAND

Macao
Harbor

Pearl River
(Chu-kiang)

●Macao

MACAO

TAIPA ISLAND

COLOWAN I.

South China Sea

MACAO

Portuguese Enclave

"Historic Macao" is the phrase which sums up the chief appeal of this overseas province of the Republic of Portugal. Macao, founded in 1557, bears testimony to that phenomenal rise of the Portuguese in the 16th and 17th centuries, which took their flag into every continent. But after the first great impetus was spent, Macao's fortunes declined, and the colony never again reached its early prosperity. But Macao is still rich in historical associations and in its old-world charm.

GEOGRAPHY AND POPULATION

The province lies on the coast of China, at the western tip of the Pearl Estuary, some 40 miles to the east of Hong Kong. It comprises a small peninsula, joined to the mainland by a low, narrow, and sandy isthmus, and two small islands, Taipa and Colowan.

The 1960 census showed a total population of 169,000. Just under 8,000 were Portuguese, and the rest Chinese, except for a few foreigners. Since 1960, a steady influx of Chinese has brought the population to over the quarter-million mark Many of the locally born Portuguese, called Macanese, have some Chinese blood.

CLIMATE

The climate is monsoonal, hot and humid from May to September, during which period 82 percent of the average annual 85 inches of rainfall occurs. The winter is cool with occasional cold spells; the autumn, dry and sunny.

GOVERNMENT

As part of Portugal, Macao elects one deputy to represent the province in the National Assembly at Lisbon; Macao enjoys considerable financial and administrative autonomy. The Governor, an official appointed from Lisbon, is responsible for the administration, except for the Magistracy which is subject to the Judiciary at Lourenzo Marques in Mozambique.

The municipal administration is called *Leal Senado* or Loyal Senate, a title awarded to it in 1640 at the time of the restoration of the Portuguese monarchy after the mother country had been subjected to 60 years of Spanish rule. Macao had during that period been loyally devoted to Portuguese interests. The *Leal Senado* consists of seven members; four are elected, and three are appointed by the Governor.

EARLY HISTORY

The Portuguese reached Malacca in 1511, and the Pearl River in 1513. Chinese exclusiveness discouraged trading relations until Portuguese successes in the suppression of piracy won Chinese permission in 1557 for them to settle in Macao.

The official name of the new settlement was "City of the Name of God." Macao, the name commonly used, comes from *A-Ma-gao*, meaning the port of A-Ma, a goddess to whom an ancient temple in the city was dedicated.

Trade flourished, especially in carrying silk to Japan in exchange for Japanese silver. But when, in 1639, Japan adopted a policy of seclusion under the Tokugawa Shogunate, this trade came to an end and Macao's fortunes declined. Nevertheless, the city remained the only place in China where foreigners might live; so, when, in the 18th century, Western and American trade with China grew, Macao played an important role as the headquarters of their merchant houses. Its eminence as the foreign port in China remained until the founding of Hong Kong in 1841.

In its early days, Macao was held by the Portuguese on payment of an annual rent. But in 1887, the province was ceded to Portugal by a Treaty of Friendship and Commerce.

RECENT HISTORY

Macao was the home of the Chinese revolutionary leader, Sun Yat-sen, who practiced medicine in that city after qualifying as a professional in Hong Kong in 1892.

During the Second World War, Macao did not fall into Japanese hands. The city sheltered so many refugees of all races that its population was swollen to over half a million.

A TOURIST MAGNET

With so much history behind it, and having a pronounced European flavor, Macao holds substantial attractions for the tourist. There is the magnificent facade of St. Paul's Church, originally called the Church of the Mother of God. This edifice was largely built by Japanese Christians at the end of the 16th century, and was part of the old Jesuit College. There are the Camoens Gardens, where tradition says—probably inaccurately—that the great Portuguese poet wrote part of the *Lusiads*. There is the Kun Yam Temple, an edifice dedicated to the Goddess of Mercy, in which the first treaty between the United States and China was signed on July 3, 1844.

St. Raphael's Hospital goes back to 1569. The first lighthouse on the China coast was built on the Guia hill in 1864. Macao is also a free port and an inexpensive shopping center.

WATERFRONT Clusters of fishing junks lie at anchor in Macao Harbor; the hills behind them are Communist China. The wide thoroughfare is lined with business offices and hotels. A ferry is moored by the covered wharf. Pedicab drivers wait for fares at the end of the pier.

GAMBLING CASINOS

Undoubtedly the most popular attractions in Macao are the gambling casinos, of which the chief ones are The Sea Palace, anchored alongside a pier in the Inner Harbor, and the elegant Estoril Hotel. There are also two rather small, dirty, gambling casinos patronized by local workers.

Fan tan is played by filling a receptacle at random with a great number of small discs. The receptacle is emptied on the table and a croupier takes away the discs four at a time. The players have placed bets, guessing whether one, two, three, or no discs will remain when the last group of four has been removed. The amazing thing here is that when the heap is about half cleared, and something like 60 or 70 discs remain, some people seem to know what the result will be.

Slot machines, so-called one-armed bandits, are much in evidence.

In the gambling casinos in Macao, the stakes are not high, and may be as low as one Hong Kong dollar—17½¢ in U. S. currency; but some tables operate at a minimum stake of 100 Hong Kong dollars, or $17.50 in U. S. currency.

The bars and restaurants are equipped so that the devotee of chance may be served without losing an opportunity to place a bet.

RELIGIOUS AFFILIATIONS

Catholicism is very strong among the Portuguese; many churches date back to the earliest days. The bulk of the Chinese retain their old Confucian, Buddhist, Taoist, or animistic beliefs; their religious festivals are marked by the colorful processions.

INDUSTRY

The chief industry is fishing. Some 20,000 people are employed in some hundreds of sailing junks. Latterly, the Chinese Communist authorities have placed restrictions on the use of their territorial waters which surround Macao. The export of fish is mainly to Hong Kong.

With the Communists entrenched on the mainland, it is difficult to surmise what the future holds for Macao.

GEORGE B. ENDACOTT

MONG-TAK SCHOOL A Chinese kindergarten. "Mong-Tak" means good character and indicates that the school's aim is to build character.

IN BRIEF

AREA — Six square miles, about a tenth of the area of the District of Columbia.

TERRAIN — The islands of Taipa (1.4 square miles) and Colowan (2.5 square miles), as well as the narrow peninsula on which the city lies, have many low, rocky hills.

FLORA AND FAUNA — Native life was that of the Chinese mainland; extensive urbanization has limited it to birds, insects, weeds, etc.

CLIMATE — Hot and wet, with some relief provided by southwest sea breezes. Average rainfall is about 85 inches a year. The mean monthly temperature never falls below 60°F.

CAPITAL — Macao city had a population of about 160,000 in the 1960 census.

POPULATION — Almost 169,000 inhabitants in the 1960 census. The population is increasing slowly, because of the Chinese refugees entering Macao in the hope of reaching Hong Kong.

ETHNIC GROUPS — Most of the people are Chinese, with about 8,000 of Portuguese background.

LANGUAGES — Portuguese and Chinese, chiefly in the Canton and Kwantung dialects.

RELIGION — Confucianism and Buddhism predominate. In the 1960 census, there were about 20,000 Christians and 29,000 of no religion.

DATE OF INDEPENDENCE — In 1557, Portuguese rule began, and since then Macao has never been autonomous. It is now occupied under a treaty signed March 26, 1887.

FORM OF GOVERNMENT

Colonial. The city is, formally, an Overseas Province of Portugal and sends one Deputy to the Portuguese National Assembly. The Governor is appointed from Portugal. The judiciary is subject to that of Mozambique. There has been no significant native authority, but recently three Portuguese residents of Macao were appointed to the *Leal Senado,* or Loyal Senate, which administers the municipality.

EDUCATION

The standard of schooling is high, with an enrollment in all grades of some 55,000. There are about 117 primary and secondary schools of which 29 are run by Catholic missions. There is one Catholic seminary, but no higher educational facilities. Literacy is low; about one-third of those over 15 are illiterate.

HEALTH FACILITIES

In 1961, there were seven doctors and seven pharmacists associated with hospitals; also several charitable clinics and some private practitioners. Sanitation has controlled the dangerous tropical diseases; diphtheria, typhoid, and skin diseases still occur.

CULTURAL FACILITIES

The six daily newspapers—one in Portuguese and five in Chinese—had a circulation of 19,000 in 1962; one person in nine gets a paper every day. The ten cinemas had an annual attendance of 4.8 million. There are two theaters; one Portuguese, the other Chinese.

CURRENCY AND FINANCE

The *pataca,* revalued in January 1965, is equal to five Portuguese *escudos* or about 22¢ in U.S. currency. Estimated revenue and expenditure were balanced at about $6.1 million in 1962.

INDUSTRY AND PRODUCTION

Traditionally makers of firecrackers, most of which are destined for the American market. A recent development has been the growth of light industries to help provide for the Chinese influx. These industries are chiefly textiles, matches, plastic ware, and joss sticks. Factories in Macao also produce shoes, cigarettes, porcelain, teak and camphor chests. There is no heavy industry. Tourism, gambling, and transit trade services provide significant portions of the city's income.

CROPS: Negligible. Most food must be imported.

LIVESTOCK: Pigs and chickens for local consumption only.

FISHERIES: Exports to Hong Kong are worth about $1 million a year.

TRADE

Macao is a free port and most of its trade is transit trade handled by Chinese merchants. Chief exports are firecrackers, which accounted for 80 percent of the total in 1962, cotton prints, cigarettes, Chinese wine, and small consumer goods, such as umbrellas, cosmetics, and shoes. Imports are mainly food, fuel, and raw materials. Unfavorable trade balances are partially offset by tourism, services, and remittances.

1962:	IMPORTS	$7,420,850
	EXPORTS	$3,713,485
	DEFICIT	$3,707,365

TRANSPORT

ROAD: Villages on Taipa and Colowan are connected by roads.

AIR: A Hong Kong company maintains an amphibious shuttle service between Macao and Hong Kong.

SEA: Four ferry steamers and four hydrofoils ply between the continually dredged Inner Harbor of Macao and Hong Kong, a distance of about 40 miles. The outer harbor is silted up. Large ships can no longer be accommodated.

COMMUNI-CATION

There were over 2,600 telephones and 5,500 licensed radios in 1962. There are two radio stations; both broadcast in Portuguese; one carries Chinese programs. Post and telegraph services are government-operated.

FUNERAL PROCESSION Preceded by a sedan chair, a draped casket is borne on the shoulders of eight men and is followed by a decorous file of mourners. The sedan chair is used to carry a picture of the dead person. No one rides in the chair. The man in white is the son of the deceased and is the chief mourner. He wears a white band around his head as a sign of mourning.

THAILAND
KRA PENINSULA
Kangar
Kota Bharu
LANGKAWI
AlorStar
Kuala Trengganu
Georgetown
PENANG ISLAND
MALAYA
Ipoh
TAHAN 7,185
Kuantan
Kuala Lumpur
PAHANG
Seremban
MALAYSIA
Port Swettenham
TIOMAN
Malacca
Johore Bahru
Straits of Malacca
SINGAPORE ISLAND
Singapore
Kuching

South China Sea

Sulu Sea
Kudat
PT. KINABALU 13,455
Jesselton
SABAH
Victoria
SINGATARAN
Sandakan
LABUAN
BRUNEI
Beaufort
Miri
Celebes
SARAWAK
Sea
Tawau
SIBU
RAJANG
KAPIT
KALIMANTAN, INDONESIA

MALAYSIA and SINGAPORE

Peoples in Search of the Future

Created in an effort to solve specific racial, economic, and political problems, Malaysia represented an experiment in planning a nation. Established in 1963 as the Federation of Malaysia, the nation united Malaya, Sarawak, Sabah, and Singapore. It was the hope of the leaders of the merging areas that their peoples would come to think of themselves as Malaysians, not as Malays, Chinese, or other racial groups, as only Singapore's Chinese formed a majority where they lived.

This hope was not realized: on August 9, 1965, Singapore left the Federation. This reduced the number of states in the Malaysian federal union from 14 to 13: the 11 states of the former Malaya and Sarawak and Sabah.

THE PROBLEM OF NATIONAL UNITY

All of Malaysia is roughly equivalent to half the size of Texas. Its three areas, Malaya, Sarawak, and Sabah, contain varying proportions of Malays, Chinese, Indians, Pakistanis, Ceylonese, and Bornean tribes, totaling about eight-and-a-half million people. Its capital, Kuala Lumpur, is the former capital of Malaya, the state which served as the nucleus of the Malaysian Federation. The Premier of Malaysia is Tengku (Prince) Abdul Rahman, who previously served as the Premier of Malaya.

Achieving national unity remains Malaysia's most pressing problem. Throughout the country, the Chinese are the retail merchants and rice millers. They constitute a majority of the inhabitants of the large cities. Most Malays live in rural areas, earning their living as small-scale farmers of rice and rubber or as schoolteachers and government servants.

THE CORE AREA OF MALAYA

Malaya, of which the state of Malaysia is an expansion, derived its name from the indigenous inhabitants of the narrow Malay Peninsula which extends southward from the Asian mainland into the geographic heart of insular Southeast Asia, but Malays do not form a majority of its population. Among some 7,500,000 people, about 44.6 percent are Malays and 37.2 percent are Chinese.

Kuala Lumpur, Malaysia's capital and the former capital of Malaya, is a city of 316,000. It was a small tin-mining camp in the 19th century and still has many narrow and crooked streets. Kuala Lumpur, however, probably also has the most rapidly changing appearance of any city in Southeast Asia. Tall modern buildings and a new elevated roadway contrast with the city's most famous landmark, its Moorish-style railroad station.

Tengku Abdul Rahman was Malaya's first and only Premier and has been Prime Minister of Malaysia since its inception. One of 45 legitimate children of the Sultan of Kedah, who had eight legal wives, the Tengku, as he is universally and affectionately known, was educated at Cambridge in England and is a lawyer by training. A civil servant in his younger years, the Tengku, who was born in 1903, has always been interested in advancing the welfare of the poorer Malays in his country. His chief asset is an almost uncanny ability to reconcile differences among others. Extremely easy-going, he is unquestionably the most widely respected—and loved—man in Malaysia.

SARAWAK AND SABAH

Sarawak and Sabah are 600 miles from Malaya, on the northern coast of the island of Borneo. Indonesia controls the rest of Borneo, except for the British protectorate of Brunei.

The Borneo tribesmen known as Ibans, or Sea Dyaks, are the largest group in Sarawak. Others include the Land Dyaks and the Melanaus. The Kadazans, or Dusuns, are the most numerous people in Sabah. There are far fewer Bajaus and Muruts. Many tribesmen of these regions still live largely as did their ancestors centuries ago. The

SINGAPORE'S CITY HALL
The star and crescent on the flag of Malaysia indicate the Islamic character of the nation.

Ibans, who dwell in the famous multi-inhabitant Borneo longhouses, were once head-hunters, some of them as recently as World War II. The Land Dyaks of Sarawak practice a primitive "slash-and-burn" type of agriculture, in which they burn off the jungle growth to raise two or three years' crops before moving on to another location. Sabah's mountain-dwelling Muruts practice a similar type of shifting cultivation.

Both the Chinese and the Malays of Malaysia are more advanced culturally and economically than any of the indigenous peoples of Sarawak and Sabah. Politically, the peoples of Sarawak and Sabah lagged far behind those of Malaya and Singapore at the time of Malaysia's formation. Sarawak held its first elections in 1959, but Sabah had never held state-wide elections. In addition, neither territory had trained personnel for government administration. Until 1946, Sarawak was the personal possession of the Brooke family—descendants of Sir James Brooke, who was given the territory by the Sultan of Brunei in 1839. Sabah was administered by the British North Borneo Company from 1882 until 1947.

SINGAPORE *Junks moored in the Singapore River are built to an ancient pattern, but contemporary developments are evident in the worn-out tires used as bumpers, and in the neat license numbers emblazoned on the side of the craft. The Victorian architecture across the river is a reminder of the days when Sir Stamford Raffles was building Singapore into the "Crossroads of the Orient."*

Sarawak has a population of 777,000, and is roughly equivalent in area to the state of Louisiana. The capital of Sarawak is Kuching.

Sabah has a population of 455,000 people, and is roughly equivalent in area to the state of South Carolina. The capital of Sabah is Jesselton.

SINGAPORE

The island of Singapore lies off the southern tip of Malaya. The island is 27 miles long and 14 miles wide, and has an area of 217 square miles, being roughly equivalent in area to one-fifth of the state of Rhode Island. It is connected to the mainland by a causeway.

Singapore has a population of nearly two million people—75 percent Chinese, 12 percent Malay, 10 percent Indians, Pakistanis, and Ceylonese, and 3 percent Eurasians. The Chinese control its economy.

One of the busiest seaports in the world, Singapore, which became a British possession in 1819, long served as a transshipment port for exports from, and imports to, Indonesia, Burma, and Thailand, as well as to Malaya and the northern Borneo territories. The end of colonial rule found the other Southeast Asian states wanting to control their own foreign trade; Singapore, therefore, has increasingly emphasized industrialization. Its labor force is probably the most skilled and energetic in Southeast Asia.

The city, with still much lush vegetation in its outlying areas, also has some of the world's most impressive low-cost public housing. Singapore functions as one of Britain's most important naval bases.

In August 1965, Singapore seceded from the Malaysian Federation. The secession was in fact a forced one, the initiative coming from the Malaysian national leadership of Tengku Abdul Rahman. The more conservative Malay-dominated central government in Kuala Lumpur had become alarmed by the possibility that Singapore's Chinese, the shrewdest and most aggressive in Southeast Asia, would come to dominate the whole Federation. The main objective of Malaysia's formation had been to contain the Chinese.

The growth of Communist strength among Singapore's Chinese was also alarming. Moreover, the Singapore government, a constituent part of the Malaysian Federation, had taken a somewhat active role in foreign affairs, and was not always in agreement with the central government. But the most important reason, probably, was that the political leadership feared that Singapore Prime Minister Lee Kuan Yew might shortly prove successful in his bid to assume leadership of the Chinese in the whole Federation.

UNIVERSITY OF MALAYA The new buildings in Kuala Lumpur are strikingly modern. The former campus of the University of Malaya in Singapore is now known as the University of Singapore. Both institutions maintain very high standards.

*LEE KUAN YEW   Generally regarded as a lead-
ing Chinese political figure, Lee is Prime Minister of
Singapore, and was chiefly responsible for having
brought Singapore into the Malaysian union. A
Socialist since his student days, and long active in
the trade union movement, he has led Singapore in
the enactment of the most advanced social welfare
legislation in southeast Asia. He is a graduate of
Cambridge University. He speaks Chinese, English,
and Malay with equal fluency.*

LEE KUAN YEW

Born in 1924 into a Chinese shipping family, Lee graduated from
Cambridge University with a degree in law. He returned to Singapore in 1950, had a flourishing law practice, and entered politics in
1955. He became the Secretary-General of the People's Action Party,
a Socialist group. In this post, he was elected as the Premier of Singapore when in 1959 Britain granted internal self-government to the
colony. A dedicated anti-Communist, he brought Singapore into Malaysia in 1963 in spite of opposition from the extreme left.

PROBLEMS OF LANGUAGE

The thorniest areas in the sensitive relations among Malaysia's
many groups are language, education, and religion. Malay was scheduled to become the sole official language of the former Malaya in 1967,
but Sarawak and Sabah, where only a minority of the people speak
Malay as their first language, wish to keep English, too.

RELIGION

Although Islam is the official religion of Malaysia, a majority of
the inhabitants of Singapore, Sarawak, and Sabah follow other faiths.
Half the people of the former Malaya are Muslims and take their religion very seriously. They do not eat pork, for example, the favorite
meat of the Chinese. A few Chinese are Christian, but most of them
adhere to a mixture of three faiths: Confucianism, Taoism, and Bud-

dhism. Most of the Indians are Hindus, although some are Muslims, Sikhs, and Parsis. The overwhelming majority of Borneo peoples are animists, possessing a primitive belief in a life-force that inhabits rocks, trees, mountains, and other objects. Animism is very widespread among the less-developed peoples of Southeast Asia and still influences even many otherwise more sophisticated peoples.

PRE-BRITISH HISTORY

Present-day Malaysia was inhabited as early as 50,000 B.C., according to archaeological findings in the Niah Caves in Sarawak. The ancestors of the present-day Malays, however, did not begin to arrive until about 2,000 B.C. This first wave of Malay migrants maintained

ISLAND VILLAGE   *The houses of this small fishing community of Lima are built on stilts to accommodate the rising tides. Shrimp are the main catch. The growth of Western influence is evident in the striped factory-made shirt worn by the small boy who is poling his perahu across the water.*

A DUSUN GIRL OF NORTH BORNEO

BAJAU CHIEF This chieftain, armed with an elaborately carved kris, is head man of a tribal farming group in the hills, near the west coast of Sabah.

DUSUN GIRLS These young ladies, members of the largest of Sabah's tribes, are playing the sompoton, a bamboo instrument with strings arranged around a cylindrical sound box. Their elaborately embroidered gowns are decorated with coins. The jewelry illustrates a common custom in southeast Asia: resources are not banked, but are invested in jewelry worn by women of the group.

BORNEO ABORIGINES   Small bands of primitives, whose ancestors are believed to have reached the Malay Peninsula long before the pre-historic entry of the Malay groups, still lead secluded lives in the jungles of the interior. A variety of percussion instruments is used to produce music.

TRIBAL DANCERS   In hand-woven sarongs and embroidered batik blouses, these girls from Sarawak demonstrate the dances of their people during the independence celebrations of 1963. Fans made from the feathers of tropical birds emphasize the movements of hands and heads. Heavy ear-bobs have elongated their ear lobes.

a fairly high level of civilization which they brought with them from southwest China. A second wave of even more highly developed Malays started to come around 250 B.C. These Malays knew how to work metals; they gradually merged with the preceding peoples.

In pre-British times, Chinese, Indian, Indonesian, and Thai cultures all influenced what is today Malaysia. Indian traders brought goods, Hinduism, Buddhism, and ultimately Islam—the religion which flourishes today in Malaya.

Srivijaya, an ancient Indonesian empire which came into being in the eighth century, extended its influence over much of Malaysia. Thailand controlled the three northernmost Malay peninsula sultanate states until as late as 1909. But in modern times, it was Britain which made the greatest impact on Malaysia. The first Westerners to arrive, however, were the Portuguese, who captured Malacca in 1511. The Dutch seized the same port in 1641, but subsequently lost it to the British, who began their conquest of Malaysia with the acquisition of Penang in 1786.

BIRTH OF A NATION

The racial problems that plague Malaysia today stem back to previous centuries. During the 19th century, Britain established control over the Malay Peninsula and the island of Singapore. Unlike other European colonies in Southeast Asia, colonial Malaya lacked a nationalist movement against foreign rule. This was because of a delicate racial balance between the Malays and Chinese. The Chinese controlled important sectors of the economy and were better educated. Many Malays feared that departure of the British would mean political domination by the Chinese. For their part, the Chinese appeared content to make money and to prosper as individuals.

World War II changed many political attitudes. Early in the war, Japan easily gained control of the area, dimming the general image of the strength and durability of British rule. Many Malays and Indians performed tasks under the Japanese that had previously been reserved for Englishmen. But the Japanese conquerors treated the Chinese badly, partly because of the conflict between mainland China and Japan.

Anti-Japanese resistance stemmed mainly from the Chinese and was Communist-directed.

After the war, Britain sought to establish a more centralized government for Malaya, proposing that Malays and Chinese be accorded equal citizenship status. Malay fears of Chinese domination were again aroused by this proposal, and the first Malay nationalist political organization was formed, the United Malays National Organization. Predominantly Chinese, Singapore remained a separate British Crown Colony.

Opposed to British rule and continuation of capitalism, Malaya's Communists resorted to armed revolt in 1948, after they failed otherwise to disrupt the economy. The government declared an "emergency" that did not officially end until 1960. At its height, the Chinese Communist revolt included more than 10,000 terrorists, who obtained food and information from rural Chinese "squatters" on the edges of the jungle. More than half a million persons had to be resettled in "new villages."

Probably the main reason for the failure of the insurrection was its almost wholly Chinese character. The "anti-colonialism" of the Communist rebels, moreover, was deflated by Britain's grant of independence to Malaya. Independence came on August 31, 1957.

FORMING THE FEDERATION

Singapore, long Malaya's main port of entry and exit, was not part of the newly independent state; nor were the three other British-controlled territories of Sarawak, Brunei, and Sabah. Although Malaya began its independence in fine economic shape, its prosperity was wholly dependent upon the export of rubber and tin. The idea of merging with Singapore and the other territories was considered as a means of diversifying Malaya's economy.

In Singapore, however, three out of four persons are Chinese, and a merger would have markedly increased the Chinese percentage of Malaya's population. The Malays feared becoming a dominated minority in their homeland. As a result, Singapore had no choice but to

MALAYSIA'S PRIME MINISTER *Tengku Abdul Rahman is one of the chief architects of the Malaysian union, holds several portfolios in the government, and was previously Prime Minister of Malaya. Head of the majority Alliance Party since the early 1950's, the prince, or tunku, has been guiding Malaya toward independence during most of his career. Of royal blood, he began his career in an obscure position in the attorney-general's department. He has won the trust and respect of the Malays. He received a bachelor's degree at Cambridge in 1925. He is now 62.*

move forward on its own toward independence, gaining self-government in 1959. Soon afterward, in 1961, pro-Communist elements in Singapore's ruling People's Action Party began to oppose the moderate leadership of Premier Lee Kuan Yew and eventually broke away from the party. Lee's government retained only a single-seat margin in the legislature. Now Malayans began to fear the possibility of a "Chinese Cuba" next door to them. Communist strength was also increasing in nearby Indonesia. In addition, Indonesia was approaching success in a campaign to acquire Dutch-held West New Guinea. Both Malaya and Singapore feared that Indonesia would soon try to absorb Sarawak, Brunei, and Sabah.

The desire for economic diversification coupled with the fear of Communist expansion again led to talks of merger. In mid-1961, Malayan Premier Tengku Abdul Rahman proposed forming a federal state of Malaysia. Malayan political leaders realized that the Malay percentage of the population in the proposed Federation would decline, and that the Chinese percentage would increase, but they believed that the various non-Chinese peoples of Borneo would cooperate with the Malays to prevent Chinese political domination. Malaysia was born September 16, 1963—but without Brunei, which decided not to join the new state.

Indonesian opposition was expected; but the hostile attitude of the previously friendly Philippine Republic surprised Malaysia's political leaders. Indonesia claimed that the true will of the peoples of Sarawak and Sabah had not been determined. The Philippines refused to recognize Malaysia because of its own historic claim to Sabah, a claim that lacked any visible support within Sabah. The three states agreed to ask the United Nations Secretary-General to determine whether the peoples of Sarawak and Sabah wanted to join Malaysia. Subsequently, the U.N. mission to North Borneo supported the Malayan position.

INDONESIAN HOSTILITY

Claiming that Malaysia was created by the British as a means for maintaining their influence in the area, Indonesia, in 1963, began a campaign to "crush Malaysia." As a result, the new nation has had to divert some of its vital resources and energies from economic development to national defense. Malaysians find it difficult to see how Indonesia can justify paratrooper and seaborne landings on the peninsula proper, territory that has never been in dispute.

Successful solution of its various internal problems may not be enough to save Malaysia in its present territorial form if Indonesia's military opposition increases or if Indonesia finds new allies within Malaysia.

Most of the fighting between Malaysians (and their British allies) and Indonesian guerrilla infiltrators has taken place in the northern Borneo state of Sarawak. For its defense, Malaysia has relied heavily on Great Britain and increasingly also on the United States for aid in the form of equipment. Malaysia's leaders have tried to expand their country's own military forces, but they have done so reluctantly and somewhat modestly. Malaysia realizes that money spent on arms is not money spent on economic development.

MALAYSIA'S ECONOMY

Economic factors were among the most important ones leading to the establishment of the Malaysian Federation. For the Borneo peoples, union with Malaya represented a means for speeding up economic development. Malaya has had the most rapidly expanding gross national product and per capita income in Southeast Asia, and the average Malayan's standard of living is the area's highest. For their part, the Malayan leaders hoped that accession of Brunei, Sarawak, and Sabah would help diversify their economy, which depends heavily on rubber and tin. But Brunei, rich in petroleum deposits, failed to join the Federation. As a result, the only new major resource to which Malaya gained access was timber from Sabah's rich timberlands. Both Sarawak and Sabah also grow rubber, adding to the national wealth but not aiding diversification of the economy. Singapore benefited more from the union. Probably the most industrially advanced area in Southeast Asia, it maintained access to Malaya proper as a market for its manufactured goods.

Malaysia today leads the countries of the world in the production of rubber and tin, producing 40 percent of the world's natural rubber and more than 30 percent of its tin. Malaysia's ranking among rubber producers has improved steadily as a result of a replanting program of high-yielding strains. But Malaysian rubber must still cope with competition from synthetic production. The extent of Malaysia's dependence on rubber is seen in the fact that the industry engages more than half the adult labor force. Hundreds of thousands of other persons are indirectly supported by this key sector of the economy. In addition, the export duty on rubber is a major source of government revenue.

Malaysian production of various goods is organized in different ways. Half the country's rubber is produced on large estates, while the other half comes from small holdings operated by Malay farmers. These men receive both technical and financial assistance from the government. About half of Malaysia's tin is mined by dredging with the more expensive equipment limited to European-owned mines. Most other mines, particularly those which are Chinese-owned, use simpler equipment. Oil palm, like rubber, is grown both on estates and by small

MURUT TRIBESMEN   Famous for their skillful use of the six-foot-long blowpip charged with poisoned darts, these tribesmen demonstrate the use of the weapon durin independence celebrations in Sabah. Only recently have these mountain tribes bee persuaded away from cannibalism. A Murut will decorate the handle of his elaborate carved kris with hanks of human hair. The men wear bird feathers in their headdres As suggested by the wrist watch worn by one of the tribesmen, the Muruts are no moving toward involvement with modern ways. They have been reduced in number b cholera, small-pox, and malaria. There are probably no more than 5,000 Muruts toda

holders. Practically everything grown or extracted in Malaya proper is also produced in Sarawak and Sabah, but in lesser amounts and usually less efficiently. In addition, Sabah is a major producer of timber, while Sarawak ranks first among nations of the world in pepper growing.

Malaysia's rice farms have the highest yield per acre of any in Southeast Asia. But because much of the land is mountainous and unsuitable for rice-growing, the country produces only about 60 percent of the rice needed to feed its people. In its quest for self-sufficiency, the government has greatly expanded the area under cultivation, conquering swamp and jungle.

Government incentives have attracted much foreign capital to Malaysia's budding industries. Except for Singapore, however, manufacturing activities are limited, and center mostly on the processing of rubber and tin.

GOVERNMENT

The pace of both social integration and economic development depends in part on the efficiency of Malaysia's political institutions. The fact that Malaysia has a federal form of government should allow a sufficient degree of local autonomy to satisfy important regional inter-

BULTAN MOSQUE The largest mosque in Singapore, this is the religious center for the city's Muslim minority. From the balconied minarets at the corners of the building, the muezzin chants his call to prayer.

ests. The Federation is centrally governed by a Parliament, with a Prime Minister responsible to a House of Representatives elected by the people. A second chamber, the Senate, is partly indirectly elected by the state legislatures and partly appointed by a paramount ruler. The ruler is chosen by the sultans of the nine peninsular Malay states from among themselves.

A coalition of parties known as the Alliance has been the ruling political party since 1957. The Alliance includes the United Malays National Organization, the Malayan Chinese Association, and the Malayan Indian Congress. There are affiliates, slightly differently composed, in both Sarawak and Sabah. The government party in Singapore is the much more leftist People's Action Party.

PROBLEM OF A NATIONAL CULTURE

Malaysia's is a mixed society; it has not yet developed a single national culture. There are in fact several Malaysian cultures, ranging from the very modern to the ancient (but not always primitive) dancing and handicrafts of the diverse Borneo peoples. The British and the Chinese brought aspects of their highly developed cultures with them in colonial times, but both groups were mainly concerned with matters of commerce—hardly at all with the arts.

The Malay culture of the peninsula is much like that of Indonesia. The peoples of east coast Sumatra (in Indonesia) and the western coast of the Malay peninsula have much more in common than most Sumatrans and most Javanese within Indonesia. The traditional Malay *wayang kulit,* or shadow play, is every bit as popular among Malaysian Malays as it is among Indonesians. The Malays, as do the Indonesians, make beautiful *batik* cloth, the patterns of which are produced by a special wax process. Such *batik,* used for shawl, skirt, or dress, is among the finest cloth in the world.

Poor immigrants are not usually carriers of the finest in their culture. So it was with Malaysia's and Singapore's Chinese. Chinese opera, however, and of course Chinese cuisine, in Malaysia is considered, as it is elsewhere, among the world's very finest.

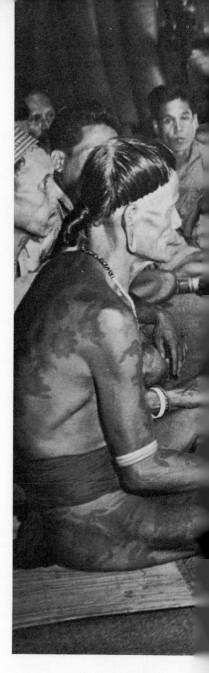

IBAN LONGHOUSE *The Ibans of Sarawak are famous for their multi-family longhouses which may house as many as 50 families. Such a house becomes the village itself. Each family's private apartment opens onto a wide corridor in which most of the community activities are carried on. Here, government officials have arrived after a long trek into the hills and are beginning to collect census data on an Iban farming village. The extensively tattooed elders of the tribe are entertaining their official guests with cooling drinks in the grass-matted community corridor. Most of the younger members of the tribe, who are respectfully looking on, have eschewed tattooing.*

The modern has inevitably invaded Malaysia and Singapore. Both Malay and Chinese films are popular with those who speak these languages. Western movies are popular in the bigger cities; they are less so farther from the areas of greatest foreign impact.

EDUCATION

Malaysia is trying to do two things through its schools. The regime

is attempting to raise the educational level of the country, and to draw the country's diverse peoples closer together as a result of exposure to a common education. There are major problems, however—the most important being the different languages spoken in the country.

The government's goal is for all Malaysian children to attend the six-year primary school. This goal is steadily being approached. Primary school instruction may be in Malay, English, Chinese, or Tamil, but

Malay and English must be taken as compulsory subjects. About one out of three children goes on to secondary school, where instruction is only in English and Malay.

Ultimately, the government hopes that all instruction will be in Malay, but the non-Malay-speaking Chinese and Bornean peoples are opposed to this.

Malaysia and Singapore both spend a quarter of their budget on education. Malaysia's expenditure on education has more than doubled since independence came in 1957. One-tenth of the capital outlay in the government's present Five-Year Plan is for new school buildings.

THE FUTURE OF MALAYSIA

History will pass final judgment on Malaysia's attempt to intermingle peoples of many races. There is no doubt that internal strains exist. But will Indonesian opposition increase divisive tendencies, or will it unite the Malaysian peoples against a common external foe? And should not living together over a long period increase the heritage of shared experiences that forms the essence of national identity?

RICHARD BUTWELL

WINNOWING RICE   In Kedah, three sarong-clad girls pour rice into an open mesh basket. As it is agitated, the grains fall on the straw mat and the chaff remains behind.

IN BRIEF

AREA
128,562 square miles. Malaya, 50,700 square miles, is a little larger than New York State. Singapore, 217 square miles, is about a fifth the size of Rhode Island. Sabah, about 29,388 square miles, is slightly smaller than South Carolina. Sarawak, about 48,250 square miles, is the size of Louisiana.

TERRAIN
Malaya, on the Kra Peninsula, is mostly mountainous; six ranges run north and south, with peaks rarely over 7,000 feet. There is a limited amount of coastal plain which is often swampy, and some inland plateau country. Sabah and Sarawak, on Borneo Island, are a jumble of mountains, with swampy coasts and a few fertile upland plains.

FLORA
Tropical rain forests, with many varieties of orchids and evergreens, cover about three-quarters of Malaya and nearly all of Sabah and Sarawak. Bamboo, palms, rattan and other lianas, mangroves, reeds, and grasses.

FAUNA
Tigers, leopards, monkeys, gibbons, wild cattle, deer, elephants, rhinoceros; numerous birds, snakes, lizards, and crocodiles.

CLIMATE
Equatorial with an average temperature of 80°F. and about 75 inches of rain a year. As much as 198 inches of rain fall in parts of the east coast. Humidity is always high, with frequent thunderstorms. No noticeable change of season. More bearable conditions are found in some highland areas.

CAPITAL
Kuala Lumpur, with 316,000 inhabitants, is the federal capital.

OTHER CITIES
Singapore, with 1.73 million inhabitants in 1961, is the chief port and commercial center and has extensive internal autonomy. Kuching, capital of Sarawak, had a population of 50,700; Jesselton, capital of Sabah, had 21,500. Other cities of importance are: In Malaya, Penang, 175,000; Ipoh, 80,000; and Malacca. In Sabah, Sandakan, 29,300, and Victoria. In Sarawak, Sibu, 29,600.

KING   In 1960, Tuanku Syed Putra ibni Al-marhum Syed Hassan Jamalullail, known by Malaysians as Yang Di-Pertuan Agong, was elected supreme head of Malaysia for a five-year period. Previously, he had been the ruler of the state of Perlis. When a term as King is concluded, one of the other Malay state rulers succeeds to the throne. Jamalullail is about 46 years old. He was educated in the Malay schools; is widely traveled; is an excellent tennis player and a good golfer.

QUEEN   Tuanku Budriah binti Al-marhu[m] Tengku Ismail, known by Malaysians as Ra[ja] Permaisuri Agong, shared the ceremonial r[e]sponsibilities of her husband, who was head [of] state. She is now a little over 40. She attend[ed] Malay School, and subsequently the Anglo-Ch[i]nese Girls' School. The former Queen is a stro[ng] supporter of the Girl Guide Movement, count[er]part of the Girl Scouts, and is an active su[p]porter, in general, of social work.

POPULATION   Well over 10 million. Estimates of local governments in 1962 were: Malaya, 7.5 million; Singapore, 1.73 million; Sarawak, 777,000, and Sabah, 455,000. Population increase is rapid. The annual rate of increase is 3.3 percent for Malaya, almost 4 percent for Singapore, 2.9 percent for Sabah, and 2.5 percent for Sarawak. Density is 134 persons per square mile in Malaya.

ETHNIC GROUPS   There are over 4 million Malays, 4.3 million Chinese, 950,000 Indians and Pakistanis, and 900,000 or so in various tribal groups. The tribes include the Kadazans, Bajaus, Bruneis, Muruts, and Suluks of Sabah, and the Sea Dyaks, Land Dyaks, and Melanaus of Sarawak.

LANGUAGES   Malay is the primary official language. English and Chinese are widely used. Tribal languages are used locally.

RELIGION   Islam is the official religion, but freedom of religion is constitutionally guaranteed. The Chinese usually practice Buddhism, Confucianism, and Taoism. Indians and Pakistanis are Hindu or Muslim; the tribal people are animists. Christians are a small minority.

DATE OF INDEPENDENCE   Malaysia was formed September 16, 1963, when Singapore, Sabah, and Sarawak joined Malaya in forming the new Federation of Malaysia.

FORM OF GOVERNMENT   Constitutional elective monarchy. Malaysia is composed of 14 states: Singapore, Sabah, Sarawak, and the 11 states of the former Federation of Malaya. The Head of State, or *Yang di Pertuan Agong,* is elected for five years by part of the Conference of Rulers, which includes the heads of the 14 states. (The heads of state for the nine traditional Malay states of the Malayan peninsula are hereditary Muslim sultans—these nine rulers elect the *Yang di Pertuan Agong.* Heads of state from Singapore, Sarawak, Sabah, Penang, and Malacca are not hereditary sultans and do not participate in the election of the monarch.)

Executive power is in the hands of a Prime Minister and his Cabinet. A 50-member Senate has 22 members appointed by the monarch, and two members elected from each state legislature. The popularly elected House of Representatives has 104 members from Malaya, 15 from Singapore, 16 from Sabah, and 24 from Sarawak. Malaysia is a member of the Commonwealth of Nations and the United Nations.

EDUCATION   Diverse languages and cultures as well as rapid increase in numbers hinder educational development. Close to 22 percent of the national budget was allocated to education in 1964. In 1962, Malaya had 1.4 million pupils in more than 5,600 schools with over 51,000 teachers. In 1961, Singapore had almost 422,000 students in 650 schools with over 13,600 teachers. During 1962, Sabah had about 63,600 students in over 470 schools, and Sarawak had 114,500 in over 975 schools. About half of those over 15 are literate in

Singapore and Malaya, but less than a quarter are so in Sabah and Sarawak.

HEALTH FACILITIES

In 1960, there were over 1,850 doctors, 485 dentists, 1,825 midwives, and 150 pharmacists. Health services are well developed for Asia and improving rapidly. The death rate was halved between 1953 and 1963; malaria is under control and cholera is practically eliminated. Life expectancy is about 57 years in Malaya.

CULTURAL FACILITIES

Malaya had 28 daily newspapers in 1960; Sabah and Sarawak had eight each; and Singapore had nine. Total circulation was almost a million, ranging from one paper for every 40 people in Sarawak to better than one for every four people in Singapore. Of the 575 books published from Malaya and Singapore in 1962, over 300 were new. In the same year, 27 films were made in Singapore. There are at least 175 cinemas, 20 of them mobile, with an annual attendance of about 100 million. Each area has its own broadcasting system; *Radio Malaya* alone broadcasts in English, Malay, Tamil, and three Chinese dialects. Television stations began operation in Singapore and Kuala Lumpur in 1963; both are government operated and provide non-commercial programs of education, information, and entertainment.

CURRENCY AND FINANCE

The Malaysian dollar is equal to 4.48 grains of fine gold, or 32.67¢ in U.S. currency. Malaya's budget was estimated at about U.S. $345 million in revenue and close to $355 million in expenditure for 1963, with over a third of the amount used for economic development. Singapore had revenues and expenditures of almost $120 million in 1962, with almost half of the 1963 budget allocated to economic development. Sabah's 1963 revenues were estimated at almost $29 million, expenditures at nearly $36 million. Sarawak's 1963 revenue estimate was slightly over $22 million, expenditure almost $25 million. Centralized financing is being deferred. Tax structures, local needs, and local governments vary considerably. Government expenditure per person in 1963 was about $34.30 in Sarawak, $50.64 in Malaya, $66.97 in Sabah, and $76.67 in Singapore.

INDUSTRY AND PRODUCTION

The export of raw materials and Singapore's shipping trade were the traditional mainstays of the economy before federation. However, the government is strongly encouraging industry and, since 1958, over a hundred new industries have been started in Malaya alone. The emphasis is chiefly on light industry and consumer goods, such as food, drugs, tires, textiles, building materials and so forth. Most enterprises have fewer than 20 employees. Heavier industry includes petroleum refineries, aluminum rolling plants, and a steel-making project. The economy is reasonably stable, and fairly rapid progress is expected by most observers. The Gross National Product, about $2.9 billion in 1961, allows one of the highest living standards in Asia. Per capita income in 1961 was estimated at $266 in Malaya, $433 in Singapore, $233 in Sabah, and $183 in Sarawak.

CROPS: The world's largest rubber producer, Malaysia exported rubber worth $492.4 million in 1962. About two million persons are supported by the rubber industry in Malaya alone. Rice, coconuts, oil palm, fruit, and tea are other important crops. Sarawak is the world's largest producer of pepper, exporting almost $8 million worth in 1962. After rubber and rice, lumber is Malaysia's next crop in economic importance; half of the product is exported and exports were worth over $70 million in 1962.

LIVESTOCK: Cattle, buffalo, goats, sheep, pigs, and poultry.

FISHERIES: Fishing, extensively practiced from small boats offshore and by hand methods in streams and paddies, does not fill local needs and fish are imported. Malaya's catch in 1962 was about 170,000 tons.

MINING: Close to a third of Malaysia's exports are mined. Malaya is the world's largest tin producer, providing 58,600 tons in 1962. Iron, 6.5 million tons in 1962, bauxite, about 575,000 tons, petroleum, 57,274 long tons, and gold are produced in significant quantities. Considerable reserves await development.

TRADE

The chief exports are crude rubber, tin, timber, spices, iron ore, and petroleum. Principal imports are machinery, iron

FISHERMEN *Everyone on the island of Ketam, which lies off the northwestern coast of Malaya, depends on fish for a livelihood. One man is cutting the catch in slices to be dried in the sun.*

and steel, transport equipment, textiles, foods, and manufactured goods. During 1962, Sabah's imports were about $78 million, its exports $72 million, with the deficit covered by the 1961 surplus. Sarawak's imports were about $130 million, its exports $133 million. Malaya's imports were $800 million, its exports $856 million. Singapore's imports were $1.37 billion, its exports $1.17 billion, with a good portion of the deficit being covered by such invisible transactions as service and shipping charges and tourism.

1962: IMPORTS	$2,375,000,000
EXPORTS	$2,230,000,000
DEFICIT	$ 145,000,000

Until 1962, Malaya had a favorable balance of trade, but Singapore has consistently had an adverse balance. Malaysia is now facing balance of payments difficulties—partly because Indonesia's policy of "confrontation" has led it to cease all trade with Malaysia. Foreign exchange reserves have dropped because of the deficit; Malaysia has moved to increase exports and to cut imports by producing goods formerly imported and by curtailing consumption of luxury products.

TRANSPORT

ROAD: Malaya had almost 7,700 miles of government-maintained road in 1962, most of it hard surfaced. Over 253,000 motor vehicles included almost 37,000 trucks and buses and over 88,000 motorcycles. Singapore had about 500 miles of road and almost 118,000 vehicles, including over 28,000 motorcycles. Sabah had about 1,050 miles of road, less than half of it hard surfaced, while Sarawak had about 850 miles, mostly gravel or earth surfaced.

RAIL: Malaya has about 1,025 route miles of railway in its system, to which Singapore is connected. Sabah has a 116-mile railway; Sarawak has none.

WATERWAY: Unimportant in Malaya, inland waterways are the main arteries in Sabah and Sarawak. Rivers, especially the Kinabatangan in Sabah and the Rejang in Sarawak, carry small cargo, passenger, and tow boats.

AIR: Malayan Airways provides extensive internal service to the 14 states. International air lines serve Kuala Lumpur, Singapore, Penang, Kuching, and Jesselton.

SEA: Singapore is the fifth largest port in the world, receiving over 11,000 vessels in 1962. Penang, Malacca, Port Swettenham, and four smaller ports serve Malaya. Sandakan, Labuan, Jesselton, and five smaller ports serve Sabah, while Sarawak's shipping goes mostly to Kuching, Sibu, or Miri.

COMMUNI-CATION

Over 700,000 licensed radios and unknown numbers of unlicensed ones were in use in 1962. Over 100,000 telephones are in use. Postal, telegraph, cable, and wireless services are well developed.

MONGOLIAN PEOPLE'S REPUBLIC

Land of the Blue Skies

On a high plateau in the heart of the Asian continent lies the "land of the blue skies"—Mongolia, seldom visited by outsiders from East or West. In the 12th century, the world trembled before the thundering hooves of Mongol conquerors. But that was 800 years ago and it has been centuries since the Mongols have played a major role on the world stage.

Mongolia is a vast country—about 1,600 miles long from east to west, and 800 miles wide, embracing an area that is more than twice the size of Texas and is larger than Germany, France, and Italy combined. The terrain rises almost a mile above sea level.

COMPOSITION OF THE POPULATION

In this remote land live about one million people, 75 percent of whom are nomads. The population is homogeneous. There are a few thousand Chinese (who ethnically are no relation to the Mongols), a very small number of Russians, and several thousand Kirghiz and Kazakh tribesmen. There are, however, nearly 400,000 Mongols resident in the Soviet Union (mostly the so-called Buryat Mongols) and about 1,500,000 Mongols who inhabit Inner Mongolia, across the border in China.

A PASTORAL LAND

For the most part, Mongolia is still a pastoral country, just as it was when the horsemen of Genghis Khan set out on conquest from their capital of Karakorum and overran China, the empires of central Asia, India, Russia, and even portions of central Europe. Today most Mon-

BALL GAME *These youngsters in modern dress are practicing volleyball without a net. Although their home is near the capital city, these nomadic families still live in yurts. The round yurt, chiefly constructed of padded felt, is effective protection against the harsh winter and high winds of the steppes. The yurt is easily portable. These present-day yurts are covered with white waterproof canvas, a modern improvement.*

gols tend herds of horses and sheep.

The country lies in the latitude of southern Quebec and New England. It has an extreme continental climate, with winter temperatures often 50 and 60 degrees below zero; in summer, highs reach 90 degrees and more.

Mongolia has good grass pasture lands, but much of the region is deficient in water. Grain is grown both by dry farming methods and irrigation.

One-third of the country is largely composed of grassland plateaus; another third is mountain lake and forest land; and the Gobi Desert covers roughly another third of Mongolia. *Gobi* is a Mongol word which means a low-lying arid region. The Gobi is notable as a region where many dinosaur eggs and skeletons have been discovered. It is also a region of rare animals including the Przhevalski horse of which only a few score are believed to exist. In recent years, oil has been discovered in the Gobi, and a dozen or more wells have been brought into production.

A COMMUNIST POLITY

Mongolia is a Communist country. Its regime dates from 1921 when a Mongol Communist named Sukhebator (Red Warrior) succeeded in establishing power with the aid of Soviet armed forces. Just

before World War I, imperial Russia had established a protectorate over Mongolia, and Communist Russia has maintained a similar role to the present day.

Before the Communists took power, Mongolia was a theocracy, headed by Jebtsundama Hutukhtu, a Living Buddha. The country was dominated by Buddhist lamaseries; an estimated third of the population was associated with the great Buddhist establishments. The Communists permitted Hutukhtu to continue as nominal ruler until his death in 1924. Despite government campaigns, Buddhism is still strong.

Little was done by way of communizing the country until after World War II. Mongolia continued its predominantly tribal, nomadic character, nine-tenths of the population living in *yurts*, or conical tents, moving frequently during the year as they changed pasture for their animals.

COLLECTIVIZATION

Irrigated state grain farms have been set up. Livestock herding has been put on a collective basis. Meat processing, leather working, flour milling, glass, milk processing, coal mining, small-scale metal working, textile plants, and wood working industries have been introduced.

Communism has attempted to collectivize the tribal herds; a nominal 90 percent have been socialized. Plowed farming is almost entirely a state operation; in 1960, nearly 80 percent of the six million acres were under cultivation. In that year, 17 million head of cattle were collectively owned, and more than five million head privately owned.

FOREIGN AID

In recent years, especially since the establishment of the Communist regime in China and the rise of Soviet-Chinese rivalry, a vigorous effort has been made to introduce Communist institutions. Both Russia and China have provided large-scale aid to Mongolia, totaling $100 to $200 million a year.

AN BATOR   *Mongolia's capital, the "Town of the Red Warrior," has well de- ed, modern buildings, broad avenues, new factories, and new apartment houses.*

ARCHERS *Herdsmen of a small, nomad settlement engage in an archery contest, shooting at a sandbag tossed on the ground 100 yards away. Mongols have excelled in archery for more than a thousand years. Their bows, unlike the English longbow, are not straight but have a double curve which makes it possible for a short bow used on horseback to waft an arrow as far as from a longbow used on foot. The Mongolian bow is made up of layers of horn, sinew, bark, and wood.*

TRANSPORTATION AND INDUSTRY

A railroad, built with Soviet aid, links Mongolia with both Russia and China. Mongolian trade is carried on almost exclusively with China, Russia, and the Soviet satellites.

There is some production of copper, aluminum, gold, wolfram, and uranium. In 1960, there were 162 industrial enterprises, employing about 25,000 workers with output valued at 567 *togruks,* roughly $125 million. Agricultural production was valued at about the same, based

HORSE RACE *Mongols are fond of horse racing, archery, and wrestling. Horse r in Mongolia, however, are different from horse races in the rest of the world. A may be run over a course that exceeds 37 miles, and is designed to test stamina ra than sprinting ability. The jockey, strangely enough, may be a girl, and generall jockey, whether male or female, is older than 10 years. Occasionally a teen-ag allowed to ride; but in important races, the age limitation is strictly followed. Mo say they do not want a jockey strong enough to force the horse; they want a rider merely guides the horse, while the race itself brings out the animal's natural willing heart, and capacity. Some hours after the race, the four winning riders will ca around the grandstand area, each one accompanied by a herald in a gown of silk. A grandstand, the herald will chant a poem of his own composition, celebrating the h and his jockey. Then the prizes will be awarded.*

on livestock herds of 23 million, almost entirely sheep and horses. The Mongol Five-Year-Plan called for establishing 100 new industrial enterprises by 1965, and for increasing production 110 percent.

EDUCATION

Before 1924, more than 95 percent of the people were illiterate. Today, half of the population remains illiterate, but the percentage is rapidly being reduced by a system of general education. Under Russian influence, a phonetic Cyrillic alphabet was introduced in 1950.

HEALTH CONDITIONS

Public health measures have vastly increased life expectancy and have reduced infant mortality. However, winter respiratory diseases still take a heavy toll. The diet, almost exclusively meat (sheep) and milk products made of mare's milk (cheese, *kumiss* or lightly fermented mare's milk) is deficient in greenstuffs and fruit.

POLITICAL ORIENTATION

In the Sino-Soviet dispute, the regime favors Moscow; but Chinese influence is active and intrigue is common, causing repeated political purges as the Moscow-oriented government of Premier Yi Tsedenbal seeks to hold firm control.

A substantial pan-Mongol movement exists; it is dedicated to the reuniting of the Buryat Mongols and the China-ruled Inner Mongols in one Greater Mongolia.

Mongolia maintains diplomatic relations with most of the Asian states, with all of the Communist countries, and with a few European states, including England. She is most eager to establish diplomatic relations with the United States.

ULAN BATOR

Ulan Bator (formerly Urga), the capital, has a population of about 160,000 and has expanded enormously in the past decade. Using Soviet funds and Chinese labor, large-scale urban housing, modern government buildings, a water supply system, sewers, electric lights, and a telephone system have been installed; and an opera house, two good hotels, several museums, a university, and other educational institutions have been established.

Ulan Bator is the site of the ancient Gandun Monastery, seat of the Buddhist church—once populated by an estimated 10,000 monks. Gandun is still in service, but its monastic population has been reduced to a few hundred. In Ulan Bator, the Palace of the last Bogodo, Hu-tukhtu, may still be seen.

KARAKORUM

The most famous relics in Mongolia are at Karakorum, the capital built according to the plans of Genghis Khan by his sons and grandsons. A portion of the ancient site of the imperial *yurt* has been preserved, as well as the enormous monastery of Erdeni Jo which dates back to the 15th century. This edifice has been turned into a museum.

HARRISON E. SALISBURY

IN BRIEF

AREA	604,095 square miles; larger than Alaska. Landlocked.
TERRAIN	Chiefly plateau country, 3,000 to 5,000 feet above sea level. Mountains, the highest being in the Altai range, are situated in the south and west, and along the Siberian and Manchurian borders. Steppes and the Gobi Desert stretch across the southeast. Prairies, fertile valleys, and large lakes characterize the north and west.
FLORA	Forests, chiefly larch, cedar, and pine, are found in the northwest mountains. Prairie and steppe vegetation, except in scrub areas of the Gobi.

PACK TRAIN   *Mounted on a shaggy, long-tailed Mongol pony, this trailsman leads his camels through Mongolia's snow-covered wastes. He is dressed in a sheepskin robe and fur-lined cap, clothing much the same as that used 700 years ago by the hordes of Genghis Khan. The Mongolian camel develops a heavy coat in cold weather; its large, flat feet are as effective in traversing snowy terrain as they are in walking over sandy desert.*

FAUNA   Antelope, wild horse, wild camel, marmot, fox, squirrel, and
                   wolf.

CLIMATE   Dry, windy, and cold, much like Siberia. Temperature ranges
                   from 12°F. below zero to 64°F. in Ulan Bator, which gets
                   only nine or ten inches of rain a year.

CAPITAL   Ulan Bator (formerly Urga); 160,000 inhabitants in 1963.

OTHER CITIES   Khobdo, Choibalsang, Nalaikha are medium-sized towns.

POPULATION   1,080,000 estimated in 1965. Annual rate of increase is very
                   high at 3.1 percent. Density is about two persons and 40
                   herd animals per square mile.

ETHNIC GROUPS   Most of the population is Mongol, the Khalka and other
                   Mongol tribes comprising 76 percent of the population.
                   Kazakhs, Kirghiz, and Chinese make up the remainder.

LANGUAGES   Mongolian. Chinese and Russian are in limited use. Al-
                   though Mongolian has been written for centuries, a new
                   phonetic alphabet, based on Russian Cyrillic letters, was in-
                   troduced in 1950.

RELIGION   Buddhist Lamaism, strongly influenced from Tibet, was uni-
                   versal until 1921. The society is now much more secular,
                   although two monasteries with 110 lamas remain.

DATE OF   On March 31, 1921, a provisional government proclaimed in-
INDEPENDENCE   dependence. The Mongolian People's Republic was pro-
                   claimed November 26, 1924.

FORM OF   Communist. The 1960 constitution vests power in the Great
GOVERNMENT   People's *Khural,* to which 290 members were elected for
                   three years in 1963. Everyone over 18 may vote. The Prime
                   Minister is always the First Secretary of the People's Revolu-
                   tionary (Communist) Party and leads the seven-man Polit-
                   buro, or executive organ. The Communist Party has about
                   45,000 full members; its youth organization is composed of
                   over 70,000 members; the closely associated labor unions
                   have close to 90,000 members. A much higher proportion of
                   the people is represented within the power structure than is
                   usual in Communist countries. Mongolia is a member of the
                   United Nations.

CAMEL TENDER

SHEEP HERDER

WORKER IN COMMUNITY MILK HOUSE

CLERICAL WORKER

WRESTLERS Here, at the opening of a tournament in Ulan Bator, wrestlers perform the leaping, arm-flapping ceremonial dance. Each wrestler wears heavy boots, a small, tight loin cloth, and a pair of sleeves that meet across the shoulders, forming a kind of abbreviated jacket. The traditional hats worn by the wrestlers will be removed when the bout starts. Each wrestler is accompanied by his silk-robed herald. The match is ended when any part of a contestant's body touches the ground.

EDUCATION

In 1961, there were almost 125,000 students in 429 elementary and 15 secondary and vocational schools. An additional 40,000 students were expected by 1965, as schooling was extended to nomad and rural areas. The National University had 2,500 students and 200 instructors; another 1,200 students were in agricultural and teachers' colleges. Less than five percent of those between nine and 50 years were reported illiterate in 1956.

HEALTH FACILITIES

There were 870 doctors in 1961, an increase of over 500 since 1956. The country had 8,500 hospital beds and 700 doctors in training in 1961. Health is rapidly improving. Deaths dropped from 11,800 in 1955 to 9,900 in 1958 despite the rapid population increase.

CULTURAL FACILITIES

The 30 newspapers and 20 magazines were said to have a total circulation of 600,000 in 1964. About one in ten people sees the Communist Party's daily paper. Publishing is chiefly text and technical books. Traditional music, folk plays, and poetry—especially extemporaneous verse—are a part of daily life. Recently introduced art forms, notably the film, novel, opera, ballet, and theater, are widely followed.

CURRENCY AND FINANCE

The *togruk* is held at par with 22.5 Soviet kopeks or, at the official rate, 25¢ in U.S. currency. Budget estimates for 1962 expected revenues of $340 million and expenditures of $338 million, or over $330 per person.

INDUSTRY AND PRODUCTION

Industry accounted for a third of the national production in 1960. Electric power production, the basic necessity for increased industry, was to be quadrupled by 1965. Development has, so far, concentrated on light industry, especially the processing of animal products.

CROPS: About 1.1 million acres were planted in 1961, and 330,000 tons of wheat were harvested. Another 750,000 acres were to be brought under the plow by 1965.

LIVESTOCK: Sheep, goats, yak, cattle, horses, and camels. The total livestock population is estimated between 23 and 25 million head. About 84 percent of the total area is pasture land; herding and associated pursuits occupy 75 percent of the people.

FISHERIES: Lake and river fisheries are capable of large-scale development. Exploitation is slow, partly because Mongols are only gradually acquiring a taste for fish.

MINING: Coal production reached 770,000 tons in 1962. Oil fields at Sain Shanda yielded 28,600 metric tons in 1960. Gold, tungsten, and uranium are mined.

TRADE

Chief exports are cattle, horses, wool, hides, meat, and butter. Imports are largely consumer goods. The Soviet Union and China are the principal trading partners.

1960: IMPORTS $97,000,000
EXPORTS $72,000,000
DEFICIT $25,000,000

TRANSPORT

ROAD: There were over 5,200 miles of motorable road in 1960. Horses and camels are extensively used for transport.

RAILROAD: About 870 miles of track. A spur line connects Choibalsang with the Soviet Transiberian Railway; the chief track connects Ulan Bator with Peking and the Transiberian line.

WATERWAY: Steamers serve on the Selenga and Orkhon rivers.

AIR: A national line provides service from Ulan Bator to Peking and to Irkutsk in the Soviet Union. Chinese flights also serve Mongolia.

COMMUNI-CATION

All services are government-owned and operated. There were 25,000 radios, one radio station, 10,500 telephones, over 185 post offices, and 25 telegraph offices in 1962.

TIBET

HIMALAYA MTS.

Jumla

DHAULAGIRI
26,810 FT.

ANNAPURNA 26,492 FT.

GAURI SANKAR EVEREST 29,028 FT.
23,440 FT. MAKALU
27,790 FT.

Pokhara

KANCHENJUNGA
28,146 FT.

Kodari

Katmandu

SIKKIM

GANDAK

KOSI

Hetaura

Birganj

Biritnagar

INDIA

NEPAL

The Himalayan Kingdom

The Himalayan kingdom of Nepal lies between India and Communist-occupied Tibet. Completely landlocked and cut off from the rest of the world by its mighty mountains, Nepal has been until recently a sealed book, a land of mystery and romance, whose rulers actively discouraged foreign visitors and foreign ways. Until 1951, probably no more than a few hundred Europeans had ever set foot in Katmandu, the capital, and fewer still had ever seen the interior.

The isolation of Nepal ended in 1953 with the opening of a road linking Katmandu to India. This and other factors such as the development of regular commercial air service to Katmandu, Nepal's admission to the United Nations in 1955, and the opening of the American, Soviet, and Chinese Embassies during the past few years have jolted the kingdom out of medieval seclusion.

A SPECTACULAR LAND

Nepal, which is about the area of the state of Wisconsin, has a population of about 10 million. One of the most mountainous countries in the world, it is a land of spectacular scenery—replete with palaces and pagodas, tigers and rhinoceroses, smiling rice-clad valleys, dense swampy jungles, and gigantic snowy mountains· Within its borders are five of the world's highest peaks—Everest, Kanchenjunga, Makalu, Dhaulagiri, and Annapurna, all above 26,400 feet.

A VARIED CULTURE

The culture of Nepal is richly diversified, drawing on that of the Mongoloid tribes of Tibet and the Indo-Aryan peoples of northern India. Nepal is the home of the fierce Gurkhas and the hardy Sherpas, as well as of a number of other small ethnic groups.

Nepal, sacred to the Buddhists as the birthplace of Buddha, is also sacred to the Hindus as the source of the rivers flowing into the Holy

Ganges. Hinduism and Buddhism are practiced here, not only as separate religions, but in many parts of the country in a synthesized form.

Many languages are spoken; those used in the lower Himalayan valleys belong to the Indo-Aryan family of tongues; those in the Great Himalayas are of Tibeto-Burman origin; between these two, there is a zone of mixed idiom.

HISTORY AND GOVERNMENT

In 1769, a band of Gurkhas led by Prithwi Narayan—descendants of people who originally came from India—conquered the Katmandu Valley, laying the foundation of the present state of Nepal. In 1814–15, the Gurkhas were defeated by the British and were obliged to accept a British Resident. Under the treaty with the British, who fixed the limits of Nepal, the Gurkhas were allowed to remain in control of the country, with some power vested in the British Resident.

In 1854, the Gurkhas invaded Tibet; for almost 100 years after, the Tibetans continued to pay an annual tribute to the King of Nepal.

From about 1850 to 1950, the Nepalese King was merely a figurehead, and the hereditary, autocratic Prime Ministers of the Rana family wielded supreme power.

In 1950, as a result of a palace revolt, the King regained his position of authority. In February, 1951, the late King Tribhuvana proclaimed the country to be a constitutional monarchy. Eight years later, in February, 1959, a new Constitution, which provided for a bicameral legislature with a representative lower house, was proclaimed by King Mahendra.

During the following spring, the arduous process of polling Nepal's scattered population was begun; and in May, 1959, the country's first elected government, headed by B. P. Koirala, leader of the Nepali Congress, took office.

KING MAHENDRA

On December 15, 1960, in a surprise sweep, King Mahendra, dissatisfied with the activities of the elected government, suspended the

HIS MAJESTY   *One of the last of the world's absolute monarchs, King Mahendra acceded to the throne in 1956, at the age of 36. Ever since, he has made various efforts, sometimes unsuccessful, to lead his country toward democratic government. He speaks English, Hindi, and Nepalese.*

Constitution and jailed Prime Minister Koirala and other members of Nepal's 19-month-old government. The King now rules his mountain kingdom directly, aided only by a new Council of Ministers which functions under his chairmanship.

THE HIMALAYA REGION

Nepal may be roughly divided into four regions: the High Himalayan country, the Katmandu Valley, the Inner Terai, and the Terai.

The Himalayan region, along the Tibetan border, is mostly over 15,000 feet high. It is uninhabited except for scattered settlements in the mountain valleys. Most of the mountain-climbing Sherpas who have taken part in Himalayan expeditions come from the northern part of Solo Khumbu. Thamey, a village in the same district, is the birthplace of Tenzing who, with Edmund Hillary, stood for 15 minutes on the summit of Mount Everest in 1953. In Khumbu the biggest village is Namche Bazar, site of the world-famous Monastery of Thyangboche.

Despite the fact that the land is rough and stony and the weather bitterly cold much of the year, the Himalayan people engage in agriculture and sheep raising. Wheat and barley are grown in Khumbu, mostly at between eight and ten thousand feet. Potatoes, the biggest crop of the Sherpas, are grown at up to 14,000 feet. In summer, the Sherpas take their herds of sheep, goats, yak, and chowries (a cross

between a yak and a cow) up to the higher mountain pastures.

In 1955, a cheese factory was built in the Langtang Valley, with technical aid from Swiss dairy experts and economic aid from the Food and Agricultural Organization of the United Nations and the Colombo Plan. The unusually rich milk of the chowries (with a butter content

MAIN STREET OF PATAN *A suburb of the capital, Patan is two miles from Katmandu. Ancient temples and statues line Darbur Square. A Hindu temple stands on the left.*

(Courtesy P. P. Karan and University of Kentucky Himalayan Expedition.)

of eight percent compared with five percent for a standard Swiss milk) produced a cheese described as rivaling that of the better Swiss products. The cheese is carried down the mountains to Katmandu on the backs of coolies—a journey taking seven to ten days. A second cheese plant was opened at Thodung in East Nepal in 1957.

THE KATMANDU VALLEY

In the southern part of the Himalayan region, there are several fertile and densely populated valleys, including Katmandu, the heart of the country. Located at an altitude of 4,500 feet, Katmandu Valley, with an estimated population of over one-half million, is the administrative, economic, and cultural center of the kingdom.

Katmandu is inhabited mainly by Newars, an indigenous people who speak a quasi-Tibeto-Burman language. They are highly skilled craftsmen and merchants and control much of Nepal's commerce. From about the 13th to the 19th centuries, Nepalese metal work, painting, sculpture, architecture, and literature were entirely the work of the Newars.

All three of the Valley's main towns—Katmandu, Patan, and Bhadgaon—have a glorious history. Their art and architecture bear witness to the cultural achievements of the Nepalese, who managed to harmoniously combine the Buddhist-Lamaism of the north with the Hinduism of the south.

In Katmandu, as in the other Himalayan valleys, farming is typically conducted on small fields with primitive implements. In this subsistence economy, rice is the leading crop. The soil is fertile, and the cultivated slopes are carefully terraced to reduce erosion; but the farmer, despite all his labor, has difficulty making ends meet, struggling, as he does, under an almost impossible system of land tenure. Most of the land belongs to a few wealthy landlords, and most farmers are merely tenants who must turn in a large share of their crop for rent.

BAREFOOT PORTERS
Used to carrying packs long distances through the wilds of Himalaya, these porters follow marked footpaths across the mountains and old bridges across rivers.

SHERPA FAMILY *They live 13,000 feet up in the Himalayas, a height at which only the hardiest humans can survive. The man wearing a hat is a professional mountaineer. He has brought his client, a Swiss geologist, to meet his family. The sturdily built stone house indicates comparative prosperity. The slightly slanting timber roof has been designed to hold a heavy covering of snow which will serve as insulation from the cold during the winter.*

ARCHITECTURE AND THE ARTS

Countless temples and shrines are to be found in the Katmandu Valley. The earliest of these are the *stupas*, located in the vicinity of Katmandu. Here, too, are the renowned temples of Swayambhunath and Buddhanath, with their gilt figures, bronze statues, guardian beasts, and sacred pillars.

In Katmandu itself, richly decorated pagodas, palaces, and houses front on open squares. The pagodas, square in plan and usually built of brick, are several stories high with roofs of tiles or copper gilt. Carved and painted woodwork featuring images of deities and floral ornaments cover the exteriors.

The art treasures of the country are displayed in a museum at Katmandu. The Durbar Library and others house fine collections of manuscripts. The arts of Nepal have long been cultivated: wood carving, brassware, bronze statues, painting, and religious items, such as prayer wheels and banners.

THE INNER TERAI

The zone of the Inner Terai consists of the Churia Hills and Bhabar. This entire section is sparsely populated; large areas are almost uninhabited.

The Churia Hills, geologically a continuation of the Siwalik Range of India, are covered with timber and savanna grass. South of the Hills is the gravelly and fairly steep Talus Slope known as the Bhabar. Here, great rivers swirl down from the Himalaya; during periods of heavy rain, these rivers bring down millions of tons of silt and stone from the ragged contours of the higher mountains. Dense arboreal growth flourishes in the porous soil of the Bhabar.

THE TERAI

South of the Bhabar and Churia Hills is the Terai, a low, fertile alluvial plain—20 miles wide at its broadest point.

The northern part of the Terai, bordering the forests of the Bhabar and Churia Hills, is a marshy region in which malaria is endemic. South of this belt lies rich agricultural land, some ten miles wide, which stretches along the Indian frontier.

INDUSTRY AND POWER

Biratnagar and Birganj are the chief centers of factory industry. Jute, cotton, sugar, matches, and processed foods are the chief industrial products. However, in Nepal, the bulk of the manufactured goods are not produced in factories, but are cottage-made. Cottage industries— or homemade products—include sugar, textiles, tobacco, wood, metalwares, and rice.

Because of its rugged topography and abundant precipitation, Nepal is well supplied with potential water power. India's huge multi-purpose Kosi Project, which includes construction of a dam in Nepal a few miles from the Indian border, will eventually irrigate a million acres of land and supply hydroelectric power to much of the Terai region.

TRANSPORTATION

Most roads are exceedingly rough and steep. The 87-mile road linking India and Katmandu, opened in 1953, is more suitable for jeeps than for ordinary cars. There are only 63 miles of narrow-gauge railroads.

An electrically operated aerial cableway (similar to a ski lift), on which cargo is transported in baskets, links Katmandu Valley with the railhead at Amlekganj. With American aid, the capacity of this aerial cableway has been more than doubled.

The government plans to construct motorable roads to link the mountain districts and the Terai with Katmandu. With Chinese aid, a road linking Katmandu with Lhasa is under construction. Soviet ex-

SIVA'S GOLDEN TEMPLE   Pashupatinath Temple, particularly sacred to Hindu Nepalis, is situated about two miles from Katmandu. Above the entrance is a representation of four-armed Siva, the Destroyer, bearing a trident. The god Kartick is represented below the symbol of the sun. The god Ganesha, with the face of the elephant, appears below the symbol of the moon. (Courtesy P. P. Karan and University of Kentucky Himalayan Expedition.)

perts have completed surveys for an East-West Highway across the country. When completed, this road program will not only stimulate trade, but will make Nepal more accessible to sightseers, and will help develop a tourist industry.

At present, the only efficient and quick means of transport within Nepal is by air. The Royal Nepal Airlines link Katmandu with such outlying towns as Biratnagar and Pokhara. Katmandu is also connected by air with Delhi, Calcutta, and Patna, in India, and with Dacca in Pakistan.

FOREIGN AID

The lack of a common language and of mass communication media militates against national unity, and political stability is constantly threatened by economic distress.

A plan for economic development is under way with foreign aid from India, the United States, the Soviet Union, China, Switzerland, Israel, and other countries. Among the important projects completed under American aid are: a new College of Education in Katmandu, installation of a radio-telephone network in the capital, navigational aids at the air fields, and the multi-purpose Rapti Valley Project (similar to the TVA). Projects to foster agricultural and village development are being carried out mainly with the help of India.

STREET VENDOR   This boy is selling yoghurt in the streets of Katmandu. Like the man behind him, the lad carries his wares on a pole from street to street. (Courtesy P. P. Karan and University of Kentucky Himalayan Expedition.)

RECLINING VISHNU   *The second god in the Hindu trinity, Vishnu the Preserver, is honored by worshippers at the Feast of Narayan, held annually during July. This 33-foot effigy of gray stone is set in a nest of stone serpents and lies in the middle of a pond. During the festival, the feet and the head of the statue are covered with flowers, holy oil, and red and yellow powder. This shrine, particularly holy to Hindus, is an object of pilgrimage to all but the King of Nepal. Since the King is regarded as an incarnation of this god, he would die if he gazed upon this holy effigy.*   (Courtesy P. P. Karan and University of Kentucky Himalayan Expedition.)

EDUCATION

The traditional schools offered a restricted curriculum which stressed religious learning and classical education. Modern education, as distinguished by a broader curriculum and improved methods of teaching, did not reach Nepal until near the end of the 19th century. Currently, great efforts are being made to expand the school system. In 1962, there were 215,000 students in primary schools and an additional 34,000 in higher schools. English is taught from the third grade. Tribhuwan University at Katmandu is developing with aid from India and the United States.

PRESS, RADIO, AND CINEMA

Daily papers are published at Katmandu in Nepali and English; there are other publications in these languages and in Hindi. *Radio Nepal* broadcasts in several languages. Prior to 1950, there were no cinema houses in Nepal, but now there are several in Katmandu. Indian films are very popular.

PRADYUMNA P. KARAN

IN BRIEF

AREA Landlocked. 54,563 square miles, slightly larger than Arkansas.

TERRAIN Mountainous, with dense swampy jungles. Across the south lies the 20-mile-wide Terai, a region of plain and swamp. The greater part of the country, a band across the center, is Inner Himalaya and Siwalik hill country; the region is broken by many sharp mountain ranges and traversed by high, fertile valleys, notably the Katmandu Valley. Along the northern border lies the High Himalaya, with five of the world's highest mountains, including Mount Everest. Mountain snows feed several great river systems, including the Kali, Karnali, Gandak, and Kosi.

FLORA Rain forests of the Terai largely overgrown with broadleaf evergreens, rhododendron, and bamboo. Some savanna areas are covered with 15-foot elephant grass which is practically impassable. There are hardwood and conifer forests in the mountains.

FAUNA Tiger, rhinoceros, elephant, wild boar in the southern swamp and forest land; snow leopard, bear, deer, wild sheep, and mountain goats in the Himalayas.

CLIMATE Arctic above 15,000 feet; alpine between 7,000 and 15,000 feet; temperate or subtropical below 7,000 feet. Most of the rain falls during the summer months, averaging about 58 inches a year. The east receives sufficient rainfall, but drought sometimes affects the west. Temperatures in the Katmandu Valley average 50°F. in January, 78°F. in July.

CAPITAL Katmandu; approximately 195,000 inhabitants.

OTHER CITIES Patan, population 135,000; Bhadgaon, 85,000. Both cities are essentially part of the Katmandu urban area.

POPULATION 9,550,000 (estimated in 1962). Rate of population increase is estimated at 1.8 percent per year. Density is 174 persons per square mile.

ETHNIC GROUPS The population is a complex intermixture of Tibeto-Mongolian tribal groups from the north, and Indo-Aryan groups

GURKHAS ON PARADE   *Nepal's famous warriors are recruited mainly from the Gurung and Magar tribes of the Inner Himalaya. The Nepalese Army includes 20,000 regulars. Here is a group on the Katmandu Parade Grounds. Both Britain and India jealously guard their right to seek soldiers from among these stalwarts. Britain maintains eight Gurkha battalions; India, twelve. The salaries of these mercenaries, remitted to their families in Nepal, are one of the mainstays of Nepal's economy.*

from the south. The Newars, concentrated in the Katmandu Valley, dominate commerce. Warrior tribes, from whom the Gurkhas spring, include the Gurung, Magar, Rais, Limbus, Sunwars, and Thakurs. In the south are the tribes of the Tharus; in the north, those of the Bhutias. The mountaineering Sherpas are one of the Bhutia tribes.

LANGUAGES   Nepali, the official language, is derived from Sanskrit but has extensive Tibeto-Burman borrowings. It is the native tongue of about 55 percent of the people, and the second language of 30 percent. English is used by most government and business officials. Linguistic diversity is a serious national problem; Hindi, Pahari, Newari, Magarkura, Gurungkura, Kiranti, Marthili, Bhojpouri, and numerous Bhutia dialects are used by groups of significant size.

RELIGION   Pauranic Hinduism, or traditional Hinduism, is the dominant faith in the south; Mahayana Buddhism dominates in the more sparsely populated north. Both faiths are followed by many people of the central region. A cult of considerable influence invests each mountain with its own deity, who rules the neighborhood of his own peak. Christian missions are admitted to the country, but conversion is forbidden.

DATE OF INDEPENDENCE   In 1769, a Gurkha king conquered and unified the Katmandu Valley area. Although Britain controlled foreign affairs for a century, formal independence has been maintained since the conquest.

FORM OF GOVERNMENT

Constitutional monarchy. On December 16, 1962, a new "Constitutional Monarchial Hindu State" was proclaimed, superseding the 1951 constitution. The 1962 document recognizes the village *panchayat* (council) as the basic unit of democracy. Village panchayats elect district panchayats, whose members elect zonal panchayats. These bodies elect 90 members to the national panchayat. Royal nominees (as many as 15 percent of the elected members) and representatives of professional groups also sit in the national panchayat. Executive power is vested in the King, who selects his own Council of Ministers from the national panchayat. Since 1955, Nepal has been a member of the United Nations.

EDUCATION

In 1961, there were almost 3,200 primary schools, with 150,000 pupils and 4,250 teachers. Almost 560 secondary and technical schools enrolled over 63,500 students with 3,150 teachers. More than 600 new teachers were in training in 15 teachers' institutions. Higher schools and colleges enrolled over 5,550. In 1960, Tribhuvan University was founded. About 12 percent of the population is literate.

*MAIN STREET OF KATMANDU
The gateway leads to Hanuman Dhoka Square, the center of the capital. Two modern hotels and the best shops line the sides of New Road, as this avenue is called. The gaily painted cycle rickshaw waits for a fare. The government-operated Emporium, which sells Nepali handicraft products — wood-carving, metalwork, and hand-woven fabrics — to tourist customers, stands just inside the gate. The representations of protective deities are mounted on the gates of the city.*

HEALTH FACILITIES

In 1960, there were 128 doctors, two dentists, 27 nurse-midwives, and one pharmacist in Nepal. Malaria remains an extremely serious problem in the Terai area, while tuberculosis is endemic in mountain areas. By the end of 1965, three new hospitals (with a total of 360 beds) and ten health centers will be completed.

CULTURAL FACILITIES

In 1960, 13 daily newspapers had a circulation of 7,000, or less than one paper a day for every thousand people. *Radio Nepal* broadcasts from Katmandu in Newari, Hindi, Nepali, and English.

CURRENCY AND FINANCE

The Nepalese *rupee* weighs 171 grains of fine gold and is valued at 13¢ in U. S. currency. Both Nepalese and Indian rupees circulate; the two currencies are freely convertible at a rate of 160 Nepalese rupees to 100 Indian rupees. Budget estimates for fiscal 1964 expected revenues of over $34 million and expenditures of $38.4 million. Revenues include $16.25 million in foreign aid, $11 million coming from the United States.

INDUSTRY AND PRODUCTION

Agriculture accounts for about 90 percent of the Gross National Product and employs 90 percent of the people. The GNP, roughly estimated at $517 million in 1961, is made up of a per capita product of $53 per year. About 15,000 industrial workers are employed in jute, sugar, rice, and timber processing mills, and in paper, plywood, cotton, wool, cement, cigarette, match, glass, and ceramic factories. Industrial development is hindered by primitive transport and limited power development. In 1963, Nepal had an installed capacity of almost 10,000 kilowatts; four hydroelectric power stations were under construction and several more were in the planning stage. Forests are probably the natural resource that can be most easily developed. One-third of the total area is forested; products include many varieties of valuable timber, resin, turpentine, dyes, medicinal herbs, and drugs.

CROPS: Rice, corn, millet, wheat, potatoes, oilseed, tobacco, jute, sugar cane, fruits, and vegetables are the chief crops. Area under cultivation is only a little over one acre per person. By 1963, almost 250,000 acres were irrigated, and irrigation works for another 350,000 acres were in progress.

LITTLE SHOP *The window screens and frames of this small store, in Hanuman Dhoka Square in Katmandu, are the work of Newari craftsmen, famous through all Asia for their skill. The Nepali girl is waiting for customers at a general store which sells spices, oils, sugar, tobacco, etc.*

LIVESTOCK: Cattle, buffalo, yak, sheep, goats, pigs, and poultry.

MINING: Talc, mica, lignite, coal, copper, and iron are mined in amounts too small to be commercially significant. When transport becomes available, deposits of copper, iron, mica, limestone, lead, zinc, gold, cobalt, and nickel can be developed.

TRADE

The chief exports are rice, grain, raw and manufactured jute, oilseeds, hides and skins, *ghee* (clarified butter), timber, medicinal herbs, cattle, and tobacco. Imports are mainly cotton and woolen cloth, petroleum products, salt, machinery, medicines, paper, shoes, cement, iron and steel, spices, and consumer goods. About 95 percent of the trade is with India.

1960: IMPORTS $37,378,900
EXPORTS $17,009,200
DEFICIT $20,369,700

Nepal's balance of trade is actually favorable; invisible transactions—pensions and remittances of Gurkha soldiers, remitted earnings of Nepalis working in India, and foreign aid—more than offset the apparent deficit.

TRANSPORT

ROAD: Pack animals or porters on foot are the only means of transport over 2,500 miles of trail. There are about 770 miles of motorable road; only 200 miles of it usable in all weathers. About 30 trucks and buses a day use the key road, a 87-mile highway from Katmandu to Birganj, on the Indian border. Some 900 miles of road are under construc-

FLOUR MILL *The millstone is turned by running water. Grain from the hanging basket falls through the hole in the center of the turning millstone. The flour piles up in powdery masses around the stone's edge.* (Courtesy P. P. Karan and University of Kentucky Himalayan Expedition.)

tion with U. S. and Indian aid; this includes an East-West Highway at the foot of the mountains. A road from Katmandu to Tibet is being built with Chinese aid. An 18-mile ropeway from Hetaura to Katmandu, once the only freight route to the capital city, has been expanded with U. S. aid funds to carry 25 tons an hour.

RAILROAD: There are 63 miles of narrow-gauge line which connect two towns on the plains with the Indian rail system.

AIR: The Royal Nepal Airline Corporation links Katmandu with 12 of the larger towns, also with Calcutta, Delhi, and Patna in India, and with Dacca in East Pakistan. Another 23 air strips are under way or have been completed. Development of air transport is given first priority, partly because road and rail construction is very difficult and very expensive in Nepali terrain.

SEA: All ocean freight is transshipped through ports in India.

COMMUNI-CATION

In 1964, there were about 2,500 telephones, mostly in Katmandu. U. S.-built telephones link Katmandu with 34 important towns; a radio network links the capital with 26 towns. Human carriers are heavily relied on. Perhaps 15,000 radios are in use. A network of 56 wireless stations is under construction with U. S. and Indian aid funds. Post, telephone, radio, and telegraph services are government-operated.

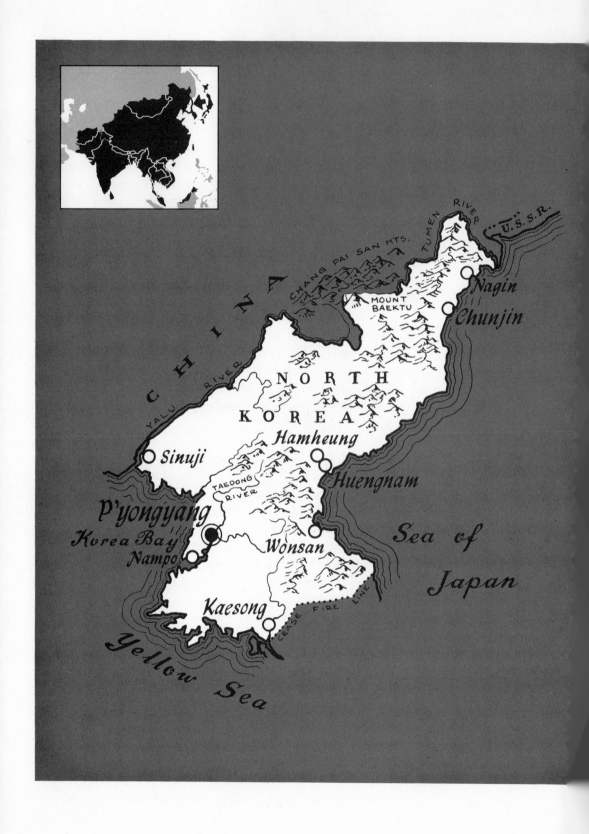

CHINA

CHANG PAI SAN MTS.

TUMEN RIVER

U.S.S.R.

Nagin

MOUNT
BAEKTU

Chunjin

YALU RIVER

NORTH

KOREA

Hamheung

Sinuji

Huengnam

TAEDONG
RIVER

P'yongyang

Sea of

Korea Bay

Wonsan

Japan

Nampo

Kaesong

CEASE FIRE LINE

Yellow Sea

NORTH KOREA

Aggressive Stronghold of Communism

The end of a 35-year period of colonial rule by the Japanese, during which many Korean nationalists died for independence, marked
the beginning of Korea's dependence upon the United States and
Soviet Russia. When, at the close of World War II, Japan surrendered
unconditionally on August 14, 1945, Russian armies had already landed
in northeast Korea and were rapidly moving southward. About a month
later, American troops disembarked in the southern half of Korea.

The objective of the military occupation of Korea's two halves,
separated by the 38th parallel, was to disarm the Japanese. Sadly, however, the demarcation still stands nearly two decades later like a fixed
national frontier, exposing the scars of the fratricidal Korean War.
Once again, Korea became trapped in the struggle for the balance of
power, as she had been in the 20 centuries of her recorded history. Yet
never before had the country been divided against itself as it is today.

For the Korean people, the accidental 38th zonal division has
meant an increasing antagonism between the two sectors. The two
opposed ideologies, the different aims and methods of government, and
a striking contrast in the social, economic, and political life of north
and south may perpetuate two Koreas. North Korea accuses the south
of being the puppet of American imperialism; South Korea accuses the
north of being the puppet of Russian imperialism. Each sector is bent
on the elimination of the other, and seeks the unification of Korea—but
according to its own pattern of government. Consequently, not even
postal exchange has existed between the two states since their creation
in 1948.

THE GRAND VISTA OF 1967

Whereas South Korea suffers under an extremely low per capita
income—low even by Asian standards—and is heavily dependent for
survival upon U.S. aid, North Korea is the showcase of Communism in
the Far East. In 1964, the then 53-year-old Premier Kim Il-song boasted

that by 1967 (the final year of the Seven-Year Plan) a self-sufficient economy would "ensure not only a bountiful material standard of living for the 12 million population in the North but also for the 25 million Southern compatriots." Kim declared that per capita industrial output in North Korea would surpass Japan by 1967. He said that production would be so far advanced that the income tax for the working class would be abolished, and that the country could then commence an 11-year, tuition-free compulsory educational system. He prognosticated that by 1967 the per household real incomes of factory and white collar workers would increase 1.7 times, and that of farmers twice, as against 1960.

And in fact, although like all controlled figures of Communist countries, there is no way of confirming North Korean statistics, the standard of living appears to be relatively high. In 1959, seven Japanese newspapermen who visited North Korea reported that the farmers, the factory hands, and white collar workers were leading a decent life, financially and culturally. The average manager's monthly salary was around 150 *won* (U.S. $150). Per capita income rose 2.2 times in 1960 as against 1956, and the workers' savings increased 2.2 times in 1957 and 4.5 times in 1958 compared with 1956. Joan Robinson, a noted British economist who visited North Korea in October 1964, reported that the difference in standard of living between urban and rural areas is very narrow. Miss Robinson concluded that the level of a farmer's income in North Korea was "well above the Chinese average." North Korea's first Five-Year Plan was fulfilled earlier than the schedule called for.

PHYSIOGRAPHY

North Korea covers approximately 47,000 square miles, an area approximately the size of New York State. On the west, it faces Communist China across the Yellow Sea; on the east, Japan across the Sea of Japan; and on the south, meets the constriction of the 38th parallel. About 500 miles of its northern boundary are almost entirely river lines backed by rugged mountain chains along Communist China. Only 11 miles of its northeastern frontier touch Siberia. This solid attach-

KAESONG *This ancient city, located in central Korea, served as the capital of the country during the Koryo dynasty (935-1392). The hills lie about 50 miles northwest of Seoul on the 38th parallel, the cease-fire line between the two parts of Korea.*

ment to Asia makes North Korea a continental rather than an insular foreland.

The topography is predominantly rough and mountainous. Only 25 percent of the land consists of plains.

On the west coast, the granary of North Korea, lie broad rice fields. The northeastern highlands are suitable for dry-field one-crop agriculture and extensive forestry.

PHYSICAL CHARACTERISTICS OF THE KOREANS

Mongoloid in character, Koreans are physically somewhat taller than the Japanese, but slightly shorter than northern Chinese. North Koreans are generally taller than their southern brothers, male height averaging five feet, five inches, and female five feet, four inches. Koreans have black straight hair, high cheek bones, dark oblique eyes, and a tinge of bronze in the skin.

THE KOREAN LANGUAGE

The ethnic character of the Korean is clearly reflected in his language. Korean, regarded as an Altaic tongue, is polysyllabic and contrasts sharply with Chinese and Japanese. It is the only language spoken throughout Korea. During the 15th century, Koreans invented a phonetic alphabet of 14 consonants and 10 vowels called Onmun, probably the only alphabet originated in the Orient. The official script in North Korea is Onmun. The use of characters and terms from Chinese, in the past considered the classic language, has been abolished. The adoption of Onmun should facilitate the campaign against illiteracy.

RELIGION

The underlying religion has been shamanism, a form of animistic nature worship. Buddhism was introduced in 373 A.D. in P'yongyang, by way of China, and later passed on to Japan. Not until the 14th century did Confucianism become the state religion.

In 1885, the first American Presbyterian missionary arrived in Korea. By 1935, there were over a half million Christians of all denominations. As late as 1949, it was estimated there were 2,000 churches in North Korea but they were suppressed by Communist anti-religious policy. In North Korea, no one religion is identified with any particular geographic area.

SOCIAL CUSTOMS

The Confucian idea that women are inferior to men is less loosely held in the north than in the south. According to Confucian concept, a boy and girl who have reached the age of seven should not sit together, but this dictum is not maintained in the north where the equality of the sexes is more or less conceded.

REGIONAL DIET AND HOUSING

The normal diet consists of rice, fish, vegetables, fruit, and a small amount of meat, milk, eggs, and dairy products. Millet is used as a substitute by those who cannot afford rice. Dried fish is a common food. Tea and rice-boiled water are the national beverages.

The typical house is a one-story structure built in the shape of an "L" or a "U" with an inside court. The better-constructed houses have walls of masonry for the first four feet, and walls of plaster reinforced by timber for the remainder. Rooms are small and cramped. Floors consist of flat stones covered with successive layers of clay, and are surfaced with oilpaper. Heat is conducted from one room to another underneath the floors by means of flues which connect with an inside fireplace.

REGIONAL DRESS

Traditional native dress is made of white cotton or silk, which is padded in winter. Men wear baggy trousers tied at the ankle; a tunic with a short, colored satin vest covers the torso. Men also wear a long coat. Elderly gentlemen wear high-crowned, finely woven, horsehair hats.

Women are dressed in full, long, and often colorful skirts, and in long-sleeved, high-waisted jackets. Feet are shod in padded white stockings and gondola-like slippers.

In urban areas, most Koreans are garbed in Western clothing.

NORTH KOREA VERSUS SOUTH KOREA

There are significant variations in the essentially homogeneous culture of Korea. North Koreans are generally regarded as more energetic and aggressive than South Koreans. Northerners are hard workers and possess a high degree of initiative. It is a commonplace in Korea for a Southerner to cynically remark that the North Korean is coarse, uncouth, and a troublemaker. The North Korean, on the other hand, is often contemptuous of the South Korean, considering him lazy, effete, and narrow-minded.

Since 1948, three of nine South Korean presidents and premiers have been of North Korean origin. More importantly, since 1946 the political, social, and economic control of South Korea have been to a substantial degree in the hands of North Koreans, 2.3 million of whom sought refuge in South Korea.

NEW RAIL LINE   *The new Haechu-Hasong (South Hwanghae Province) broad gauge railway about 50 miles long was built in 75 days to comemorate the thirteenth anniversary of Liberation Day on August 15, 1958. It is decorated with flowers, flags, and a portrait of Premier Kim. The cheering throng is composed largely of students and volunteers who worked on the project after school and working hours. The signs written in the native tongue on the front of the train and on the arch say "The Opening Ceremony of Haechu-Hasong Broad Gauge Railway."*

PREMIER KIM IL-SONG

The background of Kim Il-song, Premier of the Democratic People's Republic of Korea since its inception, suffers from a lack of authentic records. The story of his life is encrusted with legend. According to his official biography, Kim was born in 1912, near P'yongyang, into a lower-class family. At the age of 13, he migrated to Manchuria and there joined the Communist Youth League (Komsomol). In 1929, he served a term in jail. In 1931, he joined the Communist Party and led an anti-Japanese guerrilla contingent, called the Korean People's Revolutionary Army. From 1934 to 1939, Kim's partisan contingent waged almost 6,000 surprise attacks on the Japanese.

When Kim's detachments were pushed into Siberia, he transferred into the Soviet Communist Party. For heroic service in the Stalingrad battle in 1942, he was awarded the Stalin Medal and the rank of major. In August, 1945, he entered North Korea behind Soviet tanks. On October 3rd of that year, he was introduced to the public as a Korean leader.

There is a persistent rumor that the present Kim Il-song assumed the alias of an older Kim Il-song, a nationally renowned hero of the Korean resistance.

STRIFE FOR POLITICAL HEGEMONY

Kim Il-song's seizure of power would not have been possible without the full support of the 40,000-man Soviet occupation forces. There were roughly five factional groups contending for leadership in the political arena: (1) Kim and his ex-partisan comrades; (2) the 30,000 or so Soviet-citizen Koreans led by Ho Ka-ui, a Communist Party official; (3) the Yenan faction from China numbering several hundred revolutionaries with Kim Tu-pong as their leader; (4) the internal Communist group headed by Pak Hon-yong (the founder of the Korean Communist Party in 1925 in Seoul); and (5) the nationalists with Cho Man-sik, a Christian teacher, as their leader.

Through the classic stages of revolution, violence, and purge, Kim's faction crushed the nationalist group in 1946; then, the Russianized Korean leaders in 1950; the Pak faction in 1953; and, finally, the strong Yenan rival faction in 1958.

GROWTH OF COMMUNIST PARTY

Ever since its founding in September, 1946, the Korean Workers' Party (KWP) has concentrated on strengthening its membership and its organization. In 1949, the membership, increased to 700,000, included 8 percent of the population. The peasant cardholders constituted 62 percent of the membership; workers, 20 percent; white collar class, 13 percent. In September, 1961, the total membership rose to 1,311,563. The ratio of workers had grown to 30 percent in contrast with 17.3 percent in 1956.

Today, about one person in eight is a party member. When compared with the ratio in other Communist parties, the KWP is the highest in the world; Indonesia has one member to every 85 persons; Communist China, one to 45; Italy, one to 27; the Soviet Union, one to 22.8; North Viet Nam, one to 22; Czechoslovakia, one to 9.4.

THE CABINET

The North Korean government that emerged in 1948 was structurally a miniature of the Soviet political setup and was covertly controlled by the Soviet Union. In North Korea, no sharp demarcation is drawn between the legislative and the executive authority, although the framework of the government, the allocation of powers, an ostensibly popular base, and provisions, regarding individual rights are outlined in the constitution. The highest source of State power is the Supreme People's Assembly (Parliament), a body "elected" every two years by the people. In theory, it exercises supreme governing power within the State, but, in actuality, the Assembly is a rubber stamp because the Cabinet can negate the will of the legislature.

The Cabinet is composed of the Premier, eight Vice-Premiers, 20 Ministers of the State, and five Chairmen of various Commissions—a group of 34 executives. In practice, an inner circle, comprising 11 top-level Ministers chosen from the Cabinet, make the decisions. All of the members of this inner circle are Kim's ex-partisan associates.

FARMER

As in all Communist countries, the 11-member Politburo of the Central Committee of the KWP stands at the pinnacle of the party, and at the top of North Korean society as a whole, formulating the goals and policies which determine the direction of the State. The Politburo represents the corporate expression of national doctrine, and constitutes the infallible word of the State. The 11-member Politburo is, of course, interlinked with the 11-man inner circle of the Cabinet.

Surrounding Premier Kim, the Politburo includes President Ch'oe Yong-kon, an ex-partisan leader of northern Manchuria, who is titular head of the State; the first Vice-Premier Kim Il, a partisan leader of eastern Manchuria and regarded as the No. 2 man; Senior-General Kim Kwang-hyop, Minister of National Defense, once a partisan lieutenant in Kim Il-song's partisan army; Foreign Minister Pak Song-ch'ol; Internal Minister Sok San; and Agricultural Minister Pak Chong-ae, a woman. Premier Kim's position is that of Chairman of the Politburo, of the Central Committee of the Korean Workers' Party, and Commander-in-Chief of the Armed Forces with the rank of Marshal.

LAND REFORM

A decree on land reform "confiscated and distributed freely for ownership by those who till it" all land owned by Japanese, by Korean landlords, and by religious organizations. In 1946, over 2.5 million acres of land—about 56 percent of the farmland of North Korea—were distributed among 725,000 households. The size of the allotments was based on the number of laborers in the family and the ages of those in the family whom the produce of the land would feed.

In contrast with Communist China's law on land reform, North Korea prohibited the disposal of these grants while recognizing the farmers' private ownership of the land. A law stipulates that distributed lands "shall not be bought, sold or rented for tenancy, or mortgaged." The decree successfully prevented a capitalistic trend among the peasants, and also cut in half by one stroke the proportion of poor peasants in the country—from 40 percent in 1945, to 20 percent in 1946.

THE KOREAN WAR AND COLLECTIVIZATION

The U.N. estimated that North Korean casualties in the civil war were no less than 520,000 men and one million civilians. Property damage included 25 percent of the total arable land; 50,000 farming households were left without land; 32 percent of the labor force was lost. Under these circumstances, the recovery of the private farming system, without extraordinary State expenditure, was well-nigh impossible. Thus the war was directly responsible for State intervention in agriculture.

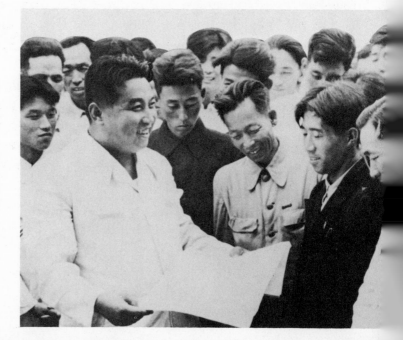

KIM IL-SONG *Premier and Chairman of the Korean Communist Party, Kim is pictured at the age of 51 in the Hwanghai Iron Works during September, 1962. He is discussing methods of steel production with senior workers.*

It was against this background that Premier Kim, in 1953, called for the collectivization of agriculture on a "voluntary basis." By December of that year, there were 806 cooperatives; and by August of 1958, no farm remained in private hands. Some 13,300 cooperatives, each composed of an average 80 households, had been established. In 1958, coinciding with the introduction in China of the "Commune System," the government announced that a new amalgamation had been completed, reducing the number of cooperatives from 13,309 to 3,880. Each cooperative had been enlarged to include, on the average, 300 households. The area of each cooperative now averaged 1,225 acres.

INDUSTRIAL EXPANSION

At the end of the Five-Year Plan in 1960, the total grain output was reported to be 3.8 million tons, making the country self-sufficient in food. By 1961, the total industrial output—increased 2.6 times as against 1956—included 9.7 billion kilowatts of electric power; 10 million tons of coal; 970,000 tons of steel; 1 million tons of pig and granulated iron; 630,000 tons of chemical fertilizer; 2 million tons of cement; 200 million meters of fabrics.

FOREIGN AID

All the economic miracles of the postwar development cannot be entirely attributed to planning strategy, or to the people's enthusiasm for hard work, or to the national character. Aid totaling $550 million from Socialist countries helped to give North Korea a start. The Soviet Union was entirely responsible for the development of the North Korean electric power station. Communist China built almost all the railways, and supplied the locomotives, not to speak of the massive irrigation projects supported by China with one million Chinese "volunteer soldiers." Hamhung, the second largest city, was built by East Germany; a number of coal mines by Poland; several automobile and machine plants by Czechoslovakia; pharmaceutical factories and the biggest Unsan cement plant by Rumania; chemical plants by Hungary; furniture factories by Bulgaria. Some 50,000 horses and dairy cows were supplied by Mongolia.

EDUCATIONAL SYSTEM

In 1964, a quarter of the 12 million people were involved in full- or part-time education, of one sort or another. In 1964, as many as 97 work-and-study colleges were functioning. By 1967, North Korea plans to have in operation 128 institutions of higher learning. A system of nine-year tuition-free education was started in 1963.

TRADE RELATIONS

In theory, private trading is allowed, but in practice business is strictly under the control of the Party–Trade Ministry complex. North Korea maintains trade relations with 44 countries of which only 13 are Communist. Trade goes on with Great Britain, West Germany, France, Switzerland, Holland, Belgium, Italy, Australia, Japan, Brazil, Uruguay, Chile, Bolivia, to name some. The trade figures per country are not available, but in 1962, the bulk of North Korean exports went to the Soviet Union. Total trade with Great Britain amounted to 240,000 pounds sterling in 1962.

THE CAPITAL CITY

P'yongyang, population one million, is the capital city and the largest in the country. It is located on both banks of the Taedong River, about 120 miles northwest of Seoul. It was founded in 427 A.D.

P'yongyang is a modern city with broad, tree-lined streets. It is a city without slums. Within it, there is a stadium, a deluxe hotel, and a number of theaters.

WORK LAWS AND POPULATION

Abortion is illegal, primarily because of an acute labor shortage. Women workers, who constitute 49 percent of the labor force, are entitled to a paid maternity leave of 77 days: 35 days before and 42 days after delivery.

From 1946 to 1960, the proportion of farmers declined from 74 percent of the work force to 44.4 percent. This meant a shift of about 20 percent, or 200,000 persons, from rural to urban centers between 1953 and 1960.

The labor system requires a work day of eight hours and a work week of six days. However, there is a six-hour day in the heavy industries and in occupations that involve a health hazard. Workers receive holidays with pay for 15 days during a year; in heavy industry, holidays run to a full month. Some 300 rest homes have been established for workers in ill health. In 1963, there were about 10,000 nurseries subsidized by the State with a capacity for some 600,000 children of working mothers.

RELATIONS WITH FOREIGN COUNTRIES

Officially, North Korea has diplomatic relations of one sort or another with over 25 countries, of which 13 are Communist and the rest either the neutral or non-aligned countries of Asia and Africa. However, North Korea maintains semi-official relations with about 44 countries in the form of trade and cultural interchange. No diplomatic relations are maintained between the United States and North Korea, nor are there any postal arrangements. North Korea is not a member of the United Nations.

Relations with the Afro-Asian bloc have been stepped up, and are increasingly significant.

In the Sino-Soviet dispute, North Korea has been clearly pro-Peking for the following reasons: (1) geopolitical contiguity; and (2) the support given by Communist China during the Korean War. North Korea, of course, maintains diplomatic relations with the Soviet Union, but Premier Kosygin's visit to P'yongyang in 1965 failed to woo Premier Kim to the Moscow position. As to the Viet Nam War, North Korea is completely in accord with Peking's bellicosity and has reportedly signed an agreement of economic assistance to the Viet Cong which also includes the shipment of war materiel into Viet Nam.

KIWON CHUNG

IN BRIEF

AREA   46,814 square miles, a little smaller than Mississippi.

TERRAIN   The northern half of a 600-mile long peninsula, North Korea is almost entirely covered by mountains. Many short rivers provide great electric power potential but little river transport, except on the Yalu River. The average elevation above the sea level is 1,600 feet. Main mountain ranges extend along the north and the eastern coast line. The highest mountain, called Paekt'usan, or the Whitehead (9,000 feet), lies on the border with Manchuria.

FLORA   Forests, partially depleted, are similar to those in Manchuria and Mainland China, and contain over a thousand different plants. Larch, spruce, oak, alder, pine, and fir are common.

FAUNA   Wild boar, leopard, lynx, tiger, bear, deer, and wolves, pheasants and other birds.

CLIMATE   Weather is very similar to that of Maine, with cold, dry winters and heavy rains during June and July. Temperatures average −5°F. in January in the mountains, reaching 68°F. in August.

CAPITAL   P'yongyang, about 940,000 inhabitants (1961).

OTHER CITIES   Kaesong is the second largest city; Chunjin and Huengnam, the chief ports. Sinuji is the center of lumbering and mining; Hamhung is important for its manufacture of chemicals.

POPULATION   11.04 million estimated in 1963. Annual rate of increase is about 2.3 percent. Density is close to 236 persons per square mile.

ETHNIC GROUPS   Koreans are a homogeneous group. There are no indigenous minority peoples.

LANGUAGE   Korean, an Altaic language, is written in a phonetic script. It is probably the first language to be printed in movable type, invented in Korea in 1234 A.D.

RELIGION   Before the ascendancy of Communism, Buddhism, Confucianism, and Christianity were the dominant faiths. A minority followed *Chondokyo,* a monotheistic combination of shamanism, Confucianism, and Buddhism.

P'YONGYANG   *A view from the Taedong River. At the end of the Korean War in 1953, the city had been completely razed as the result of bombardment. The reconstruction is still in progress with an apparent purpose, as Premier Kim says, "of making P'yongyang city a socialist showcase in the Far East."*

DATE OF INDEPENDENCE	On August 8, 1945, Soviet troops arrived to end Japanese rule. On September 8, 1948, the Constitution was approved.
FORM OF GOVERNMENT	Communist. A Supreme People's Assembly was installed in 1948 to represent both South and North Korea, but actual power rests with the Politburo. The Korean Workers' Party has a Central Committee of 85 full members and 50 candidate members, which elects the 11 members and 4 candidate members of the Politburo. The chairman of the Politburo is Premier of the country and exercises dictatorial power. North Korea is not a member of the United Nations.
EDUCATION	In 1963, almost 9,200 schools were attended by 2.55 million students, of whom 214,000 were in colleges and universities. There are 97 universities. 140,000 part-time worker-students attend 27 junior colleges. Kim Il-song University, with 20,000 full-time students, has a teaching body of 1,700. About two-thirds of the advanced students study technical and engineering subjects. Since the Communist takeover, North Korea has virtually eliminated illiteracy in a decade.
HEALTH FACILITIES	Medical care is provided by the state. The government reports that between 1945 and 1960, the average life span was increased by 20 years. Among the most prevalent diseases are typhoid fever, dysentery, intestinal infections, flukes, tuberculosis, smallpox, venereal diseases, the plague, and rabies. As of 1962, there were 15,874 doctors and resident doctors and 167 public hospitals.
CULTURAL FACILITIES	All public expression is controlled by the state. The chief publications are *Minju Choson* (*Democratic Korea*), the government newspaper, and *Nondong Sinmung* (*Labor News*), the Communist Party organ. There are 29 daily newspapers and a few hundred journals with 26 publishing houses. About 60 periodicals and over 1,000 books are pub-

lished each year. There are 238 libraries and 150 museums. In 1961, there were about 600,000 radios, or one for every 17 or 18 persons. The largest broadcast station is the Korean Central News Agency that relays the broadcasts of all Socialist countries. The agency broadcasts in six foreign languages, including English. In 1962, there were 19 theaters and 531 cinemas. Several hundred mobile theater troupes function as one of the main propaganda channels for the government policy.

CURRENCY AND FINANCE

The *won*, adopted in 1959, is worth close to $1.00 in U.S. currency at the official rate. The government budget for 1963 expected revenues of $1.17 billion, and expenditures of slightly over $1.16 billion.

INDUSTRY AND PRODUCTION

Heavy industry accounts for about 50 percent of the national product. Questionable data from official sources indicate a rise of 10 percent in the national income during 1962, together with a 36 percent rise in steel production, an 18 percent rise in coal, a 37 percent rise in textiles, and an 18 percent rise in consumer goods. Western estimates of basic production for 1962 were: 15.2 million metric tons of coal and lignite, 2.38 million metric tons of cement, 1.2 million metric tons of pig iron, 1.65 million metric tons of crude steel, 11.4 billion kilowatt hours of electric power, and important quantities of copper, lead, zinc, and tungsten.

CROPS: About 44 percent of the populace remained on the land in 1960. All small peasant holdings were collectivized in the 1950's. Farming has been largely mechanized; for example, it is stated that almost 95 percent of the plowing is done by machine, and that fertilizer factories and irrigation projects are well developed. In 1963, there were 18,000 tractors in use. Grain production of five million tons, mostly rice, was claimed in 1962. Barley and other grains, vegetables, flax, hemp, tobacco, and fruit are also raised.

LIVESTOCK: Cattle, pigs, sheep, goats, rabbits, poultry, and slikworms.

FISHERIES: The catch was 690,000 tons in 1960. There is some whale fishing off the east coast.

MINING: Iron, coal, lead, copper, zinc, tungsten, mica, phosphates, graphite, gold, and silver are mined. Oil wells began to produce in 1957.

TRADE

Before partition, the metals, fertilizers, electric power, and manufactured goods of the north were exchanged for the foods and light industrial products of the south. By 1960, about 60 percent of the trade was with the Soviet Union, 30 percent with China, and 3 percent with non-Communist countries. Precise data on trade are not released. Exports today consist mostly of metals, minerals, chemical products, machines, and marine products. Imports consist mostly of fuel, oil, aluminum, construction materials, and rubber.

TRANSPORT

ROAD: The road network is in bad condition and mostly unpaved. Statistics are not available. However, about a third of the settlements are totally dependent on road transport, so bad roads are a serious problem. Trucking carried 17.7 million tons of freight in 1961.

RAILROAD: About 3,100 miles of track had been rehabilitated and were in use in 1964. An international through-train connects P'yongyang with Moscow and Peking.

WATERWAY: About 3.5 million tons of cargo were carried on inland waterways in 1961. The Yalu, the main navigable river, carries small boats for about 430 miles from its mouth.

AIR: Government planes serve P'yongyang, Chunjin, and Hamhung. International connections are available only to Peking and Moscow.

SEA: The chief ports and best harbors are on the east coast. On the west coast, Nampo, the port for P'yongyang, has been dredged and expanded since the partition of the country. The country had three modern merchant ships totaling 5,370 gross tons in 1962, and expected to have a fleet of 36,500 gross tons by 1967.

COMMUNICA-TION

All services are government-controlled, none are fully developed; information is withheld. Communication with non-Communist nations is practically non-existent. North Korea does not even belong to the Universal Postal Union, responsible for the exchange of international mail.

CHINA

Lao Cai

FAN-
SI-PAN

SONG COI

Lang Son

VIET NAM

Hanoi

Bien Dien Phu

(NORTH)

Haiphong

Nam Dinh

Gulf of
Tonkin

L
A
O
S

ANNAMITE

M
O
U
N
T
A
I
N
S

Vinh

Dong Hoi

CEASE-FIRE LINE OF 1954

VIETNAM
(SOUTH)

NORTH VIET NAM

Militant Communist Base

Viet Nam, the largest of the three nations carved from the area formerly known as French Indo-China, is part of the "Rice Bowl of Asia." In shape, it has been likened to a peasant's carrying-pole, extending north-south, from each end of which is suspended a rice basket. All of Viet Nam covers about 129 thousand square miles—a little greater than the size of New Mexico.

Viet Nam is long and narrow, running about 1,000 miles south from the Chinese border to the Gulf of Siam. The width varies from 50 miles at the narrowest part to 300 miles at the broadest.

The centers of population and agricultural production are concentrated in two areas: the deltas of the Red River in the north and the Mekong River in the south. Connecting these two areas is a narrow backbone of mountains and a shallow coastal plain. These three regions are referred to today as North Viet Nam, Central Viet Nam, and South Viet Nam.

TERRAIN, NATURAL RESOURCES, AND FAUNA

Nearly half of the land area is covered with profuse forests of bamboo, cedar, and pine, and with lesser quantities of rosewood, ebony, and sandalwood. Viet Nam's known mineral resources include coal, phosphate, zinc, tin, and iron ore. Extensive beds of peat have been found in the swamp areas of South Viet Nam. The forests and jungles abound in elephant, tiger, panther, gaur, wild bear, black bear, peacock, pheasant, and stag. Fish and other seafood are plentiful and varied.

CLIMATE

Viet Nam is a tropical country. South Viet Nam has a pure monsoon climate, affected by the seasonal winds (monsoons) of India and Southeast Asia. As in the North, there are only two seasons; but unlike the North, these seasons differ from each other by being dry or wet.

Humidity is high throughout the year; but almost all of Saigon's 80 inches of rain comes during the wet season, between April and October. In North Viet Nam, the winter is cool and damp; droughts, floods, and typhoons occur frequently and affect the patterns of life.

A BACKGROUND OF EXPLOITATION

Most of the history of Viet Nam has revolved around relations between the Vietnamese and the Chinese. For many centuries, the Vietnamese feared China because of its power and admired China for its culture. Although the Vietnamese were ruled by the Chinese from the second century B.C. to the tenth century A.D., they accepted much of the dominant culture without becoming entirely absorbed. After finally freeing themselves from Chinese control in 939 A.D., they remained independent until the mid-nineteenth century, when they were conquered by the French. The authoritarian nature of the Vietnamese government was retained by the French colonial administration; although those in power had changed, the essential nature of authority had not. And from the very start of the French occupation, nationalist uprisings occurred.

In 1940, when France was defeated in Europe, the Japanese moved swiftly to gain control of the Indo-Chinese peninsula; and Viet Nam, Cambodia, and Laos became a base for subsequent Japanese military activities in Southeast Asia.

RECENT HISTORY

At the end of World War II, an independent Vietnamese government (the "Democratic Republic of Viet Nam") was established under the Communist leader, Ho Chi Minh, then leader of the Viet Nam League for Independence (Viet Minh). In March, 1946, the French recognized the new government as a free state within the French Union.

However, the French and Viet Minh leaders were unable to agree on an interpretation of this pact; and in December, 1946, hostilities broke out in Hanoi between French and Viet Minh forces. During the next eight years, French armies were able to win and keep control

DOWNTOWN HANOI *This is a main street of the Tonkinese section of the capital. It is the part of town the French colonialists usually called "the native quarter." This picture was taken in 1954. Today, there are few cars left in Hanoi. The city, judged by previous standards, is quite drab.*

of the major cities in Viet Nam, but much of the countryside was held by the Viet Minh, which fought a highly successful guerrilla war against the French.

In March 1949, in an attempt to attract non-Communist nationalists away from the Viet Minh, the French restored to power the former Emperor of Annam, Bao Dai, then living in exile. A new state of Viet Nam was created, supposedly independent within the French Union.

However, Vietnamese nationalists, always suspicious of French motives, soon became convinced that the French were not sincere, and most of them refused to cooperate with the Bao Dai regime. Those who did were called "colonialists" and "members of the French club," while the French damned all their opponents as "Communists." In actual fact, only a handful were truly Communists. The Nationalists were united in their hatred of French colonialism, but differed widely among themselves on points of political philosophy.

TRIBESWOMAN *One of the few foreign devices which the people of the Man tribe of North Viet Nam have found valuable is this obsolete Singer sewing machine, operated by a foot treadle. Her own garments and those of her children attest to her skill. In a mountainous area where electricity cannot be expected to arrive for years, this machine is economical and effective; only the needle and the belt may need replacement.*

In April 1954, representatives of France, the "Democratic Republic of Viet Nam," the State of Viet Nam, Cambodia, Laos, Communist China, the Soviet Union, Britain, and the United States met at Geneva to discuss the problem of bringing the war in Indo-China to an end. During the course of this conference, the Viet Minh captured the vital French fortress at Dien Bien Phu; and the French, discouraged and weary of the war, signed a cease-fire with the Viet Minh at Geneva on July 20. The State of Viet Nam refused to sign the agreement, as did the United States.

With the end of the fighting, a new era began for Viet Nam. The accords provided for a division of the peninsula at the 17th parallel, and for the withdrawal of all French forces to areas south of that line and of all Viet Minh forces to the north of that line. An International Commission for Supervision and Control, composed of representatives of Canada, India, and Poland, was set up to supervise the withdrawal and to make sure other provisions of the armistice agreement were carried out. The Final Declaration of the Geneva Conference also provided that a political settlement in Viet Nam should be effected "on the basis of respect for the principles of independence, unity and territorial integrity" by "free general elections by secret ballot" which would be held in July 1956, under the supervision of the International Commission.

However, these elections were not held, since the Government of the State of Viet Nam, which became the Republic of Viet Nam in October 1955, did not consider itself bound by the Geneva agreements (which it had not signed) and because the governments of the two halves of the country could not agree on the basis for "free general elections."

PEOPLE OF THE MAN TRIBE *This family lives on a hilltop about 50 miles west of Lao Cai, near the Chinese Communist frontier in North Viet Nam. Every detail of their dress and hair-style is designed to distinguish them from the people of the tribe on the next hill. The husband, home with his donkey from a trading trip, wears workers' clothing on the trail.*

AREA AND POPULATION

The Democratic Republic of Viet Nam (hereafter referred to as North Viet Nam) is a Communist state composed of 29 provinces of North Viet Nam and four from Central Viet Nam. Its total land area is roughly 63,000 square miles, comparable in size to Florida. Six million acres are cultivable; practically all of this area is devoted to the growing of rice.

In 1965, the population was estimated to be about 18 million; 90 percent of the people were concentrated in the delta area of the Red River and on a plain running down the coast. Population densities run as high as 2,600 persons per square mile. About 85 percent of the population is Vietnamese; the remainder is composed of various ethnic minorities. Whereas the Vietnamese are highly concentrated in the delta and plains regions, the minorities are spread through the mountainous regions which comprise 80 percent of the total land area.

HANOI

Hanoi, the capital, located on the Red River, is about 60 miles inland from the coast. The Chinese who founded it called it Dong Kinh (Tongking), *Capital of the East*. Today the city's population runs over 800,000.

Hanoi is an important transport and communications center, connected with the port city of Hai Phong. Canals crisscross the city and give it an attractive appearance. Its streets are lined with small shops and factories. Its industrial establishments manufacture explosives, tile, porcelain, and bicycles. The city's University, the oldest in Indo-China, has faculties of law, medicine, pharmacy, letters, and sciences. A Far Eastern museum, established by the French, contains notable collections of fine arts and archaeology.

RELIGION

The majority of North Vietnamese are Buddhists and Confucians, although there are about 800,000 Roman Catholics. The tribal minorities—the Thai, Meo, Muong, Nung, Tho, Man—are mostly animists or spirit-worshipers.

INFLUENCE OF THE COMMUNIST REGIME

Under the impact of Communist rule, the family has changed—although the full impact of the new order cannot be appraised as yet. The redefinition of the individual's political status makes him first a citizen, and secondly a family member; his loyalties are due primarily to the state and not to the family. "The extended family," which has played a predominant role in the social institutions of the Vietnamese, is slowly being changed. "The extended family," consisting of the immediate family and the close relatives, represented a unit of production, ownership, and management which is incompatible with Socialist doctrine since all economic factors are under state control.

Thanks to the agricultural reform program started in 1953 land ownership has become more evenly spread. However, the villager who received his land through the redistribution program was made dependent for his ownership on the continued existence of the government of North Viet Nam. This fact has enabled the government to exercise more control over the peasants. That the peasants are hostile toward governmental agricultural policies was shown during the food crisis of 1961–62 when, instead of delivering the imposed quotas to the government agencies, the farmers secreted much of their produce and sold it on the black market.

LE DUAN   Younger than any of the other top men in North Viet Nam, Le Duan is in his middle forties. He is a protege of Ho Chi Minh, and is reported to be a close friend of the old leader. Since 1960, he has headed the Communist Party organization as First Secretary of the Lao Dong. Prior to that time, he directed the Viet Minh in South Viet Nam and is believed to be better acquainted with that area than any other major figure in the Communist Party.

HO CHI MINH

The low level of industrial development has slowed the growth of a politically active and significant proletariat. The government's emphasis on rapid industrialization has an ideological as well as a practical purpose: as the proportion of industrial production in the total national income increases, workers will become numerically more significant.

For a short while, discontent with governmental policies was voiced by intellectuals. However, the government has so tightened its control that those who seek to effect change must work within narrowly prescribed limits—which means from within the Lao Dong (Communist) Party.

HO CHI MINH

North Viet Nam has been a part of the Communist world since the Geneva Conference of 1954. However, over the years, its loyalty has wavered between the Soviet and Chinese camps. Ho Chi Minh, leader of North Viet Nam since its creation in 1945, and founder of Vietnamese Communist Party, is the ranking Communist among Asian Communist leaders.

The North Vietnamese leader was born in 1890. When 21, he left Viet Nam as a cabin boy on a French ship. He was arrested and jailed several times in Europe because of his radical ideas.

About 1920, he helped found the Communist Party of France.

His book on French colonialism brought him recognition in his native land. After attending a university in Moscow, he was sent to Canton, China, where he organized a Communist anti-colonialist youth group, the original basis of his present power.

Until World War II, Ho worked for many years as a clandestine agent in Asia under direction from Moscow. During this period, he was jailed for two years in Hong Kong.

Born Nguyen Van Thanh, among the many names under which he went were Nguyen Tat Thanh and Nguyen Ai Quoc; "Ho Chi Minh," too, is a pseudonym.

POLITICAL ORIENTATION

In recent years, the younger element in the leadership, led by Party First Secretary Le Duan, has shown marked pro-Chinese tendencies. During 1964, North Viet Nam followed the Peking line in Communist politics, maintaining a militant posture in international affairs. Its policy toward South Viet Nam was shown in the January 1961 creation of a "National Liberation Front" to carry on "the people's struggle" south of the 17th parallel.

RICE PADDY   A water buffalo snatches a quick mouthful from the dike around a paddy field being prepared for seeding.

A WOMAN COAL MINER   This 22-year-old is
typical of the women miners at Cam Pha, North
Viet Nam, and earns almost as much as her fiance,
foreman of the mine.

HEROES OF LABOR   The medals worn by
this man and woman indicate that they have
exceeded required production quotas. The
Communists use this technique of recognition
and reward as an incentive.

Since 1959, North Viet Nam has infiltrated an estimated 90,000
Communist troops into the South. Today, considering all their battle
losses, they comprise over half of the hard core of red forces fighting in
South Viet Nam. At the same time, North Viet Nam has furnished
troops, technicians, and military equipment to the Pathet Lao forces
which have been striving to subvert the Royal Laotian Government.

The Viet Cong, North Viet Nam's agents in the South, are given
little chance at this point of effecting a conquest of the southern republic. Rather, North Viet Nam's ambitions in South Viet Nam appear to
be aimed at encouraging the emergence there of anti-American and

pro-neutralist elements, particularly among Buddhist and civilian politicians.

EDUCATION

In 1963, a little over two million children received primary education, and some 49,600 students were enrolled in secondary schools. Almost 16,000 students were involved in higher education. The educational system has been thoroughly overhauled by the Communists to enable the allocation of substantial amounts of classtime to ideological indoctrination. There is also greater emphasis on technical subjects today than was formerly the case, and as a result, purely academic subjects have suffered. Vietnamese is now the language of instruction, replacing the French used during the colonial period.

FEMALE SOLDIER   A long-haired soldier of the North Vietnamese Army awaits inspection. She wears citations for bravery in battle.

DEVELOPMENT OF INDUSTRY

At the time of partition, virtually all of the major industry of Viet Nam was located in the north. North Viet Nam inherited the development of large deposits of coal, iron, tin, zinc, and chromite from the French, as well as the two major industries, cement and textiles. Between 1954 and 1957, the existing plants, having been rendered obsolescent or damaged by war, were re-equipped with Sino-Soviet aid. Concentration was primarily devoted to the rapid development of industry and on rapid technical change, rather than on industry to improve agricultural production. In 1961, it was officially announced that industry for the first time had contributed more to the national income than agriculture.

TRANSPORTATION AND COMMUNICATIONS

The North's transportation and communications systems suffered serious damage during the war; after partition, rehabilitation of the road system was given high priority. By 1963, with Sino-Soviet aid, 546 miles of railroads and 4,000 miles of highways had been restored.

A Chinese airline now provides transportation services between Peking and Hanoi twice a week.

The official government organ, *Nhan Dan,* the newspaper of the Lao Dong (Workers') Party, has a circulation of 100,000. There are also two other daily papers.

FINANCIAL SITUATION

Primary emphasis in the North Vietnamese economy has been on developing industry and financing this development as much as possible from the agricultural sector. In agriculture, the emphasis has been first on "cooperativization," followed by collectivization along Russian lines. Peasant resistance, however, has slowed this trend. State control of the economy is virtually complete, dominating 85 percent of all agriculture, 90 percent of all handicraft industry, as well as all factory industry, and virtually all wholesale and retail trade.

The value of factory production nearly doubled between 1960 and

1963, with electrical power, ferrous metals, chemicals, fertilizers, glassware, and pottery showing the greatest increases. Foreign trade, like that of South Viet Nam, showed a heavy imbalance; in 1963, exports totaled $92,000,000 and imports $156,000,000. No reliable budget figures are available.

CULTURAL ASPECTS OF NORTH AND SOUTH VIET NAM

The Vietnamese are basically dwellers of the plain, who have preferred the easier, sedentary life of the river valleys and coastal areas to the jungles and forested plateaus. Over centuries of recorded history, the Vietnamese have developed an architectural style, literature, music, and art heavily influenced by Chinese models. In recent years, however, the Vietnamese have begun to develop independent forms of artistic expression reflecting not only their Chinese background, but harmonious forms of structure and painting which blend East and West in agreeable synthesis. Vietnamese lacquer paintings are highly impressionistic; as one Vietnamese critic has said, they "seek to express the unseen spirit and are thus as much symbolical as conventional."

Modern Vietnamese music is much influenced by Western forms; in South Viet Nam, jazz and rock-and-roll are in vogue, although in North Viet Nam, these Western phenomena, as in most Communist states, are officially frowned upon.

WESLEY R. FISHEL

IN BRIEF

AREA   63,344 square miles, smaller than Missouri.

TERRAIN   The Red River has a richly fertile valley and delta. A coastal plain extending toward the south is also fertile. The remaining 80 percent of the area is heavily forested hill country, with mountain peaks in the north reaching 10,000 feet.

FLORA   Bamboo, cedar, pine, rosewood, ebony, and sandalwood. Tropical rain forests give way to evergreen and deciduous trees in the drier areas.

FAUNA   Elephant, tiger, panther, gaur, wild bear, black bear, peacock, pheasant, and stag.

CLIMATE   Tropical monsoon climate characterized by hot, wet summers and cool, damp winters; frequent droughts, floods, and typhoons. The average summer temperature is 85°F.; the average winter temperature, 62°F.

CAPITAL   Hanoi (Tongking), about 850,000 inhabitants in 1964.

OTHER CITIES   Hai Phong, 370,000 population, is the chief port.

POPULATION   About 17 million in 1964. Average density is about 268 per square mile. The Vietnamese are concentrated on about 20 percent of the land—in the Red River delta or on the coastal plain, where the density may reach about 2,600 persons per square mile. Annual rate of population increase is estimated at three percent.

ETHNIC GROUPS Close to 85 percent are Vietnamese. Minorities include almost two million tribally organized Thai, Meo and Yao, Muong, Nung, and Tho, as well as some 60,000 Chinese in the cities.

LANGUAGE   The majority speaks Vietnamese, a tonal language long written with Chinese characters and still heavily influenced by Chinese patterns. Tribal tongues are also in use. French is spoken by many of the educated urban people.

RELIGION   The Vietnamese majority combines the Buddhist faith and the Confucian philosophy with ancestor worship. About 800,000 are believed to remain Roman Catholic. Tribal peoples are animist. Religious activity is discouraged by the state.

DATE OF INDEPENDENCE On September 2, 1945, a republic was proclaimed; it was installed north of the 17th parallel according to agreements signed July 20, 1954.

FORM OF GOVERNMENT Communist. According to the Constitution of January 1, 1960, the Democratic Republic of Viet Nam is a people's democratic state led by the working class. Actual power is dictatorially wielded by the revolutionary leader, President Ho Chi Minh, and a few close associates. A National Assembly of 366 deputies, elected in theory every four years by all persons over 18, meets twice a year, but its small Standing Committee interprets all legislation and holds executive power. The *Lao Dong,* or Worker's Party, consisted of 620,000 members in 1963; its Politburo, led by Ho Chi Minh, was composed of 11 full and two alternate members.

EDUCATION   In 1963, over two million children were enrolled in the primary school system. Almost 50,000 students were enrolled in middle technical schools (high schools). At the college level, 15,900 students were in the teachers' colleges, polytechnic institute, agriculture and forestry institute, art school, and in the economics and finance institute. In 1960, slightly over a third of the people older than 10 years remained illiterate.

HEALTH   In 1960, the government reported there were almost 2,000
FACILITIES   doctors and 22,000 hospital beds in the country. Medical service is concentrated in the chief cities and larger communes; *Lao Dong* members are said to have first call on the limited facilities. Diseases associated with malnutrition and lack of sanitation are endemic; during 1961, deaths by starvation were reported.

CULTURAL   In 1963, *Nhan Dan,* the official paper of the *Lao Dong* Party,
FACILITIES   had a circulation of 100,000. Although there are two other daily papers, *Nhan Dan* sets the tone for all cultural activities. Novels, plays, short stories, journals, and songs are expected to further state interests—artists who revealed unacceptable opinions during a relaxation of control were sent to re-education camps and were presumably reformed through hard labor.

CURRENCY AND   The *dong,* valued at approximately 35¢ in U.S. currency,
FINANCE   is held at a rate of 100 *dong* to 30.6 Soviet rubles. The budget for 1962 balanced at $605.5 million; one-fifth of that amount was used for administration and armed forces of about 350,000 men. Well over half of the budget, roughly $22 per person, was devoted to "economic construction," while less than $4 per person was devoted to social and cultural needs.

INDUSTRY AND   All business and industry are state-owned. By 1963, state-
PRODUCTION   operated agricultural cooperatives included 97 percent of

the village farmers. The 1961–65 Five-Year-Plan, aided by China and the Soviet Union, envisages production increases of rice to 7 million tons, coal to 4.2 million tons, steel plate to 160,000 tons, and electric power to 711 million kilowatt hours. The targets are perhaps optimistic—electricity production, for example, was only 350 million kilowatt hours in 1962, while steel production was 44,000 metric tons. Except for the steel works at Hanoi, most of the dozen or so new factories are for light industry—soap, glass, plywood, lamps, plastics.

CROPS: Approximately 90 percent of the population is rural. Over 90 percent of the six million acres of cultivable land is planted with rice. The paddy rice harvest was over 4.5 million metric tons in 1962; only in a good year does the crop meet subsistence needs. Sugar, corn, cotton, tea, row silk, tobacco, and vegetables are also grown. Timber and shellac are taken from the forests.

LIVESTOCK: In 1962, there were about 2.25 million water buffalo and cattle; also 4.2 million pigs.

FISHERIES: Shrimp, crawfish, and finned fish are caught from small boats and are an important source of protein.

MINING: In 1962, coal production was 2.6 million metric tons. Phosphates, tin, salt, chromite, and iron are produced. Strategic deposits of zinc, manganese, tungsten, and antimony may have been developed in recent years.

NURSERY   *Cool and comfortable, these swinging bamboo cradles are located in the nursery attached to a Communist factory. The Lao Dong (Communist) Party organizes these nurseries to free the mothers for labor purposes.*

TRIBE PEOPLE *This well-to-do family of the Man tribe are dressed in their holiday best. Their sturdy house is constructed of bamboo poles and woven bamboo screens. The men are seated on the doorstep; their women stand beside them.*

TRADE

Foreign trade is chiefly with China and the Communist countries.

1963:	IMPORTS	$156,000,000
	EXPORTS	92,000,000
	DEFICIT	64,000,000

TRANSPORT

ROAD: By 1963, with Sino-Soviet aid, war damage on about 4,000 miles of highways had been repaired and the roads returned to service.

RAILROAD: By 1963, almost 550 miles of railroad were repaired and were in use.

WATERWAY: Over 500 miles of waterway carry small ships at high water; about 330 miles are navigable in the dry season.

AIR: Government planes provide internal flights from Hanoi to Vinh, Dong Hoi, and Dien Bien Phu. The Chinese maintain service between Hanoi and Peking. There are no other regular foreign flights.

SEA: Hai Phong is the only significant port.

COMMUNI-CATION

All services are government-owned and operated. Letters are carried only to China and France; no other countries are in direct postal communication with North Viet Nam. Radio-telegraph communication is restricted to the Communist countries and to France, India, and Hong Kong.

East
China
Sea

AMAMI GROUP
(OSHIMA GROUP)   Naze

TOKARA ISLANDS

KIKAI
SHIMA

AMAMI O SHIMA

TOKUNO SHIMA

OKIERABU

IHEYA

OKINAWA GROUP

IE   Nago

KUME   OKINAWA

Shuri

KERAMA GROUP   Naha

TOKASHIKI

Itoman

ISLANDS

DAITO
ISLANDS

Pacific

SAKISHIMA GROUP   Hirara

ISHIGAKI   MIYAKO

MIYAKO GROUP

IRIOMOTE

Ocean

R Y U K Y U

OKINAWA and the RYUKYU ISLANDS

Fortress in the Western Pacific

The Ryukyu Islands guard the approaches to the Western Pacific. The archipelago stretches out in a great arc from the southern coast of Japan almost as far as the island of Taiwan. Near the southern end of the chain, Okinawa with a population of about 900,000 is the largest of the Ryukyu Islands.

For many centuries, the Ryukyus represented the outermost frontier of the Chinese Empire and of the kingdom of Japan. In recent history, the islands have loomed increasingly large in strategic importance. They were a pivotal outpost in the security system of Japan before and during World War II. Since 1945, the islands have become a key link in America's security chain in the Western Pacific and Far East.

THE OLD RYUKYUS

As physically isolated as they are, the Ryukyus have, nevertheless, been inhabited for several thousands of years. Little is actually known of the early history of the islands. The islanders dwelt mainly on Okinawa and were ruled by numerous local princes who constantly fought one another for political supremacy. The Chinese took over in the 14th century but in the 15th century, the Okinawans were finally united under a single monarch.

With political unity, a Golden Age began in Okinawa. For almost two hundred years, seamen from the Ryukyus ranged widely over the Western Pacific, trading with China, Korea, Japan, and the many lands of Southeast Asia. However, in the late 16th century, with the onset of competition from European merchants, commercial prosperity rapidly waned.

In 1609, the Ryukyuans reeled under a new blow. Warriors from Satsuma, the southernmost of the great feudal domains of Japan, brought Okinawa and the other islands under their control. The new rulers made no effort to terminate Chinese overlordship in Okinawa.

Instead, they used the islands as bases to carry on a trade with the Chinese Empire, which their own Japanese government otherwise forbade.

Okinawa was visited by Commodore Perry in 1853 during his expedition to open Japan. The Ryukyus soon became a bone of contention between China and Japan, both of which sought undisputed sovereignty over the islands. After a protracted dispute, Okinawa and its outlying areas were annexed and incorporated into the Japanese Empire in 1879.

Japanese rule was a mixed blessing for the Ryukyuans. Although the imperial regime introduced many reforms, the Ryukyu Islands were treated as poor relations in the Japanese Empire. Often neglected, the islands became notorious for their unusually low standard of living.

UNDER AMERICAN OCCUPATION

During World War II, on April 1, 1945, Okinawa was invaded by United States amphibious forces. After a bloody and frightfully destructive struggle, the large Japanese garrison was overwhelmed. When the war ended, all of the Ryukyus were placed under American military occupation.

Later on, with the rise to power of the Chinese Communists and the outbreak of the Korean War, Okinawa's strategic importance to the United States mounted. The northern islands of the Ryukyus were restored to Japanese administration in 1952; but by the Treaty of San Francisco, the United States retained military control of Okinawa, while recognizing Japan's "residual sovereignty."

A gigantic U. S. air and naval base was constructed on the island. However, under American occupation, Okinawa has enjoyed a large measure of civil administration. The government is vested in a popularly elected 29-member legislature and a Chief Executive appointed by a High Commissioner in whom ultimate power resides. The High Commissioner is nominated by the United States Department of the Army.

For many years, the occupation of Okinawa has caused trouble between the United States and Japan. Successive Japanese governments have repeatedly urged the restoration of Okinawa to Japanese civil administration.

TYPHOON DAMAGE *Everywhere in the Ryukyuan archipelago during the late summer months, typhoons are frequent. Here is downtown Naha shortly after a 1959 storm. Water ran six feet deep in the streets of the capital. Hundreds of houses were blown to slats.*

RYUKYUANS AND RYUKYUAN WAYS

"China," the Okinawan used to say, "is our father, and Japan is our mother," thus acknowledging his ethnic origin and the principal wellsprings of his culture. Historically, both China and Japan have strongly influenced the Ryukyuan way of life. In recent times, American influence has made itself felt.

The Okinawans and, to a lesser extent, the northern Ryukyuans, are most likely an ethnic blend. The early settlers were migrants from the Japanese archipelago. Over the centuries, new arrivals came from the north. During the times of the Ming and early Ch'ing dynasties, Chinese officials, merchants, and teachers also settled down in the islands, especially on Okinawa. The Chinese culture they brought made a lasting impression.

The languages of the islands are essentially Japanese dialects. The tongue of the northern Ryukyus is not too dissimilar from the language of southern Japan. Okinawan, however, is unintelligible to a Japanese. Educated Okinawans, particularly of the prewar generations, were generally familiar with Japanese, and sometimes with Chinese, the old language of officialdom and scholarship.

The Ryukyuan way of life has varied from one island group to another. In the northernmost islands, cultural influences from Japan have long been dominant; in the more remote Okinawan area, old Chinese ways have stubbornly persisted and have fused with Japanese customs. More recently, American occupation has greatly affected the manners and customs on the great island.

Equally significant have been the results of the new educational system. Basic schooling is compulsory for children throughout the islands, in both the American and the Japanese sectors. The American-sponsored University of the Ryukyus in Naha has become a center for intellectual and scholarly activity. Some Okinawans, moreover, have sought higher education in Japan and in the United States.

EARNING A LIVING

Okinawa is one of the most densely populated areas in the world. During the years of the American occupation the number of inhabitants has grown by leaps and bounds. In the early 1960's, the total population of the Ryukyus was about 1,100,000. The heavy density of population has placed a severe strain upon the resources of the archipelago.

Neither Okinawa nor the rest of the Ryukyu chain is richly endowed by nature. Until the end of World War II, a large majority of the islanders earned a living farming whatever arable lands there were. The principal crops have been rice, sweet potatoes, sugar, and soybeans. Fishing, lumbering, and handicraft work are other important occupations.

Under the American occupation, the nature of the economy has sharply changed. Large tracts of land have been removed from agriculture to be used as sites for huge airfields and military installations. The compensation paid to displaced Okinawans at first aroused bitter protests from the islanders; ultimately, a satisfactory arrangement was reached.

RYUKYUAN LEADER *Mr. Seisaku Ota was the first popularly elected chief executive Okinawa has ever had.*

The expansion of the American military base has created many new employment opportunities for the Ryukyuans. After securing jobs on the installations and in the dependent facilities, they soon were able to achieve a higher standard of living than they had ever known before. But the new prosperity has also aroused uneasiness; few islanders have to be told that an American withdrawal might quickly lead to a collapse of the economy.

To meet the needs of the growing population, American officials have worked to strengthen the economy. Light industries, handicraft production, and fishing have been encouraged. A modest foreign trade has been fostered with Japan, Hawaii, and the U.S. mainland. Yet it is doubtful whether these secondary activities will be adequate to cushion the economic shock of an American military retrenchment in the Pacific. Fear of economic disaster has induced many Okinawans, regardless of their personal and political preferences, to oppose reversion of the islands to Japan in the immediate future.

OKINAWA'S FATE

Okinawa and its sister islands have been caught in the vortex of war and contemporary power politics. There is little doubt that the islanders will not be the arbiters of their destiny; their fate will largely be determined by the outcome of the political struggle in the Western Pacific and Far East between the great powers.

HYMAN KUBLIN

IN BRIEF

All data herein refer to the 63 islands under U.S. administration.

AREA 848 square miles; two-thirds the size of Rhode Island.

TERRAIN A chain of about 140 islands and numerous islets, stretching from 80 miles south of Kyushu, Japan, to 73 miles northeast of Taiwan. The group is rugged, rocky, volcanic, with deeply indented shores. Many islands are coral-girt, with coral crags providing unusual scenic effects. The largest island, Okinawa, is about 60 miles long and 10 miles wide at its greatest girth, an area of 463 square miles.

FLORA Much open plain with sparsely placed trees. In spite of tropical climate, the vegetation is not tropical; there is little bamboo, no high grass, nor heavy, tangled undergrowth.

FAUNA Wild boar, deer, rats, bats. Venomous snakes infest most of the islands, notably the habu (*Trimeresuius*) which grows to six or seven feet.

CLIMATE Subtropical with frequent, destructive typhoons. Hot, humid, with heavy rainfall. At Naha, temperatures average 82°F. in July, 60°F. in January, with extremes of 96°F. and 41°F.

CAPITAL Naha, on Okinawa. Over 250,000 inhabitants in 1963.

OTHER CITIES Koza, 47,000; Itoman, 33,600; Itirara, 32,500; Ginowan, 29,500; Ishigaki, 25,950.

MOTHER AND CHILD
Women in the farm areas of Okinawa and Japan typically wear this type of dress.

POPULATION   1,100,000 estimated in 1962, plus 80,000 U.S. citizens. Density is about 1,041 persons per square mile, with 86 percent of the population on Okinawa. Annual rate of increase is 1.7 percent.

ETHNIC GROUPS   The populace is homogeneous. Original immigrants were from the islands of Japan; probably merged with groups from Southeast Asia.

LANGUAGES   Japanese dialects in the north; Ryukyuan, a language derived from Japanese, on Okinawa and in the south. Chinese, Japanese, and English are widely spoken.

RELIGION   The indigenous animistic cults are heavily influenced by Confucianism, Shinto, Buddhism, and Christianity. These cults hold no regular services; rites consist chiefly of seasonal celebrations and ceremonies honoring the dead.

DATE OF INDEPENDENCE   Under U.S. occupation since 1945, the islands, by a treaty signed April 28, 1952, are administered by the United States. Residual sovereignty remains with Japan.

FORM OF GOVERNMENT   Limited democracy. Veto power over all administrative action is held by the U.S. High Commissioner, who is responsible to the U.S. Department of the Army and the Secretary of Defense. On March 19, 1962, President Kennedy announced that the Ryukyuan Chief Executive was to be appointed upon nomination by the Ryukyuan legislature, that jurisdiction of Ryukyuan courts was to be extended, and that a U.S. civilian would have responsibility for civil administration as second-in-command to the High Commissioner. Local government is in the hands of a 29-member unicameral legislature, directly elected for a three-year term. The Chief Executive, chosen from the majority party, has veto power over all legislation.

EDUCATION   In 1961, there were 265 kindergartens and primary schools with over 4,100 teachers and 170,000 students. Education is compulsory and is available to all school-age children. Over 190 secondary and technical schools had a staff of over 3,250 and enrolled almost 86,500 students. The two universities and the teacher-training institutions maintained about 400 instructors and enrolled approximately 4,000 students. Literacy is general, except among the old. The 63 local school boards and the Central Board of Education are elected.

HEALTH FACILITIES

In 1962, there were 359 doctors, 98 dentists, over 450 midwives, and 140 pharmacists. Life expectancy was excellent in comparison with other Asiatic areas—about 70 years for a newborn child.

CULTURAL FACILITIES

About 15 daily newspapers have a circulation of close to 300,000. About one person in three buys a paper daily. In 1960, the 95 cinemas had an attendance of 8.1 million. In 1962, there were 14,000 television sets in use.

CURRENCY AND FINANCE

The U.S. dollar has been legal currency since 1959. The government budget balanced at about $41.79 million during fiscal 1963, included U.S. aid funds of $6.95 million and Japanese aid of $2.78 million. In 1964, Japanese aid was increased to $3.9 million.

INDUSTRY AND PRODUCTION

Prior to U.S. occupation, three-quarters of the people were engaged in agriculture or fishing. Industries consisted of food processing and handicrafts, notably handwoven fabrics and a durable vermilion lacquer which is highly esteemed in Japan for tableware. By 1961, the national income had risen to $209.2 million, or a per capita annual income of $237; 41 percent of the people were engaged in agriculture; 13 percent of the labor force, 55,000 workers, were employed by the U.S. government. By 1965, per capita annual income had risen to $330. Efforts to diversify have resulted in an oil refinery, beer brewery, rubber plant, and a $6 million cement plant. Sugar refining and salt manufacture are also significant. Electric power capacity in 1962 reached 116,000 kilowatts.

CROPS: Less than 20 percent of the land is flat enough to farm; much of that has been purchased for airfields and military installations. Sugar is the chief cash crop; rice, sweet potatoes, sago, soybeans, and fruit are the chief food crops.

LIVESTOCK: Cattle, pigs, goats, ponies.

FISHERIES: In 1962, the catch was estimated at 17,800 metric tons, 2,500 tons above the previous year. Economic importance of fishing is increasing.

MAIN STREET OF NAHA *Many modern stores line the shopping center of Okinawa's capital.*

MINING: Antimony, 102 metric tons in 1961, is the only mineral resource developed.

TRADE

The chief exports are sugar, canned pineapple, and small manufactured goods. Food, machinery, and building materials are imported. The trade deficit is alleviated by aid funds and foreign investments.

1962: IMPORTS $60,900,000
EXPORTS $43,500,000
DEFICIT $17,400,000

TRANSPORT

Naha is the chief port. The road system on Okinawa is well developed. Junks and small steamers provide communication with outlying islands. Naha has an international airfield.

COMMUNI-CATION

Post, radio, and telegraph services are well developed. About 14,000 civilian telephones are in use.

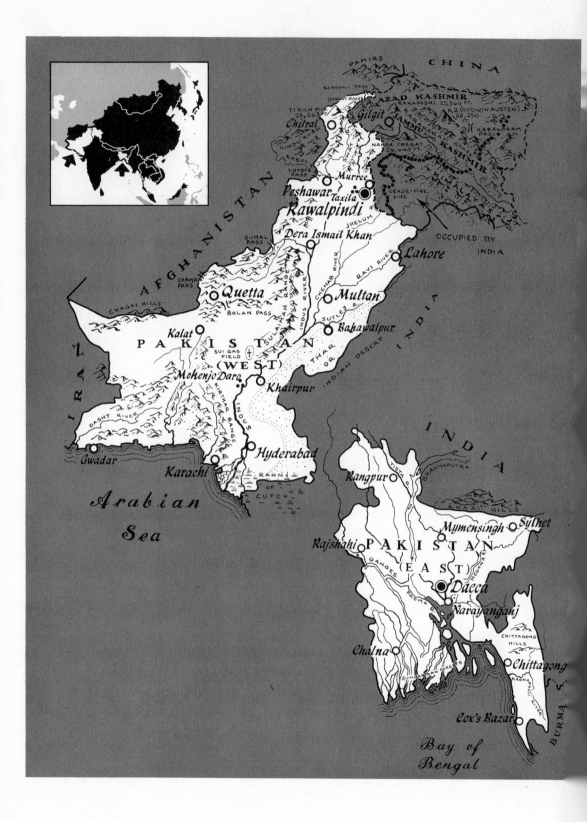

PAKISTAN

New Islamic State

Pakistan is composed of two distinct areas—provinces separated from each other by about a thousand miles. Furthermore, the peoples of West Pakistan and East Pakistan are of dissimilar racial stock, speak different languages, and live in regions in which the topography and climate are in complete contrast.

In 1947, the British granted complete independence to the Indian subcontinent· Two nations were created: one, India; the other, Pakistan. Since Muslims were concentrated on both sides of the Indian subcontinent, Pakistan was formed by making a political entity of these two widely separated and diverse regions.

In 1930, a Muslim poet and philosopher, Muhammed Iqbal, had issued a call for a separate Muslim state, soon labeled Pakistan. In 1940, the Muslim League, the political party headed by Mahomed Ali Jinnah, had subscribed to this goal in its "Pakistan Resolution." From that time on, although bitterly opposed by the Hindus and only reluctantly accepted by the British, the partition of India was inevitable.

When the subcontinent was divided in 1947, there was a large-scale exchange of peoples accompanied by mass violence. Hindus and Sikhs fled the Punjab to India; more than six million Muslims moved from India into Pakistan.

Pakistan, which in all the country's languages means *land of the pure,* reflects the Islamic goal of spiritual purity.

In area, Pakistan as a whole is roughly equivalent to the states of Texas and Wyoming combined. The entire country has a population of approximately 94 million people. Muslims make up almost 90 percent of the population. The Hindus, who constitute the largest minority, are concentrated in East Pakistan where they compose about 20 percent of the population.

Today, in Pakistan, Urdu and Bengali are national languages. Both Urdu and Bengali have literary traditions and both are enjoying

431

new life through the works of modern writers. English, taught in the schools and used in the government, is an official language, but is not widely spoken.

THE WESTERN WING

Though West Pakistan composes 85 percent of the area of the country, an area considerably larger than the state of Texas, that large region with 42 millions has a smaller population than East Pakistan. Most of the western province lies within the basin of the Indus River and its five tributaries; this is the area of the Punjab. Rainfall is slight; and the Punjab, the granary of the country, is crisscrossed with irrigation canals. Only 20 percent of the area is cultivated.

On the deserts, on the plains, and in the mountains, nomads lead their sheep and goats in search of pasture. In the higher altitudes, one encounters sparse forests and extensive orchards. The Hunza, the people of one mountainous region, ascribe their longevity to a diet of apricots. They eat the fruit both fresh and dried, and they make their bread by grinding the pits into flour.

For centuries, invaders approached India through the Khyber Pass which now lies on the border between West Pakistan and Afghanistan. This famed roadway is much less rugged and steep than would be expected.

In West Pakistan, the varied topography has served to preserve the tribal structure of the society. Many languages are in use; Urdu, Sindhi, Punjabi, Baluchi, and Pushtu are the most often heard. The major ethnic groups of West Pakistan are the Pathans, Sindhis, Punjabis, and Baluchis. All were converted to Islam many centuries ago, but each has retained its distinctive language, its distinctive dress, and its customs.

Best known to the Western world, chiefly through the tales of Kipling, are the Pathans who speak Pushtu and live mostly in the former North-West Frontier Province. A tall, blue-eyed, fair-skinned people, they are noted for their love of freedom and for their prowess in warfare. Self-appointed toll collectors at the Khyber Pass, they long resisted efforts by British forces to penetrate their homeland.

The Punjabis have a talent for administration. A comparison be-

MUSLIM WORSHIPPERS   *The Badshahi (Royal) Mosque was built by the Moghul Emperor Aurangzeb at Lahore in 1673. It has the largest open court of any mosque in the world. Here, a sea of the faithful participates in Ramadan ceremonies. During the ninth month of the Muslim year, the month of Ramadan, Muslims offer special prayers, and eat no food between sunrise and sunset.*

tween their faces on miniature paintings of the Moghul period and those of modern officials reveals startling similarities in features.

CITIES OF WEST PAKISTAN

A great new capital is under construction at Islamabad, or "City of Islam," near Rawalpindi. Many millions of dollars are being spent on buildings designed by leading architects of the world.

Ancient cities that have been uncovered by modern archeologists include Mohenjo Daro and Harappa, both on the Indus and both occupied as early as 3,000 B.C. Taxila is really three ancient cities, with ruins over an area of 25 square miles. One city was begun in the sixth century B.C. The museum houses splendid treasures of early Buddhist art.

Karachi, the largest city in the country, is the major seaport and railroad point of the country. Its wide avenues are lined with modern buildings. Karachi is now a busy city of over two million people. It is Pakistan's and Afghanistan's main seaport, and a junction point for international airlines.

Lahore, in the Punjab, is the only city now in Pakistan that was a residence of the Moghul rulers, and still has mosques, palaces, and gardens of that period. Nowadays, Lahore is a manufacturing and cultural center.

THE EASTERN WING

The terrain of East Pakistan is dominated by the great Brahmaputra River and its tributaries. The endless network of waterways in

PATHAN TRIBESMEN   The Afridi and the Orakzai are important tribes of the rugged area south and west of Peshawar. These armed tribesmen with their donkeys are approaching a village north of Kohat. There they will have their rifles or revolvers repaired, or perhaps bargain for a new one. The Afridi have long been famous for their skill in manufacturing firearms.

this delta facilitates transport by boat; but the streams offer endless ob-
stacles to the building of railways and roads.

East Pakistan, formerly the Indian province of East Bengal, may be
compared in area to the state of Wisconsin. Its population is close to
52 million. Approximately 98 percent of East Pakistan speaks Bengali.

East Pakistan is hot and humid. From June to December, while
the flooding rivers are spread out over the plain, countless villages look
like islands in a sea. On these flooded plains, rice is the major food crop.
Jute, made into gunny sacks, is the important cash crop.

Along the Bay of Bengal, a maze of forests and marshes shelters
river-swimming Bengal tigers, tree-climbing fish, pythons, and crocodiles. On the higher ground are the tea plantations, and the jungles
inhabited by herds of elephants.

Most people live in the small farming villages which are the focal
points of everyday life. The major cities are Dacca, the capital, and
Chittagong, a seaport on the Bay of Bengal.

In the two decades since independence, successive governments
have tried to promote national unity between East Pakistan and West
Pakistan. Though some progress has been made, political harmony is
lacking. So far, provincial rivalries and the lack of a common language
have been stronger than the unifying force of Islam.

THE FORCE OF ISLAM

Islam is both a religion and a way of life. In the area of Pakistan,
for centuries religious principles have dominated law, education, and
social relations. Today, strong influences from the West have affected
the fabric of the country. Many religious leaders, though powerless to
turn back the clock, still insist on trying to set up Pakistan as a theocratic
Islamic state; but since there is no agreement, even among the clergy,
on the structure of such a state, their intransigence has worked against
national unity.

It is clear that in spite of religious conservatism, the old social
structure is undergoing sharp modification, largely through the pervasive authority of the central government. When, in 1955, the several
princely states and the older provinces were merged into the single

province of West Pakistan, the power and prestige of local princes and politicians declined. In both provinces, land reforms have drastically cut down the holdings of large landowners and have turned former sharecroppers into independent farmers.

In the villages, the extended family system, that is, three generations living together, persists. Each village has its headman, its *choudhry* or *matbar,* who keeps order, settles disputes, and entertains visitors in the *dara,* or guest house. With the spread of secular education and the decrease of superstition about illness and disease, the influence of the *mullah,* the local clergyman, has declined. Nevertheless, the people still flock to the shrines of *pirs,* or holy men, both those living and those revered as saints of the past. Even many of the educated belong to *dervish* societies, whose group aim is to promote spiritual enlightenment.

As communications improve, and as public services expand, the villages tend to escape from their isolation. Nowadays, there is a growing receptivity to all forms of modernization. The tribes, particularly the nomadic ones, are less affected by the changing times, but even among these primitives some changes are apparent. One can encounter a wandering shepherd carrying a transistor radio—made in Pakistan.

BUS STOP   Buses assigned to the run between Peshawar and Kabul arrive at a station near the Khyber Pass. A typical rope bed provides a comfortable waiting place for Pakistanis most of whom are accustomed to sitting cross-legged. Every bus is gaily painted in dazzling colors with a landscape, a famous building, or a familiar scene.

CONTEMPORARY LIFE

The many aspects of the modernization of the country and its changing social and economic structures have not yet hampered traditional, picturesque customs. Special occasions still brighten the monotony of village life. They include weddings, with the bride and groom paraded on horseback and accompanied by gay music, with feasting to follow; dances distinctive to each region, especially the vigorous, warlike dance of the Pathan tribesmen; and family outings to markets, fairs, and religious shrines.

Organized sports are very popular, especially field hockey, soccer, and cricket. Folk crafts, especially weaving, silverware and copperware, wood carving, and enameled tiles, are improving in quality as they find markets abroad.

Many grow very hungry before harvest time and a very small percentage of families can afford cars or refrigerators. Nevertheless, incomes are gradually rising and the market for radios, bicycles, cooking stoves, utensils, knit goods, and many other items is constantly increasing.

MODERN EDUCATION

Today, education bears little resemblance to the former religiously oriented schooling in which the *mullah* taught boys in a *maktab*, or school, attached to the local mosque. Females remained unlettered. Learning was limited to memorizing verses from the Koran, the sacred book of Islam, and to mastering the rudiments of the three R's. Even today, such schools still exist. Comparatively few students went on to a *madrasa*, a religious school of higher learning.

Universal compulsory education, though an avowed aim of the state, is difficult to put into practice because less than 20 percent of the population is literate. Only 28 percent of the men and less than 10 percent of the women can read and write. However, today some 4.7 million children attend primary schools.

The Pakistani school system includes primary schools for ages six to 10, middle schools for ages 11 through 13, and secondary schools for ages 14 to 16. Graduates of secondary schools take examinations to qualify for clerical posts. Those continuing their education go on for two years in intermediary colleges. Successful intermediate graduates enroll in the 47 colleges attached to the country's five universities. As would be expected, college graduates—regardless of family background —move up the social ladder to good jobs in business and government.

Problems of the educational system include the too-heavy stress placed on final examinations, the necessity for educating more girls, the need for more teachers' training colleges and more technical and vocational schools.

The shortage of skilled workers remains a major industrial problem. A large reserve of labor exists among the nomadic tribes and underemployed farmers, but these groups do not yet appreciate the advantages of learning skills and of keeping regular work hours. To many Pakistanis learning is still associated with religious activity; and time is measured by the seasons, rather than by daily work hours.

AN ECONOMY IN TRANSITION

Although the national income rises each year, because of the rapid growth in population the per capita cash income remains relatively static—at something around $54.

Maintaining farm production is crucial in a land trying to develop a modern economy from a base of village agriculture. Huge dam and canal construction projects are in operation or partially completed, since much more land must be cultivated to feed a population that is both growing rapidly and is undernourished.

However, in areas that have been irrigated for a long time, the ground water rises, pushing harmful salts from the soil to the surface. Crops cease to flourish and eventually new desert areas· develop. The process of washing out the salts and lowering the water table is very costly.

HEALTH CONDITIONS

In Pakistan, the combination of inadequate nutrition, unsanitary conditions, and insufficient medical facilities results in a life expectancy of under 30 years. Although the average family spends more than one-half of its income on food, the daily intake of calories per person is still below standard requirements. Starches predominate in the form of bread and rice. The Pakistani diet lacks calcium, fats, proteins, and vitamins.

Most sanitation facilities are primitive; even the cities lack adequate sewage disposal systems; polluted water transmits typhoid fever and causes bowel disorders. However, the campaign against malaria should eradicate that disease within a few years; and a nationwide program of vaccination is gradually eliminating smallpox. The cumulative effect of these and other measures for public health accounts for the sharp rise in population to a rate of 2.16 percent a year.

ECONOMIC CONDITIONS

Pakistan's national income is well over 25 billion *rupees*, a sum equal to more than five billion dollars. The basic unit of currency is the *rupee*, worth 21¢ in U.S. currency. Both coins and paper money are used, with the banknotes issued in denominations up to 100 *rupees·*

Over three-quarters of the active workers are engaged in agriculture, about one-seventh in manufacturing and local crafts (called cottage industries), and still smaller proportions in the fields of transportation, sales and services, managerial and clerical areas, and in the professions.

Domestic trade consists largely in the exchange of goods in the village bazaars, at weekly markets in the towns, and at annual fairs. The major export items move to the seaports of Karachi, Chittagong, and Chalna. Raw and manufactured jute amounts to 65 percent of the exports by value, cotton about 10 percent, and other important items include wool, hides and skins, and tea.

Large-scale manufacturing, financed by the government largely from foreign loans, has had a phenomenal growth. There are sugar mills and plants producing fertilizers, cement, and paper, as well as factories making railroad cars, automobile tires, chemicals, pharmaceuticals, and vegetable oils.

Hydroelectric plants on the rivers in both provinces and recently developed fields of natural gas at Sui in West Pakistan and at Sylhet

STREET DENTIST   On Bunder Road in Karachi, a street dentist plies his trade. False teeth and molds are laid out. The wheeled machine is a hand-driven drill. He advertises his skill by displaying the hundreds of teeth he has extracted.

TECHNICAL SCHOOL   The industrial town of Narayanganj in the delta area of East Pakistan has a Diesel Training Center, established with United Nations assistance. These students, some of whom have never before been away from their native village, will become foremen and instructors throughout East Pakistan. Here, they listen to a lecture on the fuel injection system of the diesel engines.

FARMERS OF WEST PAKISTAN   Yoked with wood, a team of cattle pulls a primitive plow. These turbaned and bearded farmers are ethnically and culturally distinct
from their counterparts in the East. Despite their conversion to Islam centuries ago,
most farmers in East Pakistan have inherited some of the blood and much of the
culture of the Hindus.

KARACHI TRAFFIC   A camel, a donkey cart, a horse-drawn carriage, a motor rickshaw, some bicycles, cars, and crowded public buses, make up the melange of traffic
on one of the capital's busy streets.

in East Pakistan supply power for industry and lighting for the urban centers. One of the Sui gas pipelines is over 300 miles long.

The country's economic development is carried out within the framework of five-year plans. The Second Five-Year Plan runs from 1960 to 1965 and is intended to increase gross national income by 24 percent and per capita income by 13 percent. It involves spending $4.83 billion, including $2.3 billion from foreign sources.

TRANSPORT AND COMMUNICATION

In the field of transportation, air service within and between the provinces is increasingly important. Pakistan International Airlines also flies to India, Communist China, Europe, and the United States. The country's major ports, Karachi, Chittagong, and Chalna, handle ocean traffic between the two provinces and to foreign countries.

The railways of West Pakistan are three times the length of those of East Pakistan, whose waterways make railroads very difficult and expensive to build. In the east wing, inland waterways carry goods and passengers by steamer, launch, and *dinghy* (a Bengali word borrowed for English). Existing lines are improved rather than extended in both wings, because emphasis is placed on developing a network of asphalted highways. While 60,000 automobiles, 20,000 trucks, and over 10,000 buses move along 65,000 miles of road, camel caravans still transport the dairy products and wool of the nomadic tribes to market towns.

PRESS, LITERATURE, AND RADIO

Nearly 100 daily papers are published, most of them in Urdu, English, or Bengali. In general, their circulation is rather small, totaling about one paper for every 200 people in the country. The papers are smaller in size than American papers and usually have from four to eight pages. Local political and economic news predominates and advertising is scanty. The circulation of magazines of general interest and those devoted to literature and the arts, to women's interests, or to pictures is also limited. The government has legal powers to control the contents of newspapers and publications by taking action against the publishers of objectionable material.

Contemporary writing in Pakistan has been influenced by the West. Novels and short stories, which are literary forms not familiar to earlier India, are notably popular. Poetry continues to be very popular, especially in East Pakistan, and other types of writing include humor, religion, social criticism, and history. Histories are primarily concerned with the Moghul period.

KHYBER PASS   *A modern road now winds through the Khyber Pass, which has been a strategic military route since before the time of Alexander the Great. Cutting through the mountains between Kabul in Afghanistan and Peshawar in West Pakistan, this pass has been controlled for centuries by the Pathan tribes of the vicinity. Until 1947, tribesmen were subsidized by the British government of India—a form of bribery to prevent the tribesman from collecting road tolls at gun-point.*

MAN-AT-ARMS   *This is a soldier of the crack Khyber Rifles, one of the most famous units of the Pakistani Army. He serves at Jamrud Fort in the Khyber Pass.*

Pakistan developed its own film industry with a score of popular stars appearing in romantic stories loosely based on history and fable. Music and dancing are featured in these films. Both locally produced and foreign films are very popular, and Pakistan has nearly 400 movie houses.

Radio is probably the most powerful medium for reaching the masses and influencing their opinions (although *bazaar gup,* gossip in the bazaars, may give rise to all kinds of rumors).

Radio Pakistan, state-owned, broadcasts from a number of cities in 17 languages. Schedules include about 65 percent of folk music and local classical music. The balance of the programming includes news, drama, education, and special programs. Advertising is limited to a total of one hour a day. Pilot television stations came on the air at Lahore and Dacca at the end of 1964.

EARLY HISTORY

As a general background for the field of government and politics, many Pakistanis look back with pride to forbears in the Moghul period (1526–1761). Such Muslim rulers as Babur, Humayun, Akbar, Jahangir, Shah Jahan, and Aurangzeb controlled most of the Indian subcontinent during that period. Contemporary leaders seek to rival the cultural achievements of the Moghuls and to employ the force of Islam to build enduring strength in their new nation.

When the British, displacing the ruling Muslims, acquired all of India, the Muslims became a subordinate, resentful minority. While many Hindus eagerly took advantage of the new opportunities for education and government service, the Muslims remained aloof. In the second half of the nineteenth century, however, a series of Muslim revivalists, educators, and poets aroused their compatriots to the need to adapt to new conditions and to unite for a common goal.

Early in this century, when agitation for Indian independence gained momentum, some Muslim leaders joined the Hindu-dominated Indian National Congress. Then, in 1906, they founded the All-India Muslim League.

MAHOMED ALI JINNAH

Mahomed Ali Jinnah, a Karachi-born lawyer educated in England, joined with Mohandas Gandhi and Jawaharlal Nehru in promoting Muslim-Hindu unity. He was at that time president of the Muslim League, but in 1928 Jinnah concluded that the Muslims would be a weak minority in the kind of free India favored by the Hindus.

When Pakistan became independent on August 14, 1947, Jinnah was Governor General of the Dominion of Pakistan, president of the Muslim League, and head of the new country's legislative body. Unfortunately, he died in 1948 before his inspiring, forceful leadership had brought solutions to many urgent problems, including that of drafting a Constitution.

THE FIRST YEARS

The first Constitution was not completed until March 1956, after years of political bickering and inter-provincial rivalry. This Constitution of 1956 reflected the British parliamentary system in that a Prime Minister remained in office only as long as he had the support of the majority of the Parliament, but it also provided for a President of the country.

During the years to 1956, the Muslim League's position of predominant leadership declined. Tensions and disputes grew to such an extent that, in October 1958, President Iskandar Mirza stated that the

SHI'A CEREMONY *Every year, during the Islamic month of Moharrum, members of the Shi'a sect commemorate the trials of Hussain, the grandson of Mohammed. As part of the ceremony, a Muslim of Karachi walks over burning coals, fanned to a glow by attendants. The performer of this ritual remains apparently unharmed.*

EXCAVATION *Nearly 5,000 years ago, a slender, black-haired people developed a high civilization in some well-planned towns of the Indus Valley. Mohenjo Daro is now being excavated by archeologists. It was a peaceful, unfortified city of three square miles, laid out in a neat pattern of cross streets. Every street, no matter how narrow, had a brick-lined drainage system. Even the humblest dwelling was more commodious and comfortable than those in many villages of today's India. The city was destroyed about 1500 B.C. by Aryan tribes from Central Asia.*

STREET SCENE   *About a fifth of the population of East Pakistan are Hindus to whom the cow is sacred. These bullocks, allowed to roam through the main thoroughfares of Dacca, are scratching each other's heads to relieve the itch of insect bites.*

DACCA   *Huts constructed of bamboo, reeds, and matting house thousands on the outskirts of Dacca. Many of these Muslim families fled from India during the conflict of the partition period. They are being resettled in new housing communities.*

MUHAMMAD AYUB KHAN *Field Marshal Khan was born in 1907 in a small village of the North-West Frontier Province. He attended Aligarh University in India, and then entered the Royal Military College at Sandhurst, England. After a long military career, he became commander-in-chief of Pakistan's army in 1950. In appearance, speech, and manner he resembles a British officer. Khan is a forceful personality. He is an avid reader, plays tennis, bridge, chess, and is very fond of hunting.*

country was on the verge of ruin from the misrule of corrupt politicians. He dissolved the Parliament and all political parties and declared martial law. After two weeks General Muhammad Ayub Khan, head of the armed forces, ousted Mirza and took over as President, an office to which he was elected in 1960.

AYUB KHAN

Muhammad Ayub Khan was born in 1907 in a small village of the North-West Frontier Province. After graduating from Aligarh University in India, he attended the Royal Military College at Sandhurst in England and graduated from there as an officer. Prior to partition, he served with the Indian Army. He was elevated to the rank of General in the Pakistan Army in 1948, and was made a full General and Commander-in-Chief of the Pakistan Army in 1950. Tall and erect of carriage, with trimmed mustache and fair complexion, Ayub Khan is fluent in English, Pushtu, and Urdu. He is fond of playing tennis, plays bridge and chess, likes to hunt, and is a voracious reader of serious books. His wife came from a village not far from his own birthplace.

Once in power, Ayub Khan moved rapidly against corrupt politicians and officials. He named commissions to study the country's social and economic problems, and their recommendations were speedily carried out.

In October, 1959, he issued *The Basic Democracies Order* providing for a four-tiered structure of councils with both elected and appointed members. Some 80,000 "Basic Democrats," elected by adult suffrage, chose the President and the members of the legislatures. It was hoped that the councils would "prepare the base on which an upward pyramid of a sound political structure can be developed," in Ayub Khan's words.

He also hoped the councils would do away with the atmosphere of competing political parties. However, parties did return to life and attacked the regime of Ayub Khan on a number of grounds.

In 1962 a second Constitution replaced the first. Closer to the American model, it does not provide for a Prime Minister and the President has very broad powers. The National Assembly has 156 members, and each provincial legislature has 155 members.

TAXILA In the Himalaya foothills, the ruins of three ancient cities spread over an area of almost 25 square miles. These cities flourished from the fifth century B.C. to the fourth century A.D.—for almost a thousand years. Excavations of palaces, baths, government buildings, Greek temples, and Buddhist stupas have provided exhibits for a local museum. Here, the remains of a Buddhist stupa are surrounded by the rudimentary walls of the original temple complex.

FOREIGN ASSISTANCE AND FOREIGN POLICY

Pakistan receives loans and grants for its development programs from many sources. The Second Five-Year Plan is supported by several countries belonging to a so-called Aid-to-Pakistan Club. By 1964 the United States had contributed, through the Club and in other ways, well over $2 billion, exclusive of the value of military equipment.

In the field of foreign relations, Pakistan's major concern is India. India has a much larger army than Pakistan, and Pakistanis believe implicitly in its hostility to the very existence of its neighbor.

A critical dispute between the two concerns the State of Jammu and Kashmir. While India has absorbed most of the area, Pakistan insists that its inhabitants, who are mostly Muslims, must be permitted to choose whether they wish to join Pakistan or India. The United Nations has failed to resolve the dispute, which came strongly to the fore as the result of open war between India and Pakistan in the summer of 1965. The war began in Kashmir and spread to the Punjab and other areas along the common frontier.

The government of Afghanistan asserts that the Pathans, blood brothers of the Pushtun tribes on the Afghan side of the border, should be allowed to vote on whether they wish to remain in Pakistan or to set up an autonomous state of their own. The Afghans have given the name of Pushtunistan to this proposed state.

PAKISTAN AND THE COMMUNISTS

Following the Communist Chinese invasion of northeast India in the autumn of 1962, the United States and Britain rushed military supplies to India. They also extended long-term aid to increase and modernize India's armed forces. Pakistan protested vigorously. Claiming that its allies had upset the balance of strength of the two armies in favor of India, the regime announced that it would consider a more independent foreign policy.

Although successive governments had been strongly anti-communist, close relations were then sought with the People's Republic of China. Better relations with the Soviet Union were also encouraged. While remaining in CENTO and SEATO, Pakistan has drawn closer,

PLAYTIME IN DACCA   *Some of the girls play karam, a local version of checkers; others skip rope. Even at this tender age, girls and boys play separately in this Islamic society. This is a Community Development Centre, organized by the government with help from the United Nations Children's Fund.*

since 1962, to the so-called anti-imperialist and anti-colonial line pursued by the Communist bloc and the Asian and African nonaligned nations.

DONALD NEWTON WILBER

IN BRIEF

AREA

365,929 square miles. East Pakistan, 55,126 square miles, is slightly smaller than Illinois; West Pakistan, 310,403 square miles, is about the combined size of Tennessee and Texas.

TERRAIN

Most of East Pakistan is flat and wet. The Ganges and Brahmaputra rivers join to form an extensive alluvial plain and delta. To the east, the Karnaphuli River drains the Chittagong hill country. West Pakistan is arid, with plains in the south and mountains in the north. The second-highest mountain in the world, K2, lies in the Kashmir Himalayas. The waters of the five great rivers that join to form the lower Indus irrigate the southern plains.

FLORA

In West Pakistan vegetation ranges from that of pine-forested mountain valleys to arid desert and salt marsh. Bamboo, palms, and water lilies are characteristic of East Pakistan, where the famous Sundarban forests are located.

FAUNA

Tiger, including the Royal Bengal tiger, crocodile, elephant, python and other snakes, spotted deer, and yak.

CLIMATE

East Pakistan is generally warm and humid, with rains well over 100 inches a year in some parts. The driest months are November through March. The plains of West Pakistan receive only 15 inches of rain a year. Unlike the tropical monsoon climate of the east, the western wing has strongly marked seasons with cold, dry winters and warm summers.

CAPITALS

Rawalpindi, the temporary national capital, had about 340,000 inhabitants in 1961. A new national capital is being built at nearby Islamabad. Dacca, 560,000, is the second national capital and the administrative center of East Pakistan; Lahore, 1,300,000, is the administrative center of West Pakistan.

OTHER CITIES

Karachi, the chief port, has about 2,000,000 inhabitants; Hyderabad, 250,000; Peshawar, 150,000; Chittagong, 365,000.

POPULATION

Over 94 million in 1965. The annual rate of increase is 2.16 percent. Density is about 140 persons per square mile in the west wing and about 1,020 in the east.

THE VALLEY OF KAGHAN   A caravan winds through a valley of the North-West Frontier.

ETHNIC GROUPS   East Pakistan is chiefly Bengali, with some tribal peoples in the hills near the Burma border. Pathans, Punjabis, Sindhis, and Baluchis comprise most of the populace of West Pakistan. Many small tribes, such as the Urmuri, are isolated in mountainous areas.

LANGUAGES   Bengali, widely spoken in the east, and Urdu in the west are the national languages. English may be used for official purposes until 1972. Pushtu, Sindhi, Punjabi, and Baluchi are widely spoken.

RELIGION   Over 88 percent of the people are Muslims—97.2 percent in the West and 80.4 percent in the East. Almost a fifth of East Pakistan's people are Hindu. There are small groups of Buddhists, Christians, and Parsis.

PATHAN CHILDREN

DOWNTOWN KARACHI   *Wide paved boulevards and multi-storied buildings of contemporary design contrast with the dwindling number of horse-drawn carriages still used in Pakistan's largest city.*

DATE OF INDEPENDENCE

On August 14, 1947, the *Indian Independence Act* came into force. On March 23, 1956, Pakistan proclaimed itself an Islamic Republic.

FORM OF GOVERNMENT

Limited democracy. A National Assembly of 156 is composed of 75 members from each wing, plus six women who are appointed. Two Provincial Assemblies have 155 members each. All are indirectly elected. The President, who is also the supreme military commander, appoints the Cabinet. The judiciary is independent. Member of the Commonwealth of Nations, SEATO, CENTO, and the United Nations.

EDUCATION

There were almost six million students in 50,500 primary and secondary schools in 1961. Pakistan had over 193,000 teachers, with over 9,000 more being trained in 103 teachers' colleges and schools. Six universities and 241 colleges enrolled almost 140,000 students. About 19.2 percent of the people are literate. Literacy in East Pakistan is slightly higher than that in West Pakistan.

HEALTH FACILITIES

There were almost six million students in 50,500 primary and medical colleges, three are in the east wing, which has about 6,700 hospital beds. Life expectancy for a newborn child is 27 years.

CULTURAL FACILITIES

The 100 daily newspapers had about half a million circulation in 1962; of the 1,400 daily and weekly papers about 900 use Urdu, about 225 use English, and about 150 use Bengali. Of the 600 or so books published in 1960, about 450 were new. Perhaps 50 films are made each year for showing in 390 cinemas, which had a yearly attendance of 80 million in 1961. *Radio Pakistan* broadcasts news, cultural, and educational material in 17 languages. The country supports lively film industry and literary arts.

CURRENCY AND FINANCE

The Pakistan *rupee* is valued at 2.88 grains of fine gold, or 21¢ in U.S. currency. The total government budget for 1963–64 expected $1.16 billion in revenues and over $1.22 billion in expenditures. About $71.4 million was to be used on national development.

Essentially agricultural, Pakistan earns only a seventh of its income from manufacturing, and 85 to 90 percent of the people gain their living in agriculture. In 1963, national income was $5.3 billion and per capita income was $54, an increase of $3.36 since 1959. Manufactures include cotton cloth, jute goods, metal utensils, rubber tires, paper, electric wire and lamps. Jute processing is being intensively developed. Factories for processing steel, paper, cement, fertilizer, chemicals, and textiles have been recently completed.

CROPS: Rice—10 million tons in 1962–63—is the chief food crop of East Pakistan. West Pakistan grows wheat—about four million tons in 1962–63. Cotton and jute, the two important cash crops, occupy less than 10 percent of the sown land. East Pakistan grew more than a billion tons of jute in 1962–63, over 80 percent of the world crop. Other crops include tea, corn, barley, millet, sugar, and tobacco.

LIVESTOCK: Cattle, buffalo, sheep, goats, camels, and horses. Hides are an important export. Most of the 5.5 million fine goat skins produced annually are used by the European glove trade.

FISHERIES: Annual catch is about 300,000 tons; two-thirds of it comes from the flooded fields and streams of East Pakistan.

MINING: Limited production mostly in West Pakistan. Large gas fields have been discovered at Sui in the west and at Sylhet in the east; petroleum is extracted in the west. Small amounts of coal, iron, chromite, gypsum, silica sand, clay, and salt are mined.

Almost half of the 1963 exports were raw jute and jute manufactures, cotton and cotton goods. Rice, fish and fish oil, hides, tea, wool, and fruit are also exported. Principal imports are chemicals, machinery, cars and trucks, medicines, and manufactured goods.

1962: IMPORTS $738,129,000
EXPORTS $397,320,000
DEFICIT $340,809,000

ROAD: Of 65,000 miles of road, 42,000 miles were in West Pakistan (1963) as were nearly all of the 10,000 miles of all-

UNITED NATIONS CORPS *Pakistan sent 1,200 of its best troops to serve under the United Nations during the 1962-63 crisis in West New Guinea. This contingent is aboard a Pakistan ship en route to Southeast Asia.*

weather road. The 90,000 motor vehicles included some 60,000 passenger cars. Camel caravans carry some of West Pakistan's freight.

RAIL: West Pakistan has over 5,300 miles of railway; East Pakistan some 1,700 miles.

WATERWAY: East Pakistan depends chiefly on water transport. About 1,060 motor vessels and 300,000 country boats use 3,000 miles of channel (4,500 miles during monsoons).

AIR: Pakistan International Airlines provides service to 13 airfields, as well as helicopter service in the marshy east wing of the country. Twenty foreign lines serve Karachi which lies on a key route between the Far East and Europe.

SEA: Karachi in the west, Chittagong and Chalna in the east, are the chief ports. In 1963, there were 43 cargo and passenger vessels under the Pakistani flag.

COMMUNI-CATION

Post, telegraph, telephone, radio, and television services are government-owned and operated. There were 396,000 radios and 95,000 telephones in use in 1962.

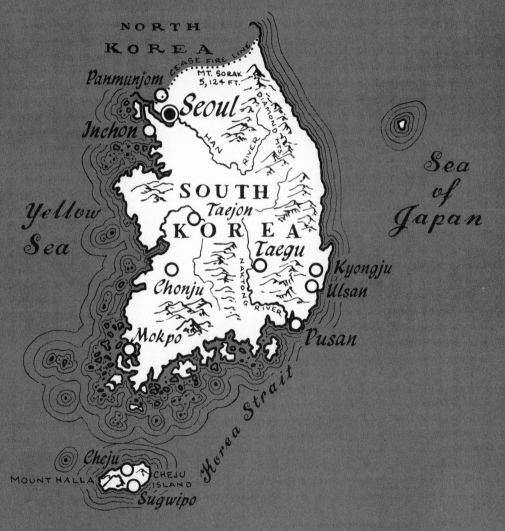

NORTH
KOREA

CEASE FIRE LINE

Panmunjom

MT. SORAK
5,124 FT.

Seoul

Inchon

DIAMOND MTS.

HAN RIVER

SOUTH

Yellow
Sea

Taejon

KOREA

Taegu

Kyongju

Chonju

NAKTONG RIVER

Ulsan

Sea
of
Japan

Mokpo

Pusan

Korea Strait

Cheju

MOUNT HALLA

CHEJU
ISLAND

Sugwipo

REPUBLIC OF KOREA

Struggling Outpost of Democracy

A look at the map of Asia leaves little doubt about the strategic importance of Korea, a land which forms a bridge between China, the U.S.S.R., and Japan. The entire S-shaped peninsula constitutes an area of more than 85,000 square miles, slightly larger than Minnesota.

North Korea, known officially as the Democratic People's Republic of Korea, occupies the larger part of the peninsula. The southern portion of the peninsula, the Republic of Korea, occupies about 38,000 square miles, an area about the size of Indiana. The Republic of Korea has about two and a half times the population of North Korea, and is, indeed, one of the most densely populated areas of the world.

HISTORICAL BACKGROUND

It has always been difficult to feed the enormous population of Korea. Nevertheless, despite the relentless struggle for survival, a most remarkable culture flourished here over a period of some two thousand years. Archaeological treasures from the period of the Three Kingdoms—the Silla, the Kokuryo, and the Paekche dynasties (57 B.C. to 667 A.D.)—attest to this.

Buddhism had been introduced under the Silla dynasty as early as 372 A.D. In 1231, the country was invaded by Mongols, and Confucianism became the official creed. That religion strongly affected the character and the institutions of the Korean people.

There were repeated attacks by foreign invaders. At the end of the 16th century, the Japanese waged war for seven years, but failed to conquer the peninsula. In 1627, and again in 1636, the country was plagued by Manchu invasions. As a result of these incursions, Korea tried to seal itself off from the outside world, and in fact remained a more or less closed book until well into the 19th century.

JAPANESE DOMINATION

It was not until 1876 that Japan succeeded in "opening" the country. The Japanese took full advantage of the factionalism which had long plagued the reigning Korean dynasty. For about two decades, China competed with Japan for the hegemony of Korea; but in 1895, China had to concede to Japan. The King of Korea became a puppet of Japan, but was compensated for his subservience with the title of Emperor. In 1905, after the Japanese had achieved a military victory over Russia, Korea was formally transformed into a Japanese protectorate. Some five years later, Japan annexed Korea, imposing its own brand of colonialism which Koreans are not likely to forget.

Although it is true that the Japanese were responsible for the modernization of the country, these benefits were dictated by Japanese ambitions. During the first decade of their control (1910–1920), the Japanese concentrated on the development of administrative machinery through which they intended to expedite the economic exploitation of Korea. Practically all key positions in the government were held by Japanese; and qualified Koreans were denied the opportunity of gaining governmental experience.

SEOUL SHOP   *This shopkeeper is hanging out freshly made noodles to dry. His finished product is displayed on the open counter.*

BUDDHIST TEMPLE This edifice, built in 982 A.D., is served by a hereditary priest. His son will assume his duties on his retirement. Both temple and priest are maintained by rents from the land owned by the religious community. Tenants must pay a third of their crop as rent.

FREEDOM IN KOREA

Japan's domination of Korea lasted 35 years. Finally, when it was clear that Japan was determined to obliterate Korean national identity, the oppressive foreign rule was deemed intolerable.

Koreans were greatly encouraged by Woodrow Wilson's proclamation of the principle of self-determination. In 1919, a nationwide peaceful demonstration for independence took place in Korea. The Japanese authorities responded by killing thousands of demonstrators. March 1st, the day on which this occurred, is still commemorated by the Korean people as a day of national remembrance.

Only at the end of World War II were the Japanese oppressors ousted. Unfortunately, the victory of the Allies did not result in the national reunification of Korea, for the Soviet Union was allowed to occupy the northern part of the country where the Russians established a Communist puppet regime.

In the southern sector, which was turned into the Republic of Korea, Dr. Syngman Rhee emerged as the undisputed leader of his people. For five decades he had struggled against the tyranny of the Japanese. It was natural that he should become the first elected President of the Republic under a presidential system established in the Korean Constitution of 1948. When elected, Dr. Rhee was 73 years old.

Syngman Rhee had professed his dedication to the principles of democracy; but despite constitutional provisions, he capitalized on the Korean need for a father image and established a highly authoritarian regime. Dr. Rhee repeatedly invoked sweeping emergency powers. Although the Constitution conferred such powers on the President, these alleged emergencies were frequent and the assumption of absolute control was, at times, quite unnecessary.

Despite Rhee's autocracy and the flagrant corruption of some of his subordinates, his popularity was so great that he encountered no difficulty in getting himself reelected three times.

POLITICAL UPHEAVAL

In 1956, however, considerable doubt was cast on the honesty of the election. Finally, in the spring of 1960, the election manipulations became so outrageous that the students sparked a revolution and forced the once revered leader to resign. He retired to Hawaii, and remained there until his death in 1965.

The government that came to power as a result of that April, 1960, student revolt was headed by Dr. "John" M. Chang (Chang, Myon), a Catholic and a man of unquestioned integrity. He tried to build a parliamentary regime on the eroded foundation of Confucian paternalism. His eagerness to break away from the discredited police state caused fears that the country was headed toward anarchy. Dr. Chang was so preoccupied with measures for liberalization that he failed to act decisively against corruptors, who took full advantage of the chaos caused by the recent political upheaval.

STREET SCENE IN
SEOUL *Korean men have
been more ready to adopt
Western clothing than have
their wives.*

On May 16, 1961, the Chang regime was overthrown by a small group of military men headed by General Chung Hee Park. For about two and a half years, the center of power was vested in the Supreme Council of National Reconstruction which was composed entirely of military officers.

However, General Park had pledged to return the country to constitutional government as soon as sufficient stability had been achieved. A Committee drafted constitutional amendments which were approved in a popular referendum by a substantial majority. In the fall of 1963, General Park resigned from the Army and announced his candidacy for the Presidency. He won by a narrow vote, but his newly created Democratic Republican Party succeeded in capturing 110 of the 175 seats in the National Assembly.

President Park was inaugurated on December 17, 1963 in an impressive ceremony. The amended Constitution went into force that same day. Since that time, considerable progress has been made toward stabilization. Although the Democratic Republican Party has a clear majority in the National Assembly, it has continued to be plagued by factionalism.

STUDENT DEMONSTRATION *The students of Korea have brought down at least one government. Here is part of a march of 70,000 students who attended a rally of the National Reconstruction Movement in Seoul in 1961.*

ETHNIC CHARACTERISTICS

In physical appearance and dress, Koreans exhibit fairly distinctive characteristics. Also, Korean food is quite different from that of its neighbors, and some dishes are definitely unique. As in most Oriental countries, rice is the most important item in the Korean diet· Koreans are very fond of *kimchi*, a strongly spiced, pickled vegetable mixture consisting usually of chopped cabbage, radishes, and hot peppers. This is produced each fall in the home, in the traditional manner, and stored in large earthenware crocks which are buried in the ground to withstand the cold and remain accessible for use by the family throughout the year.

Another favorite dish, both for Koreans and their foreign visitors, is *pulkoki*, sliced beef marinated in soya sauce and broiled on a charcoal burner.

According to anthropologists, the population of Korea can be traced to two ethnic elements in central Asia: the Tungusic and the Mongolian. Over a period of some two thousand years, these two groups have been thoroughly merged so that today the population of Korea appears remarkably homogeneous.

LANGUAGE

The Korean language is part of the Altaic or Ural-Altaic group, which accounts for its affinity to Mongolian, Turkish, and Japanese. However, this basic relationship has been overshadowed by the profound influence that the Chinese language has exerted—an influence dating back to the first Chinese invasion in 108 B.C. About a thousand years later, knowledge of the Chinese classics and the ability to write poetry in Chinese became prime requirements for appointment to higher governmental offices in Korea; and, of course, the influence of the classical Chinese language became more pronounced. This was reflected in the use of Chinese characters in written Korean.

SYNGMAN RHEE   Head of his country during the 12 years between 1948 and 1960, the first President of the Republic of Korea resigned after student riots had caused over 900 casualties and had disrupted the administration of his country. He is pictured here in retirement in Hawaii near the age of 90. He died in 1965.

The promulgation in 1446 of a Korean alphabet, known as Hangul, was an event of the greatest importance in the development of Korean culture and national identity. However, official documents continued to be recorded in Chinese characters until the end of the 18th century. Toward the end of the 19th century Hangul began to replace the Chinese characters. A few decades later, however, the Japanese overlords banned the use of Hangul in Korean schools.

Only rather recently have the merits of the more than 500-year-old Hangul come to be more widely appreciated. Korean scholars point out that this alphabet, consisting of 24 letters, is highly effective in expressing modern Korean; there are some who claim that Hangul is the most scientific writing in the world.

CULTURAL ACHIEVEMENTS

Koreans have good reason to be proud of their cultural achievements. The first moveable printing type was invented in Korea in 1234, more than 200 years before Gutenberg. The pale green Koryo Celadon ceramics, executed in inlaid clays of white and gray, with their graceful shapes and lovely designs, are regarded by connoisseurs as among the greatest achievements of the potter's art anywhere in the world.

Koreans are justly proud, too, of their rich musical tradition: royal court music, known as *A-ak;* and folk music, or *Kuk-ak*. The former is essentially Chinese; more specifically, one should note that *A-ak* is the original court music of the Chinese T'ang Dynasty (618–906 A.D.), which can no longer be heard anywhere but in Korea. The National Classical Music Institute has achieved a remarkable revival of this tradition; concerts are performed today by highly skilled musicians, dressed in nearly authentic traditional robes. The folk music, of course, with its uninterrupted tradition, is much closer to the people. Western music is also immensely popular.

FAMILY CUSTOMS

Korean family life is governed by tradition. There is considerable respect for the older members of the family. In the presence of one's

WOMEN DIVERS   *Cheju Island lies off the southern coast of Korea. Many native women of this sub-tropical isle earn their living by collecting shellfish, abalone shells, and other products from the bottom of the sea. Each diver carries a large, hollow gourd fastened to the net in which the catch is stored. The gourd acts as a buoy for the loaded net.*

elders or of an honored guest, younger individuals usually abstain from drinking or smoking.

Men and women are equal before the law, but traditional attitudes toward women have largely continued; this sometimes causes difficulty in families in which the wife or daughter has been exposed to Western customs.

In the cities, Western-style clothing is worn by most men, but many women still prefer their lovely traditional silk costumes.

One of the characteristic features of a traditional Korean house is the *ondol* floor, the smooth, wooden floor of the formal sitting room. Korean houses are generally quite cold by Western standards. Fuel is expensive and is occasionally in short supply. The heat from the kitchen oven flows under the floor, through flues covered by clay or cement. The guest of honor is usually guided to the most comfortable spot in the room.

EDUCATION

The 1948 Constitution provided for free and compulsory elementary education. Great strides have been made. The illiteracy rate is well

WOMEN ARCHERS   *An ancient and honored sport in South Korea, archery is practiced by many who compete in the annual contests in Seoul.*

under 10 percent, and further reduction is most likely.

In secondary education, Japanese disciplinarian ways have left their impact. Boys and girls wear uniforms, and they usually attend different schools. Since the end of World War II the number of universities has increased rapidly. There are now six national universities, four national colleges, and ten junior colleges. The number of private institutions has increased even more rapidly. Unfortunately, the standards in these institutions are uneven and the government has not been very successful in insisting on improvements.

Although a large number of Koreans still study abroad, the country is now well equipped to provide excellent undergraduate education. In view of the shortage of foreign exchange, it is likely that the number of undergraduates studying abroad will decline.

Korea, like many other developing countries, has a serious "drain brain" problem. A very high percentage of Koreans who acquired Ph.D.'s in the U.S. have elected to remain in the United States. The Korean Government is trying to persuade many of these skilled professionals to return to Korea by offering them more attractive positions.

ECONOMIC PROBLEMS

Although the war-shattered economy of the Republic of Korea has largely been restored, the country still suffers from numerous economic ills for which there are no quick and easy remedies. The basic difficulty stems from the fact that the economic structures of North Korea and of South Korea differ considerably. However, the two economies would complement each other to a remarkable extent were it not for the unnatural political division. The South has always been primarily agricultural. Under the Japanese, North Korea, with its substantial mineral resources, developed into the center of heavy industry.

The Japanese had no intention of developing a Korean national economy; on the contrary, every effort was made to integrate the Korean economy into that of the Japanese colonial empire. After the Japanese seizure of Manchuria in 1931, Japan, Korea, and Manchuria were tied together to form an arsenal for the Japanese war machine. By 1944, Korea contributed 100 percent of all the required cobalt, graphite, magnetite, and mica to the Japanese war economy. The country was ruthlessly exploited—for example, by the stepped-up mining of gold just before World War II.

When Korea was finally liberated, there was no opportunity to embark upon economic unification of the regions since the country was politically divided. South Korea, which had always been more densely populated than the North, could not possibly support all its people. The flight of refugees from North Korea to the South further aggravated the situation.

In recent years, the contrast in population density between North and South has been sharpened. In the South, close to 700 inhabitants occupy a square mile; whereas in the North, the average is somewhat over 200. The flight to the cities, especially to Seoul, the capital, adds to the difficulty of the situation.

RECONSTRUCTION AFTER THE WAR

Tremendous damage was inflicted during the Korean War; the property destruction has been estimated at more than three billion dollars.

CHUNG HEE PARK Korea's President took control of the government while he was an army officer. He is now the elected President.

Most Koreans are quick to acknowledge their gratitude for the foreign aid that has since been furnished, particularly by the United States, which has provided almost four billion dollars in economic assistance between 1946 and 1964, and more than two billion dollars in military assistance. The Republic of Korea has been obliged to maintain an armed security force of more than half a million men, and this has constituted a tremendous financial burden.

No responsible Korean will deny that there has been some waste in the use of economic assistance. In the past, corruption and mismanagement have been rife; but the present government is making strenuous efforts to work with maximum efficiency. President Park has made it clear that he will tolerate neither corruption nor incompetence. Economic planning has been reorganized.

Today, Korea is a developing country, but one-third of the labor force remains unemployed or underemployed. A more constructive economic relationship with Japan may be in the offing. After 14 years of intermittent negotiations, a "normalization agreement" was signed on June 22, 1965, between the two countries which is intended to restore full diplomatic relations after a lapse of 55 years. The treaty compares favorably with that concluded by other former victims of Japanese imperialism. However, Koreans have found it difficult to wipe out the memory of past humiliations by the Japanese. Many of them talk about the past when one attempts to talk specifically about the economic implications of normalization. The opposition factions have taken full advantage of this state of affairs and have engaged in obstructionist tactics in the National Assembly.

During the summer of 1965, the leaders of the Democratic Republican Party made strenuous efforts to persuade some of the opposition members of the National Assembly to support the normalization treaty. They failed to persuade the opposition, but they still had enough votes to obtain ratification of the treaty by the National Assembly. President Park signed the ratification instruments on December 17, 1965. However, at the same time, the Japanese Cabinet declared an exclusive fishing zone around Tokto Island. This was one of several indications that actual normalization was going to require a considerable amount of time and restraint on both sides.

GISBERT H. FLANZ

IN BRIEF

AREA 38,452 square miles, a bit longer than Indiana.

TERRAIN Mountainous peninsula, with narrow coastal plains and fertile river valleys. Short, swift rivers and tides as high as 33 feet on the west coast provide good electric power potential.

FLORA The forests, similar to those of mainland China, have been seriously depleted. Reforestation projects have had limited success. Bamboo, pine, oak, alder, conifers, and common deciduous trees.

FAUNA Wildlife has suffered from forest depletion. The Chindo dog is still found, but the Korean deer is disappearing.

CLIMATE Similar to that of New England, with cold winters and rainy summers. The extreme south has average temperatures of 32°F. in January and 79°F. in August. It receives about 60 inches of rain a year. Both temperatures and rainfall decrease toward the north.

CAPITAL Seoul, almost 3.5 million inhabitants in 1965.

OTHER CITIES Pusan, over 1.36 million people; Taegu, about 700,000; and Inchon, about 400,000.

POPULATION 27.226 million in 1963. The annual rate of increase is about 2.9 percent. Density is about 276 persons per square mile.

ETHNIC GROUPS   Koreans are a homogenous and distinct group probably descended from the nomadic Mongols and Caucasians of Western Asia. There are no unassimilated native minority groups.

LANGUAGE   Korean, an Altaic language, is universally spoken. It is written in Hangul, a phonetic script using 10 vowels and 14 consonants. The use of movable type for printing, which began in Korea in 1234, has helped stabilize and standardize the language.

RELIGION   Korea's indigenous faith, *Chondokyo,* has 129 churches and about 623,000 adherents; it is monotheistic and combines shamanism, Confucianism, and Buddhism. Confucianism, the official philosophy until the Japanese occupation in 1910, remains a strong influence. There are about 3.5 million Buddhists and 1.6 million Christians.

DATE OF INDEPENDENCE   On September 8, 1945, American troops landed to expel the Japanese. On May 10, 1948, the first general election was held under United Nations observation.

FORM OF GOVERNMENT   Constitutional democracy. Revolution in 1961 led to government by a military junta under General Chung Hee Park. A constitution approved by referendum in 1962 provides for a strong President and a legislature of 175 members. The political party formed by the junta leader, Chung Hee Park, won more than 100 seats in the 1963 election and he was elected President.

EDUCATION   In 1961, there were more than 4.74 million students in over 6,840 primary and secondary schools staffed by almost 88,400 teachers. Almost 10,400 more teachers were being trained in 18 institutions. The 77 higher education institutions had 136,000 students and over 7,000 instructors. The campaign against adult illiteracy was carried on through some 3,100 folk schools with over 292,000 pupils. By 1960, over 82 percent of the total population was literate.

HEALTH FACILITIES   In 1961, there were over 7,700 doctors, 1,340 dentists, 4,730 midwives, and 5,000 pharmacists. More than 3,000 herb doctors also served the populace. By 1960, life expectancy was over 52 years for a newborn baby.

KOREAN ELDER *This venerable smoking his long pipe is wearing the kat, a hat made of horsehair and tied under the chin with a black string. The kat indicates he is the senior male member of his family. Beneath it, he wears a skull cap; under the skull cap, his hair is tied into a knot.*

HILLTOP HERMITAGE
Small Buddhist shrines like this are perched on the hills and cliffs of the east coast area. Because of its scenic grandeur, this region is sometimes called the "Switzerland of Korea."

CULTURAL FACILITIES

The 34 daily newspapers had a total circulation of 1.5 million in 1962—or about one paper for every 18 people. About 3,700 books were published in 1962; over half of them dealt with technology and social science. About 113 films were produced in 1962 for showing in almost 500 cinemas with an annual attendance of 79 million. Some 1.6 million radios and 32,000 television sets were in use. The traditional and highly developed musical and operatic arts are well supported; modern art forms such as the novel flourish.

CURRENCY AND FINANCE

The *won* is valued at 270 to $1.00 in U.S. currency, or about 1.3 *won* to the U.S. cent. The 1963 government budget was $638 million in expenditure, $348.5 million in revenue. Foreign grants covered about $207.7 million of the deficit. Over $161.5 million went for national defense. On an average, taxes take 15 percent of individual incomes.

INDUSTRY AND PRODUCTION

At partition, South Korea was primarily agricultural and most industry was north of the 38th parallel. Rapid industrialization was, therefore, mandatory. Progress has been considerable, but two-thirds of the people still depend on agriculture, which provides 40 percent of the Gross National Product. The national income in 1962 was almost $1.86 billion, or over $71 per person. Although manufacturing is chiefly concentrated in light consumer goods, the country was self-sufficient in electric power, cement, and textile production by 1964. Manufacturing had risen 14.5 percent over the previous year and a sound industrial base was gradually appearing in spite of serious inflation and unemployment.

CROPS: The rice crop, grown on 60 percent of the cultivated land, was 3.13 million metric tons in 1962. Other crops are barley, wheat, cotton, tobacco, soybeans, hemp, potatoes, ginseng, fruit, vegetables, and silk from silkworms.

LIVESTOCK: Chiefly cattle, pigs, and poultry. The once-flourishing livestock industry is being gradually revived; but draft animals still predominated in the early 1960's and development of food animals was slow.

FISHERIES: The 1962 catch was over 450,000 metric tons. Fish constitutes 85 percent of the nation's protein food. Some whaling is done.

MINING: South Korea has the world's largest tungsten deposit. Other mineral deposits are small. Coal accounts for about half of the mineral output; iron, copper, kaolin, lead, graphite, asbestos, gold, and silver are also mined.

TRADE

Fish, silk, rice, and mineral products are the chief exports. Although mining provides less than two percent of the Gross National Product, it accounts for a third to a half of the country's foreign exchange earnings. The trade deficit, partly covered by foreign aid, has been decreasing. Exports passed the $100 million mark in 1964.

1962: IMPORTS $387,818,000
EXPORTS $ 56,702,000
DEFICIT $331,116,000

TRANSPORT

ROAD: There are about 16,250 miles of road, which carried about 32,400 cars and trucks in 1962.

RAILROAD: About 1,880 miles of railway are in operation.

SEA: Pusan is the chief port. There are 10 all-weather ports and 27 secondary ports.

AIR: Korean Air Lines provides service between the major cities, to Cheju Island, and to Tokyo. International flights arrive from Hong Kong, Tokyo, and Taipei.

**COMMUNI-
CATION**

Koreans had almost 140,000 telephones in 1962. Radio, postal, telegraph, and cable services are well developed.

SIKKIM

Principality in the Himalayas

Sikkim is a tiny country located between India and Tibet. It covers an area of less than 3,000 square miles, and can be compared in size to the state of Delaware.

When its first *Chogyal* or King was consecrated in 1642, Sikkim was many times the size it is today. In the 18th century, Sikkim lost considerable territories to Bhutan and to Nepal. In the first half of the 19th century, territory was annexed to India through the British East India Company. During the 1880's Sikkim's Chumbi Valley was handed over to Tibeto-Chinese authorities by the British authorities in India. This transfer is still disputed by Sikkim.

PHYSICAL CHARACTERISTICS

The country is composed of mountain ridges interspersed with gorges and valleys, the highest level reaching to over 28,000 feet above the sea. Kanchenjunga (28,146 feet) is the third highest mountain in the world. The land contains more than a dozen peaks above 20,000 feet. There are lakes in Sikkim 12,000 feet above sea level. Some forests are 12,000 feet high. Potatoes grow in this land at a level of 13,000 feet.

The river Tista, originating in the Tashi-drag glaciers in the north, and fed in its journey to the south by the scores of small tributary streams, forms the artery of irrigation, as well as of drainage. The monsoon from the Bay of Bengal adds volumes of rainwater all through the year. In this watershed a great variety of climates, fauna, and flora are encountered.

In this miniscule country, man meets the entire gamut of climate on this earth. In altitudes of 15,000 feet an arctic climate prevails; those between 15,000 and 7,000 feet are alpine areas. The valleys and plains below 7,000 feet have a temperate and subtropical climate; and those at 1,000 feet have a temperature of 100 degrees Fahrenheit and even more.

GANGTOK CINEMA *Sikkim's first movie house, completed in 1964, is partly owned by the Maharaja. So far, Indian soldiers, stationed in Sikkim, have been the chief customers.* (Courtesy P. P. Karan and University of Kentucky Himalayan Expedition.)

VARIED FLORA AND FAUNA

The vegetation follows a similarly variegated pattern. The country grows maize, millet, cardamon, potatoes, apples, bananas, fir, bamboo, juniper, magnolia, rhododendron, bougainvilla, roses, lilies, and more than 600 varieties of orchid. In Sikkim, the naturalist can find Himalayan bear, snow leopard, panda, tropical civet, otter, musk deer, barking deer, wild pig, Himalayan owls, many varieties of colorful birds, myriads of butterflies and moths, carp, trout, buffalo, and yak.

THE RACES OF SIKKIM

Within this polychrome of nature live many races who speak many languages. The first people to live in Sikkim were the Lepchas, who now form a minority. Later came the Tibetans with their Mahayana Buddhism, known today as the Bhutias. With the Tibetans there also came some Tibeto-Mongoloids like the Tsongs and the Magars. Hindus, too, settled in Sikkim during the last century.

Today, out of a total population of 161,000, two-thirds speak Nepali. Many persons in this group are not ethnically Nepali but are of Mongoloid stock. Nearly 5,000 Sikkimese serve in the Indian Army, and a few hundred have been enlisted in the British Gurkhas.

RELIGION

Mahayana is distinguished from Hinayana (Theravada) Buddhism by its emphasis on collectivist endeavor for salvation; its rituals are predominantly esoteric, and are often misunderstood by visitors and tourists. The philosophy of Mahayana goes back to Nagarjuna who flourished during the first century after Christ. His dialectics anticipated modern rationalist thought, and his philosophy has been for centuries the subject of study in Buddhist monasteries. Sikkim is proud of her association with Mahayana Buddhism.

THE CHOGYAL OF SIKKIM   Palden Thondup Namgyal became Maharaja of Sikkim in December, 1963, a few months after his marriage. For several years previous to his accession, he had been carrying on most of the chief executive's duties in place of his aged father. He was educated in India. He is an honorary major general in the Indian Army. The Chogyal speaks English, Tibetan, and Hindi.   (Courtesy P. P. Karan and University of Kentucky Himalayan Expedition.)

ROYAL CONSORT (CYALMO)   Hope Cooke Namgyal, now 25 years of age, was married to the Crown Prince of Sikkim, now the Chogyal, or Maharaja, in March, 1963. Two years earlier, the state elders of Sikkim had formally approved this marriage between a personage of the royalty and a non-Tibetan foreigner, but the engagement could not be announced until after six months of negotiations between the governments of Sikkim and India. This attractive girl from New York had completed her studies at Sarah Lawrence College shortly before her marriage. The couple met in the mountain resort of Darjeeling, India. In 1964, the Maharani gave birth to a son, Prince Palden, but the Maharaja's two older sons by a prior marriage have first claim to the throne. (Courtesy P. P. Karan and University of Kentucky Himalayan Expedition.)

The kingdom of Sikkim was established in 1642. Since then, every King has been consecrated at his ascension, for the King of Sikkim is head of the church as well as head of the state.

Though Mahayana constitutes the established church and the government runs a special department to maintain the monasteries and the monastic educational centers, there is full freedom of worship and no disability because of faith.

Buddhists, Hindus, and Christians and animists compose the population. Most Buddhists are Bhutias or Lepchas. Most of the Hindus are immigrants from Nepal, but many Hindus also worship Buddha and the Buddhist deities. There are nearly 2,000 monks and 36 monasteries in Sikkim.

FORM OF GOVERNMENT

Sikkim is a hereditary monarchy. The rule of the previous *Chogyal* (Tashi Namgyal—1914–1963) was marked by reforms to effect equality in education, employment, and welfare. Democratic reforms enable the people to participate in the government. Reforms in land tenure and the introduction of free social services have turned Sikkim into a welfare state.

Education is free for any who cannot afford to pay the moderate fees.

INDUSTRY AND LIVING STANDARD

Sikkim's carpets and wood carvings find a good market. An Institute for Cottage Industries provides training in these crafts.

Transport has undergone mechanization; mules and ponies are being replaced by motor trucks.

Sikkim possesses a higher standard of living than neighboring countries of the region; annual average income per capita in terms of cash is nearly $189. None here are very wealthy, nor is there a class of paupers. The few beggars in Sikkim came from Tibet or India.

No picture of the life in Sikkim is complete without reference to the folksongs and festivals of its people, filled with colorful song and dance.

GANGTOK MARKETPLACE   Nepali women selling puffed rice wait patiently customers. (Courtesy P. P. Karan and University of Kentucky Himalayan Expedition.)

AN INDIAN PROTECTORATE

Sikkim is a protectorate of India. Relations between the countries are governed by a treaty signed in 1950. Under this treaty, Sikkim is fully autonomous, and India is responsible for Sikkim's defenses and its external affairs.

THE CAPITAL CITY

The country is practically entirely on an agricultural standard and few cities exist in this faraway land. The capital, Gangtok, has a population of approximately 7,000 people. Physical amenities from a European or American standpoint are somewhat primitive.

PALDEN THONDUP NAMGYAL

PALACE GUARD
Sikkim has no armed forces save for a small personal guard force for the Maharaja. This Nepali, with his hair piled up underneath his hat, is on sentry duty at the king's residence in Gangtok.
(Courtesy P. P. Karan and University of Kentucky Himalayan Expedition.)

IN BRIEF

AREA

Landlocked. 2,818 square miles, a bit larger than Delaware.

TERRAIN

A succession of deep gorges and valleys, divided by high and steep mountain ridges, and drained by the Tista River. Elevations range from about 700 feet in the plains of the south to the 28,146-foot Mount Kanchenjunga. More than a dozen peaks are over 20,000 feet. Population is concentrated in the valleys of the Inner Himalaya.

FLORA

Monsoon rain forests in the south, largely composed of broad-leaf evergreen, oak, chestnut, and rhododendron. Conifers at higher elevations. Over 4,000 species of flowering plants include 600 varieties of orchid.

FAUNA

Snow leopard, bear, panda, civet, otter, squirrel, deer, antelope, wild pig, partridge, duck, and pheasant.

CLIMATE

Arctic above 15,000 feet, alpine from 7,000 feet to 15,000 feet, temperate and subtropical below 7,000 feet. Rainfall is over 130 inches and temperatures soar frequently above 100°F. in the lowland plain. Sheltered northern valleys receive less than 20 inches of rain a year.

CAPITAL

Gangtok, 6,850 inhabitants in 1961.

POPULATION

An estimated 161,000 inhabitants in 1962. Annual rate of increase is about 2.4 percent. Density is 59 persons per square mile.

ETHNIC GROUPS

About 75 percent are *Tsongs* of Nepali origin; the remainder are Lepchas, Bhutias, and Magars, all of Tibeto-Mongolian descent.

LANGUAGES

Two-thirds of the people speak Nepali. Lepcha and Bhutia are used mostly in the north. English is the official language, but is not known to many.

RELIGION

Mahayana Buddhism, received from Tibet, has been the established state religion since the early 1600's; it is the faith of about 28 percent of the people. Hindus, usually Nepali immigrants, comprise about 60 percent. There are a few Christians and animists.

DATE OF INDEPENDENCE

Although the Namgyal family has held the throne since 1642, Sikkim has only internal autonomy. Through a treaty signed on December 5, 1950, British paramountcy devolved on India.

FORM OF GOVERNMENT

Limited monarchy. India controls defense, foreign relations, and communications. The Maharaja's administration is assisted by an Indian civil servant, the Principal Administrative Officer; Indians are in charge of important government bureaus. A State Council with purely advisory functions has 20 members, 14 of them elected. Six Council seats are reserved for Bhutias and Lepchas of the minority groups. Further development of representative government is hindered by the problem of safeguarding the rights of Lepchas and Bhutias. As a protectorate of India, Sikkim has no international status as a sovereign nation.

EDUCATION

In 1962, four high schools, five junior high schools, 12 middle schools, and the Teachers' Training Centre enrolled about 10,000 students. Only a sixth of the students were girls. Literacy rate is estimated at nine percent. In effect, education is free; those who can neither pay the moderate rate nor win scholarships are admitted on a non-paying basis.

HEALTH FACILITIES

In 1962, there were four hospitals, 16 dispensaries, a maternity center, a chest clinic, and two tuberculosis treatment centers. Medical care is free. Malaria has been eradicated; all children have been immunized against tuberculosis. A campaign against endemic diseases, particularly intestinal parasites, is in progress.

CULTURAL FACILITIES

The Namgyal Institute of Tibetology in Gangtok is a center for higher religious learning; it has a library, a museum, and a publication program in English, Sanskrit, and Tibetan. The country's 36 Buddhist monasteries are the chief cultural centers. There are no newspapers in Sikkim, only periodic government publications.

CURRENCY AND FINANCE

There is no Sikkimese currency; the Indian *rupee*, equal to 21¢ in U.S. currency, is in use. Revenue in 1963 was approximately $1.64 million. The Second Five-Year Plan, 1961-66, provides for $17.7 million expenditure on agricultural and forestry development, power, roads, industries, and public services.

INDUSTRY AND PRODUCTION

There are two sizable industrial establishments: a liquor distillery at Rangpo and a fruit preservation factory at Singtam. Handicraft products include handwoven textiles, wool blankets and rugs, copperware, and wood carvings. Per capita income is estimated at $189 per year. Valuable forest resources, about 750 square miles of mountain slope, are only partially developed because transport problems have so far proved insoluble. Electric power is being developed. The Rangni Hydel Project, completed in 1961, produced 2,100 kilowatts in 1963. Four more power stations are under way.

CROPS: Rice, grains, cardamoms, potatoes, and fruits.

LIVESTOCK: Cattle, buffalo, yak, sheep, goats, ponies, mules, pigs, and poultry. Herds of yak and sheep are the main support of the people of the high valleys of the north.

MINING: Exploitation of rich copper resources has begun. Deposits of coal, graphite, gypsum, and iron are undeveloped.

TRADE

The chief exports are cardamoms, oranges, potatoes, apples, and woolens. Main imports are machinery, cotton textiles, foods, and consumer goods. Trade figures are included with those of India, and are not separately reported.

TRANSPORT

ROAD: About 475 miles of motor road and 130 miles of village paths. Good highway connects Gangtok with Rangpo, on the Indian border. Over 325 miles of road under construction will make Natu-la Pass open in all weathers and improve communication with the north. Considerable freight is still carried by mule train.

RAILROAD: Rail service is provided from Siliguri, a point in India 72 miles from Gangtok.

AIR: Air service is provided from Bagdogra, a point in India 80 miles from Gangtok.

COMMUNI-CATION

Telephone service and full access to India's communication network is available in Gangtok.

There is no radio system originating in Sikkim.

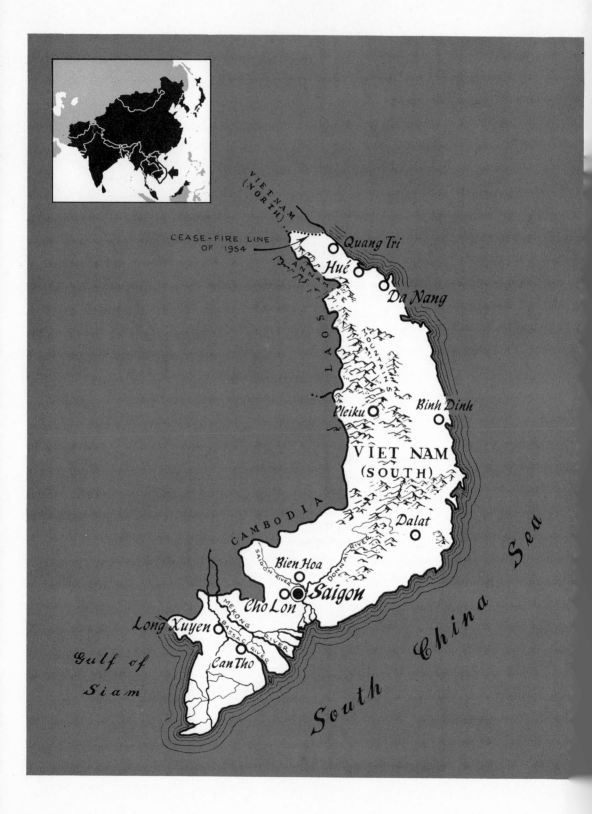

SOUTH VIET NAM

Powder Keg of Asia

For a proper understanding of this country, it is necessary that the reader refer to the article in this book on North Viet Nam, written by the same author.

During the Geneva Conference, the Prime Minister of the Bao Dai government resigned. On July 7, 1954, Ngo Dinh Diem, a prominent lay leader among Vietnamese Roman Catholics, took control, two weeks before his country was partitioned by the Geneva agreement. However, Diem found that he had little real power; he had little or no control over the National Army, nor of the police forces, which Bao Dai had sold for $1,200,000 to a private army and racket syndicate, the Binh Xuyen. Opposed to Diem were the Communists, whose followers numbered in the thousands, and the armies of two political-religious sects (the Cao Dai and the Hoa Hao) totaling more than 50,000 men. Nor could Diem count on the support of any large, organized political group.

Operating under the time-honored principle of "divide and rule," the Prime Minister split his enemies and dealt with them one at a time. First, the Chief of Staff of the Army, General Nguyen Van Hinh was maneuvered out of the country in November 1954, and replaced by a supporter of Diem. Then the Prime Minister used the Army to eliminate the control of the Binh Xuyen over the police. Then, in May 1955, Diem destroyed the power of the Binh Xuyen's army in a quick series of bloody battles. Following this, the government succeeded in breaking the military strength of the two opposing religious sects. By July 1956, the last major rebel leader was eliminated.

Earlier, on October 23, 1955, a nationwide referendum had been presented to the electorate by the Diem regime, and this resulted in the deposition of the Emperor Bao Dai and the elevation of Ngo Dinh Diem to Chief of State.

Diem's first act was to proclaim Viet Nam a republic and himself its President. In March 1956, the voters went to the polls and elected a Constituent Assembly, which wrote a Constitution for the new republic. Under the terms of this document, promulgated on October 26, the Constituent Assembly became the first National Assembly, and Ngo Dinh Diem became the first constitutional President.

COMMUNIST OPPOSITION TO DIEM

The Communists denounced the referendum on the monarchy and the two elections for the National Assembly, but were unable to obstruct the balloting. But, since 1958, the Communists have engaged in a systematic program of subversion and terrorism, and have infiltrated agents and soldiers from North Viet Nam into the country. Large numbers of South Vietnamese youth have been recruited to Communism either through terrorism or persuasion. Increasing their subversive activity month by month, the Communists, called the Viet Cong, have gained in strength and influence.

Initially, Communist terrorist acts were shrewdly directed at government welfare programs and their field representatives. Attempts were made on the lives of land reform survey agents, school teachers, malaria eradication teams, village treasurers and headmen. Sabotage was rampant. The government reacted by withdrawal and by making cautious preparations for countermeasures. Field programs were cut back; representatives traveled only with armed escorts; increased emphasis was put on military preparations—to the detriment of social and economic progress.

In addition, within the Saigon government, arbitrary and highhanded political policies attributed to Ngo Dinh Nhu, President Diem's brother, and a generally repressive approach to problems of internal security, provoked increasing resentment among the people of South Viet Nam. Mme. Ngo Dinh Nhu was responsible for maneuvering a puritanical "social reform" law through the National Assembly which banned all forms of dancing, both public and private, and made the sale of contraceptives illegal. Public uneasiness at the inroads of Viet Cong subversion was intensified by the heavy-handed measures of the regime;

FORTIFIED VILLAGE   *Plans to combat the Viet Cong involve the construction of many easily guarded, fortified centers like this, shown under construction during 1962. Each of the grass-roofed log cabins on this site is at least as commodious as a house in a small outlying hamlet. This compound will accommodate as many as 3,000 people. Because of its numbers, it pays to render this community defensible, whereas it is impracticable to do as much for a tiny community.*

and these unpopular restrictions were imposed at a time when the government needed every bit of public support.

U. S. INVOLVEMENT IN SOUTH VIET NAM

United States involvement in Vietnamese affairs was stepped up after Maxwell Taylor, Chairman of the Joint Chiefs of Staff, visited Viet Nam in the fall of 1961. He advised President John F. Kennedy that the dimensions of Communist subversive activity in South Viet Nam had grown so huge that a several-fold increase in American mili-

POLITICAL MARTYR *On June 11, 1963, the Buddhist monk, Quang Duc, poured gasoline over his saffron robe and then lit a match while thousands watched at a main intersection in Saigon. Fellow priests, present at the time, announced that his self-immolation was a protest against persecution by the Diem government. Several others followed Quang Duc's example. Less than five months after his suicide the Diem government fell.*

tary advisors and equipment was necessary, if Communism was to be successfully countered by the Saigon regime. During 1962, the number of American advisors was increased to more than 16,000 officers and men.

American involvement also took the form of pressure on Viet Nam's President to broaden the base of his government and to emphasize economic and social measures to win the grass-roots support of his people. However, contradictory advice from his brothers, upon whom Ngo Dinh Diem depended for counsel, was more influential with the reserved Vietnamese leader. As time passed, the Diem regime became increasingly intent on building military security in the countryside; the government put emphasis on demonstrations of loyalty from military and civil officials, and weeded out Communists—real or suspected—from the population.

Although a small number of Americans were killed between 1961 and 1963, in 1964 heavily intensified enemy action took the lives of 136 officers and men, approximately three times the figure for the previous three years combined.

By December, 1965, the American commitment ran to more than 180,000 U.S. personnel; and more than 1,500 Americans had lost their lives.

BUDDHIST OPPOSITION TO DIEM

On May 8, 1963, discontent with government arbitrariness, its repressive tone, and its lack of responsiveness to popular needs, erupted in the city of Hué. A crowd of Buddhists, rallied by their monks to protest governmental discrimination in favor of Catholics, marched on the local radio station. Panicky local officials ordered troops to open fire on the demonstrators. In the melée which followed, nine were killed. During subsequent weeks, the government and the rebellious Buddhist leaders tried to negotiate a compromise settlement which would preserve the regime's face and yet grant concessions to the Buddhists. But within the regime, opinion was divided as to whether it would be wiser to conciliate the Buddhists or to ruthlessly crush the opposition. Sensing this indecision, the Buddhists embarked on a campaign of violent harassment. Several monks, and even one nun, publicly burned themselves to death in dramatic displays of protest.

At the end of August, President Diem's political advisor and brother, Ngo Dinh Nhu, sent steel-helmeted riot police and special forces of soldiers into the Buddhist pagodas to arrest the rebel leaders. This proved too much for the Army chiefs. On November 1, 1963, they mounted a *coup d'état* which unseated the Diem regime. Diem and Nhu were assassinated in the aftermath, apparently on order of the generals who staged the coup.

NGUYEN CAO KY   The 35-year-old Air Force Marshal, who became Premier of South Viet Nam during June 1965, was the fourth man to hold that office in a period of six months. He advocates stepped up air raids against North Viet Nam and very stern measures against terrorists and profiteers. He is known for his flamboyant personality, owns a violet airplane, wears lavender neck scarves, writes love poetry which he is apt to recite at parties, and raises fighting gamecocks. In addition to schooling in Hanoi, Ky was educated in a Vietnamese officers' school, spent three years in French and North African aviation schools, and studied in the United States for a year. During 1964, he married an Air Viet Nam stewardess, having previously divorced the French wife who had borne his daughter and four sons.

Since then, South Viet Nam has been plagued by almost constant evidences of instability. Military leaders, Buddhist chieftains, and civilian politicians have jockeyed for positions of power, while American advisors have stood helplessly by, trying to remind their Vietnamese friends that the Viet Cong was the real enemy.

A PERIOD OF POLITICAL UPHEAVAL

The military junta, set up to govern the country after the death of Diem and Nhu, was itself ousted from power only three months later. During 1964, there were four successive changes of government effected by force. The latest *coup* occurred on January 26, 1965, when the civilian regime of Tran Van Huong, installed in October of 1964 by the military leaders, was pushed out of office by the selfsame military officers, acting in alliance with Buddhist leaders. A provisional government, more responsive to the military and to the Buddhists, was installed.

With all this political turbulence, social and economic programs have, for the most part, gone by the boards. A program of regrouping isolated South Vietnamese peasants into strategic hamlets, a program begun under the Diem regime, was reorganized by the junta; it was found that many of the supposedly secure, fortified hamlets existed only on paper. Renamed "new rural life hamlets" by the junta, these promising settlements have in numerous instances fallen into disrepair; some have even been abandoned by their inhabitants.

A program of agrarian reform, under which more than one million acres of land formerly owned by absentee landlords had been redistributed to tenant farmers and landless peasants, came to a halt. Viet Cong attacks increased in intensity and frequency.

THE COST OF CIVIL WAR

Since 1958, casualties among South Vietnamese government soldiers and loyal citizens have numbered in the tens of thousands, while Communist casualties have been estimated to be even greater. During 1964, the total of killed and wounded on both sides exceeded 50,000.

In October 1964 alone, government losses were 2,800 (of whom 700 were killed), while the Viet Cong lost about 1,600 men (including 1,100 killed).

But such figures do not in themselves fully convey the picture of what has been going on in Viet Nam. In every month of 1965, there was fighting between Vietnamese government forces and Communist guerrillas in nearly every one of the country's 45 provinces. Thousands of homes have been burned; peasants have been driven from their land by the armies of both sides. Communist sabotage has destroyed anew the Vietnamese National Railway, which was rebuilt at great cost after the Geneva armistice of 1954. An estimated 50,000 children have been deprived of their schoolrooms by Viet Cong activity. And today, the fighting continues with ever greater fury and bitterness.

VIETNAMESE SOCIETY

The Vietnamese are plains-dwellers. Over the centuries, they have left the mountains and forested plateaus to the ethnic minorities among them, preferring to cultivate their rice in placid and peaceful villages clustered in the fertile valleys and plains lying between the mountains and the sea. To most Vietnamese, the forests and the mountains have always been mysterious and dangerous regions, inhabited by savage tribes and wild animals. Although the Diem government made a systematic effort to establish the frontiers of settlement farther and farther to the west by moving more than 200,000 people from overcrowded villages to the frontiers of Laos and Cambodia, the average Vietnamese still looks upon these territories with suspicion and fear.

Vietnamese society is based largely on cooperative village organization, the village traditionally being responsible for building and maintaining irrigation works, storing rice, and redistributing certain commonly owned village lands from time to time. In the family, the father is the head, though the mother enjoys an important voice in family decisions, and usually controls family finances. Twenty years of warfare and social unrest have forced hundreds of thousands of peasants to seek refuge and work in the towns and cities. The unrest has weakened the tight traditional hold of the family on its members; nevertheless, family ties are still important, especially in the rural areas.

RELIGION

Thirty-five percent of the population of South Viet Nam are at least nominal Buddhists; a smaller number would be counted as devout pagoda-goers. Catholics comprise ten percent of the people, and Cao Daists number another eight percent. Cao Dai means *five virtues* or *five ways*. The faith was founded in 1914 by a French clerk in the colonial administration. The million-odd adherents worship Christ, the Buddha, and Confucius. They include the French novelist Victor Hugo, a certain 16th century Vietnamese poet, and Sun Yat-sen, leader of the 1911 Chinese revolution, among their patron saints. During the early 1950's the sect fielded an army of guerrillas which materially added to the disorganization faced by the Diem government during its first years of power.

Another million South Vietnamese are adherents of the Hoa Hao faith. An offshoot of Buddhism, Hoa Hao is a simple, uncomplicated religion which has had great appeal to the peasants of the Mekong delta. It has no religious hierarchy, no rituals, and no houses of worship. Its followers believe that through prayer they can communicate directly with their ancestors and with God. The religion was founded in 1939 by Huynh Phu So who claimed to be the reincarnation of the Buddha, the reincarnation of the angel Cu Da, the reincarnation of a dead Buddhist priest, and also the reincarnation of a 19th century Vietnamese patriot. This religious movement quickly took on politico-military aspects similar to those of the Cao Dai; by 1953, the Hoa Hao had perhaps 30,000 armed men in the field, divided into four major private armies. In 1955, both the Cao Dai and the Hoa Hao forces were bought off or defeated in battle by Vietnamese National Army forces; and thereafter, they ceased to be a military threat to the central government in Saigon.

POLITICAL ACTIVITY OF THE BUDDHISTS

Since May of 1963, Buddhism has become an active and vigorous

RURAL POVERTY *During the protracted guerrilla war the majority of families in the Mekong Delta have been reduced to conditions of bare survival. The new-born baby in the hammock is wrapped in a dirty blanket. The dwelling is constructed of poles, old pieces of army canvas, and grass.*

VIETNAMESE DRESS *The women of Viet Nam wear
a tight-fitting, narrow, neck-to-ankle dress with a skirt slit to
the waist on both sides. Fitted pantaloons, usually white, are
worn under the gown.*

political force in South Viet Nam. Monks and lay leaders, involved in
the agitation and intrigue that brought the Diem government to its
knees, found power to their liking. During the months since November
1963, they have maneuvered constantly to enhance the scope of their
influence. Suggestions that they have been infiltrated by Communist
agents, which are widely believed by many Vietnamese, have been in-
dignantly denied. It is arguable that Buddhist political activity has
helped the Communists by encouraging disunity in the nation.

A STEPPED-UP PROGRAM OF EDUCATION

Until the coming of the French in 1858, the Chinese concept of education dominated the Vietnamese scene. The educated man, the intellectual, has traditionally been ranked above the farmer, the artisan, the soldier, and the tradesman. The French altered this significantly by developing standard textbooks, and taking schooling out of the pagoda and the home and channeling education into formal school buildings. The French also took the revolutionary step of establishing public schools, and the still more radical step of admitting girls into schools. The French even set up a university in Hanoi to serve all of the Indo-Chinese people.

In 1954, after the peace of Geneva was agreed upon, the new government in Saigon began rebuilding 689 schools that had been destroyed during the civil war between the French and the Viet Minh. At the initiative of President Diem, a campaign was begun to build a three-room school in every one of the 5,000 villages that had no school at all. Textbooks were rewritten to make the student conscious of Viet Nam's historical past. A nationwide program in literacy was gotten under way to extend educational benefits to older citizens. Enrollments shot upward; elementary school pupils increased from some 400,000 in 1954 to almost a million and a half in 1963; secondary school students who numbered 43,000 in 1954 increased to 265,000 in 1963.

STUDENT DEMONSTRATIONS

During the colonial period, student activity had been a feature of revolutionary agitation. When Ngo Dinh Diem came to power in 1954, he was hailed as a nationalist hero by students; and when he used the National Army to drive the Binh Xuyen gang out of the capital, student groups demonstrated excitedly for him in the streets of Saigon.

Like the Buddhists, the students, too, were discontented during the last years of the Diem regime, and their street demonstrations and often violent opposition to police measures during the summer and fall of 1963 helped destroy the power of the government. Some evidence of Communist influence in the student groups was seen; but by and large, the demonstrations were simply evidence of rebellious and dissatisfied youth, led in many cases by older, "professional students," who had gained some political experience, and were in the service of dissident political, religious, or military groups.

AGRICULTURE AND INDUSTRY

Under the French, South Viet Nam was the agricultural half of the country. Partition at the 17th parallel in 1954 left South Viet Nam with only a handful of service industries, such as rice milling, distilling, brewing, ice-making, and the manufacture of cigarettes and matches. While the Diem government emphasized the importance of increased agricultural production and the introduction of new crops as a necessary base for industrialization, the government also encouraged the development of light industry. Concentrated thus far in the Saigon area, the newer industries include cotton spinning and weaving, manufacture of burlap bags, paper, tires, and various consumer goods (pens, pencils, batteries, plastic articles, paint), and assembly of radios, motor scooters, sewing machines, and bicycles.

Exploitation of coal deposits at Nong Son has made the South Vietnamese virtually independent of coal imports. And the development of the kenaf (fiber similar to jute) industry has freed them of reliance on imported bags for cement and grain.

An extensive hydroelectric plant, built by the Japanese government as part of its war reparations, has brought the promise of ample electric power to the tiny republic. But the intense guerrilla warfare being waged in the countryside has kept the Vietnamese from enjoying this boon, and the exposed power lines, stretching over 100 miles from the great dam at Da Nhim to Saigon, have offered a tempting target to Viet Cong saboteurs.

U. S. IN VIET NAM

The American involvement in Viet Nam, which began in 1950 with the sending of the Griffin Mission on foreign aid to French Indo-China, has gradually intensified over the years. In 1965, it had become

DEMONSTRATORS *Waving a Vietnamese flag, a Saigon student rallies a mob of his fellows prior to storming the government's Information Ministry in August, 1964. Three days later, the seven-month-old government of General Khanh fell, undermined by multiple demonstrations similar to this one.*

the single largest financial and human undertaking of the U.S. anywhere in the world.

Initially, the Americans were regarded as potential allies by the Vietnamese nationalists; but as the U.S. increased its military and economic aid to the French in the war against the Viet Minh from 1950 to 1954, many Vietnamese considered the Americans as pro-colonialist. After the signing of the Geneva Accords in July 1954, American assistance was given directly to the new Vietnamese nationalist regime in Saigon. As French influence dwindled between 1954 and 1956, the Vietnamese came increasingly to depend upon the U.S. as their major ally.

The expansion of Communist subversive activity after 1959 brought about a reaction from the U.S. in late 1961; the number of American military advisors was increased from approximately 700 to more than 16,000. By 1965, the American government had clearly made a firm commitment to stand by the side of the Saigon administration, and there were more than 180,000 American servicemen in Viet Nam, while American aid funds (economic as well as military) were being channeled into the little Southeast Asian republic at a rate in excess of $3 million per day.

Initially, the Vietnamese reaction to the influx of American personnel was manifestly friendly; but many feared that as the numbers of the Americans increased there would be a negative response from the Vietnamese. Little evidence of such hostility has thus far been shown. However, American ground and air operations in the countryside have involved the bombardment of villages and the unavoidable killing of civilian bystanders. This development has undoubtedly created resentment of both the Americans and the Vietnamese military as well. The Communists have attempted to stimulate anti-American sentiment by exploiting such military episodes. At the same time, responsible Vietnamese have indicated an awareness that an American withdrawal from South Viet Nam would lay open the country to a Communist takeover. As far as that can be measured, public sentiment is strongly anti-Communist; the Vietnamese leaders are willing to continue the war and bear the increasing presence of Americans as the price of freedom.

WESLEY R. FISHEL

IN BRIEF

AREA   66,293 square miles, smaller than Oklahoma.

TERRAIN   The Annamite mountain chain in central Viet Nam rises to heights of 5,000 to 6,000 feet and falls to narrow but fertile coastal plains on the east, with higher, less fertile plateaus on the west. The Mekong River forms a large and very fertile delta in the south.

FLORA   Extensive mangrove swamps and forests of bamboo, cedar, and pine, with lesser quantities of rosewood, ebony, and sandalwood.

FAUNA   Elephant, tiger, panther, gaur, wild bear, black bear, peacock, pheasant, and stag.

CLIMATE   Tropical monsoons create rainy and dry seasons which are varied; the southwest monsoon brings 80 inches of rain to Saigon and the south from April to October; the northeast monsoon, August to December, brings most of the 116 inches received in Hué and the central region. Average summer temperature is 85°F.; average winter temperature is 78°F. Typhoons are less frequent than in the north.

CAPITAL   Saigon, including Cholon, had about 1.6 million inhabitants in 1965.

OTHER CITIES   Hué, population 103,000. Da Nang, Dalat.

POPULATION   15.7 million by 1965 estimates. Annual rate of population increase is about 2.8 percent. Density averages only about 215 persons per square mile, but the population is heavily concentrated in rice-growing areas.

ETHNIC GROUPS   Over 14 million are Vietnamese. There are more than 800,000 Chinese in urban areas. About 700,000 montagnards are in numerous tribes in the highlands. Cambodians, Indians, and Europeans are other major resident minority groups.

LANGUAGE   Vietnamese. French is spoken by many; Chinese and English are widely used. Cham, Khmer, Rhade, Jarai, and others are

AO DAI FUNERAL   Tay Ninh, a town 60 miles north of Saigon, is the chief cen- of the Cao Dai sect. In this procession, a group of adherents march beside a dragon at. Mourners wield symbolic oars. The dragon boat serves to symbolically cross the of difficulties, trouble, and sorrow on its way to heaven.

used among minority groups. *Quoc ngu,* the phonetic alphabet presently used for Vietnamese, replaced Chinese ideographs during the colonial period.

RELIGION

Persons of every faith participate in ancestor worship, spirit worship, cults of local heroes and gods. Except among the hill tribes Buddhism is usually combined with animistic beliefs. Roman Catholicism and the indigenous Hoa Hao and Cao Dai sects have over a million adherents each.

DATE OF INDEPENDENCE

On July 20, 1954, accords signed in Geneva established the State of Viet Nam below the 17th parallel.

FORM OF GOVERNMENT

Theoretically a constitutional republic since October 26, 1956, the Republic of Viet Nam has actually been run by dictators or alliances of powerful individuals, usually a mili-

DELTA VILLAGE   *The sign is a warning that there may be land mines hidden nearby. Phy My is a typical village in the Mekong Delta country, where the people are subjected alternately to the appeals of the government and the pressures of the Viet Cong.*

tary clique subject to kaleidoscopic change. Following the U.S. model, the Constitution provides for separation of powers —an independent judiciary, a unicameral National Assembly, and an executive branch under a President. The President's powers are extensive—governors of the 39 provinces are appointed by him. Since before President Ngo Dinh Diem was killed in a 1963 coup, the Constitution has been more or less in abeyance.

EDUCATION

In 1963, nearly 6,300 primary schools enrolled almost 1.5 million students. Some 265,000 students attended 500 or so secondary schools. Three universities served 18,000 students. U.S. aid of $19 million had been used mostly for medical, vocational, and teacher education. Between 1956 and 1963, adult education programs made good progress against illiteracy.

HEALTH FACILITIES

In 1960, there were almost 500 doctors, 70 dentists, 600 midwives, 300 pharmacists, and about 800 traditional birth attendants in the country. The University of Saigon has a modern medical school, and a school of pharmacy, but health conditions remain inadequate. About one-sixth of those who die are children under a year old; roughly one child in 20 dies before reaching school age.

CULTURAL FACILITIES

In 1962, the 28 daily papers had a circulation of about 560,000, or one paper for every 25 persons. Over 80 percent of the more than 1,500 books published in 1962 were first editions. Ten films were made, and there were about 160 cinemas with an annual attendance of 21.2 million. Although art forms like the novel have been greatly influenced by the French, poetry, music, and drama usually follow Chinese models.

CURRENCY AND FINANCE

The *piastre* is valued on the free market at 73.5 to $1.00 in U.S. currency, or approximately 1.36 cents each, but is worth only 60 to $1.00 in import and export trade. At the market rate, budget estimates for 1964 included expenditures of $387.6 million and receipts of about $258.4 million. U.S. aid is supplemented by loans and grants from France, West Germany, Japan, and Australia. The country maintains well over 215,000 men in the armed forces; also an 83,000-man Civil Guard, and 103,000 men in Self Defense Corps.

INDUSTRY AND PRODUCTION

Apart from new factories for cement, steel, paper, and textiles, most industries process agricultural and forest products, assemble machinery, or make light consumer goods. Industrialization has been delayed by lack of power; practically all development is in the Saigon area. In 1962, less than 350 million kilowatt hours of electricity and 90,000 metric tons of steel were produced.

CROPS: Rice and rubber are the chief crops. The 1962 rice harvest, 5.2 million metric tons, doubled that of 1955. Rubber, 72,500 metric tons in 1962, mostly produced on French-owned plantations, accounts for more than half the country's exports. Tea, coffee, quinine, tobacco, spices, timber, silk, and bamboo are grown in the highlands. Corn, sugar, peanuts, jute, and kenaf crops are increasing in importance.

LIVESTOCK: In 1962, there were about 2.8 million pigs, 10 million chickens, 8 million ducks, 900,000 cattle, and 570,-000 water buffalo used as draft animals. Between 1955 and 1962, extensive and effective government programs had replaced wartime losses and allowed the people to almost double their meat consumption.

FISHERIES: By 1962, about 10 percent of the 39,000 small fishing boats were equipped with motors and the annual catch had risen to 255,000 metric tons. Used fresh or dried or made into fish sauce, fish are significant in the national diet. Shrimp, crayfish, bass, snapper, and tuna are plentiful in the coastal waters.

MINING: Small coal mines, peat beds, and extensive phosphate deposits have been developed. Lead, limestone, zinc, molybdenum, and gold deposits await further development.

TRADE

Rice and rubber account for 90 percent of the exports. Imports are chiefly metals, machinery, drugs, fertilizer, and manufactured goods. The United States, France, and Japan are the principal trading partners, with the United States covering most of the trade deficit.

1962:	IMPORTS	$262,000,000
	EXPORTS	$ 56,000,000
	DEFICIT	$206,000,000

CHAMPIONSHIP BOUT *Boxing, banned under the Diem regime, was re-introduced in South Viet Nam early in 1964. This 1965 bout between two young Chinese women is for Women's Championship in Saigon and was held under the auspices of the Vietnamese Boxing Federation. One girl weighed 90 pounds, the other 93 pounds. The bout ran for three rounds. A purse went to the winner.*

TRANSPORT

ROAD: In 1962, there were less than 9,000 miles of road. Somewhat less than half of the roads can be used only in the dry season. Over 60,000 cars and trucks and 44,000 motor-cycles and scooters were in civilian hands.

RAILROAD: About 830 miles of track were restored to service after war damage; since 1961, guerrilla activity has prevented use of some sections.

WATERWAY: Over 1,800 miles of rivers and canals carry much of the traffic in the south. Much of the system requires dredging and repair to restore full use.

AIR: Air Viet-Nam provides internal service from Saigon to 14 cities; also to Hong Kong and points in Indo-China. Passenger air traffic, over 213,000 in 1961, doubled in 1962, as surface services met guerrilla interference.

SEA: Saigon, 45 miles from the sea, is the chief port. Da Nang, second in importance, handles about a sixth as much freight as Saigon.

COMMUNICA-TION

Telephone, radio telephone, and telegraph services are government-owned. A modern telecommunications system was largely completed by 1963 at which time over 15,000 of the 18,000 phones in use were concentrated in Saigon. Most of the country is reached by government-controlled radio broadcasts. In 1961 there were 125,000 licensed radios.

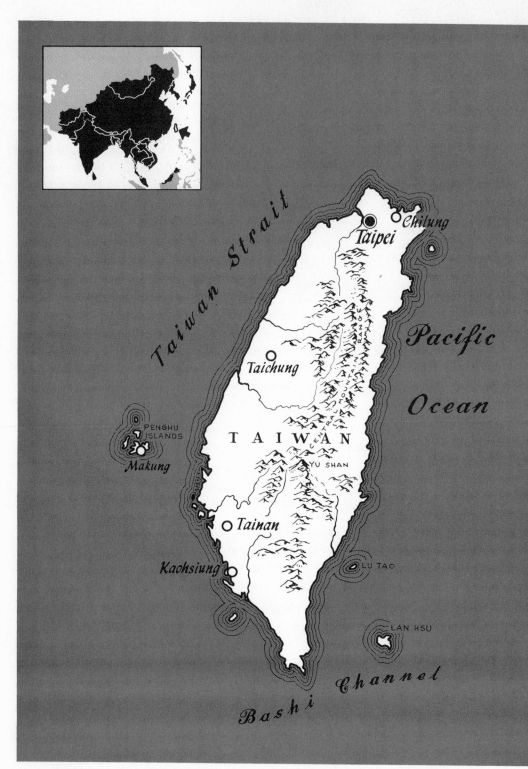

TAIWAN

Garrison of Free China

Since World War II, the island of Taiwan has been a citadel of resistance by Nationalist China against the Chinese Communists. When the forces of General Chiang Kai-shek were crushed on the mainland by the Chinese Red Army in 1949, the survivors of the debacle withdrew to Taiwan. The island has ever since embodied Nationalist hopes for recovery of power over all of China.

With the passage of time, the dreams of the Nationalists for a return to the mainland have seemed ever more illusory. Only because of the firm backing of Chiang's regime by the United States have Chinese Communist plans for subjugation of the island been frustrated. The "liberation" of Taiwan continues, however, to rank high among the political objectives of the government of Mao Tse-tung. American support of the defiant Nationalists has thus served to exacerbate relations between Communist China and the United States, and to obstruct prospects for a settlement of political differences between those nations.

THE BEAUTIFUL ISLAND

Portuguese seamen, sailing along the China coast in the 16th century, observed a large island in the offing. "Beautiful!" they exclaimed in admiration. Thus the island acquired the name of Formosa, which means *beautiful* in Portuguese. To the peoples of East Asia, however, the island has always been called Taiwan, a name of uncertain origin and meaning.

THE LAND

Taiwan lies about 90 miles off the shore of east central China. On a clear day, the mainland may be seen from the mountains. The Pescadores (Fishermen's) Islands are situated a short distance to the southwest. Several hundred miles to the northwest are the tiny Nationalist-held islands of Matsu and Quemoy, additional thorns in the side of Communist China.

507

The western part of Taiwan is a long, coastal plain. Most of the island's cities and towns are located in this region. There are also hundreds of farming and fishing villages.

The terrain rises in the central part of the island and gradually gives way to the rugged mountain ranges and thick forests which dominate the eastern half of Taiwan. This sector is not only difficult of access from the western plain, but the seaward approaches are blocked by soaring cliffs, frequently 2,000 and more feet high.

CLIMATE

Taiwan enjoys a subtropical climate throughout the year. The heaviest rains occur from May to September, a season also marked by uncomfortably high humidity. During the other months, the temperature ranges from about 50 degrees to 80 degrees.

Most of the many streams on Taiwan are short and unnavigable.

AGRICULTURE AND TIMBER

Taiwan is a moist, subtropical area. Rice is the principal crop. Its cultivation in irrigated paddy fields occupies the efforts of most of the island's farmers. Other important crops are sugar, sweet potatoes, pineapples, bananas, tea, and jute.

The forests and jungles are rich in such commercially useful timber as camphor, cypress, and bamboo. Until the outbreak of World War II, Taiwan enjoyed practically a monopoly of the production of camphor. With the subsequent development of synthetics, the importance of the island's supply has greatly declined.

THE TAIWANESE

Until some five centuries ago, when the Portuguese came to the island, Taiwan was inhabited mainly by aboriginal tribes of Malayan origin whose ancestors had migrated from south China and southeast Asian areas in early times. Warlike, uncivilized headhunters, the primitives were both feared and scorned by the Chinese.

Chinese emigrants began to settle in Taiwan during the 17th and 18th centuries. Gradually driving the aborigines into the interior, they

DRAGON DANCE   *The Chinese New Year falls in February. Taipei throngs watch the 1964 traditional dragon dance. The dragon's body which is almost 200 feet long is draped with paper or with cloth. The carved, gilded dragon's head weighs about 50 pounds and is a heavy load for the lead dancers.*

occupied the great western plain. These pioneers, whose descendants today are the Taiwanese, came mainly from the coastal provinces of Fukien and Kwantung. Transplanting their own Chinese civilization to Taiwan, they also preserved in their new home their local languages and customs, which often differed substantially from those of North China.

From 1895 to 1945, under Japanese rule, the ethnic and cultural patterns of Taiwan were strongly modified. During these years, Japa-

PEDICABS *This is Chung King Road South in downtown Taipei, one of the main streets of the capital. Here, the pedicab—a bicycle combined with a rickshaw —serves for a taxi. Fares are a matter of bargaining.*

nese customs penetrated throughout the island and Japanese was widely adopted as a second language. The Japanese rulers also took stern steps to curb the independence of the aboriginal tribes.

The last great flood of migrants poured into Taiwan after World War II. Seeking to escape from the victorious Communists on the mainland, about a million Nationalists fled to the island. Often viewed as carpetbaggers and intruders by the old-time Chinese, these refugees did not, at first, fit smoothly into island life. However, the newcomers have since emerged as the social and political élite of postwar Taiwan.

In the early 1960's, Taiwan's population approached 12 million. The population of Taiwan thus outnumbers the populations of about two-thirds of the member states of the United Nations. With one of the highest birth rates in the modern world, Taiwan's postwar population has been steadily mounting. Today more than 10 million are "Taiwanese" Chinese; the remainder are mainlanders and their offspring.

For many centuries, Taiwan was *terra incognita* to the Chinese people. Taiwan is first mentioned in Chinese records of the seventh century. When the Mongols, led by Kublai Khan, conquered China in the 13th century, they dispatched an expedition to bring the island under their sway. However, they did not occupy or administer Taiwan.

It was not until the 17th century that Taiwan made its mark upon Chinese history. During the upheavals accompanying the overthrow of the Ming Dynasty by the Manchus, Koxinga, the son of a Chinese pirate and a Japanese mother, set up a base on the island to carry on Chinese resistance against the Manchurian conquerors. He died shortly thereafter, but his successors continued to defy the Manchus until 1683, when they were finally suppressed. To this day, Koxinga is a great hero among the Taiwanese.

Chinese imperial rule was only of marginal benefit to Taiwan. For two centuries the island was poorly governed and grossly neglected. When, at the end of the Sino-Japanese War (1894–1895), Taiwan was turned over to Japan, China's rulers did not grieve deeply over their loss.

Japan, however, made a major effort to develop Taiwan into a model colony. An efficient administration was introduced; law and order were sternly upheld; and legal and judicial practices were overhauled. Public sanitation and hygiene were promoted. To expedite the economic exploitation of the island, transportation and communication facilities were improved. The Japanese, too, encouraged light industries. By introducing new crops, such as sugar, they also made agriculture more profitable than ever before.

POSTWAR TAIWAN

At the end of World War II, Japanese rule over Taiwan was terminated. Taiwan might well have remained a mere provincial outpost of the Chinese Nationalist government. But when the Communists smashed their way into power, the island became a haven and a fortress for Chiang Kai-shek and the remnants of his army.

CHIANG KAI-SHEK

Generalissimo Chiang, born in 1887, aspired to be a professional soldier, and attended the Paoting Military Academy. When the Chinese Revolution against the Manchu Dynasty broke out in 1911, he was engaged in postgraduate study in Tokyo. Chiang's participation in this historic event was merely nominal. But thereafter, he rose constantly in the Kuomintang, and upon the death of Sun Yat-sen in 1925, he quickly stepped into a position of leadership. His primacy within the Kuomintang has not been successfully challenged since.

In 1927, Chiang married for the second time; his bride was Mei-ling, the youngest of the three famed Soong sisters. Mme. Sun Yat-sen, the eldest, thereby became his sister-in-law. Mme. Chiang, who was born in 1898 and college-educated in the United States, has for many years served the Generalissimo as English interpreter, confidante, and advisor.

Chiang has often been deemed a better politician than a general. His education has been largely technical; his social and economic thinking has been strongly influenced by Confucianism. He is austere, even puritanical, in his personal habits. Two sons by his first marriage hold high ranks in the Nationalist regime.

CHAING KAI SHEK   The Generalissimo, who has already passed his 75th birthday, was trained as a professional soldier, and has been the leader of China's anti-Communists for the past 40 years.

MADAME CHIANG KAI SHEK   The first lady of Nationlist China inspects a housing project during November, 1964. She is accompanied by the wives of officers, who are residents of the project. Madame Chiang is a sister-in-law of Sun Yat Sen, "Father of the Chinese Revolution."

ROLE OF THE UNITED STATES

The outbreak of the Korean War in 1950 was a boon to the defiant anti-Communists on Taiwan. The United States ordered its powerful Seventh Fleet to patrol the Formosa Straits which separate Taiwan from the mainland. Notice was thereby served to the government of Mao Tse-tung that it would not be permitted to take advantage of the events in Korea to invade Taiwan. The American naval patrol has been maintained there ever since.

The United States also took measures to strengthen Chiang's regime on Taiwan. Large doses of economic, technical, and military aid were poured into the island. In time, the Nationalist Army has blossomed into one of the most powerful military forces in Asia. But whatever hopes Chiang may have had of returning to the mainland were firmly discouraged by the United States.

THE TWO-CHINA PROBLEM

The impasse over Taiwan gave rise to one of the knottiest political issues of the postwar era, the "Two-China" problem. Many countries, including the United States, recognize Chiang's regime at Taipei as the official government of China. Other states—in Asia, in the European Communist bloc, in the Middle East, and in Africa—sooner or later extended recognition to Mao's regime. In the coming years, it may be assumed, the Communist government on the mainland will acquire increasingly widespread acceptance by other states.

Differences also divide world opinion on the question of admission of Communist China into the United Nations. For many years, the United States has been successful in rallying sufficient support for its opposition to the acceptance of the People's Republic into the international organization. From time to time proposals have been made to include both Chiang and Mao's governments in the U.N. These suggestions, however, have been consistently rejected by both Chiang and Mao, who have insisted upon the principle of the unity of China. It seems clear that the Nationalists cannot continue indefinitely to represent China in the U.N.; but to find a formula for Chinese representation that will not wreck the international organization will be no easy matter.

THE GOVERNMENT OF TAIWAN

Two governmental systems are in operation on Taiwan, a local provincial government and a national government. Since the retreat from the mainland, the Republic of China, claiming to be the national government for all China, has set up its functions at Taipei. Although many political responsibilities are still vested in the provincial government of Taiwan, this government has been completely overshadowed by the national regime.

Technically, the government of the Republic of China is defined in a Constitution. The head of state is the President, an office held continuously by General Chiang. Actual administration is vested in a Premier. In keeping with modern Chinese republican tradition, there is a fivefold division of powers. Nominally, a party system and popular elections are in effect, but in actual practice the Kuomintang (Nationalist Party), controlled by Chiang Kai-shek, has dominated political life.

The Kuomintang has been accused of perpetuating authoritarian rule. It is indisputable that democratic government has not prevailed under Chiang's leadership. Free political activity has been discouraged; censorship has been common; and a secret police force has cowed the people.

However, more recently the Kuomintang government has become much less oppressive and far more efficient than most regimes in Asia. In justification of their frequently arbitrary ways, Nationalist leaders have argued that, since their government is at war, normal democratic processes must be suspended for the duration. It is sometimes conjectured that a relaxation of the severe political controls will occur only when Chiang has passed away.

TAIWAN'S BOOMING ECONOMY

In the postwar era, the growth of Taiwan's economy has truly been impressive. When the Nationalists moved to Taipei, the island's economy was on the verge of collapse. Sound planning, large-scale American aid (terminated in 1965), and the availability of numerous Japanese-trained professional and skilled workers facilitated rapid recovery and expansion. By the early 1960's, the Chinese on Taiwan were enjoying one of the highest standards of living in all Asia.

The mainstay of the Taiwanese economy continues to be agriculture. Cultivation of the land furnishes employment for the majority of the island's inhabitants and accounts for the larger part of economic production. Thanks to island-wide agrarian reforms, agriculture is much more profitable than ever before. Private land-owning has been encouraged, rates for land rental and of interest on farm loans have been effectively controlled, and scientific methods of cultivation have been fostered. In Asia, only the agricultural systems of Japan and Israel may be compared with that of the Taiwanese for efficiency.

The Nationalist government has attempted to diversify the economy. Many new light industries have not only helped to fulfill local consumer needs, but have also turned out surpluses for export. However, Taiwan has continued to be heavily dependent upon foreign suppliers for heavy industrial equipment.

The Nationalist government has also been active in extending transportation facilities and in promoting foreign trade. Japan and the United States are Taiwan's best trading partners.

HEALTH AND EDUCATIONAL ADVANCES

Taiwan's economic gains have been shared, albeit unequally by the people. The grinding poverty and privation, rampant in prewar China, have been drastically reduced. Schooling has been available for children of all ages; literacy is widespread; and a respectable system of higher education has been erected. Standards of public sanitation and hygiene are outstanding among Asian lands.

THE CITY OF TAIPEI

Taipei, with a population of over 900,000, is a city of striking contrasts. The traditional ways of China are juxtaposed alongside the most modern innovations, while evidences of great wealth and prosperity are constantly balanced by numerous signs of struggle and poverty. The city overshadows the rest of the island in many ways; it is the center of government, the site of many factories and workshops, and the hub of educational and cultural life. It is thus dangerous to generalize about conditions of life in Taiwan as a whole on the basis of the situation in Taipei.

TAIWAN'S FUTURE

The Taiwanese, proud of their achievements in the postwar period, are understandably uneasy about the future. Only the incorrigibly optimistic retain their dream of a triumphant return to the mainland. For the vast majority, the political future of the island remains indeterminate and a source of anxiety.

HYMAN KUBLIN

SAN TI MEN VILLAGE   *The Paiwan, an aboriginal tribe of the Taiwan hills, live in platform houses constructed mainly of grass matting and straw. Here, a woman pounds the husks off rice in a huge wooden mortar and pestle.*

IN BRIEF

AREA

13,936 square miles (including Quemoy, Matsu, and the Penghus). A little larger than Connecticut and Massachusetts combined.

TERRAIN

Shaped like a tobacco leaf, the island, which is about 240 miles long and 85 miles wide, lies about 90 miles off the China coast. The Penghus are an archipelago of small islands scattered over the Taiwan Strait, roughly 25 miles west of Taiwan. Quemoy and Matsu are small islands just off the China coast. About two-thirds of Taiwan is mountainous, with a high point of over 13,000 feet in the Central Mountain Range. Most of the population is concentrated on the broad and fertile coastal plain on the west; plains are few and narrow on the east. Numerous short, swift rivers provide hydroelectric power; none are navigable.

FLORA

Over half the land is forest, with conifers, cedar, cypress, juniper, rhododendron, maple, and camphor in the hills, and bamboo, evergreens, and palms in the lowlands.

FAUNA

Monkeys, fox, deer, rabbit, squirrel, rats, bats, birds, and snakes.

CLIMATE

Subtropical. Average rainfall is about 101 inches a year and there are frequent typhoons in the summer months. The northeast monsoon, from October to March, brings rain to the northern shores; while the southwest monsoon, May to September, brings rain to the south and west. Average temperature in the north is about 70°F.; in the south, about 75°F.

CAPITAL

Taipei, with about 964,000 inhabitants in 1962.

OTHER CITIES

Kaohsiung, 275,000; Tainan, 230,000; Taichung, 207,000; Keelung, 145,000.

POPULATION

12,117,000 in 1964. The annual rate of increase is extremely high, about 3.5 percent. Density is over 900 persons per square mile.

ETHNIC GROUPS   Chinese are the majority group. There are about 10 million "Taiwanese" Chinese, and about 2 million who have arrived from the Mainland since World War II. About 210,000 tribal people—Ami, Atayal, Paiwan, Apayao—live in the hill areas. They are of Malay-Indonesian ancestry and constitute less than two percent of the population.

LANGUAGES   Mandarin Chinese is the official language, but over half of the people speak Mingan and many use Hakka, two dialects of south China. Japanese and English are in limited use. Tribal peoples use tongues related to Malay.

RELIGION   Confucianism is dominant. It is usually practiced in conjunction with Buddhism or Taoism. An estimated six to eight million are Buddhist. Islam and Christianity are followed by small groups.

DATE OF INDEPENDENCE   On December 8, 1949, the government of the Republic of China established its capital in Taipei.

FORM OF GOVERNMENT   Authoritarian republic. Taiwan is, theoretically, a province of the Chinese Republic, but local government is effectively eclipsed by the national government-in-exile. Chiang Kai-shek, who as President is head of state, dominates the government and the Kuomintang party; administrative, legislative, and judicial functions have not been independent. Censorship and a secret police inhibit democratic processes. A state of wartime emergency officially exists. The Republic of China is a member of the United Nations.

EDUCATION   In 1963, there were almost 2,000 primary schools with 1.9 million students and almost 47,000 teachers; 430 secondary and technical schools had close to 18,000 teachers and 360,500 students; 33 universities and colleges enrolled 35,000 students. About 10 percent of the people are illiterate, but 92.5 percent of school-age children are in school. In 1964, some 22 percent of the total population was enrolled in school or college.

HEALTH FACILITIES   In 1960, there were 6,900 doctors, 975 dentists, 3,050 mid-wives, and 1,090 pharmacists. Over 400 government-operated health stations and clinics were in operation. During 1964, family planning clinics and centers were to be established.

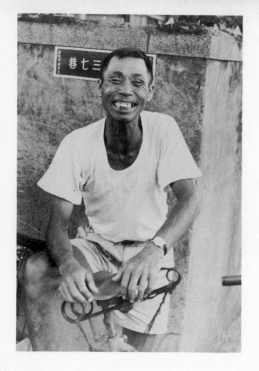

PEDICAB DRIVER *This middle-aged Chinese, waiting for a fare, is a Chinese immigrant who arrived on Taiwan with Chiang Kai-shek in 1949. He is a veteran of the Nationalist Army.*

ABORIGINES *Taiwan's majority is Chinese; their ancestors have been emigrating from China for at least 600 years. The aborigines, less than two percent of the population, live mostly in the hill regions and are related to the peoples of Malaya and Indonesia.*

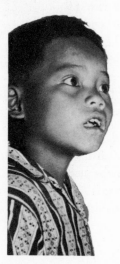

RESTORATION DAY *Every year, on October 30th, all of Taiwan celebrates the return of Chinese rule after half a century of Japanese occupation. Stilt-walkers, lion dances, and dragon dances characterize the proceedings.*

Life expectancy was about 63 years for a newborn child.

CULTURAL FACILITIES

In 1961, some 31 daily newspapers had a circulation of about 720,000; thus, roughly one person in 20 bought a paper every day. About 475 magazines and periodicals were published. In 1962, some 2,625 books were published; well over half were on literary topics and many were pirated editions. Over 550 cinemas had an annual attendance of almost 67 million and, in 1961, about one person in 20 owned a radio. Communication media are frequently subject to censorship.

CURRENCY AND FINANCE

The *New Taiwan Yuan* fluctuates in value; since 1963 it has been worth 2½¢ in U.S. currency. In 1962, over half of the provincial government revenue of about $253 million went to the national government which maintained an army of 450,000 men, an air force of 80,000, a navy of 60,000, and 25,000 marines.

INDUSTRY AND PRODUCTION

Although over half of the population was still dependent on agriculture, by 1961 the Gross National Product was over $1.42 billion and was rising at an annual rate of 7.4 percent. Per capita income was $115 a year and was rising by four percent a year. By 1964, the economy had reached the point where progress would continue without foreign aid, and U.S. economic aid was discontinued. By 1962, over 445,000 workers were employed in 52,100 manufacturing industries, the most important being based on flour-milling, sugar, tobacco, oil, iron, glass, bricks, soap, textiles, fertilizer, and cement. Electric power production was over 4.85 billion kilowatt hours.

CROPS: Rice, 2.63 million metric tons in 1962, is the chief crop. Also significant are wheat, sugar cane, peanuts, soybeans, tea, sweet potatoes, tobacco, and fruit.

LIVESTOCK: In 1961, there were 423,000 cattle, 2.4 million pigs, and 13.7 million poultry.

FISHERIES: The 1962 catch was 327,000 metric tons.

MINING: Coal and natural gas are the only minerals present in abundance. Copper and gold are mined in small amounts.

TRADE

The chief exports are sugar, textiles, rice, cement, and canned fruits and vegetables. Chief imports are raw materials and heavy machinery. Japan, the United States, and Hong Kong are the principal trading partners.

1963: IMPORTS $336,787,000
EXPORTS $357,524,000
SURPLUS $ 20,737,000

TRANSPORT

ROAD: There are almost 10,000 miles of road, mostly gravel, except for the modern north-south highway. In 1961, there were 57,600 cars, trucks, and other vehicles (including over 33,000 motorcycles) in use among the civilian population.

RAILROAD: About 590 miles of railway are operated by a government corporation. Private industries operate about 2,200 miles of track, 680 miles of it available for public use. All major points are accessible by rail.

SEA: The chief ports are Keelung in the north and Kaohsiung in the south; both can handle ships of 20,000 tons and both are being expanded. There are five smaller ports. The merchant fleet comprised over 1,700 vessels, including two passenger ships, 242 freighters, and over 1,400 fishing vessels, in 1962.

AIR: Taipei has an international jet airport served by four foreign lines and four domestic lines.

COMMUNI-CATION

Telephone, radio, radiotelephone, post, and telegraph services are government-operated and fairly well developed. There were over 120,000 telephones in use in 1962. About 609,000 radios received over 60 radio stations, half of them operated by private commercial interests. Commercial television broadcasts to 3,300 sets began in 1962.

:T FISHING   Fishermen have built a ·ker dam in a stream near Taichung. This rier steers fish coming downstream into opening of the basket-like net.

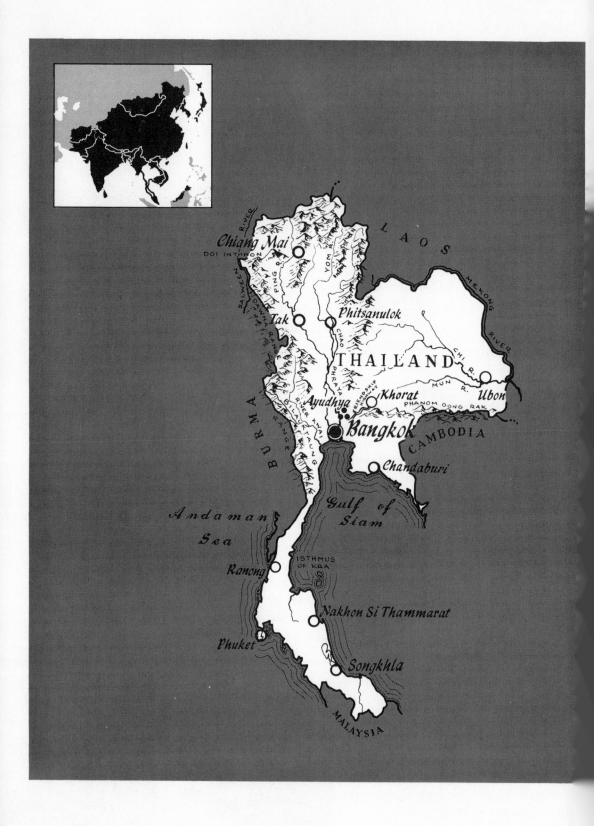

THAILAND

Land of Smiles

"In the water there is fish, in the land there is rice." This is probably the best known old Thai saying. And it tells much about the Thai people and their country.

The heartland of Thailand is its rich Central Plain, the rice bowl of the country. During the rainy season the Chaophraya River overflows its banks, bringing water to the growing rice, depositing a fine silt to fertilize the land, and turning the Central Plain temporarily into a vast shallow lake filled with fish. This rich plain makes Thailand, indeed, a land blessed with fish and rice—a land in which no one starves, and few have to worry about basic needs.

Literally, Thailand means *the land of the free* and, in fact, Thailand has never been a colony under any European power. "Siam," a name still used by some people outside Thailand, is the name of the ancient kingdom and is never used by Thai when they speak of contemporary Thailand.

WEALTH OF THE LAND

Thailand is about the size of France; its total area is about 200,000 square miles. More than half the land is forested or suitable only for grazing animals. About 20 percent is cultivated. The rest is taken up by roads, waterways, towns, or marshes and other wastelands.

Aside from the rich Central Plain, there are three other important geographic areas in Thailand: the north, the northeast, and peninsular Thailand.

The north is a hilly, heavily forested region; teak is the most famous of the fine woods felled there. Herds of wild elephant roam in this area. Captured elephants are trained to work in the lumber industry, carrying huge teak logs to streams down which the logs are floated to the Bangkok market. Occasionally an albino elephant is captured. This famed white elephant is regarded as sacred by the Thai people.

RAJDAMNERN AVENUE Modern government and commercial buildings rise along the flanks of this up-to-date thoroughfare in Bangkok. The monument commemorates the beginnings of constitutional government in 1932.

A symbol of good luck, the white elephant, when found, is offered to the King.

The north is also the home of a tiny scale insect that sucks the juices of certain trees and shrubs and produces a resinous secretion called stick lac, which is the source of shellac.

The northeast, also known as the Khorat Plateau, is a relatively barren region; its soils are poor and better suited to raising corn and cattle than rice.

Peninsular Thailand, in the south, extends 300 miles down to Malaysia. Like Malaysia, this region has extensive rubber plantations, rich tin mines, and many small coastal fishing villages. It is the rainiest and warmest part of Thailand, and the mountain ranges are covered with a dense tropical jungle in which tigers, gibbons, and brightly colored birds abound.

CLIMATE

All of Thailand lies within the tropics; the annual mean temperature is 80°. There are three main seasons: the hot, rainy season of the southwest monsoon, from May to September; the cool, dry season from October to February; and the hot, dry season from February to May. But even in the cool season, when Thai are apt to wear sweaters, the temperature hardly ever goes below 75° during the day.

LAND OF SMILES

The easygoing, fun-loving, and noncompetitive people have earned Thailand a reputation as the "land of smiles."

Sports and pastimes are popular throughout the country. Religious occasions are celebrated with festivities, fairs, bright lights, and music. Western sports, such as soccer, are widely played. But even more popular is the game of *takro,* played with a rattan ball. The people also love folk dancing, songfests, and gambling. The Thai are inveterate gamblers. They will wager on almost anything—coin tossing, card games, cockfights, kite flying, contests between Siamese fighting fish, and the national lottery.

THE THAI

Thailand has about 30 million people, of whom about 80 percent are Thai. The Thai belong to the Mongoloid race, but their culture is distinctively their own. They speak the Thai language, which is a tonal language and basically monosyllabic. In writing, the Thai use an alphabet based on an ancient Indian script. Most Thai are farmers who live in small farming villages.

THE CHINESE MINORITY

The largest minority group in Thailand are the Chinese, who number 3.5 million. The Chinese play a vital role in Thailand's economy; they serve as middlemen in internal trade and control much of the nation's industry.

In recent times, the national pride of the Chinese has been invigorated by China's growing command of international attention; many of the Chinese inhabitants of Thailand undoubtedly sympathize to some extent with the aims of Communist China.

FLOATING MARKET *The early morning market held on the klongs of Bangkok is famous for its color, profusion, and gaiety. A small channel is always kept free for midstream traffic. The sellers are women. Many will have carried the produce of the family farm for a considerable distance. The big sunshade hat rests on a thin frame so that the head is effectively insulated from the deadly sun by flowing air. Boats are laden with bananas, coconuts, pineapples, papayas, pomelos, oranges, melons, flowers, onions, cucumbers, chilis, garlic, corn, and every sort of tropical fruit and vegetable. The fruit in the baskets in the foreground is the delicious tropical "custard apple." Hot coffee and full-scale meals are passed from sampan to sampan. Such scenes have led travelers to dub Bangkok the "Venice of the East."*

The strong economic role of the Chinese and the growing nationalism of both the Thai and the Chinese have led to strained relations between the two groups. To combat tensions, the government has tried to encourage the Thai to play a greater role in trade and at the same time to encourage the Chinese to adopt Thai habits.

The education of young Chinese in the ways of Thailand has been emphasized. The government has made it more difficult for Chinese to send money "home" to China, in an attempt to focus Chinese

attention and allegiance on the country they inhabit. In an effort to combat the age-old Thai contempt for commerce, the government now requires that 75 percent of the jobs in any business be filled by Thai.

The result of these campaigns is a peculiar kind of compromise that is characteristic of Thailand. The Chinese remain dominant in most businesses, but Thai sit on the boards of directors, presumably earning their salaries by obtaining for their companies the cooperation of the government.

MALAYS AND OTHER PEOPLES

About 700,000 Malays live in Thailand, most of them concentrated in the southernmost provinces nearest Malaysia. The majority of the Malays, like the Thai, are farmers. But their language, customs, and Islamic religion separate them from the Thai.

Among the most colorful of the non-Thai peoples are 200,000 or so people of the hill tribes. These people live in the north and practice "slash and burn" cultivation. They burn off a forested hill area, plant their crops, use the land for a season or two until the fertility of the soil is exhausted, and then move on.

WESTERN WAYS

The peoples of Thailand are being caught up in the stream of modern world culture. The Thai girl in the paddy field transplants rice seedlings much as her mother and grandmother did before her, but under her old-fashioned straw hat she probably has a Western-style permanent. As she works, she is probably dreaming of visiting a relative in Bangkok, where she can see a film or shop in the capital's modern stores.

Many of the indigenous arts of Thailand have suffered from the Western impact. Machine-made cotton goods have largely replaced hand-loomed fabrics. Western dress has supplanted the sarong-like skirts once worn by men and women. Western motion pictures and modern Thai motion pictures have replaced the traditional shadow plays and folk dramas. Old poetic forms have not disappeared, but the fast-paced prose writings of popular novelists have gained a wider reading public.

Dietary habits have lost the least ground to Western influences. Most Thai still prefer boiled rice served with a hot curry of shrimp or fish to bland Western foods—although the addition of a coke to an old-style dinner is a spreading innovation.

THE SACRED CITY

Bangkok, the capital of the country, and Thonburi, its "twin city" across the Chaophraya River, constitute the only large urban centers in

AYUTTHAYA RESTORED *These three chedis, or stupas, hundreds of years old, were given new coats of cement in the early 1950's during a government-sponsored improvement program. A chedi has no entrance; it is a locked architectural jewel box built over sacred relics of the Buddha or of a consecrated ruler.*

Thailand. Among the Thai, Bangkok is known as *Krung Thep,* or "City of Angels."

The population of Greater Bangkok is around two million. In this cosmopolitan city, many foreigners, including about 1,000 Americans, live and work as representatives of governments or business concerns.

In ancient Siam the capital was regarded as the magical center of the kingdom. Here the King performed ceremonies that were be-

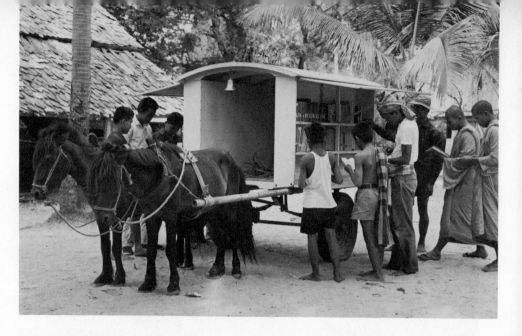

PONY CART LIBRARY *Villagers of the Khorat Plateau along the Laos border come to borrow and return books. The bell is rung to tell the village that the library has arrived. Borrowers include two young monks from the village wat. The young librarian (in the Western-style hat) is a student who devotes some of his time to this program of self-improvement for rural communities.*

lieved to ensure the welfare of the kingdom. Although the capital no longer has this mystic significance, it retains much prestige.

Bangkok today is the great administrative, cultural, commercial, and industrial center in Thailand. It is by far the busiest port in the kingdom and the site of almost all the industries that have been developed. Its commercial character has attracted many Chinese; the Chinese quarter is large, and hundreds of Chinese workshops turn out handicraft articles and small-scale industrial products.

The city has many reminders of the past, particularly its canal thoroughfares choked with sampans and barges. But in many respects Bangkok is a modern city; it has broad new. avenues, taxis, and fine hotels. Its many handsome Buddhist temples make it one of the most beautiful cities in Asia. The extensive ruins of the old capital of the country, Ayutthaya, located about 50 miles north of Bangkok, are a major tourist attraction.

TOWNS AND VILLAGES

The largest city in Thailand except for Bangkok and Thonburi is Chiangmai, which has a population of only about 65,000. Market towns with populations over 30,000 include Khorat, Lampang, Hadyai, and Nakhonsawan.

There are thousands of small villages in Thailand. Thai farmers usually build their houses in a cluster close to the village *wat*, or Buddhist temple. Thai towns are really overgrown villages. They are set apart from the surrounding rural scene by the presence of large numbers of government officials—police officials, education officials, agricultural specialists—all appointed from Bangkok to oversee affairs in the villages around the town.

RELIGIOUS BELIEFS AND PRACTICES

The Thai people are Buddhists of the Theravada school of Buddhism and accept its ideals of non-violence and non-attachment to material things. Every young man is encouraged to enter a Buddhist monastery at least once during his life, preferably for the three-month period of the Buddhist Lent. Buddhist "merit-making" is a universal Thai activity. It takes many forms, from giving food to the monks every day to freeing caged birds bought at temple fairs.

In addition to their belief in Buddhism, many of the Thai people have animistic beliefs. They believe in nature spirits, such as the rice goddess, and in the spirits of certain trees and mountains. They also believe in ghost-like spirits of the dead. All these spirits must be placated with offerings of food and flowers lest they cause mischief.

Christian missionaries have been active in Thailand for more than a century and have been given freedom to build churches, schools, and hospitals. Relatively few Thai, however, have been converted. Buddhism is so much a part of the Thai way of life that Christianity has little appeal.

SOCIAL ORGANIZATION

In ancient Thailand there were three main social classes: (1) members of the royal family and royal officials; (2) commoners; and (3) slaves. Class lines were not absolutely restrictive. Most slaves, for example, were debt slaves and could gain their freedom by paying their debt.

THE KING AND QUEEN *The King —the only King of any country to be born in the United States—is about 38 years old. He was educated in Switzerland. He is an accomplished performer on the alto-saxophone and the clarinet, and at times he broadcasts in a Bangkok combo. The Queen is the daughter of the former Thai ambassador to France, and she met her future husband at a Paris reception in 1945. When she visited the United States, she dazzled the television audience with the Thai silk dresses made for her by Pierre Balmain of Paris.*

In recent years class lines in Thailand have grown weaker. The last vestiges of slavery were abolished in 1905. The royal family is not as large or important as it once was, and official positions are now open to anyone who can acquire an education.

The most important social unit in Thai society is the primary family composed of parents and unmarried children. Married children usually establish separate homes of their own. There are no clans and no castes in Thailand.

Throughout Thai society, age is an important criterion for respect. Within the family, much respect is accorded parents. Among children, the older brother or sister receives respect from the younger.

High respect is also accorded the King and royal family and, by extension, government officials, who theoretically serve the King. Also accorded much respect are members of the Buddhist Order.

The traditional sign of respect among the Thai is the *wai*, a silent bow with the hands raised, palms together. The person who is junior or of lower status bows first and raises his hands higher than the person returning the salute. All lay persons greeting a monk, including the King, must *wai* first; indeed, the monk, because of the holiness of his role, does not even return the greeting.

EDUCATION

For hundreds of years, village temples served as schools, and village monks drilled young boys in the fundamentals of reading and writing in order to impart the basic principles of Buddhism. Government-supported education was unknown until the nineteenth century.

Then increased contact with Western countries convinced the government that it must prepare the Thai for the modern world. As a result, compulsory education was introduced in 1921.

Chulalongkorn University in Bangkok, Thailand's leading institution for higher learning, was established in 1917. Other universities specialize in law, agriculture, fine arts, and medicine. Post-secondary schools train teachers, agricultural specialists, and other vocational specialists. The national literacy rate has been raised to about 60 percent.

MODERN SCHOOLROOM   *Girls in modern dress take careful notes as a Buddhist monk in the traditional saffron robe conducts a special class in Buddhist ethics. The carved, gilded table behind the severely modern lectern holds a small statue of the Buddha surrounded by offerings of candles and flowers.*

ARTS AND CRAFTS

Some of the old arts and crafts of Thailand have survived in the modern era of mass production, mostly because they have found markets and new uses in the West. The beauty of Thai designs and colors in handwoven silks attracted Western businessmen and New York fashion designers shortly after World War II. Since then this once-dying industry has been reinvigorated.

The beauty of the work of Thai silversmiths, especially their black-and-silver nielloware designs, also attracted Western attention. This handicraft industry, which once supplied the royalty of Thailand with betel boxes, has greatly expanded. It now supplies people throughout the world with cigarette cases, bracelets, and cuff links.

COMMUNICATION

The Thai government operates a network of radio stations as well as two Bangkok and three provincial television stations. Not many Thai outside of Bangkok own radio receivers, but government provincial offices have receivers, and government news broadcasts and entertainment programs are widely heard. Fourteen Thai-language daily newspapers, two English-language dailies, and many weekly journals are published in Thailand. These publications are subject to censorship; open criticism of the government is not allowed.

HEALTH AND WELFARE

Thailand, like other underdeveloped countries in the tropics, has more serious health problems than most Western countries. Thailand has not had some of the problems of its Asian neighbors, however. Starvation, for example, is virtually unknown.

The major diseases include malaria, tuberculosis, intestinal disorders, pneumonia, and typhoid fever. Diseases associated with childbirth and infancy are common, and the infant death rate is high—about 65 per 1,000 live births. Life expectancy is around 53 years.

In recent years, the Thai government has launched extensive projects to raise health standards. Information on hygienic disposal of human wastes, on proper care of infants, and on adequate diets has been sent to villages and taught in schools.

The government launched a massive ten-year campaign to control malaria in 1951. The program was an enormous success, and in 1961 the far more difficult goal of malaria eradication was adopted. The death rate from malaria, once Thailand's leading killer, has now been cut 80 percent.

AGRICULTURE AND MINING

The economy of Thailand is based on agriculture. About half of the country's income is derived from the land. The five leading exports from Thailand in 1960 were rice and rubber, each accounting for about 30 percent of total value of exports; maize and tin, each accounting for about six percent; and teak, accounting for about four percent.

Farmers make up 85 percent of the labor force. Most farmers still use traditional methods: they prepare their fields with plows and harrows drawn by water buffalo; they plant their rice by hand; and they harvest their crops with a hand sickle. Farmers often cooperate on such tasks as repairing irrigation canals and harvesting crops.

In the past, almost all Thai villages were self-sufficient. Today, with the development of commercial farming, many items once locally produced are bought in the marketplace instead. But the old pattern survives in many areas of the country; most Thai farmers still own their own land and grow their own food. Tenant farming is not widespread.

Second in economic importance to agriculture is mining, particularly of tin. Ore from the tin mines in peninsular Thailand is shipped to Malaysia for smelting. Newly found mineral deposits are coming into greater economic prominence, and production of lead, antimony, gypsum, iron ore, and tungsten is rising.

DIVERSIFICATION AND DEVELOPMENT

The predominance of agriculture, and especially the reliance on rice farming, has led the Thai government to encourage diversification of crops and the development of industry. Corn production has in-

PARADE OF WAR ELEPHANTS

During the annual pageantry of the Surin Round Up, no effort is spared in reconstructing in all their historical detail the costumes and the equipment of the war elephants who were employed by ancient kings. In olden times, wars in this part of Asia were sometimes settled by a single contest between two kings, each of whom sat atop a battle elephant. The tiered umbrella over the howdah is the mark of royalty. With two bunches of grass, the man in the howdah signals the soldiers and the elephants which are behind him just as his royal ancestors did, except that the ancient kings were accustomed to holding peacock feathers for the purpose. The man in the lead, who is armed with a wicked-looking blade, takes the role of the king's warrior. It was he who was primarily responsible for fighting the opposing elephant under the direction of his royal master.

THAI BOXING   In this sport, participants may use fists, feet, elbows, and knees. A bout is preceded by a ceremonial prayer and a dance-like display of skill by each contestant. In accordance with tradition, the entire program is accompanied by the beat of two drums and the piping of a flute.

FIGHT WITH STAVES   *These women, armed with sticks longer than themselves, demonstrate a traditional art of self-defense. For centuries, during the era when only the wealthy and the nobles bore metal weapons, soldiers recruited from the peasantry marched into battle armed in just this fashion. The combatants wear a traditional costume for fighting: the loose lower garment is a single piece of fabric which is wound around the waist and pulled between the legs and then fastened at the belt line.*

ELEPHANT RACE   *Every year, around the end of October, there is held at Surin the only elephant race in the world. Riders use a spiked goad to drive the pachyderms to increased effort. Experts assert that the sharp hook does not penetrate far enough into the elephant's hide to injure the animal.*

creased phenomenally; corn is now the third-ranking export in value. Cassava (tapioca) production has also spurted upward, and cassava now rivals teak in export value. Between 1950 and 1958, industrial production doubled. Thailand now has cement factories, sugar refineries, liquor and beer factories, and cigarette factories. These industries have drastically reduced the need for foreign imports.

Foreign investments have been encouraged. Most industries are still on a small scale; many need government support. But a start has been made, and manufacturing now contributes an estimated 14.5 percent of the gross national product (estimated at two billion dollars in 1961).

Thailand buys most heavily from Japan, the U. S., and the industrialized countries of Western Europe. It sells its food and raw materials chiefly in Japan and Malaysia.

One important hindrance to the development of industry in Thailand has been lack of power. To meet this need, long-term plans for building hydroelectric power facilities have been developed and partly carried out. Yanhee Dam, 260 miles north of Bangkok, completed in 1963, is expected to supply some 850,000 kilowatts of electric power. The dam will also provide irrigation waters and a means for flood control.

CAVE TEMPLE This giant Buddha with its rows of attending figures sits inside a cavern in Mount Khao Luang, a 5,900-foot peak. The Buddha rests in the posture prescribed for overcoming temptation: the left arm folded, the right extended to touch the ground (to attest the good deeds of present and former incarnations). On the head is the flame-shaped sign of enlightenment.

TRANSPORTATION

Thailand's waterways are the principal highways of the country. Supplementing these waterways is a growing network of railways, roads, and airlines. The Royal Thai State Railways has trunk lines radiating from Bangkok to Chiangmai, to the Khorat Plateau, and to the Malaysian border. Modern roads total about 6,000 miles. Government-operated airlines maintain service to provincial centers and, in cooperation with the Scandinavian Airlines System, serve several cities in the Far East.

EARLY FORMS OF GOVERNMENT

Government in ancient Thailand was highly authoritarian. The King had absolute powers and was accorded the position of a god. The people were not allowed to look at him; his officials had to crawl on their hands and knees in his presence. The justification for this elevated position of the King was the important magical and religious role he played. By performing court ceremonies, the King supposedly ensured the health, prosperity, and strength of his people.

In ancient times, the Thai state held a relatively strong position in Southeast Asia. The Thai were often able to control neighboring Malayan, Cambodian, and Laotian areas. The main threat to Thailand came from Burma, which conquered and dominated Thailand for a brief period in the sixteenth century and again in 1767.

A NEW WAY OF LIFE

A new period of Thai history began with the coming of Western merchants, missionaries, and diplomats in the nineteenth century. Thai leaders soon discovered that if Thailand was to remain independent many concessions would have to be made to the powerful West. King Mongkut—of *The King and I* fame—reigned from 1851 to 1868. He began to modernize the government, and signed liberal treaties with Western countries that opened Thailand to foreign traders. King Chulalongkorn, who reigned from 1868 to 1910, and his sons Vajiravudh and Prajadhipok, who succeeded him, continued and developed Mongkut's policies. As a result, Thailand was the only state in Southeast Asia that succeeded in retaining its independence.

In 1932 a *coup d'état* led by young Western-educated Thai ended royal leadership of the Thai state. The monarchy was retained, but only as a symbol. Real control was assumed by a small group of military and civilian officials who inaugurated a constitutional regime that was supposed to bring full democracy to Thailand.

The two most prominent early leaders in the constitutional government were Pridi Banomyong, a young lawyer, and P. Pibulsonggram, a military officer usually referred to as "Pibul." In the struggles for power that ensued, the military faction won out.

Pibul became Premier in 1938. During World War II Pibul followed a strongly nationalistic program. He delayed the planned democratization of government, and in December 1941 allied Thailand with Japan. When Japan's fortunes declined during the war, Pibul retired from government. At the end of the war, a civilian government, controlled by Pridi, assumed power.

Postwar problems, including the mysterious and fatal shooting of the young King, Ananda Mahidol, in July 1946, gave the military leaders the opportunity to attack Pridi's government. They seized political control in November, 1947. Early in 1948 Pibul was chosen to resume the premiership. He remained Premier until 1957. The following year, Field Marshal Sarit Thanarat, an army strong man, became Premier. He remained at the head of the government until his death in 1963. Sarit was succeeded by General Thanom Kittikachorn.

Since 1946 the King of Thailand has been Bhumibol Adulyadej. At the time of his accession, he was not yet nineteen. He was not formally crowned as Rama IX until 1950, shortly after his marriage to Sirikit, a Thai girl whom he had met when he was a student in Switzerland. Bhumibol is the only King born in the United States. His father,

THANOM KITTIKACHORN
He became Prime Minister of
Thailand at the end of 1963.

Prince Mahidol, was a physician. Mahidol was studying public health at Harvard Medical School when he met and married a student nurse who was also a lady of the royal court.

Since 1932, the King has ruled Thailand as a figurehead. Governments have been dominated by military men and have remained authoritarian. Since 1958, the Constitution and constitutionally chosen Parliament have been abandoned. The present provisional Constitution gives broad powers to the Premier. The present constituent assembly is composed almost entirely of military men, and is appointed rather than elected. The electorate is not strong and is not aware of its potential power.

Thailand's military governments have been able to act decisively; Sarit, for example, was able to inaugurate broad economic reforms without fear of opposition. Although the military governments have been characterized by corruption and by instability of leadership, they have maintained fairly consistent policies.

FOREIGN AFFAIRS

Since the end of World War II, Thai governments have been consistently pro-Western in foreign policy. Thailand sent contingents to support the United Nations action in Korea. It was also a charter member of the Southeast Asia Treaty Organization (SEATO). Between 1951 and 1961 Thailand received about $500 million of U. S. military, economic, and technical aid.

Thailand's friendship with the West is based primarily on recognition of the power of the West and the benefits of Western aid. The

WAT PHRA KEO   *These precincts of the Temple of the Emerald Buddha, which are within the walled compound of the royal Grand Palace, contain some of the most sacred objects in Thailand. In addition to the Chapel of the Emerald Buddha, there are memorials to important white elephants, a great chedi built over relics of the Buddha, statues of venerated hermits and holy men, and a depository for ancient copies of the Buddhist scriptures. The building at left is the Royal Pantheon, which is open to visitors on only one day a year. Within it are life-sized bronze figures of the former kings of the land. To the right is a yak, one of the plaster demons stationed in pairs as gatekeepers to ward off evil spirits.*

BANG PA-IN   This pavilion, an architectural gem which is the very epitome of classic Thai style, is part of the former royal summer palace. The "sky tassels" at the peak of each gable are the tails of stylized serpents, whose bodies are carved along the edges of the roof.

NET FISHING   This Thai farmer has poled his sampan out to a net which has been set up to catch the fish in the khlong, or canal. As he lets his end of the long pole rise, the flexible bamboo pieces fastened to the four corners of his net will straighten out and will thus cause the mesh to lie flat under the surface of the water. The long pole is manageable because most of its weight is sustained by the shorter upright staff which is anchored deep in the mud. When the farmer raises the net again, he may find several fish in it.

AYUTTHAYA This city was the sacred capital of the ancient kingdom of Siam. It was abandoned in 1767, after Burmese invaders looted and burned it, destroying all records of the kingdom and putting to death the king, all the members of his court, and thousands of other Siamese. Here, recently rescued from the encroaching jungles, are some of Ayutthaya's numerous temples and sacred buildings.

Thai also fear Communist China, Communist pressures in Laos, Cambodia, and South Viet Nam, and the potential spread of Communism among the large Chinese minority in Thailand. The Chinese Communists have made some efforts to exploit sources of discontent in Thai society. They have concentrated on Thailand's economically backward provinces in the northeast, provinces that were once part of the ancient kingdom of Laos. The government of Thailand is trying to forestall trouble by improving the economy of the northeast. Thus far the attempts of the Chinese Communists to subvert or alter the pro-Western policy of the Thai government have had little success. However, since Thai foreign policy is based on self-interest, drastic changes in the world scene could lead the Thai to adopt a neutralist policy.

WALTER F. VELLA

IN BRIEF

AREA	198,250 square miles. Similar in size to the combined territory of Florida, Georgia, South Carolina, and Alabama.
TERRAIN	To the imaginative eye, Thailand is shaped like an elephant's head. There are four geographically distinct regions. The fertile central region is alluvial plain watered by the Chaophraya. The southern area on the Kra Peninsula has some fertile coastal plain and mountains which extend on the west almost to the sea. In the northeast, the Khorat Plateau lies between the mountains and the Mekong River. The northwest is mostly mountainous and forested. Farms are concentrated in its river valleys.
FLORA	Bamboo, palms, bananas, teak and yang trees, and the opium poppy.
FAUNA	Crocodiles, wild boar and buffalo, snakes and leeches, bears, tigers, black panthers, elephants, monkeys, and apes are numerous. Siamese cats have become comparatively rare.

RAFTS ON THE CHAOPHRAYA
Bamboo trees have been cut in the forests and floated down Thailand's main highway, the Chaophraya River, to Bangkok and the towns of the delta region.

CLIMATE	Mostly hot and humid. Temperature ranges between 60°F. and 90°F. Rainfall reaches 160 inches a year in the west. The rainy season of the southwest monsoon—May to September —is followed by the dry and cooler season of the northeast monsoon—November to March.
CAPITAL	Bangkok (Krung Thep) and its suburbs had 1.7 million inhabitants in 1960.
OTHER CITIES	Chiangmai, 65,000; Horat, 42,000.
POPULATION	About 30 million people in 1962. Increase is close to three per cent per annum. Density is about 151 persons per square mile.
ETHNIC GROUPS	Great majority are ethnic Thai, with traces of Mons, Khmers, and primitive hill tribes. About three million Chinese; 700,-000 Malays; over 200,000 tribal and nomadic people in the hills.
LANGUAGES	Thai dialects used by 97 percent of the people. The Chinese are usually bilingual. English is frequently used in commerce.
RELIGIONS	Theravada Buddhism, with borrowings from animism, astrology, and Hinduism, is practiced by 93 percent of the populace. There are some 700,000 Muslims; 80,000 Christians.

CHULALONGKORN UNIVERSITY *Founded in 1917, this institution is Thailand's oldest and largest university. It was named in honor of the king who outlawed slavery.*

DATE OF INDEPENDENCE

On June 24, 1932, a coup d'état turned absolute rule into a constitutional monarchy; Thais were never under Western colonial rule.

FORM OF GOVERNMENT

Limited monarchy. Known as Siam before 1939 and from 1945 to 1948. Rule is neither despotic nor democratic. An Army Field Marshal, designated Prime Minister by the King, runs the government under an interim constitution. His Cabinet is largely composed of Army officers. Twenty-six coups between 1932 and 1958 have produced very few casualties. Governments have rarely been oppressive. Member of SEATO and the United Nations.

EDUCATION

In 1961, there were almost 4.5 million students with about 133,000 teachers in over 29,000 primary, secondary, and technical schools. Close to 12,000 teachers were being trained in 30 colleges. Five universities had over 51,000 students and 3,300 instructors. In 1960, about 70 percent of those over 10 were literate. Literacy is rapidly increasing.

HEALTH FACILITIES

In 1960, there were approximately 3,400 doctors, 240 dentists, 4,800 nurse-midwives, and 850 pharmacists. In 1948, life expectancy was about 50 years; since then, sanitation, health care, and malaria control have improved. The birth rate is now over five times the death rate.

CULTURAL FACILITIES

In 1960 around 20 daily newspapers had about 290,000 circulation. One person in a hundred sees a paper every day. 1,400 new books published in 1961; most dealt with history, social science, literature, and religion. Over 50 percent of the rural population and about 70 percent of Bangkok residents see a film each week. About 20 feature-length films for

WAT ARUN   The Temple of the Dawn, one of the most famous wats of the Bangkok area, is decorated with a plaster-covered brick surface which is inlaid with myriad bits of shell, pottery, and porcelain. The inlay glints and sparkles in the sun. The narrow stair leads to the top of the main prang, or tower, which permits a wondrous view of the city's skyline and river, and of the countryside beyond. Terraced levels are supported by rows of demons which alternate with much smaller angels. Sky tassels rise at the point of each gable. The "trident of Siva," a relic of Hindu influence, appears at the top of the tower on the right.

local use are produced yearly. Traditional dance-drama and music are well supported. In 1963, broadcasts in Thai, Chinese, and English emanated from 22 radio stations to about three million radios; five television stations reached a million viewers through 120,000 sets. The government-owned *Radio Thailand* transmits in English four hours a day.

CURRENCY AND FINANCE

The *baht* is valued at 0.659 grains of fine gold or 4.8¢ in U.S. currency. Government receipts in fiscal 1963 were about $414.72 million; expenditures were $461.28 million. Over 50 percent of the budget was spent for economic development, education, and public health.

INDUSTRY AND PRODUCTION

Manufacturing—chiefly the processing of crops—accounted for only 12 percent of the Gross National Product in 1962. The GNP was $2.9 billion; per capita income in 1962, about $92. GNP has been increasing by over five percent each year but, because of population increase, individual incomes rise by only 1.7 percent a year. Industrial development has been hindered by lack of electric power. The huge Yanhee Hydroelectric Project on the Ping River began to supply power in 1964.

CROPS: About 85 percent of Thais engage in agriculture; most own their land. Three-quarters of the cultivated land is in rice, in 1962 producing 9.25 million tons. The country produces almost 10 percent of the world's rubber. In 1963, the rubber crop was worth over $91 million; 750,000 tons of corn, grown mostly for export, was worth over $40 million; tapioca, $19 million. Kenaf fiber (a substitute for jute), sugar, cotton, beans, peanuts, fruit, and tobacco are important. Forest products are teak, oak, yangwood, and lac for shellac.

LIVESTOCK: Buffalo, cattle, pigs, horses, elephants, chickens, and ducks. 12,000 elephants are used in forestry; seven million buffalo in farming.

FISHERIES: In 1960, freshwater fish were estimated at 73,000 metric tons; saltwater fish, at about 150,000 metric tons. There were 4,500 fishing boats, 3,600 of them mechanized; 940 fish and shrimp processing factories. Fisheries account for 2.1 percent of the Gross National Product.

MINING: Third among the world's tin producers, in 1962 Thailand sold about 20,000 metric tons worth $32.6 million. Tungsten, iron, gypsum, lignite, and manganese are also mined. Extensive mineral reserves remain almost untouched.

TRADE

Rice, rubber, and tin accounted for about 63 percent of the 1963 exports. Corn, tapioca, kenaf, and teak also earn significant amounts. The chief imports are manufactured goods, machinery, chemicals, and fuel.

1963: IMPORTS $592,100,000
          EXPORTS $466,900,000
          DEFICIT $125,200,000

TRANSPORT

ROAD: About a quarter of the 6,600 miles of highway is paved; much rehabilitation is needed. In 1962, the 116,000 motor vehicles included about 64,000 trucks and buses. There were also about 40,000 motorcycles and scooters.

RAILROAD: The 2,200 miles of railway are being expanded and modernized. Over a third of the country's freight goes by rail.

WATERWAY: The Chaophraya, its tributaries, and about 1,000 miles of canals (*klongs*) carry a third of the country's freight. The Mekong is also navigable. Some areas are served only by waterways or elephants.

AIR: Bangkok's Don Muang, the busiest airport in Southeast Asia, is served by 23 international airlines. Thai Airways provides service from Bangkok to 15 provincial airports.

SEA: Bangkok, the chief port, is 25 miles inland on the Chaophraya. It handles 90 percent of the imports and 75 percent of the exports. Songkhla, Phuket, and Kantang handle most of the remainder.

**COMMUNI-
CATION**

In 1962, there were fewer than 50,000 telephones in use, most of them in Bangkok. External post, cable, and telegraph services are available; internal services are limited.

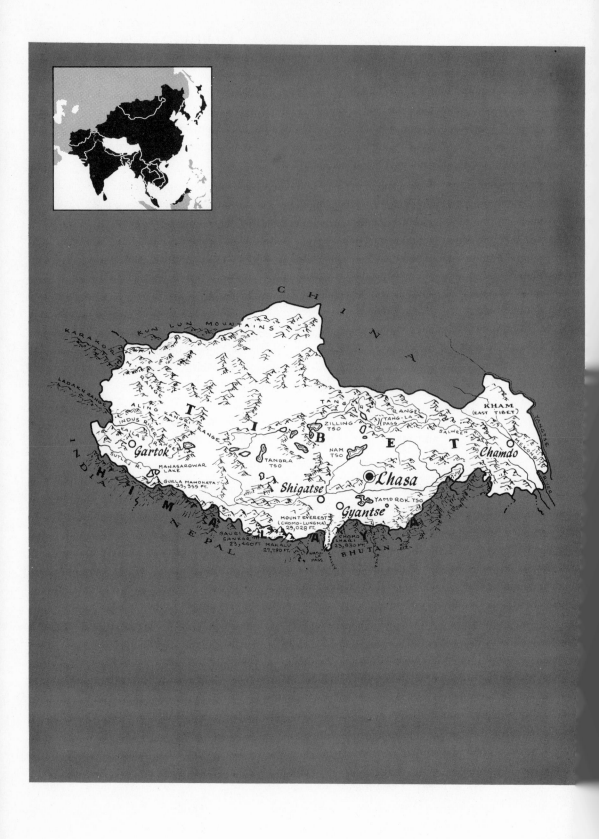

TIBET

The Roof of the World

Tibet has succeeded in capturing the Western imagination to an extent which few other countries have equaled. In large part, that is to be explained by the allure of a Forbidden Land, the exotic elements in Tibetan civilization, and the unique challenge of the Tibetan environment itself—that remote and windswept "roof of the world" where man's hardihood is put to a severe test. In the tales told of such a land, fantasy has often vanquished fact, as in the legends of "Shangri-la."

WESTERN RESPONSES TO TIBET

Reflective scholars visiting Tibet have found an added charm—the illusion of stepping back in time and experiencing life as it must have been in medieval Europe. The entire fabric of European social life was then permeated by religion no less than in Tibet. Awareness of his own heritage has helped the Westerner to understand and respond warmly to the Tibetan people. He appreciates their sturdiness, kindliness, honesty, and cheery good humor, and is particularly impressed by their consideration and care for draft animals.

CONTRASTING CHINESE ATTITUDES

In contrast, the Chinese, whose heritage has been entirely different, have always tended to look upon the Tibetan as a savage, to ridicule his way of life, and to view Tibet as a place of exile from all that makes life desirable. Today, these longstanding attitudes have been intensified by the powerful drives generated by a messianic Communism and a resurgent Chinese nationalism.

THE PLIGHT OF TIBET

Tibet, today, is being assailed as never before in the more than 13 centuries of its known history. In poignant contrast to the myriad subject peoples who have in recent years stepped forward to full nationhood, the Tibetans—a peaceful, deeply religious people—have not only lost their former independence but have been subjected to an alien military rule. Furthermore, these rulers are dedicated to atheism and are bent on stamping out the unique Tibetan way of life.

We have no certain means of ascertaining which, if any, aspects of Tibetan life have survived the Chinese onslaught. Except as otherwise noted, the description of Tibetan ways that follows must be taken to apply to the Tibet that existed just before 1950.

HISTORIC SECLUSION

Two striking aspects of Tibetan life have been, in recent centuries, the dominance of religion and the society's resistance to change. Both of these aspects have been fostered by the geographic and climatic features of the Tibetan environment.

Tibet lies on a high plateau, averaging some 15,000 to 16,000 feet in elevation. Its northern and southern borders are formed, respectively, by the Kunlun and Himalayan ranges, two of the world's most impressive mountain ranges. Almost as impressive a natural border is the river-gorge area in the east. Here the Salween, Mekong, and Yangtze rivers flow down from the Tibetan highlands, eventually making their way southward in parallel courses, forming canyons divided by sharp mountain ridges. There is no comparable natural border in the west, but distances are vast here, routes are few, and the population on both sides of the border is sparse. Thus, while Tibetan borders were by no means invasion proof—as demonstrated in turn by the Mongols, Nepalis, Dogras, British, and Chinese—they had, over the centuries, allowed Tibet an unusual degree of seclusion.

Within these borders the Tibetan terrain is far from hospitable. Nearly three-fourths of the land lies in the semi-arid Chang Tang ("northern plains") where the elevation averages nearly 17,000 feet. The eastern portion (of which Kham, the home of the warlike Khampas, is best known) consists largely of wild mountain-gorge country.

The most heavily populated area is the basin of the Tsangpo River and its tributaries. Tibet's capital city, Lhasa, lies in this area, at an altitude of 12,000 feet. The rugged and often desolate terrain, together

POTALA PALACE *Seat of the government of Tibet, this famous palace-monastery, built on a crag, rises in tiers. In March, 1959, thousands of Tibetans surrounded the palace, determined to protect the Dalai Lama from Chinese invaders. Shortly after this, the Dalai Lama fled to India.*

with the absence of roads and wheeled vehicles, contributed to Lhasa's seclusion.

A MYSTIC FAITH

In this beautiful but harsh land, man is dwarfed by nature. Not only Tibetans, but also Westerners who have traveled there, find the high altitude, thin atmosphere, raging winds, and empty immensities conducive to mystic experience. In such a land, both demons and gods can seem to have found a natural abode. In the distant past, Tibetan religion was indeed much concerned with demons. Remnants of the old religious beliefs, known as Bön, still linger, although Bön, centuries ago, largely gave way to Mahayana Buddhism, which had developed originally in India.

According to Tibetan tradition, Buddhism came to Tibet in the seventh century, during the reign of their great king, Song-tsen Gam-po, the founder of Lhasa. Under this king, Tibet became the dominant military power in Central Asia, strong enough to demand—and receive —a royal princess in marriage from both the Emperor of China and the

OUTDOOR CLASSROOM   *Tibetan refugees of all ages gather to learn to read and write. At Dalhousie, in India, they learn to read and write Hindi, using the Devanagari script.*

ruler of Nepal. Both queens were Buddhists, and it is said to be through them that this now dominant religion was first brought to Tibet and promulgated by royal edict.

Basic to the teachings of Mahayana Buddhism is the belief that the individual is destined to undergo a long series of earthly incarnations, living one life after another here on earth. Wrong actions in one life must be atoned for in later incarnations. Nirvana, or cessation of bondage to an otherwise endless series of rebirths, is to be attained only by living according to a high standard of moral conduct. To reach this final goal, the Buddha taught, involves purging the self of such sins as passion, anger, pride, hostility, and ignorance.

THE BODHISATTVA

The Mahayana ideal is the Bodhisattva, a being who has earned the right to enter Nirvana, but who compassionately refrains, accepting rebirth in order to help all sentient beings achieve enlightenment. The head of the Tibetan hierarchy, the Dalai Lama, is such a Bodhisattva. There were a number of others in Tibet, including the Panchen Lama, who was esteemed second only to the Dalai Lama.

THE LAMA GROUPS

Over the centuries, Buddhism received considerable metaphysical elaboration, and several different acceptable methods for attaining enlightenment were evolved. Several such schools took root in Tibet, each tracing its teachings to different Indian saints and mystics. The principal schools became popularly known—by the color of the hats worn by the Lamas (teachers)—as the Black sect, the Red sect, and the Yellow sect. The most influential was the Gelukpa (Virtuous People), or Yellow sect. To this reformed, celibate sect belong both the Dalai and Panchen Lamas. Fierce rivalry once characterized relations between the Red and Yellow sects, but sectarian differences do not affect the people's devotion to the Dalai Lama.

MONKS, NOBLES, AND COMMONERS

Tibetan society has been closely interwoven with lamaism. It was customary for all families to contribute at least one son to the monasteries. Monks and nuns were estimated to make up at least 10 percent of the total population. The monasteries were the principal centers of education. They had a powerful voice in running the country, and exerted, on the whole, a strong influence against change. At the same time, the monasteries represented the most democratic element in Tibetan life, offering opportunity for advancement to boys of ability, whatever their family background might be.

Society was divided into nobles and commoners. The noble families consisted mainly of descendants of the early rulers of Tibet. The ranks of the nobility were not totally determined by descent, however. Also ennobled were commoners (a) who belonged to a family into which a Dalai Lama was born; (b) who rendered unusual service to the state (as in wartime); and (c) who purchased a feudal estate where the old family line had died out.

When the Chinese attempted to gain popularity in Tibet by representing themselves as liberators of the common people from a cruel and oppressive "upper strata" and a corrupt and extortionate clergy, they had very little success. Reforms within the Tibetan social structure might seem long overdue, but the average Tibetan clearly preferred his old way of life to the "reforms" dangled before him by the Communist Chinese.

ECONOMIC ORGANIZATION

Each of the monasteries and noble families had one or more official estates from which its revenues were derived. In return, monasteries were expected to promote the welfare of the state, and a son of each noble family entered government service, without salary. The farmers on these estates held plots of land rent-free in return for services such as road work, transportation, or cultivation of the landlord's fields. Other farmers held freeholds directly from the government. These holdings could be leased, mortgaged, or even sold. Their taxes were ordinarily payable in kind. District officers received no salary, taking their pay from revenues collected in excess of those due the government.

Stores of butter, barley, and cloth were sent to Lhasa for distribution to the tax-supported monasteries. Provisions were also stored locally. In the Tibetan climate storage offered no great difficulties, and government granaries customarily held enough grain for three years. Consequently, before the Chinese Communists took over the country and emptied the granaries, famine had been unknown in Tibet.

The economy, although primitive by modern standards, was by no means unsuccessful in its own terms. The monks and lamas were denounced by the Chinese as parasites, and evicted from the monasteries. But it should not be forgotten that the lamas were teachers and that many cultural activities were carried on within the monasteries, which were also heavily involved in trade and other economic enterprises. The celibate orders also played a role in holding down the growth of the population to the point where it was in balance with the slow growth of the Tibetan economy. Tibet was free from the disastrous effects of population pressure upon scant resources. Although the system left much room for improvement, by Asian standards the average Tibetan was remarkably well housed, well clad, and well fed.

FOOD AND HOUSING

Barley, which will ripen at high altitudes, was the staple grain and basic item of food. Radishes and turnips were also grown, and some wheat where conditions permitted. Fruits and such vegetables as peas and beans were grown in sheltered valleys, but green vegetables were not greatly esteemed and were only sparingly grown. The Chinese now emphasize vegetable growing, especially cabbages. The principal sources of Tibetan wealth were their herds of sheep, goats, and yak.

The yak, a large, long-haired ox indigenous to the Tibetan plateau, was indispensable to the nomadic herdsmen, providing transport, meat, and milk products. Good use was also made of yak hides, horns, and bones. The tails, dyed red, found a ready market in India as fly whisks.

The flat-roofed farmhouses were strongly built of stone or dried brick. Supplies were stored and animals housed on the ground floor. Family quarters, above, benefited in winter from the heat generated by the animals beneath them. Chained mastiffs guarded the dwellings.

Each household provided most of its basic necessities. Women wove their own cloth. It was customary for several brothers to form a single household, sharing one wife. This kept the family estate intact and had other advantages under Tibetan conditions, where a man was frequently gone for long months on pilgrimage or on a trading expedition.

TRADE AND INDUSTRY

Nearly all Tibetans—whether nomad, villager, farmer, muleteer, monk, or noble—engaged to some extent in trade. The most important exports were gold and the high-quality Tibetan wool. Tea and rice were outstanding among imports. These products were controlled by the government. Other imports included silks and brocades from China, household goods from both China and India, and cotton cloth, iron, copper, dyestuffs, and condiments from India. Exports to China included hides, horn, and medicinal herbs. Tibetan salt was extremely important in the Indian border trade since salt is lacking throughout the southern slopes of the Himalayan range. Other Tibetan products marketed in India were bells, beads, rugs, and a square-bladed sword (*dao*) used to hack jungle clearings.

No modern industry was developed. For religious reasons, mineral resources were sparingly exploited, as the Tibetans feared that removal of minerals would impair the fertility of the soil. Recent Chinese geological surveys have reported finding a long list of minerals, notably deposits of coal, iron, graphite, and crystal. Many thousands of Chinese laborers, peasants, and soldiers are now reported to be working in Tibet. Thousands of miles of roads have been constructed, but the Tibetans report that these roads are for military use and do not benefit the Tibetan people.

THE ART OF TIBET

Tibetan culture has absorbed influences from both India and China. Indian influence has been more pervasive, but often reached Tibet only after modifications had been introduced in Kashmir or Nepal.

The Tibetans took over the Indian alphabet in use in Kashmir in the seventh century. This handsome script is no longer in use in India, but has been handed down from one generation to the next in Tibet, virtually unchanged, although the spoken language—especially the Lhasa dialect—has altered considerably during this period.

Tibetan literature, although predominantly concerned with religion and philosophy, includes works on such subjects as geography and history. Poetry falls largely into one of two categories: either folk verse or hymns and other religious poems. A prominent exception is the lyric poetry written by the sixth Dalai Lama, a gifted poet with a reputation as a libertine.

Tibetan painting was exclusively religious in theme and symbolism, which were characteristically Indian. On the other hand, these paintings are often set in landscapes which are handled in Chinese style. Indian sculptural canons of the Pala and Gupta periods, originally

brought to Tibet by Nepali craftsmen who settled in Lhasa, have remained in use. Tibetan bronze work is patterned closely on the high-quality work developed in Nepal.

In architecture, Tibet has developed a distinctive style. The magnificent Potala palace-monastery in Lhasa is world renowned. Similar but more modest structures were built throughout Tibet. These monasteries, built on crags, were both aesthetically impressive and highly functional; they also served as forts, local treasuries, and granaries.

POPULAR ARTS AND CRAFTS

Folk crafts included engraving, block-printing, and metal work. Copper, brass, and silver were often used in combination to make utensils—including bowls and beer-mugs—of a striking and distinctive Tibetan style. One unusual craft used human bones in making articles believed to possess strong magical powers.

FEMALE YAK WITH HER YOUNG The yak provides hides, milk, meat, wool, and transportation.

Tibetan dances are masked pantomimes which dramatically and colorfully reinforce the teachings of religion and morality. The dancers are always male. The principal musical instruments are drums, cymbals, clarinets, oboes, gongs, bells, and, above all, trumpets of many kinds— small ones of silver, larger ones of human thigh bones, and most striking of all, the famous deep-toned brass trumpets (sometimes 18 feet long), too heavy to be supported by a single man.

GOVERNMENTAL SYSTEM

For over 300 years, the supreme ruler of Tibet has been the Dalai Lama, in whose person spiritual and temporal rule were united. The first Dalai Lama, whose powers were spiritual only, is traced back to the 15th century· The "Great Fifth" Dalai Lama (1617–1682), who was unusually able, became a dominant figure politically as well as spiritually. The ascendancy of the Dalai Lama has in more recent times become a major unifying factor in Tibetan politics. The Dalai Lama who was forced to flee his country in 1959 is the fourteenth in this line.

In his task of governing the country, a Dalai Lama had two specially trained service corps, one consisting of 175 nobles and the other of 175 monks. He was also assisted by two Prime Ministers, one a monk and the other a layman. His *Kashag,* or Cabinet, consisted of one monk and three lay officials.

There were also two parallel secretariats: the *Yig-tsang,* dealing with religious affairs and headed by four monks, and the *Tse-khang,* or Finance Office, directed by four laymen. Each administrative department—as, for example, foreign affairs, agriculture, taxation—had two chairmen, one a monk and the other a layman.

This dualism, established centuries ago in an effort to insure a balance between the monasteries and the nobility, extended even to the offices of Chief Justice and municipal judge. From the judgment of these officials there always existed the right of appeal to the Dalai Lama himself, who was considered to be the incarnation of mercy.

THE NATIONAL ASSEMBLY

A *Tsong-du,* or National Assembly, met to consider matters of national importance, as for example the appointment of a Regent after the death of a Dalai Lama. This Regent would run the country until a new Dalai Lama was found and grew to maturity.

A nuclear group of the full Assembly, consisting of the eight *Yig-tsang* and *Tse-khang* officials and perhaps a dozen other important monks and lay officials, was almost constantly in session. This group could convene a somewhat larger number—about 30—to consider specific problems. The full Assembly of some 400 was called into session only on matters of high importance.

THE SEARCH FOR A DALAI LAMA

After the death of a Dalai Lama and the appointment of a lama Regent, a search for the Dalai Lama's new incarnation began in due course. The region where the rebirth had taken place was first determined, if possible, through various signs and portents. Sometimes the late Dalai Lama's utterances had given some useful hint. The lamas entrusted with the search—usually persons closely associated with the previous Dalai Lama—also consulted the State Oracle and sought visions by gazing at the waters of a sacred lake.

Once the area of rebirth had been narrowed down, boys born at the appropriate time were sought out and tested for their ability to

CONFERENCE   *The Dalai Lama (left) plays host to the Panchen Lama (who had been in Chinese hands since boyhood) when both young Lamas were in Peking in 1956. During their stay in Peking the Dalai Lama was made Chairman, and the Panchen Lama and a Chinese official made Vice-Chairmen, of a "Preparatory Committee for the Tibet Autonomous Region." This arrangement constituted one of many infringements of the 1951 Agreement between Tibet and China, and allowed Tibet no true autonomy, despite its misleading name and profuse Chinese promises.*

select from a number of persons and articles those which had been associated with the late Dalai Lama. This ability was considered decisive, since only a true Bodhisattva—who had freely chosen to be reborn —was believed able to recall the details of his earlier life.

The search committee kept careful records, placing their findings before the full National Assembly, which alone could issue the formal declaration that the Dalai Lama had been discovered. The child, normally about four or five years old at this time, was then enthroned in Lhasa. The Regent continued in power while the young Dalai Lama was being educated by private tutors in preparation for his duties. At 18 he came of age and was formally installed as supreme ruler.

THE FOURTEENTH DALAI LAMA

The present Dalai Lama was born in the summer of 1935. His parents were peasants in a farming community in the northeast part of Tibet, near the famous Kumbum monastery. This part of Tibet was under Chinese rule, and difficulties were placed in the way of the child's removal to Lhasa. This was in the end managed through the payment of a considerable bribe to the local Chinese warlord. The Dalai Lama was formally installed in 1940, charming European observers and Tibetans alike with his poise and dignified demeanor.

Fortunately for his country, the boy displayed unusual ability. Therefore, when the Chinese Army attacked Tibet in the fall of 1950, the decision was reached to unify the country by installing the young Dalai Lama with full powers, although he was at the time only 16. (We would consider him only 15, but the Tibetans follow the East Asian system of reckoning a child's age as one year at birth.)

The ensuing years, as he related in his autobiography, were to prove extremely difficult for the young ruler. Despite his best efforts, a crisis involving a direct confrontation between the Chinese military rulers and the Tibetan people could not be averted. There was reason to believe that the Chinese intended, by one means or another, to reduce the Dalai Lama to the status of a Chinese puppet. Had this happened, the smoldering spark of Tibetan independence might indeed have been extinguished. Instead, the Dalai Lama provided fresh inspiration to his people with his successful escape into exile in India.

TIBET'S STATUS IN THE MODERN WORLD

The question of Tibet's international position first came to world attention in 1950. Mao Tse-tung's armies then stood poised on the Tibetan border, and the Tibetans sought the aid of the United Nations.

The Chinese possess a basic conviction that the superiority of their civilization gives them valid title—whenever they are strong enough to enforce it—to all outlying areas which have ever been in a subordinate relation to the Chinese Empire at its zenith. Indeed, they seem to carry this conviction of superiority to the point of believing that any relations whatever could only have been of subordination to the greatness of China. The Tibetans, on the other hand, have an equal conviction of their own independent identity, whatever misfortunes they may temporarily have been forced to endure.

Most of the rest of the world had, before 1950, given the matter little thought. When the question was then taken in hand, it soon appeared that the complex realities of Central Asian relationships do not readily fit into the categories familiar to present-day international law. Given both legal tangles and the enormous physical difficulties involved in aiding landlocked Tibet, the United Nations finally accepted the optimistic Indian view that a peaceful solution would soon be forthcoming and shelved further consideration of the matter. It was not to be taken up again for nine years.

Meanwhile, Tibet's brave but hopelessly overmatched army was quickly routed. On May 23, 1951, Tibetan representatives had no choice but to accept a treaty which did away with their nation's sovereignty under ostensible guarantees that the Tibetans could continue to run their internal affairs in their own way, and that no changes would be made in the Dalai Lama's status. These guarantees soon proved illusory.

The Dalai Lama, aware of the probable tragic consequences of rebellion, bent his efforts toward easing the situation where possible, while keeping the people calm. Nevertheless, by early 1956, rebellion flared in the eastern province of Kham and spread to Lhasa as the Chinese tried to enforce Communist "reforms" throughout Tibet. The situation became so difficult that the Dalai Lama, when he visited India later in the year for the celebration of the 2,500th anniversary of the Buddha's birth, told Prime Minister Nehru that he wished to remain in India, in exile.

The Indian Prime Minister discussed the matter in detail with the Dalai Lama, urging him to go back to Tibet. Nehru also discussed Tibetan affairs at considerable length with Premier Chou En-lai, who was also in New Delhi. Assurances were given by the Chinese Premier that Tibet was considered an autonomous region, that it was "absurd" for anyone to imagine that China was going to force Communism on Tibet, and that all reforms would be postponed for a considerable time. The Dalai Lama had little faith in Chinese promises, but after carefully weighing the situation, he concluded that the Chinese must be given one more chance to keep their word. He returned to Lhasa, but only to find that the latest Chinese promises had no more validity than the earlier ones. Both Chinese pressures and Tibetan rebellion soon regained momentum.

THE DALAI LAMA'S ESCAPE

Matters came to a head in March, 1959, when the Chinese military commandant invited the Dalai Lama to visit a theatrical show at the Chinese camp, but insisted that he must come without his usual armed bodyguard, and that the visit be kept strictly secret. These unusual requests could scarcely be kept secret, and suspicion of Chinese motives reached a fever pitch. The populace of Lhasa, convinced that the Chinese intended to remove the Dalai Lama secretly to Peking, surrounded his palace en masse in an effort to protect his person. The situation moved rapidly from crisis to crisis. In the end the Dalai Lama, hoping to avert a general massacre, hurriedly made a dramatic escape in disguise, aided by loyal guerrilla fighters. Forty-eight hours after he had left, and before the Chinese had discovered he had gone, they shelled his palace and then turned their artillery on the city and the nearby monasteries, killing thousands of defenseless Tibetans.

The Chinese were unable to prevent the escape of the Dalai Lama, however. Decoys and false trails kept his route secret. In a monastery in the mountain fastnesses, the Dalai Lama formed a new, temporary government which was consecrated with traditional religious rites. He formally denounced the 1951 Treaty with China—all of the provisions of which had been broken by the Chinese—and issued a proclamation of the establishment of his new government. It was clear, however, that he could not safely remain in Tibet. On March 30, he crossed the Indian border, where he received asylum.

APPEAL TO THE WORLD

Once more the question of Tibet came before the United Nations, this time on the appeal of the Dalai Lama. The Chinese protested, insisting that Tibetan affairs were purely an internal Chinese matter. The U.N. resolution that was finally adopted, on October 21, 1959, did not face that question squarely, nor did it specifically mention China. It did call for "respect for the fundamental rights of the Tibetan people and for their distinctive cultural and religious life."

A legal inquiry was set in motion by the International Commission of Jurists—a non-governmental organization—which established a committee composed of judges, professors, and legal practitioners of high standing from various parts of Asia, Africa, and Europe. This Legal Inquiry Committee on Tibet issued a unanimous report of its findings in August, 1960. The Committee concluded that the Chinese were guilty of genocide against Tibetans as a religious group, and had also violated 16 articles dealing with human rights. Tibet, the Committee concluded, had been at the very least a *de facto* independent state when the agreement with China was signed in 1951, and Tibetan repudiation of the agreement was fully justified by Chinese violation of the undertakings set forth in it.

In view of the fact that the United Nations was one of the bodies to which the report was submitted, it is of particular interest that the report declared that Tibet was the legitimate concern of the United

Nations. The report, however, failed to lead to any significant action on behalf of Tibet. As the Secretary-General of the International Commission of Jurists pointed out in a foreword to this report, the only force at the disposal of either the Committee or the Commission was the force of ideas—a force which "may or may not ultimately prevail."

PLANS FOR THE FUTURE

The Dalai Lama, now still in India, looks to the time when Chinese rule will decay. We have no exact figures as to the number of Tibetans who share his exile, but there may be as many as 100,000, most of whom are living in India, Nepal, Bhutan, and Sikkim. A few are living in European countries, particularly Switzerland, and a handful can be found in the United States. The continued education of the children in accordance with their Tibetan heritage is a project upon which the Dalai Lama lays great importance.

In 1963, on the fourth anniversary of the uprising in Lhasa, the Dalai Lama published his blueprint for the establishment of constitutional government in Tibet, under the guiding principles of religion. In this document—Tibet's first written Constitution—the Dalai Lama has codified and extended his earlier efforts at reform. He has faith that on this foundation there will arise a new Tibet, open to the world, and "as happy in the modern world as old Tibet was in its isolation." Meanwhile, the Dalai Lama's faith nourishes his people's hope.

MARGARET W. FISHER

IN BRIEF

AREA
Estimated at 470,000 to 500,000 square miles, larger than Texas, Oklahoma, and New Mexico combined.

TERRAIN
A high mountainous plateau with an average elevation of 16,000 feet, with highlands in the west, the Kunlun Mountains to the north, and the Himalaya to the south. The river valleys of the south central area are more productive than the arid plateau, which is suitable only for grazing. Ridges and deep river gorges characterize the eastern border region.

MOTHER AND CHILD

LITTLE BOY

LITTLE GIRL

YOUNG WOMAN

(*Courtesy P. P. Karan and University of Kentucky Himalayan Expedition.*)

FLORA Scanty forests of birch, poplar, maple, walnut in the south. Most of the land is high plateau with sparse alpine and desert vegetation.

FAUNA Wild yak, antelope, sheep, goat, ass, marsh deer, bears, wolves, foxes, duck, and pheasant.

CLIMATE Strong winds and low rainfall (the average is only eight inches a year) combine to produce arid or semi-arid conditions through most of Tibet. The temperature of Lhasa (situated in a small river valley at 12,000 feet) varies between 5°F. in winter and a high of 80°F. in summer. Upland plateau temperatures rarely reach 65°F. in summer. Lows of −27°F. have been recorded.

CAPITAL Before 1950, Lhasa was estimated to have about 50,000 inhabitants, including 20,000 lamas, or monks.

OTHER CITIES Shigatse, with possibly 12,000 people in 1952; Gyantse, with 8,000.

POPULATION Estimates vary between one and one-half million and six million; three million people, or about six persons per square mile, may not be far wrong.

ETHNIC GROUPS Tibetans, whose origins are little known, have been united in language and culture for at least a thousand years. An unknown number of Chinese have been settled on the land since 1951.

RELIGION A form of Mahayana Buddhism, sometimes referred to—although not by Tibetans—as Lamaism. Tibetan life has long been completely dominated by Buddhism, although traces of an ancient animist faith called Bön can still be found.

DATE OF INDEPENDENCE In 1910, a Chinese army invaded Lhasa and took over the administration. In 1912, the Tibetans expelled all Chinese officials. From 1912 to 1951, Tibet exercised all the powers of a fully independent nation. On May 23, 1951, after their army had been routed, the Tibetans signed a treaty with China surrendering their independence but obtaining guarantees of internal autonomy. In March, 1951, the Dalai Lama's government denounced the 1951 treaty, stating that all its provisions had been broken by the Chinese. The Dalai Lama and his officially reconsecrated government fled to India.

FORM OF GOVERNMENT

Tibet is currently administered by China as one of the "Autonomous Regions of Nationalities." Under the Tibetan system, the Dalai Lama, the foremost of a number of reincarnating lamas, was supreme temporal and spiritual ruler. He was assisted by ministers and an executive council of high-ranking monks and laymen. A National Assembly was summoned when decisions had to be taken on particularly important matters. On the death of a Dalai Lama, the Assembly appointed a Regent. The findings of the search committee which discovered the identity of the new Dalai Lama were also placed before the Assembly, which alone could issue the formal declaration of discovery. The Dalai Lama was then installed, but the Regent continued to rule until the Dalai Lama reached majority at age 18.

EDUCATION

There are 78 primary schools in Tibet, and in Lhasa, one school roughly comparable to a high school. It is reported that about 10,000 Tibetans attend schools. Traditional education was directed chiefly toward religious needs; all monks and nobles as well as numbers of townspeople—perhaps a quarter of the population—were literate.

HEALTH FACILITIES

To some extent modern medical practice had been accepted by the people of Lhasa prior to 1950; a small British hospital had been used by the more sophisticated. Conservative religious opinion was frequently against medical innovation, but certain techniques, notably vaccination, gained wide acceptance.

CULTURAL FACILITIES

In the complete absence of newspapers, public opinion was molded by songs and lampoons and an occasional anonymous poster. All forms of art, drama, and scholarship were closely tied to religion; most cultural activities were carried on by monks in monasteries.

CURRENCY AND FINANCE

The *sang* fluctuates in value; 6.5 *sangs* equaled an Indian *rupee* during 1964, about 21¢ in U. S. currency. Monasteries served as banks for both currency and produce. Since government accounts, taxes, and budget functions were neither entirely monetary nor entirely secular, budget data are irrelevant. The Chinese occupation force has not released later data.

MONKS CHANTING
Standing in their yellow woolen hats and ceremonial robes, these monks are singing to the accompaniment of cymbals.

OLD MAN   His prayer wheel and rosary are commonly used by Mahayana Buddhists. He twirls the cylinder around and around; it is believed to send a new prayer to heaven with each rotation. (Courtesy P. P. Karan and University of Kentucky Himalayan Expedition.)

INDUSTRY AND PRODUCTION

OCCUPATIONS: Largely farming and herding, accompanied by handicrafts, especially metal work and weaving. Nearly everyone had some interest in trade.

MODERN INDUSTRY: None, prior to 1960, when the Chinese reported that Tibet's first iron and steel plant had begun to produce molten iron. A cement factory, farm implement plants, motor vehicle repair shops, and other modern facilities are reported to be in operation.

CROPS: Barley, wheat, peas, beans, buckwheat.

LIVESTOCK: Sheep, goats, yak, horses.

MINING: Small-scale surface mining of gold, salt, and borax was carried on by Tibetans; mineral resources—especially coal, iron, graphite, crystal, and copper—have been reported by Chinese surveys, and are presumably now being exploited.

TRADE   Exports were chiefly wool, hides, livestock, gold, medicinal herbs, and salt; imports were tea, rice, silk and cotton textiles, iron, copper, dyestuffs, condiments, and household goods. Balance of trade was usually favorable, with exports estimated at about $700,000 a year. Trade is now monopolized by the Chinese, with disruption of long-established trading patterns. The once-important border trade with India and Nepal was choked off after 1959, but was reopened in the summer of 1962 after a customs house had been established for Tibet.

TRANSPORT   ROAD: Until 1954, when the Chinese completed a motor road to Lhasa, all transport was by caravans of horses, yak, goats, or sometimes sheep. Since 1954, roads through Shigatse, Gyantse, and Gartok have been completed, and Lhasa connected by highway to Katmandu, Nepal.

RAILROAD: The Chinese have attempted to extend their railway system to Lhasa, but, so far as is known, without success.

WATERWAY: Coracles of yak hide were used to cross rivers and small boats plied the streams.

AIR: Air service between Lhasa and China is operated by the Chinese government.

SEA: Any ocean freight must be transshipped through China or across the Himalayas.

**COMMUNI-
CATION**   Lhasa and Shigatse have a public telephone system. The British-built post and telegraph facilities linking Tibet with India were handed over to the Chinese in 1954. The Chinese claim to have quadrupled the number of post and telegraph stations. Tibetans say the new communications services are for military purposes only.

GLOSSARY

A-AK Ancient Korean royal court music, still preserved and heard today.

AJANTA A series of caves in central India decorated with mural paintings and carvings dating from the second century B.C. to the seventh century A.D.

ANGKOR WAT Ancient temple in Cambodia where Brahma and, later, Buddha were worshiped.

ANIMISM Primitive belief that spiritual forces are embodied in natural phenomena; still practiced in many areas of Asia.

ANNAM Former name for Viet Nam.

ANURADHAPURA Ancient capital of Ceylon, founded in 437 B.C., and a leading Buddhist center for centuries.

ARAKANESE Spoken language of the Chittagong Hill Tracts of East Pakistan.

ARYANS A distinctive ethnic group. Tribal peoples who moved from distant Asia into Afghanistan and India long before the Christian era.

ASOKA'S WHEEL "The Wheel of the Law," the symbol of Buddhism. Carved on one of the pillars erected by King Asoka to record the edicts of the Buddha, this symbol is used on the national flag of India.

ASSAM Region of extreme northeastern India.

ASSAMESE A language of East Pakistan and northeastern India.

AYUDHYA Former capital of Siam (Thailand) founded in 1350, situated 40 miles north of Bangkok.

BAMIYAN Valley in central Afghanistan, long a center of Buddhism, with huge statues of the Buddha and decorated cave-temples.

BENGALI The major language of East Pakistan and the adjacent areas of India. *Also* A native or resident of Bengal.

BHIKKU A Buddhist monk of Ceylon.

BHOODAN In India, the "land-gift" movement begun in 1951 by A. V. Bhave. He and his followers walked from village to village requesting donations of farming land which were then distributed to landless peasants.

BHUTIAS Natives of Bhutan and Sikkim, of Tibetan origin. Also called Bhutanese, Drukpas.

BO TREE The tree under which the Buddha attained enlightenment.

BODHISATTVA A being destined to be ultimately reborn as a Buddha.

575

Glossary

BÖN The ancient pre-Buddhist cult of Tibet.

BONZE A Buddhist monk of China and Japan.

BRAHMA The "Creator" of the Hindu Trinity of Gods; the supreme godhead of Hinduism.

BRAHMINS Members of the highest Hindu caste.

BUDDHA The "Enlightened One." Prince Gautama, born in India about 563 B.C., left his palace and his family at the age of 29 to lead a religious life. Six years later he received enlightenment and for 45 years preached his message of human salvation.

BUDDHISM Faith developed from the teachings of the Buddha. It stresses the renunciation of materialistic goals and the pleasures of the senses, and emphasizes a deliberate striving to attain the complete peace of mind that results in the recognition of ultimate reality, or *nirvana*.

BURGHER In Ceylon, a descendant of a marriage between a European man and a Ceylonese woman.

BURNING GHAT A platform on which bodies of Hindus are cremated.

CAO DAI A politico-religious sect in South Viet Nam. An amalgamation of Eastern and Western religions, with an overlay of spiritualism, it claims over one million followers.

CARDAMOM Seeds of herbs used to prepare aromatics and stimulants.

CASTE A hereditary class distinction. In Hinduism, the four broad divisions are, in descending order of prestige, Brahmins (priests), Kshatriyas (warriors), Vaishyas (commoners), and Sudras (serfs).

CEYLON MOOR A Muslim long settled in Ceylon.

CHADRI The veil traditionally worn in public by Muslim women.

CHAMPA Ancient Kingdom of Indo-China.

CHAMS Muslims of southern Viet Nam and Cambodia.

CHINS Tribal peoples of East Pakistan, Assam, and western Burma.

CHONDOKYO An eclectic religion of Korea. The "Sect of the Heavenly Way," it was founded in the mid-nineteenth century by an apostate Catholic, and now claims over one million adherents.

COCHIN CHINA Former name of several provinces of South Viet Nam, so called by the French occupiers. One of the world's great rice-growing regions.

Glossary

COLOMBO PLAN The Consultative Committee for Economic Development in South and Southeast Asia, with 17 nations as its members. Established in 1950.

COMMONWEALTH OF NATIONS A voluntary association of some 20 nations which acknowledge the monarch of the United Kingdom as head of the Commonwealth. Many members are former British colonies. The term came into use in 1949.

CONFUCIANISM A secular philosophy derived from the teachings of Confucius, who lived in China in the sixth century B.C. He believed that each person should live in accordance with the duties imposed on him by his rank in society.

DAGOBA *See* Stupa.

DALAI LAMA The ruler of Tibet and the head of the Buddhist Yellow Hat Order in his successive incarnations.

DARI The form of the Persian language that is used in Afghanistan.

DECCAN Historical term for the southern half of the Indian subcontinent.

DERVISH Member of a Muslim religious order; *also* a religious mendicant.

DEVANAGARI The alphabet usually employed in writing Sanskrit and various vernacular languages of India; also called Nagari.

DHARMA RAJA Buddhist spiritual leader of Bhutan. Succession was dependent upon proof of reincarnation. The last *Dharma Raja* died 35 years ago.

DIEN BIEN PHU Town in North Viet Nam, site of disastrous defeat of a French force in 1954.

DRAVIDIAN An aboriginal inhabitant of the Indian subcontinent.

DRAVIDIAN LANGUAGES A language family in India, Ceylon, and West Pakistan with no established relationship to any other.

DRUK KARGUPA Red Hat Buddhist sect.

DRUKPAS *See* Bhutias.

DUARS Eight- to ten-mile deep band of plains and river valleys in Bhutan, bordering the Assam-Bengal plains of India. They control access to the strategic passes through the Himalayan foothills.

DURAND LINE Border between Afghanistan and British India established in 1893.

DYAK A name given by Malayans to an aboriginal of Borneo.

577

Glossary

DZONG Buddhist castle-monastery.

EIGHTFOLD PATH Proclaimed by the Buddha, offers eight ways of right acting and right thinking: right views, right aspirations, right speech, right living, right effort, right thought, right action, and right concentration.

EMERALD BUDDHA Figure in the Phra Keo temple at Bangkok, Thailand.

FOUR NOBLE TRUTHS Proclaimed by Buddha, the fourth is the Eightfold Path (*quod vide*). Others are the truth of infelicity, the truth of the cause of infelicity, and the truth of the cessation of infelicity.

GAUTAMA The name of the prince who became Buddha. *See* Buddha.

GOBI Vast, sandy desert in China and Mongolia.

GUJARATI Language of the old province, or region, of Gujarat in West Pakistan, and of a larger adjacent area of India, spoken by about 16 million people.

GURKHAS Hindu people of Gurkha Province in Nepal.

GURU Spiritual preceptor of Hindus.

HAKKA A people of southeastern China who intruded from the north about 1,000 A.D. (the name means "alien clans"); *also* their dialect.

HANAFI SUNNI Orthodox Muslim sect.

HARAPPA Ancient city site on the Indus River.

HINAYANA The "Lesser Vehicle," a development of Buddhist thought and doctrine which is more conservative and closer to the teachings of the Buddha than is the Mahayana, or "Great Vehicle."

HINDI A language of India, spoken by some 80 million people, and written in the Devanagari script.

HINDUISM The assimilative religion of the Indian subcontinent, with many deities.

HINDUSTANI A major language of India, called *Hindi* when spoken in India and *Urdu* when used by the Muslims of West Pakistan. Spoken by about 86 million people. *See* Hindi and Urdu.

HOA HAO A radical Buddhist reform movement in South Viet Nam, founded in 1939.

HUJREH Quarters for male guests in West Pakistan.

IBAN *See* Dyak.

Glossary

IMAMI A Muslim sect.

INDO-CHINA A term introduced by the French in the nineteenth century to designate their colonies comprised of Viet Nam, Cambodia, and Laos.

JAIN A follower of Jainism, a religion of India that resembles Buddhism and has one million adherents.

JATAKAS A vast collection of stories concerned with the various incarnations of the Buddha.

JUNK A seagoing sailing vessel.

KACHINS A people of Burma.

KADAZANS Also Dusun, inhabitants of Sabah in Malaysia.

KAFIRS *See* Nuristanis.

KALI Hindu goddess, fond of blood sacrifices.

KANA A system of syllabic writing developed in Japan in the eighth or ninth century as better suited to the pronunciation of Japanese than was the Chinese script formerly used.

KANNADA Ancient Hindu Philosopher.

KARAKUL The breed of sheep in Afghanistan which produces so-called Persian lamb skins.

KARENS A people of Burma.

KARIZ Underground tunnel used for irrigation in Afghanistan.

KASHMIRI The Indic language of Kashmir; *also,* inhabitants of Kashmir.

KHA Dominant tribe of Nepal; a military people of the Kshatriya caste. *Also* An aborigine of Laos.

KHAMPAS A warlike people of Kham, in Tibet.

KHMER EMPIRE The Empire of Cambodia from early in the Christian era into the fourteenth century.

KSHATRIYA An upper Hindu caste traditionally engaged in government and military occupations.

KUK-AK Korean folk music.

LAC Wax exuded by an insect, used to make a red dye and, when dissolved in alcohol, shellac.

LACQUER Varnish made from the sap of the sumac tree.

LAMA Buddhist monk of Tibet. Western form of the title *bla-ma.*

LAMASERY Western term applied to the Buddhist monasteries of Tibet.

LAO The major language of Laos. *Also* A Buddhist people living in Laos and adjacent parts of Thailand. Also called Loatian.

LEPCHA A Mongoloid people of Sikkim and the Darjeeling district of India; *also* their language.

LOLO A people inhabiting the southwestern borderland of China. Of Mongolian origin, they speak Tibeto-Burman tongues.

LONGHOUSE In Borneo, a dwelling occupied by all the members of a village.

MAHARAJA Title of ruler of the former princely states of India.

MAHAYANA The "Great Vehicle," a major development of Buddhist thought and doctrine. *See* Hinayana.

MALAY SULTANS Rulers of nine hereditary states within Malaya.

MALAYALAM A Dravidian language of southern India; an offshoot of Tamil.

MAN A minority people of North Viet Nam.

MANDARIN The nine grades of officials of the Chinese empire. Promotion was based on passing civil service examinations on the literary classics. Grades were denoted by different colored buttons on the hats of office. *Also* The dialect of Chinese spoken in North China; the present national

language, although originally the dialect of Peking; spoken by at least 300 million people.

MARATHI A language of India, spoken at Bombay and its vicinity by some 21 million people.

MEO A minority people of North Viet Nam.

MOGHUL A dynasty of Muslim Kings which ruled India from the sixteenth until the nineteenth century.

MOHENJO DARO An ancient city site on the Indus River.

MON A people of Burma; *also* their language.

MON EMPIRE A medieval kingdom of lower Burma.

MON-KHMER LANGUAGES A language group of the Indo-China peninsula.

MONTAGNARDS French for mountain people, applied to the hill tribes of Indo-China.

MOOR *See* Ceylon Moor.

MOSLEM *See* Muslim.

MU'ANG THAI The "Land of the Thai," the local name for Thailand.

MUEZZIN The man who calls Muslims to perform their prayers.

Glossary

MUSLIM Adherent to the religon of Islam. There are about 120 million Muslims in the countries included in this book.

NAGA SYMBOL In India, a headgear made of a crown of cobra heads.

NAGARI *See* Devanagari.

NAGAS Devils or demons (serpents), allegedly the earliest inhabitants of Ceylon. *Also* Members of a tribe in the Naga Hills of Assam.

NEGRITOS Dwarfish Negroid people of Southeast Asia and Oceania.

NIRVANA *See* Buddhism.

NUNG A tribe of North Viet Nam.

NURISTANIS A small tribal group of Afghanistan, called *Kafirs* (infidels) before their conversion to Islam in the late nineteenth century.

ONMUN The Korean alphabet.

ORIYA The language of Orissa, in India; closely related to Bengali.

OUTCASTES Casteless people in India who are denied all social rights and perform the most menial tasks; the "untouchables."

PADDY The wet field in which rice is grown; *also* the harvested rice before it is milled.

PAGODA A temple.

PAKHTUNS Also Pushtuns. A tribal people of eastern Afghanistan and West Pakistan.

PALI The language in which early Buddhist scriptures were written; not spoken today.

PANCHEN LAMA Tibetan Buddhist prelate, second in rank only to the Dalai Lama.

PARSIS Zoroastrians living in India and Pakistan.

PATHANS Tribal people of West Pakistan and Afghanistan. *See* Pushtuns.

PATHET LAO A Communist-oriented group in Laos.

PHNONG Highland tribesmen of Cambodia.

PUKHTUNWALI The unwritten "Code of the Hills" in Afghanistan.

PUNJABI Language of the region of the Punjab, now divided between India and Pakistan; spoken by about 30 million people. *Also* A native of the Punjab.

PURDAH The seclusion of women in Muslim society.

Glossary

PUSHTU Language of the Pushtuns (Pakhtuns, Pathans) of Afghanistan and West Pakistan; spoken by about 16 million people.

PUSHTUNISTAN The name given by the government of Afghanistan to the area of West Pakistan inhabited by Pushtuns.

PUSHTUNS Also Pakhtuns and Pathans. Tribal people of eastern Afghanistan and West Pakistan.

QUININE A drug, specific against malaria, made from the bark of the quininetree.

QUOC NGU The Vietnamese language written in Latin characters.

RAJ British. The period of British authority in India.

RAJA Tribal chief of ancient India, later equivalent to "prince."

RAMADAN The lunar month in which Muslims fast from sunrise until sunset.

RAMAYANA One of the two great Sanskrit epics of ancient India. Composed about 500 B.C., it contains 24,000 couplets and covers the life and deeds of the deity Rama.

SAKI Beer made from rice, popular in Japan.

SAMPAN Small, shallow-craft boat, usually poled or sculled.

SANSKRIT Ancient literary language of the Indian subcontinent.

SCHEDULED CASTES Euphemism for the outcastes of India, formerly called the "untouchables."

SHAMAN Healer or diviner, controller of the spiritual forces of nature. *See* Animism.

SHAN A people of eastern Burma.

SHELLAC *See* Lac.

SHI'A A sect of Islam.

SHINTO The indigenous religious cult of Japan, a complex of ancient Japanese folk beliefs and rituals that was put into definite form in the eighth century A.D.

SHIVAISM Religion of the worshipers of Shiva, an ancient divinity of southern India.

SIKHS Adherents of the Sikh religion, an offshoot of Hinduism founded in the seventeenth century. It differs from Hinduism in being monotheistic and in its renunciation of castes.

SINHALESE The major group of the inhabitants of Ceylon and the name of their language.

SIVA *See* Shivaism.

Glossary

SLASH - AND - BURN AGRICULTURE
The clearing of forests for planting crops; widely practiced, and with different terms used locally.

SON OF HEAVEN Title of the Emperors of Japan.

STUPA An edifice built over a relic of the Buddha.

SUDRA Lowest of the four Hindu castes.

SUKHOTAI A kingdom of Thailand from 1219 until 1350.

SUNNI The orthodox sect of Islam. *See* Hanafi Sunni

SUTTA, OR SUTRA Aphorisms, discourses, and scriptures of the several religions of India.

TAI *See* Thai.

TAMIL Language of southeastern India and northern Ceylon, spoken by about 25 million people. *Also* A Tamil-speaking person.

TAOISM A religious system of China, founded on the teaching of Lao Tze, who wrote the *Tao Te Ching* around 500 B.C. Emphasis is placed on ethical conduct.

TELEGU An important Dravidian language of southern India, spoken by some 35 million people. *Also* One of a Dravidian people of Andhra Pradesh

State in India.

TERAI A swampy, lowland belt in India, north of the Ganges River, at the foot of the Himalayas.

THAI A language group that includes Siamese and Annamese. *Also* Tribes in Burma and Thailand comprising the Laos, Shan, and Siamese (Thai).

THERAVADA *See* Hinayana.

THO An agricultural tribal people of North Viet Nam.

TIBETO-BURMAN A language group of the Indo-Chinese family of languages.

TONKIN Gulf, an arm of the South China Sea. *Also* Older name of a region of North Viet Nam.

TRANH A coarse grass covering plateau ground; sometimes stands six feet high.

TRANSHUMANCE Seasonal migrations of nomads, with their livestock, between lowlands and mountains.

TRIPITAKA Any one of the three great divisions of Buddhist scriptures. One division deals with philosophy and tradition, one with discipline, and one contains metaphysical discourses and enumerates personal duties.

UNTOUCHABLES The outcastes of India, *quod vide*.

583

Glossary

URDU A national language of Pakistan, spoken by six million people in West Pakistan; related to Hindi, but written in Arabic script.

VAISHYA The third in rank of the four Hindu castes.

VARNA Term for caste used in ancient India; the word means *color*.

VAT A temple. *Also* Wat.

VEDA The seven works comprising the Hindu scriptures.

VEDDAHS Primitive, aboriginal people of Ceylon, probably a mixture of Negrito and Australoid groups.

VIET CONG The military arm of the Communists in South Viet Nam.

VIET MINH The Communist Party of North Viet Nam.

VISHNU The "Preserver" of the Hindu Trinity of Gods.

WAKHAN CORRIDOR A narrow arm of extreme northeastern Afghanistan.

WAT A temple. *Also* Vat.

YAKKHAS Devils or demons, allegedly the earliest inhabitants of Ceylon. *See* Nagas.

YAO One of the aboriginal peoples in China.

ZEN Meditation. A sect of Mahayana Buddhism developed in Japan in the thirteenth century.

ZOROASTRIAN An adherent of the religion of ancient Iran. Small communities of Zoroastrians are found at Karachi, Pakistan, and at Bombay, India. *See* Parsis.

INDEX

Index

Index

Index

in India, 212

Jatakas, 579

Mahayana, 69, 75, 229, 478, 479-480, 483, 555-557, 570, 578, 580, 584

nirvana, 120, 556, 581

Red Hat Order, 75, 577

Shin sect, 270

in South Viet Nam, 487, 490, 491-492, 494-496, 502

Theravada, 114, 124, 132, 141, 479, 533, 547, 583

in Tibet, 555-557, 570

Tripitaka, 94, 583

in Viet Nam, 502

Yellow Hat Order, 577

Zen, 270-271, 276, 584

Bulgaria, aid to North Korea, 395

Bullfighting, in Japan, 282

Bultan Mosque (Singapore), 340

Burghers, of Ceylon, 133, 136, 141, 576

Burma, 20, 28, 29, 79-101, 171, 181, 189, 250, 305, 329, 453, 541, 545, 576, 579, 580, 582, 583

in brief, 97-101

the "Burmese Road to Socialism," 84, 98

early history, 81-82

economic modernization, 94-95, 99-101

future outlook, 96

health conditions, 95-96, 99

Japanese occupation, 83, 88, 101

the Kachins, 89-90

the Karens, 89, 90, 92

the Konbaung Dynasty, 82

minority strivings, 89-94

nationalism and independence, 83-86

political factionalism in, 87-89

the Shans, 90-94

social and cultural life, 94, 99

the Toungoo Dynasty, 81-82

under British rule, 82-83

Burmese boxing, 96

Burmese National Housing Board, 95

Burning ghats, 251, 576

Buryat Mongols, 353, 359

Buzkashi, 38, 42-43

Byodoin Temple (Uji, Japan), 273

Cairo, Egypt, 244

Calcutta, India, 238, 246-247, 257, 263

Cambodia, 20, 25, 29, 103-127, 171, 189, 303, 305, 404, 406, 546, 575, 576,

Cambodia *(continued)*
579, 581

in brief, 123-127

culture, 114, 126

early history of, 114-116

ethnic tensions, 104

forest dwellers, 108

gaining independence, 116

government of, 117-118, 124

industry and trade, 110, 126-127

modern communications, 113-114, 127

neutralism, 121-123

the people of, 103-104, 124

political structure, 118-119

relations with United States, 121

religion and family unity, 120

rise of the Khmer Empire, 115-116

social unity, 119-120

village life, 105-107

Cambridge University, 234, 235, 326, 330, 336

Canada, 171, 180, 406

Cannibalism, 338

Cao Dai, 487, 494, 502, 576

Caste system, 26, 27, 31, 132, 133, 222-225, 258, 576, 579, 581, 582, 583, 584

in Ceylon, 132, 133

Eta caste, in Japan, 26

in India, 27, 222-225, 258

Kshatriyas, 222, 576, 579

outcastes, 222-225, 581; *see also* Untouchables

scheduled castes, 224, 582

Sudras, 222, 224, 576, 583

untouchables, 27, 31, 224, 581, 582, 583

Vaishyas, 222, 224, 576, 584

Catholics, in Asia, 132, 136, 213, 217, 271, 408, 416, 487, 494, 502

Central Treaty Organization (CENTO), 20, 450, 455

Ceylon, 18, 19, 21, 28, 101, 129-145, 189, 250, 254, 575, 576, 577, 581, 582, 583, 584

in brief, 141-145

Burghers, 133, 136, 141, 576

caste system, 132, 133

communications, 137, 145

Communists in, 140

economy of, 136-137, 144-145

government of, 138-139, 143

589

Index

Index

Index

Index

Index

Index

Index

Index

Index

Index

Index

Index

Index

Index

Index

the Lama groups, 557
mystic faith, 555-556
social strata, 557-558
Tibeto-Burman, 583
Tibetology, Namgyal Institute (Sikkim),
484
T'ien Au Men (Peking), 156
Tien Shan, 17
Time Magazine, 23
Tin Hau, 200
Tokaido Rail Line (Japan), 295
Tokugawa Shogunate, 318
Tokyo, Japan, 290, 291, 475
Tokyo University, 274, 291
Tongking, 408, 416. *See also* Hanoi
Tonkin, Gulf of, 583
Tonle Sap, 104, 105, 106, 110, 122, 123,
126
Toungoo Dynasty, 81-82
Toward Freedom, 235
Tranh, 583
Transhumance, 71, 583
Transiberian Railway, 365
Treaty of Friendship, Alliance, and
Mutual Assistance (China—Soviet
Union), 169
Treaty of Nanking, 192
Treaty of San Francisco, 422
Tribhuvana, King, 368
Tribhuwan University (Nepal), 377
Tripitaka scriptures, 94, 583
Trotskyists, in Ceylon, 140
Tsangpo River, 554
Tsong-du, 562
Tsongs, 478
Two-China problem, 514
Turkomans, 35, 39, 40, 58, 59

Uganda, 250
Uighurs, 26, 173, 182
Ulan Bator (Mongolia), 357, 360, 362,
364, 365
Unani medicine, 260
Union of South Africa, 224, 231
United College, 199
United Kingdom. *See* Great Britain
United Malays National Organization,
335, 341
United National Party (Ceylon), 140
United Nations, 20, 86, 96, 98, 124, 143,
171, 184, 214, 233, 250, 252, 289,
337, 367, 397, 440, 450, 455, 472,

United Nations *(continued)*
510, 514, 519, 543, 548, 565, 567-
568
United Nations Children's Fund, 451
United States, 20, 52, 61, 79, 109, 115,
121, 170, 195, 211, 240, 247, 289,
307-308, 315, 376, 397, 421-429,
442, 450, 470, 489-491, 498-500,
504, 513-514, 523, 534, 542, 543
aid to India, 211, 247
aid to Nepal, 376
aid to Pakistan, 450
aid to South Korea, 470
aid to Thailand, 543
intervention in Laos, 307-308
involvement in South Viet Nam, 489-
491, 498-500
relations with Cambodia, 121
relations with China, 170
role in Taiwan, 513-514
in the Ryukyu Islands, 421-429
the two-China problem, 514
United States–Japan Security Treaty,
289
Universal Postal Union, 75, 401
University of Ceylon, 138
University of Hong Kong, 199, 204
University of Malaya, 329
University of Rangoon, 83, 84
University of the Ryukyus, 424
University of Saigon, 503
University of Singapore, 329
University of Southern California, 29
University of Wisconsin, 237
Untouchable, 253
Untouchables, 27, 31, 224, 581, 582, 583
Urdu, 216, 219, 227, 260, 431-432, 442,
453, 455, 578, 584
Uruguay, 396
U.S.S.R. *See* Soviet Union
Uzbeks, 35, 39, 50, 58, 59

Vaishyas, 222, 224, 576, 584
Vajiravudh, King, 541
Varna, 584
Vat. *See* Wat
Vatthana, Sri Savang, King, 307
Veda, 584
Veddahs, 135, 141, 584
Vientiane, Laos, 308-310, 311, 314, 315
Viet Cong, 121, 397, 412, 488, 489, 492,
493, 498, 502, 584

Index